Mom! Dad! Help me! Am I Gay?

Public school children are in a war zone, and do not know what to do. Hesitate to rescue them, and they will perish.

A fierce religious war is being waged in public school classrooms to drive a wedge between God-fearing parents and their children. If enemies infiltrate our schools and successfully seduce our children into atheism and sodomy, they do not have to engage us in a battle of tanks and canons. Indeed, if our own children accept the ideas of our enemies, then they become our enemies too! For it is the clash of irreconcilable ideas that make people enemies. When our children accept the evil ideas of our enemies the war has already been lost, for do we not go to war to protect our children from the evil ideas of our enemies?

The most important idea of all is God. It is upon this idea alone that truth and freedom rest. Yet our enemies' idea—that there is no God—is the idea being taught to children in public schools today. Therefore our fullest attention must be directed to our children's education until we are absolutely certain that their minds are being molded by teachers who believe in the same God in which we believe. Without doubt, the fate of public education will determine the fate of our nation—and of our children.

The enemy is smart. He knows that he can turn children against their parents and against God by getting them addicted to vile but physically pleasureable sins such as sodomy. This is why Gay Straight Alliance (GSA) clubs are being started in public schools all across America. Children have never been in more danger. The enemy knows also that children grow up to be adults, and adults vote, and he is determined to shape their minds so that they vote his way, until eventually the enemy wins all the elections and defeats America without even firing a shot.

Most Americans do not know their enemies. In fact, most Americans not only willingly submit their children to their enemies for brainwashing, but also vote to pay their enemies big salaries so that their enemies can devote themselves without hindrance to the task! Then these parents wonder why their children grow to despise them.

Who IS the enemy? What does he believe? Why are his ideas wrong and perilous? Do you know? If not, both you and your children are in grave danger. That is why you must read this book immediately.

To my Lord God and Savior

Jesus Christ

and to my country

The United States of American

and to

All the American Chlidren and Their Parents

PUBLIC SCHOOL HELL

the Humanist religion established as state church

Louis A. Turk, Ph.D.

First Edition

DAYSPRING PUBLISHER
Oklahoma City, Oklahoma

PUBLIC SCHOOL HELL

the Humanist religion established as state church

Published by: Dayspring Publisher LLC
Oklahoma City, OK, USA
http://www.dayspringpublisher.com

ISBN, print ed. 0-9779996-8-8
ISBN, PDF ed. 0-9779996-9-6
First Printing 2008

PREFACE

One Humanist preacher boldly stated what they all know: *"Every American public school is a school of Humanism."* Then he rhetorically asked, *"What can the theistic Sunday Schools, meeting for an hour once a week, and teaching only a fraction of the children, do to stem the tide of a five-day program of humanistic teaching?"* (Charles Francis Potter in *Humanism: a New Religion*). This book gives the answer to that question.

Notice the word *"every."* Potter said, *"**Every** American public school is a school of Humanism."* Can this be so? What about the public schools in the heartland of America? Are they also schools of Humanism? The sad truth is, Yes, they are. Public schools are founded on a basic atheist idea—an idea so opposed to the teachings of Christ that public schools have never been, and can never be, truly Christian. This book will expose that wicked idea for the poverty producing, education destroying lie it is.

Notice also the title of Potter's book: "Humanism: a New Religion." On page 3 of his book Potter wrote, "Humanism is not simply another denomination of Protestant Christianity....It is a new type of religion altogether." Potter spoke the truth. Humanism is the religion that underlies communism. It is altogether different from theistic religions. Yet it has ministers and religious rituals; and it even enjoys tax exempt status as a religion recognized by the U.S. government.

Notice also Potter's question: "What can the theistic Sunday Schools, meeting for an hour once a week, and teaching only a fraction of the children, do to stem the tide of a five-day program of humanistic teaching?" His implied answer is, Nothing! He is totally confident that Humanism will defeat and bury Christianity. Why is he so confident? Because Humanists are successfully exploiting a common weakness found in many people, including many Christians. You must be certain that this weakness is not found in you!

Just what is taught in that "five-day program of humanistic teaching" that Potter believes will result in the eventual triumph of Humanism over Christianity? This book will show you what humanists teach, and what the end result of that teaching has been and will be.

This book is filled with proof after proof after proof (1) that Humanism is the root problem with the Public School system of America; (2) that Humanism is the same pagan religion that underlies communism; and (3) that the Humanist religion is established as the state church of the U.S.A. in violation of the First Amendment to the U.S. Constitution. That many parents do not even realize that there is an atheist religion called Humanism, much less that its doctrines are being taught to their children in public schools, shows just how deceptively successful Humanists have been. Your children's religion has already been chosen for them without you or them knowing it.

However, it is not sufficient to know how evil Humanism is or even to know that it is established as the state church. Other writers before me have pointed out these things, but to no avail. Public education has been in crisis since the day of its founding. A constant stream of reforms have been attempted without success. The proper solution must be given, or else all efforts to correct the problem will be in vain—as they have been up to now.

All education is inseparable from religion. There is no such thing as non-religious education. Even secular education is intensely religious. Secular simply means that God is excluded, and that the religion is therefore deceitful and wicked.

America is presently engaged in a fierce civil war of religious ideas between two camps which are diametrically opposed to each other and cannot exist together in harmony. One of these camps is eventually going to overcome the other. It is a war in which no one can take a neutral stand. Atheist Humanists are presently winning and have great momentum. Act immediately or there is no hope. Our children will be the spoils of this war.

Read this book now. Many people have already lost their children to humanism. For them it is too late. Don't wait until it is also too late for your children.

Louis A. Turk
Oklahoma City

ACKNOWLEDGEMENTS

My deepest thanks to Ben Wattenberg, Charles McCombs, and Lawrence Smith for permission to quote rather extensively from their writings. Also, thanks to my sons, Samuel, Isaiah, and Caleb for proofreading the manuscript for this book many times, and for making many suggestions for improvement. Thanks also to my son, Joshua, for his math expertise in chapter 14. Thanks also to my parents for introducing me to Christ at an early age, and for teaching me to value the truth.

Table of Contents

Chapter 1

WHY THESE KILLING FIELDS?

Because Someone Planned It So

Are we sending our children to public school hell? Why is mention of God forbidden in public schools today? Why are our children failing to learn reading, writing and arithmetic? Why the mass-murder shooting sprees, the unbridled sex, and the drugs? Why are our children coming home so disrespectful and irreverent? Why is prayer no longer allowed in the classrooms or at school events? And why is the Bible banned? Who caused this horrible situation in the public school system? There is, indeed, something demonic—right out of the pits of Hell—going on in public schools.

For many children the terror in the halls of their public school is far more real and life-threatening than the Al-Qaeda. And this terror is not new. On the cover of the March 9, 1992 issue of *Newsweek* magazine was the following headline: "Kids and Guns: a Report From America's Classroom Killing Grounds." Right after home, school should be a child's first place of safety. Yet, on page 22 of this magazine, Carol A. Beck, principal of Thomas Jefferson High School in Brooklyn, New York is reported as saying, "Our *last* place of safety is the school. Next to Mother's arms, that should be the safest place." Page 24 of this same magazine reports that "Beck took a survey and found that half her students had puncture wounds of some kind." In other words, one out of every two students had been stabbed at some time or another! "These children are at war," Beck says "They worry that in the blink of an eye they could be killed—this is a reality—and they think they have to protect themselves." [Shouldn't school personnel be protecting the children? Why school children think they have to protect themselves will be discussed in a later chapter of this book.] *Newsweek* gives the Ronald D. Stephens National School Safety Center as the source for the following information which *Newsweek* called "Life on the Front Line": "An Illinois study showed that one in 12 public high-school students reported being the victim of a physical attack in school or on the way to school. One in 12 also said he'd stayed home from school one or more days out of fear."[1]

More recently the *National Examiner* reported that "A whopping 6,250 teachers are physically threatened, and 260 are brutally attacked in America—EVERY DAY!"[2] In a side bar to this article, titled "Shocking Lesson In Shame & Terror" (page 7), the *National Examiner* said:

> WARNING: Attending school in America can be dangerous to your health.
>
> In fact, it may be deadly.
>
> The Centers for Disease Control in Atlanta says violence is a major threat to our nation's public health and safety.
>
> "It's become an epidemic," says James Mercy of the CDC. "We were stunned when we saw the numbers."
>
> Here, from the CDC and other agencies, are some of the risks kids face in school every day:
>
> —More than three million violent incidents occurred last year in the nation's schools.
>
> —Almost 100,000 kids a day show up with handguns, rifles, sawed-off shotguns, knives, razors and clubs. Many carry these weapons for their own protection. One of five routinely carry weapons.
>
> —Nearly 160,000 youngsters skip school daily out of fear they'll be gunned down or caught in the crossfire.
>
> —Forty kids a day are either killed or wounded by gunfire at school.
>
> —Twenty-four percent of suburban and 23 percent of urban students say there are gangs in their schools.

---

1 "Kids and Guns: A Report from America's Classroom Killing Grounds," *Newsweek*, March 1992, 29.

2 "The Blackboard Jungle—America's Schoolyards Are Tragic Killing Fields Where no Child is Safe," *National Examiner*, 1993, 9 November 1993, 7.

—A mind-boggling 52 percent of students know someone their age who has tried to commit suicide—20 percent know someone who succeeded.[3]

"It's Not Like That In My Little Town, Is It?"

Many people think that these problems are confined to the big cities. Not so.

> Says Bill Martin, a spokesman for the National Education Association: "It's not an issue [that is] centered on the large cities anymore." Texas A&M's Kingery, whose research shows an alarming rise in the number of children who carry guns in rural Texas schools agrees. "It's a myth that rural schools are safe havens from the problem," Kingery says, "All the people who are taking their kids out of urban schools and moving to rural areas are living on false hope."[4]
>
> "The threat of violent crime is very real to millions of American schoolchildren. A national survey conducted by the U.S. Bureau of Justice Statistics last year [1991] showed, for instance, that more than 400,000 students between the ages of 12 and 19 say they have been the victims of violent crime, and that younger children are more likely to report victimization than older teens."[5]

Public schools all across America have become armed camps filled with terror. The following statistics are from a flyer titled "The Guns Have Got to Go!" published by the Oklahoma City Public Schools:

> According to a U.S. Centers for Disease Control Survey, 135,000 guns are carried into schools across this country each day.
>
> According to the same survey, 1 in 5 high-school aged youth has carried some type of weapon in the last month, and 1 in 3 boys has carried some type of weapon to school in the last month.
>
> The survey shows that 2.5 million U.S. teenagers carry guns and other weapons.[6]

It is difficult for schools to find time to teach reading, writing and arithmetic when they must teach such courses as "How to Survive a Drive-By Shooting."

> Cities like Oakland and Los Angeles, and even small towns such as Cokeville, Wyo., have started DBS (drive-by shooting) drills and "drop drills," teaching kids how to hit the floor when gunfire breaks out. It's a sad day when DBS replaces the ABCs, but for many kids, the No. 1 lesson is staying alive.[7]

And it will keep getting worse and worse as long as we allow the very people that caused the problems to fix them using the same methods that caused them.

From Many Murders To Many Mass Murders

"In 1996, nearly 93,000 juveniles were charged with violent crimes—a number 60 percent higher than a decade ago. In 1996 alone, more than 2,000 juveniles were charged with murder."

Rapidly gaining in popularity have been mass-murder shooting sprees. On October 1, 1997, a seventeen year old Pearl, Mississippi public school student walked into his own mother's bedroom, and stabbed her to death with a butcher knife. Then he took a gun to Pearl High School and killed two of his classmates and wounded seven others.[8] "On December 1, 1997, a 14-year-old student was arrested after three students were killed and five others wounded in a hallway at Heath High School, West Paducah, Kentucky. One of the injured girls is paralyzed."[9] On February 2, 1998 a ninth grade honor student at Frontier Junior High in the small town of Moses Lake, Washington shot and killed a teacher and two students, and wounded a third stu-

---

3 Ibid.

4 Ibid., 25.

5 Ibid., 29.

6 *The Guns Have Got to Go* (Oklahoma City: Oklahoma City Public School District, 1992), 1.

7 Eloise Salholzwith and Barbara Kantrowitz, "How to Keep Kids Safe," *Newsweek*, 9 March 1992, 30.

8 Brian Cabell, "Teen Blames 'Demons' in Pearl, Mississippi, Killings," *CNN Interactive*, 4 June 1998, Http://cnn.com/US/9806/04/woodham.trial.index.html.

9 Fiona Steel, "A Growing Problem," *The Crime Library Web Site* (1999)*Calm Before the Storm—the Littleton School Massacre*, Http://www.crimelibrary.com/serial4/littleton/6.htm.

dent. "On March 24, 1998, in Jonesboro, Arkansas, two boys, Andrew Golden, 11, and Mitchell Johnson, 13, opened fire on teachers and students as they left a middle school building during a false fire alarm. Four girls and a teacher were killed and 10 people were wounded."[10] On April 24, 1998 a 14 year old student of Parker Middle School in Edinboro, Pennsylvania "opened fire at an eighth-grade dance at a banquet hall late Friday, killing Gillette [a teacher] and slightly wounding two teen-age boys and a second teacher."[11] A photo accompanying this article shows him sitting in a police car after being arrested, smiling and obviously very proud of himself. "On May 19, 1998, an 18-year-old honor student opened fire in a parking lot at a high school in Fayetteville, Tennessee. A classmate who was dating the student's ex-girlfriend was killed."[12] "On May 21, 1998, a 15-year-old boy opened fire at a high school in Springfield, Oregon. Two teenagers were fatally shot and 20 people were injured. The boy's parents were found slain in their home."[13] The morning of

> Tuesday, April 20, 1999 started much the same as any other day in the middle-class town of Littleton, Colorado. None could know, as they went about their normal business, that beneath the calm, an anger had been raging in the hearts and minds of two young men, Eric Harris, 18, and Dylan Klebold, 17. At 11:35 a.m. on that fateful Tuesday, the 110th anniversary of Adolf Hitler's birth, the two teenagers began a rampage through the corridors of Columbine High School that ultimately ended their lives. In their wake they left 13 dead, 25 injured, many seriously, and a town shaken to its core.[14]

On May 20, 1999, six students were injured at Heritage High School in Conyers, Georgia by Thomas Solomon, 15, who was reportedly depressed after breaking up with his girlfriend. On November 19, 1999, Victor Cordova, Jr., 12, shot and killed 13 year old Araceli Tena in the lobby of Deming Middle School, Deming, New Mexico. On December 6, 1999, Seth Trickey, 13, shot and wounded four students with a 9mm semi-automatic handgun at Fort Gibson Middle School in Fort Gibson, Oklahoma. On February 29, 2000, a six-year-old boy shot and killed six-year-old Kayla Rolland at Buell Elementary School, Mount Morris Township, Michigan. On March 10, 2000, Darrell Ingram, 19, killed two students as they were leaving a dance sponsored by Beach High School, Savannah, Georgia. On May 26, 2000, Nate Brazill, 13, shot and killed a teacher, Barry Grunow, at Lake Worth Middle School, Lake Worth, Florida. On September 26, 2000, two students were wounded by the same gun during a fight at Woodson Middle School in New Orleans, Louisiana. On January 17, 2001, a student was shot and killed in front of Lake Clifton Eastern High School in Baltimore, Maryland. On March 5, 2001, Charles Andrew Williams, 15, firing from a bathroom at Santana High School in Santee, California, shot and killed two and wounded 13 others. On March 7, 2001, student Kimberly Marchese shot and wounded student Elizabeth Catherine Bush, 14, in the cafeteria of Bishop Neumann High School, Williamsport, Pennsylvania. On March 22, 2001, Jason Hoffman, 18, shot and wounded a teacher and three students at Granite Hills High School in Granite Hills, California. On March 30, 2001, Donald R. Burt, Jr., 17, shot and killed another student in Gary, Indiana. On November 12, 2001, Chris Buschbacher, 17, took two hostages at Caro Learning Center, Caro, Michigan, before killing himself. On January 15, 2002, a teenager wounded two students at Martin Luther King, Jr. High School in New York, New York.[15]

"Nearly a million U.S. students took guns to school during the last academic year [1997], according to the Parents Resource Institute for Drug Education (PRIDE)"[16] in spite of all the newly installed metal detectors, increased police patrols, etc. So school violence is not a problem that promises to go away any time soon.

---

[10] Ibid.

[11] "Classes Resume Monday After Middle School Shooting," Associate Press, *CNN Interactive*, 26 April 1998, Http://cnn.com/US/9804/teacher.killed/index.html.

[12] Steel, "A Growing Problem."

[13] Ibid.

[14] Fiona Steel, "Hidden Rage," *The Crime Library Web Site* (1999)*Calm Before the Storm—the Littleton School Massacre*, Http://www.crimelibrary.com/serial4/littleton/index.htm.

[15] "A Time Line of Recent Worldwide School Shootings," *Infoplease.Com* (2002), Http://www.infoplease.com/ipa/A0777958.html.

[16] "Survey: 1 Million Students Took Guns to School in '97," Reuters Limited, *CNN Interactive*, 19 June 1998, Http://ccn.com/US/9806/gun.school.survey/index.html.

Is Your Unmarried Daughter Still a Virgin?

Most likely your unmarried daughter is not a virgin if she has been very long in the public school system of America. And if she still is a virgin, she very likely will not be one for long unless you take immediate steps to prevent her defilement.

> A recent Harris poll of U.S. teenagers indicated that more than half have had intercourse by the time they are 17—primarily because they felt pressure from their peers. "My friends say, if you haven't done it, you're not in with the 'in' group," says Nekell McGrith, a 16-year-old sophomore at Harry S. Truman High School in the Bronx.[17]
>
> The statistical portrait of sex and the American teenager will stagger many parents. Each year for the past decade, more than a million teenage girls have become pregnant. Even though the teenage-pregnancy rate has remained fairly steady for the last few years, it is still very high—indeed, it is the highest in the Western world. The number of illegitimate births has soared. In 1984, 56 percent of teen births were out of wedlock, compared with only 15 percent in 1960. About 500,000 teenagers actually become mothers each year; the rest of the pregnancies end in miscarriages or abortions. A shocking one-third of all abortions performed annually in this country are done on teenage girls.[18]

Those statistics were for 1984. A more recent study reported in the March-April 1992 issue of *Public Health Reports* revealed that five years later the situation continued to grow alarmingly worse.

> Births to unmarried women totaled 1,094,169 in 1989, a 9 percent increase from 1988, accounting for 27 percent of all births. This was the fifth consecutive year that nonmartial births increased by 5 percent or more; births to unmarried women have risen more than 60 percent in the past decade.[19]

In other words, one out of every four babies born in the USA is born of a father who does not love him enough to marry his mother! This baby will be called hurtful names, and will most likely grow up in poverty. Illegitimacy is a tragedy beyond comprehension, and its effect on those babies will be awful. Had the teenage mothers who aborted their babies allowed them to be born instead the number of illegitimate births would be even more astronomical! But for those babies, their mothers also have no love, and murdered them in cold blood.

Morality is rapidly going out of style in the USA, with even former President Clinton known as an unashamed adulterer by the whole world. The news media plays down the importance of fornication and even adultery. But are these sins really insignificant? Consider this:

> Every minute, five people between the ages of 10-24 are infected with HIV, the virus that causes AIDS.... at least one-third of the 30 million HIV carriers are under 24.... Every day, 7000 young people ages 10-24 contact HIV—nearly five a minute and 2.6 million a year. By the year 2020, there will be more than 40 million orphans under age 15 in the 23 countries most affected by HIV. Most of them will have lost their parents to AIDS.[20]

Obviously, sexual immorality is not just wrong—it is extremely dangerous. Sex should be an extremely private experience, but it has extremely public consequences, affecting everyone. Therefore, sexual conduct is everybody's business, and to punish immoral sexual conduct is necessary and right and just. What children are being taught by teachers in sex-education classes in public schools today is extremely improper and wrong and harmful.

Is Your Child Gay?

In the October 2005 issue of Time magazine there was an article titled "The Battle Over Gay Teens" in which it was stated, "the gay movement is responding to the emergence this decade of hundreds of thou-

---

17 "Kids and Contraceptives," *Newsweek*, 16 November 1987, 56.

18 Ibid., 54–55.

19 "National Center for Health Statistics Data Line," *Public Health Reports* 107, no. 2 (March-April 1992): 233.

20 Jill Dougherty and The Associated Press, "U.N. Alarmed by Spread of HIV Among Young People," *CNN Interactive*, 22 April 1998, Http://cnn.com/HEALTH/9804/22/un.aids/index.html.

sands of openly gay youths."[21] Yes, the gay movement is responding with glee to its phenomenal success in instilling its ideas in our youth! The change in America's morality has been profound. I am 60. I did not know what a homosexual was until I was well into my twenties. I knew not even one person that claimed to have attraction to his or her own sex. I read a few articles about homosexuals, but so far as I know, I never met a homosexual until I was in my forties. Now every child is being asked to decide if he or she is gay, lesbian, bi-sexual, transexual, or heterosexual. Obviously, children are very easily confused by such questions, especially if they are being encouraged to choose something besides heterosexual. As a result hundreds of thousands of children—most likely including yours—are being seduced into sodomy. Do you realize what this means? I am in a dilemma—how can I inform you of the great danger homosexuals pose to your children in public schools? Ephesians 5:12 says that "...it is a shame even to speak of those things which are done of them in secret." ***But the fact is that it is absolutely vital for you to immediately know what shameful sins are presently being taught to children in public schools.*** Your children have very likely already been exposed to such immoral teachings, and their very lives are at stake. MassResitance.org, a pro-family website which opposes the teaching of sodomy to school children, is a good place to learn more about what is happening. I urge you to spend a few hours examining the photographs and documents on their website. You will be shocked and deeply disturbed to learn what public school children are being taught. An extremely vile pornograpic booklet titled *Little Black Book—Queer in the 21st Century*[22]

> ...was distributed to hundreds of kids (middle school age and up) at Brookline High School, Brookline, MA, on April 30, 2005. It was written by the Boston-based AIDS Action Committee, with help with the Massachusetts Department of Public Health and the Boston Public Health Commission.
>
> The event that day was designed for children and their teachers across Massachusetts, organized by the "Gay Lesbian and Straight Education Network" (GLSEN). This is the group that runs "Gay-Straight Alliance" clubs in public schools across the country. You must ask yourself: What kind of person would write this? What kind of person would give it to kids? Where is this movement headed?

Publications like this *Little Black Book* are being distributed at public schools all across America. To get the answer to, "Where is this movement headed?" go to this page of the American Civil Liberties Union (ACLU) website: http://www.aclu.org/getequal/scho/alliance.html

Click on all the links on the left of that web page, and you will see that the ACLU is working together with GLSEN to coordinate the organization of Gay Straight Alliance (GSA) clubs in public schools all across America. So, there is no way that your school will escape this.

The homosexual behavior encouraged in the *Little Black Book* mentioned above causes boys to get feces on their bodies and in their mouths. Not only is such behavior extremely dangerous health wise, but it also causes guilt, shame, and self loathing. Once a child commits this sin he or she feels like damaged goods that no one but other homosexuals would want. Thus he or she becomes trapped—enslaved to the sodomite community. Virtually every family in America has been harmed by this wicked movement to promote sodomy as a righteous alternative lifestyle. The author has a Christian friend whose son was seduced into the sodomite lifestyle, became infected with AIDS, and died a horrible death at a very young age. His funeral was the saddest I have ever attended. God pity us if we don't take immediate steps to rescue our children from this Satanic movement. More will be said about this in later chapters.

What Is Done To Solve These Problems?

Public schools are championing three solutions for these problems: (1) freely available condoms, (2) metal detectors and anti-gun legislation, (3) legislation to punish parents for their children's misbehavior.

---

21 John Cloud, "The Battle Over Gay Teens," *Time*, 2002 October 2005, Http://www.time.com/time/magazine/article/0,9171,1112856,00.html.

22 http://www.massresistance.org/docs/issues/black_book/black_book_inside.html

Freely Available Condoms

Children are told to use condoms as a solution to sex problems. But "twenty-three percent of female students say they've been raped or sexually assaulted."[23] Are we to expect that the rapist will put on a condom before raping his victim? Also, many teenagers refuse to wear condoms because it just doesn't feel as good, and our children are being taught that if it feels good do it. Sixteen year old Vantra, a sophomore baton majorette at L.G. Pinkston High School in Dallas is a case in point. Contraceptives have been available on her campus since the mid-1970's. In fact,

> she received birth control pills from the clinic as a ninth grader but gave them up because she could not remember to use them. "It'd be a problem because I get so busy," she says. She went back on the pills two months ago, supplementing them with a barrier foam as protection against forgetfulness, but soon yielded to her 16-year-old boyfriend's request that she not use anything. They have sex "more than" twice a week, Vantra says.
>
> Vantra's case underscores a frustrating reality: making contraceptives available to children is not necessarily insurance against pregnancy.[24]

And it definitely is not insurance against fornication; in fact, it is condoning and encouraging it. As Dr. Teresa Crenshaw, a member of the U.S. Presidential AIDS Commission and past president of the American Association of Sex Educators said, "Saying that the use of condoms is 'safe sex' is in fact playing Russian roulette. A lot of people will die in this dangerous game."[25]

> Human papilloma virus (HPV) is the most common ***incurable*** STD in the United States. ...***When condoms are used properly and consistently, which only occurs between 5 and 40 percent of the time, they still serve as ineffective barriers against STDs. Condoms, whether used correctly and consistently or not, do not prevent the spread of HPV.***
>
> Federally funded sexual health organizations and the Centers for Disease Control, however, continue to promote condoms as effective STD barriers. They briefly mention sexual abstinence as a tool for STD prevention, before campaigning for the "consistent and correct" use of condoms as sufficient STD deterrents.
>
> Those concerned with public health should strongly encourage the only guaranteed method of conquering this public health epidemic—sexual abstinence until entering into a lifelong, monogamous marriage with an uninfected partner.[26] [Emphasis added.]

According to the Center For Disease Control and Prevention

> In the United States, ***more than 65 million people are currently living with an incurable sexually transmitted disease (STD)***. An additional ***15 million people become infected with one or more STDs each year***, roughly half of whom contract ***lifelong*** infections.[27] (Emphasis added.)

Sixty-five million people is approximately 20 percent of the US population—one out of every five people! The Center for Disease Control and Prevention estimates that "in 1994, the direct and indirect costs of the major STDs and their complications were estimated to total almost $17 billion annually." As the song says, "sin will cost you far more than you will want to pay." The use of condoms obviously has not prevented the spread of STDs, and the risk of infection with an STD is extremely high when engaging in any sexual activity outside of marriage to an uninfected person of the opposite sex.

---

[23] "Shocking Lesson in Shame and Terror," *National Examiner*, 9 November 1993, 7.

[24] "This is a Good Place—a Clinic in Dallas Copes with Teenage Sexuality," *Newsweek*, 16 February 1987, 61.

[25] "Condom Warnings -- Beware!!!" *Pro-Live America*, Http://www.prolife.com/CONDOMS.html.

[26] Heather Farish and Yvette Schneider, "The Human Papillomavirus (HPV) Epidemic: Condoms Don't Work," *PhysiansForLife.Org* (2005), Http://www.physiciansforlife.org/index.php?option=content&task=view&id=756.

[27] "Tracking the Hidden Epidemics: Trends in STDs in the United States 2000," *Center for Disease Control and Prevention*, Http://www.cdc.gov/nchstp/dstd/Stats_Trends/Trends2000.pdf.

Metal Detectors and Gun Legislation

To cope with the violence, "The Guns Have Got to Go" flyer previously quoted also states: "Metal detectors are in use at Oklahoma City school athletic events, as needed, at high schools and middle schools during the day." But metal detectors can not stop truly motivated bullies from perpetrating violence. An obvious problem with metal detectors is that if their sensitive level is set too high it will detect even the metal in zippers; and if set too low will miss some knives and guns.

> The initial purchase price of a portal metal detector is almost insignificant compared with the ongoing personnel costs to operate the equipment in a complete weapon detection program.... It should be noted that the only way these schools are able to avoid huge waiting lines, even with this much equipment and this many officers, and still get everybody to class on time is by a complete restructuring of their class periods. There is a significant staggering of first period start times so that the students arrive over a 90-minute period. On average, NYC school safety officials estimate that they fund approximately 100 additional security officer hours a week for each of their schools that screen for weapons.
>
> To make any metal detection program effective, school access during the rest of the school day, during off-hours, and during special activities needs to be tightly controlled. A motivated student can defeat a lax system. If there is a comprehensive metal detection program at the front entrance to the school, but the back entrance through the cafeteria is unguarded, the funding and efforts put into a well-meaning program can be wasted.[28]

If too many students are stopped because their belt buckles trigger the alarm it slows or stops movement through the equipment and makes many students late to class. Time and money restraints, therefore, prevent setting sensitivity levels high enough to prevent all weapons from passing.

> "The biggest lessons to learn from this [mass murder at Columbine High School] is we cannot use steel and concrete to make our kids safe," said Marc Stine, principal of Rangeview High School in Aurora.... "The sad thing is that, if they'd had metal detectors at Columbine, the first fatality might well have been the metal detector operator," Denver Public Schools spokesman Mark Stevens said.[29]

Just a day before the rough draft of this chapter was written, another student was stabbed at Northwest Classen High in the Oklahoma City school district, proving once again that metal detectors cannot take the will to murder out of depraved hearts. And where there is a will there is a way. A gun or knife is not necessary to kill. A pencil, pen, or rat-tailed comb can be used to stab. Even a chair or bare hand or foot can also be used as a weapon to kill. At Taft Middle School in Oklahoma City a large girl once attempted to strangle her principle with his own tie! Perhaps ties should be banned, and tie detectors installed at school entryways!

Legislation To Punish Parents

"School officials are discussing with lawmakers *new legislation that would make parents legally liable and subject to civil and criminal penalties if their children bring weapons to school*"[30] [Emphasis original!]. Public schools refuse to discipline children, thus making them into monsters. They even tell the children that if their parents spank them they should call the police to report child abuse. Then when the children do evil, it would seem that the public school officials themselves should be punished. But no, they make the parents responsible! Always they punish the innocent instead of the wrongdoer—the wrongdoer must be protected at all costs! All parents are threatened by such stupid legislation, and had better take steps to prevent such legislation from becoming law. Obviously, punishing parents will not prevent children from being violent, and this is especially so if the parents are not allowed to discipline their children.

---

[28] Mary W. Green, *National Criminal Justice Reference Service Web Site*, September 1999*The Appropriate and Effective Use of Seurity Technologies in U.S. Schools—a Guide for Schools and Law Enforcement Agencies* (Washington, D.C.: U.S. Department of Justice, Office of Justice Programs, National Institite of Justice, 1999), Http://www.ncjrs.org/school/ch3a_5.html.

[29] Tustin Amole, "Security is Under Siege: School Officials Feel Handcuffed Providing Safety for Students" (Denver: Denver Rocky Mountain News, 1999), Http://osiris.colorado.edu/~glenn/media/rmn/0422sec15.shtml.

[30] *The Guns Have Got to Go.*

A true life example from a small Oklahoma town. A certain girl was repeatedly told (along with all the other students in her class) that spanking was child abuse, and that she should report her parents to the police if they spanked her. This severely interfered with her parent's ability to discipline her, as each time discipline was attempted she warned them that she would phone the police if they spanked her. She rapidly became a problem at home (even hitting her mother in the face) and at school. Soon a school official phoned her dad, "Mister, your daughter is totally out of control and causing a lot of trouble at school. We expect you to get her under control soon." Her dad answered, "Lady, I can take care of this problem tonight, so that it will never happen again. But if I do, are you going to report me to the police as a child abuser for spanking her?" Her answer, "Yes, we will." His response, "Well in that case, I cannot help you even if she tears your school building to the ground. You have caused this problem, now you will have to live with it." Her dad was right—he was being blamed for the problems caused by the very hypocrites accusing him of causing them!

Condoms, metal detectors, anti-gun laws, and punishing parents. Obviously, public school officials are merely treating symptoms, while letting the spiritual disease which is causing these symptoms continue to destroy our children. It is vital that we determine the spiritual disease which is causing these symptoms. What spiritual disease is this which compels our children to fornicate and murder?

It Doesn't Have To Be This Way

Students of our parents's day certainly had more restraint. Even a casual student of history, or a person who just listens to his parents and grandparents talk about the way things used to be, knows that the people of the United States used to be far less violent and far more moral.

> In the 1940's, teachers listed littering, gum chewing and defying the dress code as their main disciplinary problems. Today, teachers' top concerns are assault, rape and robbery, surveys say.[31]

The author's father-in-law and his classmates left their rifles outside on the school porch with full permission of the school authorities. It never entered anyone's thoughts that the guns might be stolen or used to commit murder; and they never were. To a very great degree, students could be trusted in those days. But a rapidly growing number of today's students cannot be trusted. They are fundamentally different in their hearts—different in world-view and culture and values and morals. Why? What evil force compels them to selfishness, dishonesty, immorality, and even murder or sodomy or other wickedness? If we can just determine the cause of these sins of the heart—and find an effective cure, or (better yet) prevention—our schools won't have to remain prisons.

---

31 "Blackboard Jungle," 7.

Chapter 2

WHO IS RESPONSIBLE?

Humanists Planned It and Did It

Violence, immorality, and lack of learning to the extent found in the public schools of America today does not happen without cause. It is made to happen by the execution of well-thought-out plans.

Unmasking the Culprits

Let us call to the witness stand a leader of the very people responsible for our schools's problems. Let him with his own words expose and incriminate both the movement in which he is a leader and the spiritual disease it spreads. The main reason our children are not learning reading, writing and arithmetic, is because they are being taught something else instead. Listen to this amazing admission from Morris B. Storer. one of the foremost spokesmen of the people who are destroying our schools:

> Why in the face of this [swelling rate of violent crime, disorder and cynicism, drugs and abandonment in schools], a symposium on ***humanist*** ethics?... Because ***humanists*** have an especially heavy responsibility for these things today.... ***Humanism*** has to face special responsibility in this area because a large majority of the educators of America and of the western world are ***humanist*** in their outlook. The faculties of American colleges and universities are predominantly ***humanist***, and a majority of the teachers who go out from their studies in the colleges to responsibilities in primary and secondary schools are basically ***humanist***, no matter that many maintain a nominal attachment to church or synagogue for good personal or social or practical reasons. Critics of ***secular humanism*** are apt to hold responsible (for the problems in the schools) not simply the ***humanist*** educator, but the educator's ***humanism***.[32] [Emphasis added.]

It behooves parents to study the above quotation carefully and seriously. Nothing their adversaries could have written would have so exposed the religious/political philosophy called humanism as the cause of the startling decline in the health of education in America as has those words of their own humanist leader, Morris B. Storer, found in his "Editor's Preface" to *Humanist Ethics: Dialogue on Basics.* That book, published by Prometheus Books, is composed of papers submitted to a symposium on humanist ethics by 20 of the foremost Humanist leaders in the world. Storer most likely did not intend for his words to be read by critics. He was addressing devout humanists, warning them to prepare their defenses.

Prometheus Books is the publisher which publishes books for the American Humanist Association, including *Humanist Manifesto I & II.* Storer is not just a humanist but is also a Humanist (with a capital H)—that is, he is not just a humanist in philosophy, but is also a member of (and leader in) the highly influential American Humanist Association. When the subject is humanism, he knows what he is talking about. As Storer so clearly states, humanist educators teaching and practicing humanist principles in the classrooms are responsible for the disastrous moral virus which is debilitating America's public schools. Humanism is a spiritual and mental AIDS.

Astoundingly, humanists never seem to learn from their failures—humanism is even the "cure" humanists prescribe to treat the symptoms humanism has caused! They argue that the reason humanist education has failed for decades is only because it has not yet been allowed pure implementation. Thus they work fervently to force the whole bottle of humanism down the throat of their chronically ill patient, and the condition of education in America gets progressively worse in a rapidly tightening downward spiral. One would think that humanists would consider how much better things used to be, and would want to return to sanity. But not so.

---

[32] Morris B. Storer, ed., *Humanist Ethics: Dialogue on Basics* (Buffalo, New York: Prometheus Books, 1980), 1–2.

The rate of juvenile delinquency and violent crime perpetrated by children has increased dramatically since moral absolutes and discipline were removed from the schools. From 1950 to 1977 the arrest rate for the age group under 18 increased from 200 to 6,500 per 100,000—an increase of 3,200%!

"Interviews with juvenile justice officials around the country indicate that the age at which youngsters are committing serious crimes is declining steadily, and that cases that seemed like bizarre anomalies a few years ago are now becoming more common. According to crime figures compiled by the Federal Bureau of Investigation, based on reports from 11,249 agencies in 1985, youths age 15 and younger were responsible for 381 cases of murder, and non-negligent manslaughter, 18,899 robberies and 2,645 rapes. Further, children age 12 and under were responsible for 21 of the killings, 436 of the rapes, 3,545 aggravated assaults and 1,753 robberies, the FBI said. Daniel P. Dawson, chief of the juvenile division for the ninth circuit state attorney's office in Orlando, Florida, said, 'Not only is the age dropping at which kids are getting involved in crime, but the violent crimes are being committed by younger and younger kids. Four or five years ago, even two or three years ago, it was very unusual to see a child younger than 12 or 13 in the system, particularly with multiple charges. Now you see kids age 7, 8, or 9 come in with a whole string of burglaries.'" (*International Herald Tribune*, Feb. 5, 1987)

Almost two decades ago the U.S. Senate Committee on the Judiciary published a report entitled *Our Nation's Schools—A Report Card*, which concluded that the "level of violence and vandalism is reaching crisis proportions which seriously threatens the ability of our educational system to carry out its primary functions."

Further, by every standard, learning has declined in this same period. In April 1983 a special government report entitled *A Nation At Risk* was published. It stated: "Our nation is at risk. Our once unchallenged preeminence in commerce, industry, science, and technological innovation is being overtaken by competitors throughout the world....The educational foundations of our society are presently being eroded by a rising tide of mediocrity that threaten our very future as a Nation and a people." The report stated that the sharp decline in learning in American schools happened in one generation. The report noted that "The College Board's Scholastic Aptitude Tests (SAT) demonstrates a virtually unbroken decline for 1963 to 1980. Average veral scores fell over 50 points and average mathematics scores dropped nearly 40 points. (William Jasper, "Who Shall Teach?" *The New American*, Sept. 28, 1987). The McGuffy's Fourth and Fifth grade readers of the 1800s provide a real challenge to many college students today.

Is all this mere coincidence? Come now! But what does the liberal humanist say about such things? He continues to pooh pooh the need for the Bible, prayer, moral absolutes, and discipline and proposes, instead, more sex education, more buildings, more teachers, more psychology, more moral license, more counselors, more relativism, more entertainment, more months in school—more MONEY![33]

The Spiritual Disease They Spread

But what is Humanism? Most people have never heard of either humanism or Humanists. Except in literature addressed to their own group, Humanists seldom identify themselves as Humanists. They realize they must hide both their own identity and the identity of their philosophy which is so adversely changing our schools and our country. You see, humanists have an agenda they know most Americans would fiercely oppose if they just realized it's far-reaching significance. Humanists are fighting a spiritual war of sedition against Christianity and against the USA. They plan to subdue this nation by proselytizing our children to their Godless religion. Consider carefully the following statement of John Dunphy from *The Humanist* magazine:

> I am convinced that the battle for humankind's future must be waged and won in the public school classroom by teachers who correctly perceive their role as the proselyters of a new faith: a religion of humanity that recognizes and respects the spark of what theologians call divinity in every human being. These teachers must embody the same selfless dedication as the most rabid fundamentalist preachers, for they will be ministers of another sort, utilizing a classroom instead of a pulpit to convey humanist values in whatever subject they teach, regardless of the educational level—preschool day care or large state university. The classroom must and will become an arena of conflict between the old and the new—the rotting corpse of Christianity together with all its adjacent evils and misery, and the new faith of humanism, resplendent in its promise of a world in which the never-realized Christian ideal of "love thy neighbor" will finally be achieved.
>
> Then, perhaps, we will be able to say with Tom Paine that "the world is my country, all [Hu]mankind are my brethren, and to do good is my religion." It will undoubtedly be a long, arduous, painful struggle, replete with much sorrow and many tears, but humanism will emerge triumphant. It must if the family of humankind is to survive.[34]

The title of Dunphy's article is "A Religion For the New Age." Dunphy correctly calls humanism "a new faith: a religion." Humanist public school teachers are "proselyters of a new faith." A proselyter is a person who works to convert people from one religion to another. Humanist school teachers are working zealously

---

[33] David Cloud, "Humanists Are Never Wrong," *O Timothy* 10, no. 9 (1993): 6.

[34] John J. Dunphy, "A Religion for the New Age," *The Humanist*, January/February 1983, 26.

every day in classrooms all across America converting their students from Christianity to the atheistic religion called humanism.

"Congressman Pete Stark, Humanist of the Year, has served in Congress since 1973. A senior member of the powerful Ways and Means Committee, he is currently the Chairman of its Health Subcommittee. Stark previously served as the subcommittee's Ranking Minority Member from 1995 to 2006 and as its Chairman from 1985 to 1994....In March, 2007, Stark made history by becoming the first member of Congress to ever publicly acknowledge the lack of a god belief, going on record as identifying as a nontheist."(http://www.americanhumanist.org/conference/awardees08.php)

The American Humanist Association, a very dangerous and highly organized organization, virtually identical to the Communist Party in beliefs and goals, is the leader in promoting humanism in this country. The American Humanist Association is an international organization operating under the umbrella of the International Humanist and Ethical Union. The Humanists' goal is to make humanism the government and religion of the world. That is the reason you must carefully read (and reread) all of this book. You *must* be informed of the facts about humanism which humanists hide from you—facts which are vital to both your children's survival and to the survival of the values and culture and morals which made the United States the greatest nation in history. ***It cannot be emphasized enough that what is presently happening in public school classrooms is more important than anything else that is happening in America.*** Public (socialist) education is America's hole in the dike, through which a flood of philosophical and pagan doctrinal pollution is drowning out the Christian culture which made this country rich in both material and spiritual blessings. If we do not plug this hole soon, nothing else is going to matter.

Do These Organizations Actually Exist?

Unfortunately, yes they actually exist. Humanism is no conspiracy theory; it is a real conspiracy.

Here is the URL for the International Humanist and Ethical Union:

www.iheu.org

And here is the URL for the American Humanist Association:

www.americanhumanist.org

The following letter was recently posted on the American Humanist Association website.[4] If you are a real doubter, and if you are reading this book soon enough, you can try to attend The IHEU 17th World Humanist Congress and the AHA 67th Annual National Conference. In the following letter, note carefully and remember the names of the speakers and the organizations they represent. Note especially Peter Stark.

> E Pluribus Unum:
> Reclaiming Humanist Values
>
> The IHEU 17th World Humanist Congress and the AHA 67th Annual National Conference
>
> When: June 5-8, 2008
>
> Where: Washington, D.C. at the L'Enfant Plaza Hotel
>
> Join the International Humanist and Ethical Union and the American Humanist Association for the 17th annual World Humanist Congress in Washington DC at the L'Enfant Plaza Hotel. This exciting event will be held June 5-8, 2008, with extended activities June 4 and 9.
>
> Plenary sessions include topics on human rights, bioethical issues, religious reform, freedom of conscience and expression, Humanist approaches to social problems, and many others.
>
> Speakers include IHEU President Sonja Eggerickx, AHA President Mel Lipman, Maryland State Senator Jamie Raskin, Feminist Majority Foundation President Eleanor Smeal, Rob Boston of Americans United for Separation of Church and State, Lori Lipman Brown of the Secular Coalition for America, and many others to be announced. Accepting the Humanist of the Year award is U.S. Representative Pete Stark, the first openly nontheist member in Congress.
>
> The IHEU World Humanist Congress is a triennial event that has been held in France, India, and the Netherlands. The last Congress held in the United States was 20 years ago. Don't miss this rare opportunity to participate in this unique conference and meet Humanists from around the globe.
>
> Keep checking our website for more updates on the conference schedule, speakers, and Humanist awardees.

4 http://www.americanhumanist.org/conference/

Chapter 3

WHAT IS HUMANISM?

A Pagan Religion

Humanism is first and foremost a religion. It is a religion because it attempts to answer the religious questions all humans ask: Is there a God? What is our origin? What is right, and what is wrong? What is our purpose in life? Is there life after death? How can I be saved? That humanism is a religion is easily seen by inspecting the definitions and proclamations of humanism written by Humanist leaders. This chapter will examine these definitions and proclamations in relation to the fundamental religious questions they attempt to answer. Also, since the significance of error is easier to see if contrasted with truth, Humanism will be contrasted with Christianity in each case, giving the Christian position first.

Religious Questions Humanism Tries To Answer

The most fundamental religious question of all, of course, is:

Is There a True and Living Creator God?

God is an undeniably religious topic. A doctrine concerning God is the most fundamental element of any religion.

True Christians Believe In the True and Living God

God is declared to exist in the very first verse of the Bible: "In the beginning God...." (Gen. 1:1), and the Bible reveals to us God's attributes and will, using the word "God" 4,110 times.

The reality of God is clearly seen—even by atheists—in the incredibly intricate design of all God's creation.

> For the invisible things of [God] from the creation of the world are clearly seen, being understood by the things that are made, even his eternal power and Godhead; so that they are without excuse. (Rom. 1:20)

It does not take much intelligence to realize that random chance could not produce such a creation no matter how many billions of years one allows for it to do so. How many billions of years would you have to wait for random chance to produce a personal computer? *It would never happen*, you rightly answer. Yet the simplest one-celled animal is far more complicated than the most advanced super-computer—and is alive! Where there is such amazing design there is an amazing Designer.

However, though nature clearly reveals that God exists and is super-naturally intelligent, nature is unable to reveal to us the spiritual attributes of God. Science is also unable to reveal to us the spiritual attributes of God. "God is a Spirit" (John 4:24), but science can only deal with matter. God cannot be made the object of scientific experiments. Because of this, science cannot reveal the complete truth about God—that is why God revealed Himself to us in the Bible.

The Bible declares that faith in God is essential to finding and pleasing God:

> By faith Enoch was translated that he should not see death; and was not found, because God had translated him: for before his translation he had this testimony, that he pleased God. But without faith it is impossible to please him: for he that cometh to God must believe that he is, and

that he is a rewarder of them that diligently seek him. (Heb. 11:5-6)

True Christians have believed God's Word, and have been rewarded with becoming personally acquainted with him. They no longer just believe God exists, they ***know*** He exists.

Humanists Do Not Believe In the True and Living God

Humanists claim to base everything on science. Since there is no scientific evidence to disprove the existence of God, one would think that Humanists would therefore not have a position concerning God. Wrong! Very wrong! Humanists have strong, continually preached doctrinal beliefs concerning God—beliefs they cannot prove, but accept on blind religious FAITH. Statements such as the following are found often in Humanist writings:

> Sigmund Freud said the widespread belief in a father-god arises from psychology. Tiny children are awed by their fathers as seemingly all-powerful protectors and punishers. As maturity comes, fathers grow less awesome. But the infantile image remains buried in the subconscious, and attaches to an omnipotent, supernatural father in an invisible heaven.
>
> That makes sense to me. It says the father-god is just a figment of the imagination. ***But you can't prove it's true....*** Is there a personal God waiting to reward me in a heaven or punish me in a hell? ***I don't know***—but I doubt it.[36] (Emphasis added)

So, Humanists do not know that God does not exist, and certainly cannot prove it. Obviously their belief that God does not exist rests on pure FAITH alone.

Still, Humanists are far from neutral concerning God. Indeed God occupies a major portion of their thoughts. They hate the true and living God with a burning passion. Though they claim to be atheists or "non-theists," they cannot get God out of their minds. *Humanist Manifesto II*, Section 1, states:

> ... traditional dogmatic or authoritarian religions that place revelation, God, ritual, or creed above human needs and experience do a disservice to the human species. Any account of nature should pass the tests of scientific evidence; in our judgment, the dogmas and myths of traditional religions do not do so. Even at this late date in human history, certain elementary facts based upon the critical use of scientific reason have to be restated. We find insufficient evidence for belief in the existence of a supernatural; it is either meaningless or irrelevant to the question of the survival and fulfillment of the human race. As nontheists, we begin with humans not God, nature not deity.[37]

Of course, such talk is pure deception. Placing God first does not place Him above human needs. Indeed, the first and most basic needs of man are to be rescued from the wages of sin, to be given eternal life, to have a relationship and be in fellowship with God, and to have an eternal purpose for living. God alone can supply those needs.

Also, as will be shown in this book, there *is* scientific evidence that God exists. On the other hand, there is zero scientific evidence that God does not exist. Of course, humanists do have a multitude of atheist doctrines—mere myths—cloaked as scientific evidence.

Humanist editor Morris B. Storer writes:

> What is humanism, and who is humanist? For our purposes I will identify as "humanist" all who, in the basic deliberations and action decisions of their lives, have set aside faith in revelation [the Bible] and dogmatic authority [God] (if they ever had it), and have settled for human experience and reason as grounds for belief and action, putting human good—the good of self and others in their life on earth—as ultimate criterion of right and wrong, with due concern for other living creatures. It has been estimated that as many as thirty million Americans—around one out of every seven—are of this mind, but the number is probably much larger. And the world population of humanists defined in such limited terms, may be numbered at close to a billion, remembering that 95% of China's 700 million were reared to a mix of humanist Confucianism, naturalist Taoism, and atheistic Buddhism, and that the Soviet Union's 250 million population have been officially committed to a somewhat corrupted mode of Marxist humanism by fiat of a dictator State.[38]

Notice in the above quote that Storer includes Confucianism, Taoism, and Buddhism—the religions espoused by the so-called "New-Age Movement"—right along with Communists as fellow humanists. All of

---

[36] James A. Haught, "Commentary: Is There a God?" in *Secular Humanism Online Library* (Amherst, New York: Council For Secular Humanism, 1996), Http://www.SecularHumanism.org/library/haught_08_96.html.

[37] Paul Kurtz, ed., *Humanist Manifestos I & II* (Buffalo, New York: Prometheus Books, 1981), Http://www.humanism.net/documents/manifesto1.html and http://www. humanism.net/documents/manifesto2.http.

[38] Storer, *Humanist Ethics: Dialogue on Basics*, 2.

these philosophical religious systems deny the existence of a true and living creator God, who is separate from the universe He created. Instead they teach that the universe itself is God—that God is not a living person, but is just the dead natural forces. This idea is called pantheism. Humanists call these dead natural forces "Evolution."

Harvey Lebrun, founder of the Chapter Assembly of the American Humanist Association, refers people seeking a definition of Humanism to the

> Statement of Purpose preamble to the Bylaws of the American Humanist Association, which declares the philosophy of Humanism to be—*a nontheistic world view that rejects all forms of supernaturalism and is in accord with the spirit and discoveries of science.*[39] (Emphasis original).

That statement is half true, half lie. The lie is that Humanism is in accord with the spirit and discoveries of science. The so-called "science" Humanism preaches is the "theory" of macro-evolution, which is mere faith, not science. No scientist has ever seen dead matter birth life. Nor has any scientist ever witnessed an animal of one kind give birth to an animal of a different kind. Evolution is not science, nor is it reason; it is superstition. This will be discussed in more detail in a later chapter. Nevertheless, it obviously is true that Humanism preaches atheism, which also is not science, but is a religious doctrine based on faith.

Lebrun goes on to say that one of the "four basic principles, the raison d'etre of the American Humanist Association" is

> No belief in, reliance upon, or subservience to supposedly supernatural powers or their effluvia, such as a god or gods, a soul separate from the body, immortality, sin, answered prayer, or divine revelation.[40]

That is a very strongly stated religious belief. It is interesting to note that no attempt whatsoever is made to give proof for such a belief. Definitely this is not a statement of science, but of religion. Lebrun and his humanist friends are not scientists but mere ***Human-Theory Thumpers***. Evolution is their ***dogma***.

Another document from the American Humanist Association web site is titled "What Is Humanism?" and is written by Fredrick Edwords. According to a biography on the Infidels.Org web site—the name of this web site shows just how arrogant Humanists are—, Fredrick Edwords is the current executive director of the American Humanist Association, editor of the *Humanist* magazine, and is also a Humanist minister.[41] He describes Humanism as defiance of God.

> The Secular Humanist tradition is a tradition of defiance, a tradition that dates back to ancient Greece.... Prometheus stands out because he was idolized by ancient Greeks as the one who defied Zeus. He stole the fire of the gods and brought it down to earth. For this he was punished. And yet he continued his defiance amid his tortures. This is the root of the Humanist challenge to authority.
>
> The next time we see a truly heroic Promethean character in mythology it is Lucifer in John Milton's Paradise Lost. But now he is the Devil. He is evil. Whoever would defy God must be wickedness personified. That seems to be a given of traditional religion. But the ancient Greeks didn't agree. To them, Zeus, for all his power, could still be mistaken.
>
> Imagine how shocked a friend of mine was when I told her my view of "God's moral standards." I said, "If there were such a god, and these were indeed his ideal moral principles, I would be tolerant. After all, God is entitled to his own opinions!"[42]

Lucifer—the Devil himself—is a "truly heroic Promethean character" for Humanists to model themselves after because he defies God?! If, as Humanists insist, God does not exist, then why bother defying Him? What a waste of time and life.

Edwords continues:

> Only a Humanist is inclined to speak this way. Only a Humanist can suggest that, even if there be a god, it is OK to disagree with him, her, or it. In Plato's Euthyphro, Socrates shows that God is not necessarily the source of good, or even good himself. Socrates asks if something is good

---

[39] Harvey Lebrun, "Humanism with a Capital H," reprint, 1973 (Amherst, New York: American Humanist Association, 1994), Http://www.americanhumanist.org/humanism/lebrun.html.

[40] Ibid.

[41] "Brief Biography of Fred Edwords," in *Library: Modern* (Amherst, New York: American Humanist Association, 0198), Http://www.infidels.org/library/modern/fred_edwords/edwords-bio.html.

[42] Frederick Edwords, "What is Humanism?" *American Humanist Association Home Page* (1989) (Amherst, New York: American Humanist Association, 1989), Http://www.humanism.net/definations/humanism.html.

> because God ordains it, or if God ordains it because it is already good. Yet, since the time of the ancient Greeks, no mainstream religion has permitted such questioning of God's will or made a hero out of a disobedient character. It is Humanists who claim this tradition.
>
> After all, much of Human progress has been in defiance of religion or of the apparent natural order.... [Humanists] recognize the Promethean defiance of their response and take pride in it. For this is part of the [Humanist] tradition.[43]

"Such questioning of God's will" is not new. It began in the Garden of Eden. The book of Genesis records the origin of humanism as follows:

> Now the serpent was more subtle than any beast of the field which the LORD God had made. And he said unto the woman, Yea, hath God said, Ye shall not eat of every tree of the garden? And the woman said unto the serpent, We may eat of the fruit of the trees of the garden: But of the fruit of the tree which is in the midst of the garden, God hath said, Ye shall not eat of it, neither shall ye touch it, lest ye die. And the serpent said unto the woman, Ye shall not surely die: for God doth know that in the day ye eat thereof, then your eyes shall be opened, and ye shall be as gods, knowing good and evil. (Gen. 3:1-5)

Satan's appeal to mental pride has not changed. And to believe him is to worship him—and to suffer horrible loss.

At its November 6, 1996 meeting in Mexico City, "the Board of the International Humanist and Ethical Union approved the following 'minimum statement' of Humanism:"

> Humanism is a democratic and ethical life stance which affirms that human beings have the right and responsibility to give meaning and shape to their own lives. It stands for the building of a more humane society through an ethics based on human and other natural values in a spirit of reason and free inquiry through human capabilities. It is not theistic, and it does not accept supernatural views of reality."[44]

Notice once again that this is merely a statement of ***faith*** concerning basic religious issues. There is nothing scientific about this statement at all.

What Is Our Origin?

People of all ages want to know how humans and this universe came into being. Where did we come from? This is—and will forever be—a religious subject, for it is impossible to reproduce the creation of the universe in a laboratory. Either we accept God's explanation of how the universe began, or else we must accept the speculations (human-theory thumping) of some men who were not there when it happened, and do not know. Everyone at some point in life decides who they will believe. What a person decides to believe concerning the origin of the universe determines that person's worldview. A "worldview" is the foundational belief which one uses as a basis for determining all other beliefs. A person's worldview drastically influences every area of his life.

The Christian Worldview

The Christian worldview is found in Genesis 1:1, the very first verse in the Bible: "In the beginning God created the heaven and the earth." Christians believe the revelation of God's Word in this matter of origins, and base every aspect of their lives upon it. Looking at the world from this view, it is logical to believe that since God created the heaven and the earth, then God must exist. And since God exists and the Bible is "given by inspiration of God" (2 Tim. 3:16), then the teachings of the Bible concerning sin, immortality, Heaven, Hell, redemption, salvation, and everlasting life are also true.

The Humanist Worldview

The Humanist worldview is just the opposite of the Christian one. Humanists choose NOT to believe the revelation of God's word concerning creation, and instead base every aspect of their lives upon the "theory"

---

[43] Ibid.

[44] Board of the International Humanist and Ethical Union, "IHEU Defination of Humanism" (Amherst, New York: American Humanist Association, 1996), Http://www.humanism.net/definitions/iheu-def.html.

of macro-evolution (either Charles Darwin's version or else someone else's modification of Darwin's theory). Of course, Darwin did not originate the theory of evolution, but only made an old pagan myth look "scientific."

According to a document on the American Humanist Association web site, early in 1977 the AHA established itself as a major force in the creation-evolution controversy by issuing "A Statement Affirming Evolution As a Principle of Science" and sending copies of it to every major school district in the country.[45]

Thus Humanists clearly not only believe in evolution, but also intend that every child in America be taught evolution.

It is important to note that Bible-believing Christians do believe in ***micro***-evolution (change within a kind of animal or plant). It is ***macro***-evolution (change from one kind into another kind) that Christians deny. Mate two mongrel dogs and you never know what the babies will look like, except for one certainty—the babies will all be dogs. Humanists want us to believe that a new ***kind***—a non-dog—might be born. Furthermore, Humanists believe and teach our children that change within a kind proves that change from one kind into another kind also happens. Their belief is simply not in line with what is observed day by day in the laboratory of life. Since it is macro-evolution that Humanists generally mean when they refer to evolution, macro-evolution is what will be meant in this book also, unless stated otherwise.

Looking at the world from the false macro-evolution worldview, it appears logical to believe that there is no such thing as a real, living, prayer-hearing-and-answering God, no sin, no immortality, no Heaven, no Hell, no redemption, no salvation, and no everlasting life.

Humanists are atheists in the sense that they reject the true and living creator God. ***This does not mean that Humanists do not believe in a god—for they do believe in a god, though they deny it.*** The "natural force" that they claim created life and all the life forms is their god. They call him (or her or it) **EVOLUTION.** Though no one has ever seen him (or her or it) in action, Humanists insist he (or she or it) exists. Evolution is their "spook in the machinery," their idol, and they worship him (or her or it) with a fervent blind faith. Humanists are, in fact, polytheists, for they also worship themselves.

What Is Right, and What Is Wrong?

Like it or not, we have to make decisions concerning right and wrong virtually every day of our lives. Should I lie about my age? Should I sleep with this person? Should I cheat my neighbor? Should I murder my unborn baby? These are religious decisions for which scientific experiments cannot provide direction.

Christians Believe There Is Righteousness and Sin

Christians believe that since God created all things, He certainly knows what is good for humans, and what will cause them harm. His laws are therefore authoritative, and, though in our youth or inexperience we may not understand them, we are wise to obey them for our own good. Most people go through a time during their teenage years when they question God's moral laws, but the pain this causes eventually convinces wise people that God must be right after all. This accepting the truth of God's law is called maturing. True Christians believe that God is right when He says that murder, rape, sodomy, adultery, fornication, stealing, and lying are sins.

---

[45] Lloyd Morain, "Chapter 9: The American Humanist Association," in *Humanism as the Next Step*, reprint, 1954 (Amherst, New York: Humanist Press, 1998), Http://www.americanhumanist.org/publications/morain/chapter-9.html.

Humanists Deny There Is Righteousness and Sin

Humanists reject the Ten Commandments and the very concept of sin because they reject God Himself. Boasts Fredrick Edwords,

> Religious Humanism is usually without a god, without a belief in the supernatural, without a belief in an afterlife, and without a belief in a "higher" source of moral values.
>
> Humanism's rejection of the notions of sin and guilt, especially in relation to sexual ethics, puts it in harmony with contemporary sexology and sex education as well as aspects of humanistic psychology.[46]

Harvey Lebrun declares that two of the basic principles held by Humanists are:

> 1. No belief in ... sin.
> 2. Commitment to individual and social ethics that are based on changing human experience, compassion for other human beings, and concern for the related world of humankind and Earth—rather than on supposedly divine injunctions, church pronouncements, divine rewards and punishments in this or a future life, and so forth.[47]

Now it is these ideas—that there is no sin, that nothing is absolutely wrong, and that God is not the final authority concerning right and wrong—that make humanism so purely wicked and evil. To the Humanist, morality is whatever he wants it to be. What the Humanists call "new morality" is what the Bible calls "sin." The following quotes from Humanist writings demonstrate this fact clearly.

Humanist Morality Rejects/Belittles Marriage

Humanist (im)morality means a total breakdown of the home. Humanist writer Tom Flynn states the Humanist stand concerning marriage very bluntly:

> For my money, matrimony remains a corrupt, misogynistic, and outmoded institution. The need to do away with it is as real today as it was in the 60s.... Today, it seems foolish to expect that many persons will find the same partner physically, emotionally, and intellectually fulfilling throughout a long life of profound and often unpredictable personal development. Divorce and remarriage are easier than they were, say, half a century ago, a reform for which freethinkers and humanists deserve much credit.... Perhaps our battle cry should be "Legitimize bastardy!"[48]

Misogynistic means hateful of women. According to those who have swallowed humanist dogma, to marry a woman means you hate her, but to rob her of her virginity, give her a bastard baby, and then desert both her and the baby is to love her and liberate her. Humanists have confused love with lust and have confused liberty with licentiousness. Obviously, it is actually the Humanists that are hateful of women.

Humanist Morality Encourages Adultery and Sodomy

Humanists encourage teenagers to have sex before marriage, and encourage husbands and wives to be unfaithful to their mates, and encourage everyone to have sex with multiple partners of either sex. One of the most important Humanist documents is "The New Bill of Sexual Rights and Responsibilities" which states:

> Repressive taboos should be replaced by a more balanced and objective view of sexuality based upon a sensitive awareness of human behavior and needs. Archaic taboos limit our thinking in many ways. The human person, especially the female, has been held in bondage by restrictions that prescribed when, where, with whom, and with what parts of the body the sexual impulse could be satisfied. As these taboos are dispelled and an objective reappraisal ensues, numerous sexual expressions will be seen in a different light. Many that now seem unacceptable will very likely become valid in certain circumstances. Extramarital sexual relationships with the consent of one's partner is being accepted by some. Premarital sexual relationships, already accepted in some parts of the world, will become even more widely so. This will very likely also be true of homosexual and bisexual relationships. The use of genital associations to express feelings of genuine intimacy, rather than as connections for

---

[46] Frederick Edwords, "What is Humanism?"

[47] Lebrun, "Humanism with a Capital H."

[48] Tom Flynn, "Legitimize Bastardy!" *Secular Humanist Bulletin* 12, no. 2 (Spring 1996) (Amherst, New York: Council for Secular Humanism, 1996), Http://www.SecularHumanism.org/library/shb/flynn_12_1.html.

physical pleasure or procreation alone, may then transcend barriers of age, race, or gender.[49]

In other words, Humanists believe that for humans to live lower than dogs and pigs is the way it ought to be.

Humanist Morality Advocates Pornography

On every moral issue Humanism takes a stand against the morality of God's Word. If Humanism is moral, than the Bible is immoral (and, of course, Humanists say it is). Pornography is another example of Humanist (im)morality. Humanist Wendy McElroy has written several books on the subject of pornography, including, "*XXX: A Woman's Right to Pornography* ... and *Sexual Correctness: The Gender-Feminist Attack on Women*."[50] Writing in the humanist magazine *Free Enquiry*, McElroy states her humanist moral position:

> As a "pro-sex" feminist, I contend: Pornography benefits women, both personally and politically.... Pornography benefits women politically in many ways. Historically, pornography and feminism have been fellow travelers and natural allies. Although it is not possible to draw a cause-and-effect relationship between the rise of pornography and that of feminism, they both demand the same social conditions—namely, sexual freedom.
>
> Pornography is free speech applied to the sexual realm. Freedom of speech is the ally of those who seek change: it is the enemy of those who seek to maintain control. Pornography, along with all other forms of sexual heresy, such as homosexuality, should have the same legal protection as political heresy. This protection is especially important to women, whose sexuality has been controlled by censorship through the centuries.[51]

There is a little bit of truth to what McElroy says: pornography and Humanist feminism *are* fellow travelers. That is another reason why no true Christian woman can be a part of the misnamed Woman's Liberation Movement (it should be called the Woman's Enslavement Movement).

The rest of what McElroy says is lies. Pornography does not benefit women, either personally or politically. To the contrary, pornography results in women being degraded, abused, raped, beaten and murdered. Pornography stirs up vile and selfish lusts in both men and women, thus causing them to break their marriage vows, to become prostitutes spreading destructive diseases, and to do many shameful, abominable acts.

Pornography is not free speech anymore than lying is free speech. Pornography is no more protected by the Bill of Rights than rape. True freedom provides opportunity to do right, not the opportunity to abuse and degrade fellow human beings.

Humanist Morality Advocates Murdering Children

Humanists love to put the word "children" in the names of their organizations so that people will think they love children. However, the fact is that Humanists hate children so much that they try to prevent them from even being born. Failing in that they try to kill them in any manner possible. Specifically, Humanists advocate murdering children by abortion, infanticide, and assisted suicide.

Murder by Abortion. Says the American Humanist Association about its own self:

> The AHA was the first national membership organization to endorse elective abortion. Further, leading abortion-law reform groups of the time were top-heavy with humanists, most notably the Religious Coalition for Abortion Rights (now the Religious Coalition for Reproductive Choice) and the National Association for the Repeal of Abortion Laws (now the National Abortion Rights Action League).[52]

---

49 Lester Kirkendall, "New Bill of Sexual Rights and Responsibilities," *The Humanist*, January/February 1976 (Buffalo, New York), Http://www.humanism.net/~documents/sexual-rights.html.

50 Wendy McElroy, "A Feminist Defense of Pornography," *Free Inquiry* 17, no. 4 (Fall 1997) (Amherst, New York: Council for Secular Humanism, 1997), Http://www. SecularHumanism.org/library/fi/mcelroy_17_4.html.

51 Ibid.

52 "Frequently Asked Questions (FAQS) About the American Humanist Assocation" (Amherst, New York: American Humansist Association, Yr. on web 1997), Http://www.humanism. net/information/faqs.html.

McElroy, the same Humanist that advocated pornography in the quote above, reveals the humanist principle underlying abortion as follows:

> The liberal principle "a woman's body, a woman's right" underlay arguments ranging from abortion rights to lifestyle freedoms like lesbianism.[53]

This idea, that a woman's body is her own to do with as she pleases, is very popular today, but is simply a falsehood. The Bible tells us the truth in 1 Cor. 6:18-20:

> Flee fornication. Every sin that a man doeth is without the body; but he that committeth fornication sinneth against his own body. What? know ye not that your body is the temple of the Holy Ghost which is in you, which ye have of God, **and ye are not your own**? For ye are bought with a price: therefore glorify God in your **body**, and in your spirit, which are **God's**.

God owns us in two ways. First, He created us, and therefore we are His—spirit, soul, and body. Second, He became a human by being born of a virgin so that He could die for our sins. He gave himself to be crucified in order to purchase us with his own blood (Acts 20:28). By sinning we sold ourselves into the bondage of sin, but Jesus paid the ultimate price to buy us back.

> Forasmuch as ye know that ye were not redeemed with corruptible things, as silver and gold, from your vain conversation received by tradition from your fathers; but with the precious blood of Christ, as of a lamb without blemish and without spot. (I Pet. 1:18-19).

Murder by Infanticide. Many people have already been so influenced by Humanist doctrines taught to them in public school "life skills" (sin skills) sex classes that they do not believe that abortion is murder. Humanism does not murder only the unborn, but the partial born are also murdered. The Religious Coalition for Reproductive Choice, the group the American Humanist Association said is "top-heavy with humanists" (see quote above), is pro-partial-birth abortion. This is the procedure in which a baby is delivered feet first, so that when all of the baby has exited but its head, a medical instrument is pierced into the baby's skull at the base of the neck, and its brains sucked out. If they did this an instant after the head emerged, they would be arrested for murder. It is, in fact, murder even if it is declared legal by corrupt judges. The Religious Coalition for Reproductive Choice ended an article which they fittingly titled "Partial Compassion" (it certainly isn't full compassion, and in fact isn't true compassion) by exhorting readers to write then President Clinton to ask him to veto the partial-birth abortion ban bill sponsored by the Republican majority congress:

> President Clinton has vowed once again to veto any ban on late-term abortions that does not include both a life and health exception for the woman. Please call or write the White House, citing bill S6/HR1122, to let him know you support that position.[54]

The "life and health exception for the woman" is pure hypocrisy—the baby is already born except for its head; its legs, body and arms are already out. The head would easily follow in a few seconds. The real danger to the mother is not the birth of the baby's head, but the partial-birth abortion procedure itself, which requires the doctor to insert his hand or an instrument inside the mother to force an always risky breech birth. This procedure is nothing less than pure, premeditated, cold-blooded murder of a full-term baby. In July of 1998 the Republican-majority House voted 296-132 to overturn President Clinton's veto of a bill banning partial birth abortion, but on Friday, September 18, 1998, the Republican led Senate failed by three votes to reach the two thirds majority needed to do the same. Fifty-one Republicans and 13 Democrats voted to overturn the president's veto, while 32 Democrats and 4 liberal (humanist) Republicans voted to sustain it. So the murder continues.

But Humanists are not content to murder only the pre-born and partially born: they also want to murder the completely born. The murder of an already born child is called "infanticide," and has always been murder in the USA. But Humanists intend to change that law. Infanticide is a logical position for a humanist

---

53 McElroy, "A Feminist Defense of Pornography."

54 Jay Heavner, "Partial Compassion," *Web Site of Religious Coalition for Reproductive Choice* (1996) (Washington, D.C.: RCRC Publications, 1996), Http://www.rcrc.org/pubs/speakout/lateterm.html.

to take. Humanist leader Joseph Fletcher (the author of the book *Situation Ethics*), writing in a volume titled *Infanticide and the Value of Life*, says truthfully, "It is reasonable, indeed, to describe infanticide as post natal abortion."[55] It is clear therefore that the Humanists who have really studied this issue realize that abortion is the same thing as infanticide. If infanticide is murder, then abortion is murder also. Humanists advocate murdering unwanted babies during the first year of life after birth. In the book just referenced (*Infanticide and the Value of Life*) Arval A. Morris submits "Proposed Legislation" which states:

> Section 1. Authorization of euthanasia. Subject to the provisions of this Act it shall be lawful for a qualified physician, or his professional medical agent, as authorized by a qualified physician's written statement, to administer euthanasia to a qualified child for whom the child's parent or guardian previously has made a written declaration voluntarily requesting euthanasia for the qualified child and which declaration is lawfully in force at the time of administering euthanasia.[56]

Murder by suicide. Brags the American Humanist Association about itself:

> In 1974, long before the activism of Dr. Jack Kevorkian and the Hemlock Society, the National Commission for Beneficent Euthanasia was established as an AHA program. It issued through the Humanist magazine the groundbreaking statement, "A Plea for Beneficent Euthanasia." The document was signed by medical, legal, and religious leaders and called for "a more enlightened public opinion to transcend traditional taboos and move in the direction of a compassionate view toward needless suffering in dying." As a result of this, the ideas it presented are now a regular part of public discourse.[57]

Humanists are masters at renaming words with names that sound exactly the opposite of the real meaning of the word. In this case they have renamed murder as euthanasia. "Euthanasia" means "a painless, happy death." It sounds good—better to die happy than to die sad, right? However, it will not have such a happy ring if it is one of your own loved ones—a mate or parent or child—that is talked into committing suicide by a humanist doctor such as Dr. (Death) Kevorkian.

Paul Kurtz, the author of *Humanist Manifesto II*, tells the following interesting story:

> Prometheus Books, the leading secular humanist and freethought publisher in the world, is no doubt familiar to most readers of Free Inquiry. Prometheus was recently subpoenaed to appear at the Oakland County, Michigan, criminal prosecution trial of Jack Kevorkian. Dr. Kevorkian has helped twenty-seven people to die—people who were terminally ill and/or suffered great pain and requested the right to commit suicide. He has thus far been acquitted of all efforts to convict him.
>
> The Oakland County prosecutor's office has scheduled two trials. The first, which began in February 1996, involves the deaths of Merian Frederick and Dr. Ali Khalili, who died a month apart in 1993 by breathing carbon monoxide gas supplied by Dr. Kevorkian. He is being tried ex post facto under a now-expired law that banned assisted suicide. A second trial is scheduled to begin in April 1996. Dr. Kevorkian is being prosecuted for the deaths of Marjorie Wendt and Sherry Miller, which occurred in 1991. Prometheus Books was subpoenaed to appear in the first trial because it has published Dr. Kevorkian's book, *Prescription Medicide: The Goodness of Planned Death* (hardcover 1991, paperback 1994).[58]

How fitting that Dr. Death is a Humanist! He really fits in with that group. "Planned Death" is so "good" to Humanists, that they just can't wait to help someone die. Humanists hate life; they don't even want humans to be conceived. But if a human is conceived, they plan to see him dead before birth if possible, at birth if not, during his first year of life otherwise. Else, just as soon as they catch him in pain or depressed, or weak—zap! Loving, kind people that Humanists are, some how some way they are going to "help" people die—prematurely. They have such "compassion," and "love" humanity so! They claim to be pro-choice, but give the babies they abort no choice. No, they are not pro-choice. They are pro-death.

Again it is important to remember: ***right*** and ***wrong*** are religious issues, and it is obvious that Humanism is a religion, for it deals with religious issues only, and not with science as it pretends.

---

55 Joseph Fletcher, *Religioethical Issues*, ed. Marvin Kohl (Buffalo, New York: Prometheus Books, 1978), 17.

56 Arval A. Morris, "Proposed Legislation," ed. Marvin Kohl, in *Infanticide and the Value of Life* (Buffalo, New York: Prometheus Books, 1978).

57 "Frequently Asked Questions (FAQS) About the American Humanist Assocation."

58 Paul Kurtz, "Notes from the Editor: Jack Kevorkian on Trial," *Free Enquiry* 16, no. 2 (Spring 1996)*Notes from the Editor* (Amherst, New York), Http://www.SecularHumanism.org/ library/fi/kurtz_16_2.html.

What Is Our Purpose In Life?

Why are you alive? What is your purpose in life? What are you doing here on this big ball called earth? Is there any good news to encourage you in the right direction? Everyone needs a purpose in life lest he be constantly frustrated and confused. Everyone needs to know why they are here and what they should be doing. But again, these are religious questions which science cannot answer. Christianity answers these questions, and so does Humanism—but with irreconcilably opposing answers.

The Christian Purpose of Life

Christianity teaches that humans exist to worship and serve their Creator, who loved them, and gave Himself for them. Christians are to worship God by loving Him with all their hearts, obeying His commands, and fulfilling the Great Commission which He gave them in Mat. 28:18-20. Millions of Christians (the author included) testify to the fact that serving Christ brings not only joy and peace, but also a marvelous sense of eternal importance and significance to life. The word "eternal" needs to be emphasized in the last sentence, because eternal importance and significance is something Humanism obviously cannot give. According to Humanism, once you die life is over. But according to the Bible of Christianity, once you die conscience existence continues forever.

The Humanist Purpose of Life

Humanism also endeavors to provide people with an answer to the question, What is the purpose of life? There is a document on the website of the American Humanist Association titled "Friends of Religious Humanism." This document, as its name implies, solicits people to become members of a Humanist organization called Friends of Religious Humanism. According to this document

> the Friends of Religious Humanism is an organization founded by Edwin H. Wilson, Lester Mondale, and others in 1962 as the "Fellowship of Religious Humanists" to advance humanism within the Unitarian-Universalist denomination and to promote religious humanism in general.... The FRH office is located in Humanist House, which also contains the offices of the American Humanist Association.... Mira Poudrier is the office manager for FRH and oversees the publication of *Religious Humanism*, the FRH semi-annual journal.... The friends of Religious Humanism is an affiliate organization of the Unitarian Universalist Association. Our stated purpose is as follows: "To promote and encourage the religious, ethical and philosophical thought and life of our members and society. To this end, (we) shall arrange lectures, encourage writing, publish periodicals and other literature, hold discussion groups, seminars and conferences, endeavoring to provide both inspirational materials and scholarly studies which apply the scientific spirit and methods to the materials of ethics and religion."[59]

In an effort to encourage people to join The Friends of Humanism, this American Humanist Association document gives the following testimony from a man named Peter Samson:

> "YES: Humanism can be religious; indeed, the most meaningful and livable kind of humanism is itself a religious way of understanding and living life. It offers a view of [people] and [their] place in the universe that is a religious philosophy ... overarching and undergirding it all, there can be a haunting sense of wonder which never leaves one for whom life itself is a mystery and miracle. Where did we come from, why are we here, where are we going with all the effort, frustration, the grief, the joy? To be caught up in this sense of wider relatedness, to sense our being connected in live ways with all the world and everyone in it, is the heart dimension of religion, whatever its name."[60]

So, the leaders of Humanism also agree that Humanism is a religion. But what is their answer to the question, "What is the purpose of life?" Their answer may surprise you. Edwords gives the Humanist answer to our question as follows:

> One dances for the sheer joy of the activity. It is the process more than the product that counts. And this is how the Humanist good life is to be lived.
>
> So, when someone asks a Humanist, "What is the purpose of life?" the Humanist should answer, "Life is not purpose, life is art." The meaning is found in the doing.

---

59 "Friends of Religious Humanism" (Amherst, New York: American Humanist Association, Yr. on web 1997), Http://www.humanism.net/frh/html.

60 Ibid.

This is a revolutionary and truly unique way of looking at the world. It is a way that finds the question of cosmic purpose irrelevant.[61]

So, to a Humanist, life has NO purpose! Humanists are here, but they don't have any idea why. Therefore they devote themselves to trying to create the "Humanist good life," by ignoring their duties to God, family, and country, and living for their own selves, indulging in illicit sex, drugs, alcohol, getting rich, buying new cars and houses, etc., because they think the only heaven they will ever have is the one they create for themselves here on earth. Not only do humanists have no purpose, they also have no hope for the future. No hope for seeing again their loved ones that pass into eternity before them. No hope for an improvement over this life. No hope at all. They are, as the Bible puts it, in the condition of "having no hope, and without God in the world" (Eph. 2:12).

And what if they are unable to create their "good life?" What if their labors don't make them rich? What if their immorality causes them to get AIDS? What if their unfaithfulness causes the destruction of all the relationships in life that really matter? What if their "quality of life" does not match their expectations? Well they have an answer for that also—suicide! Just as they use contraception and abortion to prevent having to share wealth with children now, so humanists depend on death to deliver them from the consequences of their depraved lifestyle later. Christianity offers a much cleaner, and rewarding life in the here and now, plus eternal life and Heaven. Humanism offers something it can seldom deliver in the here and now, then everlasting death. Humanist leader Fredrick Edwords puts it like this:

"What is the promise of Humanism?"

Well, we already know what we can't promise. As sober realists and no-nonsense straight-shooters, we're experts in throwing the wet blanket of rationalism over the fondest hopes of our fellows. We know the "bad news," but what's our "good news," what is the gospel of Humanism?... The promise of Humanism is a good life here and now.... But now we can ask, if this is the promise of Humanism—if this is the promise of liberal religion—is it a promise limited only to the affluent, the intelligent, the educated? If so, then are we making a promise we can't always keep? This is the criticism leveled against us by the otherworldly religions. While we say that they can't keep their otherworldly promises, they explain that they turned to this other world because we Humanists didn't keep our worldly promises.... And when, in those rare instances, we find that the realization of the promise is futile, as in the case of an agonizing terminal illness, Humanism offers the freedom to exit this life at will and with dignity. This is voluntary euthanasia, an area of great importance to Humanists, so much so that there will be two major workshops on this topic at the national conference of the American Humanist Association next weekend.

So, in the end, the promise is not a perfect one. But we admit that. Others may seem to offer more perfect promises, but can they deliver? I have no evidence that anyone has ever gotten to heaven, realized Nirvana, or merged with God. But I see evidence every day that the promise of the good life is no mirage.[62]

So, if Humanism should not work, and instead turns our lives into messes, let us be comforted to know that the Humanists are conducting workshops to show us the best way to commit suicide! Unfortunately, after reading stacks and stacks of Humanist books, magazines, and other literature in preparing to write this book, I have found no evidence whatsoever that there is no God. So I think I'll pass on the suicide. True Christianity doesn't drive one to suicide, but I can certainly understand how Humanism or Humanist Christianity (often called liberal—that is, phony—Christianity) might.

Let us be very blunt. Not only is the promise of Humanism not a perfect one; it is a mirage in spite of what Edwords says. And I see evidence every day that the Humanist promise will never be attained for the general population by any godless, humanist, socialist economic system. Humanism NEVER fulfills its promise to the masses. The humanist economic system, socialism, is economic gambling—there are a few winners at the expense of a huge multitude of losers, with most of the money going into the pockets of the casino state. The casino state then magnifies the winner, to lure in more sucker voters, totally ignoring the multitude of suffering losers. Witness the poverty brought upon every country that has tried communist

---

61 Fredrick Edwords, "The Promise of Humanism," in *Library: Modern* (Amherst, New York: American Humanist Association, 1989), Http://infidels.org/library/modern/fred_edwords/promise.html.

62 Ibid.

humanism, or Buddhist humanism, or any other brand of socialist economy. In country after country humanists advocate socialism in spite of the fact that it unfailingly fails. Under socialism the wealth always ends up in the hands of a few corrupt government officials and their friends, while everyone else lives in poverty. The closest that humanity has ever come to a good life materially has been attained here in the USA as a result of our Christian heritage and the free enterprise system based upon it.

Humanism has a gospel, and humanism claims to give people purpose of life. Humanism is therefore a religion. But the Humanist religion's gospel is false, and its purpose of life leaves one without hope and without God.

Is There Life After Death?

Since all men know that they will someday die, this is a question of great interest to everyone. Science, however, has never been able to give an answer to this question one way or the other. This, therefore, is an immensely religious question.

Christianity Says There Is Life After Death

The Bible very clearly declares that upon dying believers in the Lord Jesus Christ go to Heaven, and unbelievers go to the Lake of Fire:

> For whatsoever is born of God overcometh the world: and this is the victory that overcometh the world, even our faith. (1 John 5:4)

> He that overcometh shall inherit all things; and I will be his God, and he shall be my son. But the fearful, and unbelieving, and the abominable, and murderers, and whoremongers, and sorcerers, and idolaters, and all liars, shall have their part in the lake which burneth with fire and brimstone: which is the second death. (Rev. 21:7-8)

Humanism Says There Is No Life After Death

What about immortality? Does Humanism take a purely scientific stand by avoiding this purely religious question? Absolutely not! Declares Humanist Manifesto II:

> Promises of immortal salvation or fear of eternal damnation are both illusory and harmful. They distract humans from present concerns, from self-actualization, and from rectifying social injustices. Modern science discredits such historic concepts as the "ghost in the machine" and the "separable soul." Rather, science affirms that the human species is an emergence from natural evolutionary forces. As far as we know, the total personality is a function of the biological organism transacting in a social and cultural context. There is no credible evidence that life survives the death of the body. We continue to exist in our progeny and in the way that our lives have influenced others in our culture.[63]

Where is their proof that modern science discredits the existence of a separable soul? They give none, for they have no proof to give! Nor can they show us an experiment proving that humans emerged from natural evolutionary forces—or even that such forces exist. Again, this is purely a religious doctrinal statement. No proof is given to back up this superstitious faith. Humanists give no credible evidence that there is no soul, nor that the soul does not survive the death of the body. Clearly the Humanist movement is based on religious faith, and not on scientific fact. Humanism is a pagan religion pure and simple. There is nothing scientific about it.

How Can I Be Saved?

The subject of salvation certainly is a religious subject if ever there was one. It implies that there is something to be saved from. More than anything else humans want to be saved from the horrors and uncertainties of death and whatever follows death. They want to be saved from the penalty God said would

---

63 Paul Kurtz, *Humanist Manifestos I & II.*

result from sin—specifically eternal torments in Hell and the Lake of Fire and Brimstone. So far science has not been able to prevent life from leaving a body, nor give life back to a dead body. Nor is there any indication that science will ever be able to do so. So, Humanists are unable to offer science as a solution to this problem. They can only offer a religious answer, and they do.

Let us contrast Christian salvation with Humanist salvation.

Christian Salvation

The Bible teaches that we cannot save ourselves; only God can save us. "For by grace are ye saved through faith; and that not of yourselves: it is the gift of God: not of works, lest any man should boast" (Eph. 2:8-9).

God took upon himself a human body by being born of a virgin. "Behold, a virgin shall be with child, and shall bring forth a son, and they shall call his name Emmanuel, which being interpreted is, God with us" (Mat. 1:23). As a human, He "was in all points tempted like as we are, yet without sin" (Hebrews 4:15). Being sinless, He was able to die for our sins on the cross of Calvary. 1 Corinthians 15:1-4 tells us that the gospel (meaning "good news") is "how that Christ died for our sins according to the scriptures; and that he was buried, and that he rose again the third day according to the scriptures." God's promise to us is

> that if thou shalt confess with thy mouth the Lord Jesus, and shalt believe in thine heart that God hath raised him from the dead, thou shalt be saved. For with the heart man believeth unto righteousness; and with the mouth confession is made unto salvation.... For whosoever shall call upon the name of the Lord shall be saved. (Rom. 10:9-13)

The believer in the Lord Jesus Christ is instantly passed from death unto eternal life, and knows it.

> And this is the record, that God hath given to us eternal life, and this life is in his Son. He that hath the Son hath life; and he that hath not the Son of God hath not life. These things have I written unto you that believe on the name of the Son of God; that ye may know that ye have eternal life, and that ye may believe on the name of the Son of God.... And we know that the Son of God is come, and hath given us an understanding, that we may know him that is true, and we are in him that is true, even in his Son Jesus Christ. This is the true God, and eternal life. (1 John 5:1-20)

Humanist Salvation

Humanism, as is to be expected, teaches just exactly the opposite of what the Bible says. Declares *Humanist Manifesto II*, "No deity will save us; we must save ourselves."[64]

Now that is an interesting statement, remembering that Humanists don't believe in sin or Hell—how can they save themselves from something if it doesn't exist? Many of the signers of *Humanist Manifestos I and II* have already gone on to meet their Maker. Why didn't they save themselves? The above statement from *Humanist Manifesto II* shows again just how proud, conceited, and foolish Humanists are.

In conclusion, Humanism is a religion, based not on science, but on faith. Two more quotes from documents from the American Humanist Association web site will further confirm this point. Says Beverly Earles in "Friends of Religious Humanism": "Humanism is religion come of age."[65] And says the executive director of the American Humanist Association, in his essay "What Is Humanism": "Religious Humanism is 'faith in action.'"[66] Did you catch that? Humanism is religion. Humanism is not science, but "**faith**" in action.

---

[64] Ibid.

[65] "Friends of Religious Humanism."

[66] Frederick Edwords, "What is Humanism?"

The Religious Status of Humanism Matters

If humanism is scientific, then it would surely be wrong, even stupid, to oppose it. However, ***if humanism is merely a religion, then for public schools to teach humanist doctrines constitutes the establishment of a state religion, and is therefore illegal according to the First Amendment to the Constitution.***

"UUs Continue to Protest Impending War with Iraq in Large Numbers—Demonstrations held in New York, San Francisco. (Boston, Feb. 19, 2003) During January and February, across the United States and around the globe, demonstrations which oppose pre-emptive U.S. military action against Iraq have continued, with Unitarian Universalists participating in large numbers in organized marches, rallies, and demonstrations. On January 31, UUA President William Sinkford joined nearly 400 UUs from the greater Los Angeles area in a candlelight vigil against pre-emptive military action in front of the Westwood Federal Building. On February 15, an estimated 350,000-500,000 people participated in a demonstration in New York City. Hundreds of UUs from across the US and Canada attended" (http://www.uufh.org/newsdetail.html?key=101&back=). Is this using tax exempt status to influence politics?

Chapter 4

IS HUMANISM REALLY A RELIGION?

Yes! A Communist-Like Religion

Can a Communist-like organization that denies the existence of God and seeks political dominion over the whole world properly be called a religion? The answer is a resounding "YES!" Remember that Communism itself is a religion. Here is how the late FBI director J. Edgar Hoover described Communism:

> Communism is more than an economic, political, social, or philosophical doctrine. It is a way of life; a false, materialistic "religion." It would strip man of his belief in God, his heritage of freedom, his trust in love, justice, and mercy. Under communism, all would become, as so many already have, twentieth-century slaves.[67]

Elizabeth Gurley Flynn, one of the founding members of the ACLU later became the head of the Communist Party USA.

That description applies equally to Humanism. Humanists are very dangerous religious fanatics, and pose an even greater threat to the USA than do radical Islamists. The Humanist religion is more dangerous than Islam because Humanists have a much larger following in the USA than does Islam, because it has infiltrated our government, schools, and communications media, because its loyalty is not to the USA but to an international headquarters (International Humanist and Ethical Union), and because it has succeeded in hiding itself behind a thin veneer of false science. Humanists leaders present themselves as scientists instead of as the ministers of darkness they actually are. Humanism is what the Apostle Paul described as "science falsely so called" (1 Timothy 6:20).

Actually, to be very accurate, humanism (with a lower-case h) is the religious upon which communism is built, and the American Humanist Association (upper-case H) is an organization almost identical to communism that is promoting the same materialist religion here in the USA, and around the world. Humanism is also the religion of the Unitarian-Universalist Church, which is why you see Unitarian ministers at so many Left-wing rallys and demonstrations, along with the ACLU lawyers, NOW women, Act Up sodomites, and, of course, Michel Communist-Health-Care Moore.

Perhaps the one subject Humanist leaders discuss most frequently among themselves is humanism as a religion. Privately among themselves, they plot and plan how to proselytize the members of other religions. And quietly in courts of law, they demand tax exempt status as non-profit religious organizations. But this religion status of humanism is the very last subject they want discussed in public. Why? ***Because by vigorously promoting separation of theistic religion and state, they have succeeded in obtaining court orders totally expelling God and theistic teachings from public schools.*** Only humanist atheistic views of such religious doctrines as the origin of the universe and man, discipline, morals, etc., may now be taught in the tax-funded schools of America. God has been expelled. Prayer is banned. The Bible is deemed pornography. They have almost

---

[67] J. Edgar Hoover, *Masters of Deceit* (New York, New York: Affiliated Publishers, 1958), vi.

total control of what our children are taught, and they are using this control to brainwash our children in their dogma.

But humanists realize that if enough Christians and other theists ever realize that humanism is a religion also, then Christians might successfully demand that humanist doctrines too be banned from public education! A near fatal blow would therefore be stuck to humanism in the USA. Thus humanists virtually never call humanism a religion when speaking or writing in public forums. Always publicly humanists refer to humanism as "science" and to humanist doctrines as "scientific facts." Just how scientific humanism actually is is a topic of major importance. However, since humanism as science will be discussed in the next two chapters, this chapter will be confined to discussing humanism as a religion. Is Humanism really a religion?

Humanists Declare Humanism a Religion

As has already been shown, Humanist leaders know that Humanism is not science, but is religion. In this chapter more Humanist leaders will be quoted to prove this fact beyond any shadow of doubt. The best way to learn the truth about this issue is to read the books and other publications Humanists wrote for their own—writings meant to be read only by other Humanists or by people interested in becoming Humanists. Humanists know that God-fearing people are very unlikely to read such books.

Lucien Saumur has written a book titled *The Humanist Evangel* to teach Humanists how to spread Humanist beliefs and gain converts to Humanism. This book was first published in 1982 by Prometheus Books in Buffalo, New York, a publishing arm of the American Humanist Association, and therefore voiced the official position of the American Humanist Association. Listen to what Saumur says about humanism being not science but a religion:

> But then if ***humanism cannot be defined positively as humanitarianism, socialism, or science***, must it be defined negatively as anti-religious? Is humanism just an "anti-religion"? Must it be anti-religious because it opposed to some religions? Was Christianity an anti-religion because fought so bitterly against the religion of Islam?
>
> What is it that proposes to explain human nature and purpose if not religion? Is humanism not in fact a religion? Why can it not be so even though it is competing with other religions, with every other religion?
>
> Is it not only as a religion that humanism can have an identity? Is it not only as a religion that humanism can be defined simply and clearly as something distinct from everything else? That it is not a duplicate of something else? That it is defined as something positive rather than as what it is not: that it is defined for what it is for, rather than for what it is against?
>
> Evidently, ***humanism, being a religion, can be classified with other religions. It shares the essential characteristics of a religion.*** But it is not those other religions: ***it is a religion*** essentially different from every other religion, it is itself; it has an identity. And it is in describing this essential difference that the identity may be defined.[68] [Emphasis added.]

It is clear then that Humanist leaders know what every American needs to know: "Humanism cannot be defined positively as … science.… it is a religion." Humanist leaders all know this, but they don't want the American people to know it, for that would mean the end of the domination of Humanist influence in America.

Edward L. Ericson is a humanist minister and the author of *The Humanist Way: an Introduction to Ethical Humanist Religion*. In a forward to Ericson's book, Isaac Asimov, famous writer and past president of the American Humanist Association, says that Ericson is the Humanist minister that preformed his marriage ceremony.[69] After giving an extended history of Ericson's personal involvement as a leader in the religious humanist movement (he was president of the American Ethical Union), Ericson makes the following statement:

> With this extended association spanning three continents, imagine my astonishment to read in the press from time to time that Humanist religion does not exist. It is said to be merely a "myth" invented by extremists of the Fundamentalist right! Some of those who subscribe to this "explanation" grudgingly concede that a few attempts to organize Humanist congregations have been undertaken but usually with the implication that such efforts have been unsuccessful or short-lived.

---

[68] Lucien Saumur, *The Humanist Evangel* (Buffalo, New York: Prometheus Books, 1982), 16.

[69] Edward L. Ericson, *The Humanist Way: An Introduction to Ethical Humanist Religion*, foreword by Isaac Asimov (New York: The Continuum Publishing Company, 1988), vii-ix.

> Yet if one counts the total number of Ethical Culture societies and fellowships and then adds the Unitarian Universalist churches and societies that are explicitly or predominately Humanist in orientation and practice, plus the various congregations of the Society for Humanistic Judaism—all existing examples of Humanist religious organization in the United States and Canada—the sum of such congregations would be in the hundreds. To that number must be added the members-at-large of the Fellowship of Religious Humanists and the considerable body of religious Humanists within the American Humanist Association, an "umbrella" organization that includes both the religious and the non-religious. (In the case of the Unitarian Universalist churches and fellowships an exact estimate of members is not possible, since there exists a gradation from societies that are explicitly Humanist in orientation to those in which more traditional theistic views prevail.) So while the religion of Humanism in North America is small when compared to other religious movements, it can hardly be dismissed as a myth created by its enemies.[70]

Mr. Ericson could hardly have stated the facts more clearly—HUMANISM IS A RELIGION.

The Supreme Court Declares Humanism a Religion

As seen above, the statement that humanism is a religion is not just a baseless accusation of the Fundamentalist Right as humanist journalists would have us believe. Indeed, in the writings Humanists intend to be confined to fellow humanists and humanist sympathizers, Humanists freely admit—even brag—that humanism is a religion. But it is the ***legal*** status of humanism in the USA that is of crucial importance. The fact is that the Supreme Court has ruled Humanism to be an officially recognized religion, and furthermore has granted Humanist organizations full non-profit-organization, tax-exempt status. Mr. Ericson explains:

> Having no God to propitiate, nontheistic religious devotion is directed toward other ethical and spiritual ends. In a footnote to a 1961 Supreme Court decision that extended the full protection of the freedom of religion clause of the First Amendment to a nontheistic Ethical Humanist (a member of the Washington, D.C., Ethical Society), Justice Hugo Black observed: "Among religions in this country which do not teach what would generally be considered a belief in God are Buddhism, Taoism, Ethical Culture, Secular Humanism and others."
>
> The decision in this case (Torcaso v. Watkins) held that a nontheist is entitled to the same rights of conscience under the Constitution as a believer in God. The Court did not "establish" Humanism as the preferred religion of the secular state as some right-wing Catholic and Fundamentalist polemicists have since absurdly contended. The Court only assured to Ethical Humanists and other nontheists the same rights that Baptists, Lutherans, Catholics, and other religious citizens have always claimed for themselves. A contrary decision would have reduced Humanists and all other nontheists to second-class citizens whose full liberty of conscience would be infringed upon. (The government's refusal for many years to accept nontheists as conscientious objectors under the military draft resulted in prison terms for many—a grievous example of religious discrimination on the basis of theology.)
>
> Unfortunately, in the footnote quoted above, Justice Black did not help to clarify matters by referring to Humanist religion as "Secular Humanism." The use of this combination of terms in the Supreme Court's Torcaso decision has since confused the distinction between the secular, and religious types of Humanism.
>
> The confusion came about in the following manner. Shortly before the Supreme Court heard the Torcaso case, a congregation of religious Humanists in California had won in state courts their claim to be a church, a decision that was argued in the Torcaso case as a precedent. Unfortunately, a legal brief that cited the precedent referred to the California congregation as "Secular Humanists," an ambiguous and problematic conjunction of terms to use when referring to a religious body. But Justice Black apparently accepted the label as an accurate and usual designation, and the practice ever since of identifying Humanist religion as "Secular Humanism" has stirred endless misunderstanding and befuddled public comprehension.[71]

Mr. Ericson has inadvertently made an extremely important point! All humanism—even "Secular Humanism"—has been officially recognized as a religion by the Supreme Court of the United States of America. Secular does not mean "non-religious" as so many people think; rather it simply means "excluding God." Not only do most Humanists consider humanism—even that called "secular humanism"—a religion, so does the United States government. Therefore court rulings declaring legal in public schools the teaching of only humanist doctrines concerning such religious subjects as the origin of the universe and of man constitutes the "establishment of a religion" by the United States government.

Ericson's claim that the Supreme Court did not establish humanism as the "preferred religion" of the United State in the Torcaso v. Watkins case is true but deceptive. Ericson is implying that even now humanism has not been established as a preferred religion, and that is not true. In later rulings the Court protected the teaching in public schools of humanist doctrines (e.g. evolution), while banning the teachings and practices of other religions (e.g. the Genesis account of creation and prayer). The following is a statement of present law taken directly from the American Humanist Association web site:

---

[70] Ibid., 9–10.

[71] Ibid., xiii-xiv.

> Schools may teach about explanations of life on earth, including religious ones (such as "creationism"), in comparative religion or social studies classes. In science class, however, they may present only genuinely scientific critiques of, or evidence for, any explanation of life on earth, but not religious critiques (beliefs unverifiable by scientific methodology). Schools may not refuse to teach evolutionary theory in order to avoid giving offense to religion nor may they circumvent these rules by labeling as science an article of religious faith. Public schools must not teach as scientific fact or theory any religious doctrine, including "creationism," although any genuinely scientific evidence for or against any explanation of life may be taught.[72]

It is what is taught in the science class as scientific fact—truth provable in a scientific laboratory—that is important. Evolution, which is merely a dogma—an unprovable religious teaching—of the Humanist religion, should not be allowed to be taught in science class as a proven scientific fact to the exclusion of all debate on the matter, as is now the case. Freedom of speech is essential for truth to prevail. But there is no freedom of speech in the classrooms of public schools today. Instead, public "schools may not refuse to teach evolutionary theory," but "public schools must not teach as scientific fact or theory any religious doctrine, including 'creationism.'" Note that creationism may not even be taught as "scientific theory!" So, humanist religious dogma must be taught as scientific fact even though it isn't, but creationism may not even be taught as scientific theory even though it is the absolute truth.

According to the American Civil Liberties Union (ACLU),

> though social studies classes can survey creation-of-the-world beliefs, U.S. Supreme Court rulings (Epperson v. Arkansas, 1968 and Edwards v. Aguillard, 1987) have made clear that creationism may not be taught as science in public schools because it is a religious dogma.[73]

The ACLU is one of the most important of all Humanist organizations, so we see once again that Humanists leaders know the untruth of their denial that Humanism has been made the state religion of the USA. U.S. Supreme Court rulings have declared evolution to be science (truth), and have declared creationism be in opposition to science (error). Court rulings, therefore, have in fact made Humanism the established state church of the USA in violation of the Bill of Rights. We the people are forced against our wills by taxation to fund a religion which is opposed to everything we believe to be true and sacred. No religion should be so funded, even if it is the true religion. It is wrong to force people to fund teachings they cannot with a clear conscience endorse.

Let us, now call to the witness stand Paul Kurtz, who "in 1973 … took the initiative, as editor of *The Humanist* magazine, in drafting the landmark consensus statement, *Humanist Manifesto II*."[74] We will have him read to us from his preface of that document that was published together with *Humanist Manifesto I* as a small book titled *Humanist Manifesto I & II*. Wrote Kurtz: "Humanism is a philosophical, ***religious***, and moral point of view as old as human civilization itself"[75] [Emphasis added].

Humanist Manifesto I Declares Humanism a Religion

Perhaps the scariest declaration of Humanism as a religion is found in *Humanist Manifest I*. In *Humanist Manifest I*, not only is Humanism boldly declared to be a religion but is also shown to be one and the same with Communism in basic ideology and goals. Note that even the word "manifesto" is used in naming the document. Remember the *Communist Manifesto*?

Boldface italic emphasis has been added to the words religion, religious, etc. in the following excerpt from *Humanist Manifest I* so you can note how often they are used, and how clearly Humanism is declared to be a new "religion" for this age.

> The time has come for widespread recognition of the radical changes in ***religious*** beliefs throughout the modern world. The time is past for mere revision of traditional attitudes. Science and economic change have disrupted the old beliefs. ***Religions*** the world over are under the necessity of coming to terms with new conditions created by a vastly increased knowledge and experience. In every field of human activity, the vital movement is now in the direction of a candid and explicit humanism. In order that ***religious humanism*** may be better understood we, the undersigned, desire to make certain affirmations which we believe the facts of our contemporary life demonstrate.…

---

[72] "RELIGION IN THE PUBLIC SCHOOLS: A Joint Statement Of Current Law," *The American Humanist Association*, April 1995, Http://www.americanhumanist.org/press/Religionpublicschools.html.

[73] "Creationism," in *Threats to Civil Liberties* (New York: American Civil Liberties Union, 1996), 1, Http://www.aclu.org/about/right4.html.

[74] Storer, *Humanist Ethics: Dialogue on Basics*, 3.

[75] Kurtz, *Humanist Manifestos I & II*, 2.

Today man's larger understanding of the universe, his scientific achievements, and his deeper appreciation of brotherhood, have created a situation which requires a new statement of the means and purposes of ***religion***. Such a vital, fearless, and frank ***religion*** capable of furnishing adequate social goals and personal satisfactions may appear to many people as a complete break with the past. While this age does owe a vast debt to traditional ***religions***, it is the less obvious that any ***religion*** that can hope to be a synthesizing and dynamic force for today must be shaped for the needs of this age. To establish such a ***religion*** is a major necessity of the present. It is a responsibility which rests upon this generation. We therefore affirm the following:

First: ***Religious humanists*** regard the universe as self-existing and not created.

Second: Humanism believes that man is a part of nature and that he has emerged as the result of a continuous process.

Third: Holding an organic view of life, humanists find that the traditional dualism of mind and body must be rejected.

Fourth: Humanism recognizes that man's ***religious*** culture and civilization, as clearly depicted by anthropology and history, are the product of a gradual development due to his interaction with his natural environment and with his social heritage. The individual born into a particular culture is largely molded to that culture.

Fifth: Humanism asserts that the nature of the universe depicted by modern science makes unacceptable any supernatural or cosmic guarantees of human values. Obviously humanism does not deny the possibilities of realities as yet undiscovered, but it does insist that the way to determine the existence and value of any and all realities is by means of intelligent inquiry and by the assessment of their relation to human needs. ***Religion*** must formulate its hopes and plans in the light of the scientific spirit and method.

Sixth: We are convinced that the time has passed for theism, deism, modernism, and the several varieties of "new thought."

Seventh: ***Religion*** consists of those actions, purposes, and experiences which are humanly significant. Nothing human is alien to the ***religious***. It includes labor, art, science, philosophy, love, friendship, recreation—all that is in its degree expressive of intelligently satisfying human living. The distinction between the sacred and the secular can no longer be maintained.[76]

Eighth: ***Religious humanism*** considers the complete realization of human personality to be the end of man's life and seeks its development and fulfillment in the here and now. This is the explanation of the humanist's social passion.

Ninth: In place of the old attitudes involved in worship and prayer the humanist finds his ***religious*** emotions expressed in a heightened sense of personal life and in a cooperative effort to promote social well-being.

Tenth: It follows that there will be no uniquely ***religious*** emotions and attitudes of the kind hitherto associated with belief in the supernatural.

Eleventh: Man will learn to face the crises of life in terms of his knowledge of their naturalness and probability. Reasonable and manly attitudes will be fostered by education and supported by custom. We assume that humanism will take the path of social and mental hygiene and discourage sentimental and unreal hopes and wishful thinking.

Twelfth: Believing that ***religion*** must work increasingly for joy in living, ***religious humanists*** aim to foster the creative in man and to encourage achievements that add to the satisfactions of life.

Thirteenth: ***Religious humanism*** maintains that all associations and institutions exist for the fulfillment of human life. The intelligent evaluation, transformation, control, and direction of such associations and institutions with a view to the enhancement of human life is the purpose and program of humanism. Certainly ***religious*** institutions, their ritualistic forms, ecclesiastical methods, and communal activities must be reconstituted as rapidly as experience allows, in order to function effectively in the modern world.

Fourteenth: the humanists are firmly convinced that existing acquisitive and profit-motivated society has shown itself to be inadequate and that a radical change in methods, controls, and motives must be instituted. A socialized and cooperative economic order must be established to the end that the equitable distribution of the means of life be possible. The goal of humanism is a free and universal society in which people voluntarily and intelligently cooperate for the common good. Humanists demand a shared life in a shared world.

Fifteenth and last: We assert that humanism will: (a) affirm life rather than deny it; (b) seek to elicit the possibilities of life, not flee from it; and (c) endeavor to establish the conditions of a satisfactory life for all, not merely for the few. By this positive moral and intention humanism will be guided, and from this perspective and alignment the techniques and efforts of humanism will flow.

So stand the theses of ***religious humanism***. Though we consider the ***religious*** forms and ideas of our fathers no longer adequate[77], the quest for the good life is still the central task for mankind. Man is at last becoming aware that he alone is responsible for the realization of the world of his dreams, that he has within himself the power for its achievement. He must set intelligence and will to the task.[78] [Emphasis added]

The religious doctrines presented in *Humanist Manifesto I and II* are discussed in other chapters of this book. The point of importance to be emphasized here is that *Humanist Manifesto I* professes to be (and obviously is) the statement of faith and aims of a "religion." It claims as its purpose "to establish...a vital, fearless, and frank religion." Four times it refers to "religious humanism." Sixteen times it uses the terms "religion" or "religious." Note also that all its theses are religious in nature. They discuss issues one would expect to be discussed in a Sunday School class at church, though they admit that their religious

---

[76] Please reread this important statement number seven, which is true! Everything in life is religious, including philosophy, science, and public education. Humanists usually lie about this fact, but here they tell the truth. This proves that Humanist leaders know that evolution is a religious teaching. Let this fact sink deep into your memory.

[77] This is an inadvertent admission by Humanists that the USA was founded on Christian principles, and not on humanist principles as Humanists so often claim.

[78] Kurtz, *Humanist Manifestos I & II*, 7–11.

beliefs and forms are not the same as the religious beliefs and forms of the founding fathers of this country. The evidence that humanism is a religion is thus overwhelming.

The chilling truth: the United States of America has combined with the Humanist church in direct violation of the first amendment to the Constitution. The citizens of the USA are now forced by taxation to support the propagation of a pagan atheistic religion which despises everything Christianity stands for. Oppression of free speech in public schools began years ago. Teachers may no longer teach the Genesis account of creation, but are forced to teach the humanist religious doctrine of evolution. Freedom of religion is denied to public school teachers and public school students. When we enter the school yards, we are no longer a free people. If you do not believe this important fact, you definitely need to read the rest of this book and open your eyes—**especially you need to wake up to the religious oppression your children are experiencing every day they attend public school**.

This December 3, 2007 screen shot of the Communist Party USA web site shows the American Civil Liberties Union (ACLU)at the very top of the list of organizations recommended by the Communist Party USA for protecting civil rights. The ACLU is perhaps the most important arm of the American Humanist Association. Both groups have often had the same head. Elizabeth Gurley Flynn, a communist was one of the founding members of the ACLU. She later went on to become the head of the Communist Party USA.

We will close by letting Roy Wood Sellers, professor of philosophy at the University of Michigan, and the man who wrote the initial draft of Humanist Manifest I, tell us what Humanism is:

> Is Humanism a religion, perhaps, the next great religion? Yes, it must be so characterized, for the word, religion, has become a symbol for answers to that basic interrogation of human life, the human situation, and the nature of things—which every human being, in some degree and in some fashion, makes. What can I expect from life? What kind of universe is it? Is there, as some say, a friendly Providence in control of it? And, if so, what then?[79]

[79] Bob Green, "Sixty Years Of A Humanist Manifesto," *Humanists of Utah*, May 1993, Http://www.humanistsofutah.org/1993/artmay93.html.

Chapter 5

IS HUMANISM SCIENCE?

No! It Is Science Falsely So Called

As shown in the previous chapter, if Humanists are to remain in exclusive control of public education, it is vital for them to keep the American public ignorant of two facts: (1) that humanism is indeed being taught in public schools, and (2) that humanism has been officially declared a religion by the United States Supreme Court. As long as Humanists can keep the American public ignorant of these two facts they will be able to continue to monopolize public education to brainwash generation after generation of American youth with their atheistic propaganda, until eventually the majority of Americans will become humanists—and humanism will reign victorious over theism.

But if enough Christians are alerted soon enough to what the Humanists are doing, there is still a chance that Humanism could lose its present monopoly of public education, and in fact suffer a tremendous defeat which would set back its agenda for many decades.

Therefore, in public Humanists almost never identify themselves as Humanists or even as humanists, and almost never identify their beliefs as humanism. Instead they claim to be "scientists," and claim that their beliefs are "proven scientific facts." Furthermore, Humanists label those who disagree with them "opponents to science" whose teachings are based on "unproven religious faith." One specific example of this is their zealous insistence that the theory of evolution is proven scientific fact (and therefore undeniably true), while belittling the Genesis account of creation as a mere religious fable (and therefore undeniably false). So foundational is the theory of evolution to Humanist doctrines that we will devote all of the next chapter to it.

First, however, we must examine Humanist positions on issues in general to see if Humanists actually do determine their positions by applying the scientific method to the issues as they claim. To do this we will go again to the literature that they intended to be read only by other humanists and not by the general public.

Marvin Zimmerman's Testimony

We call to the witness stand Marvin Zimmerman, professor of Philosophy at the State University of New York at Buffalo. Humanist editor Morris B. Storer has recognized Mr. Zimmerman as among "the most careful and realistic thinkers, the lifetime students, the most articulate writers in the field" of humanist ethics.[80] Zimmerman, as a leader in the Humanist movement, knows humanists far better than do most men. What has been his observation? Are humanists scientific? Mr. Zimmerman answers our question in his essay titled "How 'Humanist' are Humanists?" as follows:

> Are humanists scientific? Do humanists practice what they preach? Humanists have claimed their superiority to supernaturalists in their belief in scientific method and empirical truth.... Unfortunately, in practice, humanists often misuse science or do not even pretend to use it at all, in taking positions on a variety of issues.[81]

That is certainly a surprising opinion to be expressed by a Humanist leader. Could Mr. Zimmerman please give us a concrete example? Yes, he obviously can, for in his essay he proceeds to do so:

> In fairness to the humanists, a lack of sophistication and historical insight into the judicial tyranny developing in our country characterizes a much larger segment of our people. But it does seem more prevalent in liberal, secular, and humanist quarters, and probably because of the recent thrust of the Supreme Court decisions in their direction. Compounding the error of accepting decisions on a basis of emotion rather than evidence, humanists have been indifferent to this abuse and growth of judicial power by the Supreme Court, a usurpation of the legislative and executive functions.

---

[80] Storer, *Humanist Ethics: Dialogue on Basics*, 3.

[81] Ibid., 262.

Almost anyone can claim to be scientific in ethics, but whether one actually looks to experience and scientific evidence is an entirely different matter. Thus, whether humans are equal, races are equal, men and women are equal, different cultures are equal, and in what ways are difficult questions to analyze scientifically. Yet, they seem to be easily answered by humanists (and others) and in anything but a scientific fashion. Thus, though there is evidence against belief in equality in all these areas, such suggestions are met by cries of racism, sexism, chauvinism, prejudice, and so on. New absolutes are proclaimed, even as old absolutes are rejected.

There is overwhelming evidence that humans are different in more ways than they are the same, whether physically, mentally, culturally, or educationally. Most are not qualified to practice medicine, law, engineering, police work, firefighting, teaching, et cetera. Yet the reality of ability and achievement or merit is being ignored in order to promote the illusion of equality by use of quotas, reverse discrimination, goals, executive and judicial decrees, charges of discrimination or what have you. In general, many humanists have condoned, if not advocated such measures.

In the name of equality, innocent individuals are being penalized because of their race or sex, and others rewarded because of their race or sex, all this under some form of quota system. Humanists who should be in the forefront of the battle against this new form of original sin, have barely voiced their opposition. Though humanists oppose discrimination against atheists, blacks, and females, they condone, if not accept, discrimination against theists, whites, and males.[82]

Being obviously upset by the hypocrisy he sees in humanist circles, Mr. Zimmerman proceeds on to yet another example of humanist hypocrisy concerning science:

Most humanists oppose capital punishment, not on the basis of scientific evidence that it does not deter crime, but on grounds indistinguishable from religious faith or dogma, namely emotions. They accept blindly the claim that capital punishment does not deter killing because people who kill are too emotional to even consider the consequences of their actions. What about the calm premeditative killer and even the emotionally disturbed? What is the effect of capital punishment on recidivists? They accept the argument that innocent people might be executed and that minority groups make up a disproportionate number on death row. They ignore the fact that most of the victims of crime are also innocent people and also minority members. The issue is not whether the data supports capital punishment, but whether the humanists have taken a stand against capital punishment without regard to the data or scientific method.

Even apart from capital punishment, the humanists' attitude toward crime appears to be based on sentimental emotions rather than reason. They express sympathy for rehabilition, parole, and prisoners' rights, whether or not supported by evidence, and a virtual disregard for victims of crime. In spite of the increasing evidence that the use of parole, rehabilitation, and prisoners' rights have been ineffective for the most part and, as a matter of fact, tend to increase crime, the humanists continue to support them.[83]

Still not content, Mr. Zimmerman continues to give example after example of humanists being unscientific. Unfortunately, space considerations forbid giving all of them here. One more will have to suffice:

Humanists seem to buy the antinuclear energy hysteria, an area in which science would seem to be most relevant and yet has been mostly ignored. Though so many activities are far more dangerous to life and limb (e.g., coal mining, automobile driving, flying in airplanes, or merely crossing a city street), the humanists succumb to the emotions rather than to reason.[84]

Zimmerman concludes his testimony with this sweeping condemnation of humanist hypocrisy (to which we can only say, Amen):

Again and again, on issue after issue, it seems clear that the humanists have failed to practice what they preach, and can hardly be distinguished from the supernaturalists whom they ridicule for being unscientific.[85]

Lucien Maumur's Testimony

It is extremely important that it be proven that humanism is not science. This is important because if humanism is not science then it must be religion. Humanist leaders know that not only is humanism not science, it is not even scientific. It is pure blind faith. Lucien Maumur in his *Humanist Evangel* confirms this:

To achieve a positive role while being anti-religious, humanists are led to pose as the defenders of science against religion. They do so by proclaiming the rationality of science against the alleged irrationality of religion. Yet in this role they fail to be particularly rational; nor are they particularly effective defenders of science. While they proclaim their rationality, they fail to do exactly what a rationalist should do, which is to give a reason. Their opponents, who are accused of being irrational, often display more rationality than they do: their opponents give more reasons than they do! Because of their obsession, these self-proclaimed rationalists firmly believe that they have cornered the market on rationality. In spite of their boast, they cannot recognize reason when they are face to face with it, and thus they dismiss their opponents without a trial and with further accusations of irrationality and superstition. Dialogue is always difficult, and as a result the humanists are usually ignored and thus remain a small and ineffective self-righteous group.

---

82 Ibid., 263.

83 Ibid., 264.

84 Ibid., 268.

85 Ibid.

> Those who pose as the defenders of science against religion are oblivious of the fact that they convince no one and that, to the contrary, they create ill feeling and confirm their opponents in their convictions. But why should these humanists care about the effect of their actions as long as they are doing their appointed duty, which is to proclaim the True Faith?
>
> They never stop to notice that they are not performing any better than the most fanatical of their opponents. While they claim that science contradicts religion, their faith in science has the same kind of absolute quality as does the faith that their more fanatical opponents have in their God. They worship science like others worship gods. They could rightly be accused of having enthroned science as a new superstition or as a new myth.
>
> Furthermore, the attempt of humanists to link religion to anti-science and to pose as defenders of science, in hope of defining itself positively, turns against humanism. While it is true that it is no longer defined negatively, it is no longer defined distinctively either. Thus humanism, in its role as the defender of science, becomes a subordinate part of the scientific establishment. And because it badly overplays its role, it is often unwanted in this part. Thus, when it is defined as the defender of science, the identity of humanism is no better but worse than when it is defined as either humanitarianism or socialism.[86]

Well and truthfully said! Except that humanists do not "worship science like others worship gods." Rather, humanists worship an imaginary creator force they call Evolution as their god—a idol they made with the hands of their mind. They have never seen, heard, smelt, felt, or tasted Evolution, and he, she, nor it has never answered a prayer. But humanists "got faith." Evolution is really slow, they say—takes billions of years to do anything. Evolution is the slowest god in history! If you like to see things happen, worship Jesus.

The Plain Truth

The basic theme of this book is that humanist doctrines being taught in public schools constitutes a violation of the principle of separation of church and state. Humanists know this is true. A few theists also know this, and they are trying to make this known to the public. This has so shaken the Humanist leaders that they are now writing articles and books denying that humanism is a religion. While they used to call humanism "religious humanism," the term "secular humanism" is now used. More than ever, humanists are stressing that humanism is based on science. Next time you read such claims, remember the above quotes, and don't be deceived. Humanism is not substantiated by scientific facts at all (as will be shown in the next chapter). Humanism must be taken on blind faith. It is not science, but is the same pagan religion which underlies communism.

---

86 Saumur, *The Humanist Evangel*, 13–14.

Humanist "science" is the same kind of superstition as practiced by the wizards of the false religions mentioned in the Old Testament. Humanist religious dogma such as "The Big Bang," abiogenesis (spontaneous generation of life from dead matter), the evolution of animals of one kind into a different kind, etc., are all unprovable (because they are not true), and are merely human philosophy which has become the religion of atheists. In no way are any of humanism's evolutionary doctrines provable by the scientific method. Humanists love to use big words to make people think they are highly educated, and to prevent people from questioning them. But make them present their ideas in plain and simple language that people can understand, and humanist dogma become laughable. That is why humanists don't want creationism taught in public schools---humanism cannot survive rational questioning.

Chapter 6

IS EVOLUTION SCIENCE?

No! It Is Religious Dogma

The theory of evolution is not science, as many people have been led to believe, but is the core faith belief held by the atheistic religion called ***humanism***. The doctrine of the origin of the universe and life is the most basic of all religious doctrines. Humanists call their doctrine of origin "Evolution." All humanist teachings revolve around and rest upon the evolution frame and world-view. Rejecting God as the frame upon which to build a satisfactory idea-system, humanists place their faith in a mysterious dead natural force, which—say they—causes all things to evolve upward from dead matter into life, and from the simple to the complex. Upon this unprovable belief humanists base every aspect of their lives. Sir Julian Huxley, world famous evolutionary biologist, former head of UNESCO (United Nations Educational, Scientific, and Cultural Organization), and a signer of *Humanist Manifesto II*, explained this intimate relationship between humanism and evolution as follows:

> If the situation is not to lead to chaos, despair or escapism, man must reunify his life within the framework of a satisfactory idea-system. To achieve this, he needs to survey the resources available to him, both in the outer world and within himself, to define his aims and chart his position, and to plan the outline of his future course. He needs to use his best efforts of knowledge and imagination to build a system of thought and belief which will provide both a supporting framework for his present existence, an ultimate or ideal goal for his future development as a species, and a guide and directive for practical action and planning.
>
> This new idea-system, whose birth we of the mid-twentieth century are witnessing, I shall simply call **Humanism**, because it can only be based on our understanding of man and his relations with the rest of his environment. It must be focused on man as an organism, though one with unique properties. **It must be organized round the facts and ideas of evolution**, taking account of the discovery that man is part of a comprehensive **evolutionary process**, and cannot avoid playing a decisive role in it.[87] [Emphasis added.]

The Significance of Evolution

The significance of evolution is this: if evolution is true, then the Bible is not true, and there is no God. It is amazing how many Christians cannot see this obvious fact. Certainly the humanist leaders of the world are not so blind. Sir Julian Huxley clearly stated the atheistic implication of evolution as follows:

> Darwinism removed the whole idea of God as the creator of organisms from the sphere of rational discussion. Darwin pointed out that no supernatural designer was needed; since natural selection could account for any known form of life, there was no room for a supernatural agency in its evolution.... I think we can dismiss entirely all idea of a supernatural overriding mind being responsible for the evolutionary process.[88]

Since the theory of evolution is being taught daily to our children in public schools, and since Humanism is the religion espoused by the United Nations, it is very important that Americans understand more about Humanism and its theory of evolution.

The Root Idea of Evolution

The root idea of evolution is that living beings can come into existence out of non-living matter without parents. In the past, this basic premise of evolution was called spontaneous generation. Humanists boast that humanism caused the scientific revolution that brought in all the advancements in medicine in the past 100 years. However, that is not true. In fact, scientists' rejection of the Bible and belief in the humanist doctrine of evolution kept the medical world blinded to the true cause of disease for hundreds and hundreds of years. Unwilling to accept God's account of creation, and being unable with their naked eyes to see small

---

87 Julian Huxley, ed., *The Humanist Frame* (New York: Harper & Brothers, 1961), 14.

88 Julian Huxley, "At Random: A Television Preview," in *Evolution After Darwin*, in *Issues In Evolution*, ed. Sol Tax, 3 (Chicago: University of Chicago Press, 1960), 45.

creatures reproduce, they reasoned that dead meat just "spontaneously generated" flies, and that germs had no parents but just evolved from naturally occurring chemical processes.

> The story of the theory of spontaneous generation is one of the most fantastic in all biology. Thompson says: "If longevity of a belief were an index to its truth, the theory of spontaneous generation should rank high among the veracities, for it flourished throughout twenty centuries and more. We cannot trace the history of the theory in detail, but the story may be recommended to the psychological historian as a labyrinth of error, with glimpses of truth at every turn.
>
> The belief in spontaneous generation is recorded In literature back as far as Anaximander (611-547 B.C.). He believed that eels and other aquatic forms are produced directly from lifeless matter. His pupil Anaximenes (588-524 B.C.) "introduced the idea of primordial terrestrial slime, a mixture of earth and water, from which, under the influence of the sun's heat, plants, animals and human beings are directly produced—in the abiogenetic fashion," says Osborn in "From the Greeks to Darwin." Diogenes and Xenophanes ... also believed in spontaneous generation. Then came the "father of natural history," Aristotle (384-322 B.C.), who fostered this idea so strongly that it has persisted for more that twenty centuries.[89]

Louis Pasteur, the father of modern medicine, dared to question the evolution dogma. Under his microscope, Pasteur observed the opposite of evolution, and suspected that spontaneous generation (also called abiogenesis) of living beings from dead matter was not a reality. Furthermore he believed that species did not evolve into new species, but rather came from parents of the same kind as themselves. (This is called biogenesis, and is what the Bible teaches in Genesis chapter one.) Pasteur realized that if he were right, different kinds of germs caused different diseases, and by determining a germ's kind and learning how to kill that kind, the disease it caused could be cured. Pasteur declared, "It is in the power of man to make parasitic illnesses disappear from the face of the globe, if the doctrine of spontaneous generation is wrong, as I am sure it is."[90] On April 7, 1864, six years after Charles Darwin published his *Origin of Species*, and after Pasteur had endured years of opposition, ridicule and outright hatred from evolutionary pseudo-scientists, he lectured in a large lecture room of the Sorbonne concerning his famous experiments. He began by alluding to the significance of his experiments to the creation/evolution conflict.

> Great problems are now being handled, keeping every thinking man in suspense; the unity or multiplicity of human races; the creation of man 1,000 years or 1,000 centuries ago, the fixity of species, or the slow and progressive transformation of one species into another; the eternity of matter; the idea of a God unnecessary. Such are some of the questions that humanity discusses nowadays.[91]

Then he explained his famous experiment, disproving abiogenesis (spontaneous generation). He showed two flasks. Both contained portions of the same organic broth. Both had necks open to the air. Months before, the broth in both had been sterilized by heat. But the neck of one pointed upward, while the long neck of the other curved downward, then upward, like a swans neck. "Why does one decay," he asked, "while the second remains pure?"

> The only difference between them is this: in the first case the dusts suspended in air and their germs can fall into the neck of the flask and arrive into contact with the liquid, where they find appropriate food and develop; thence microscopic beings. In the second flask, on the contrary, it is impossible, or at least extremely difficult ... that dusts suspended in air should enter the vase; they fall on its curved neck.... And, therefore, gentlemen, I could point to that liquid and say to you, I have taken my drop of water from the immensity of creation, and I have taken it full of the elements appropriated to the development of inferior beings. And I wait, I watch, I question it, begging it to recommence for me the beautiful spectacle of the first creation. But it is dumb, dumb since these experiments were begun several years ago; it is dumb because I have kept it from the only thing man cannot produce, from the germs which float in the air, from Life, for Life is a germ and a germ Life. Never will the doctrine of spontaneous generation recover from the mortal blow of this simple experiment.... No, there is now no circumstance known in which it can be affirmed that microscopic beings came into the world without germs, without parents similar to themselves. Those who affirm it have been duped by illusions, by ill-conducted experiments, spoilt by errors that they either did not perceive or did not know how to avoid.[92]

Note carefully what Pasteur said: "there is now ***no*** circumstance known in which it can be affirmed that microscopic beings came into the world without germs, ***without parents similar to themselves***." Amazingly, in spite of Pasteur's conclusive evidence against evolution, humanists still insist that evolution is no longer theory but proven fact! Desperate to believe there is no God, they frantically cling to any straw of evidence for evolution, no matter how fraudulent. For example, Charles Darwin's *Origin of Species*, gave

---

89 "The Origin of Life," by Carolina E. Stackpole, in *Biology*, vol. 6 of *The Outline of Knowledge*, ed. James A. Richard (New York: J.A. Richards, Inc., 1924), 227–8.

90 Beverley Birch, *Louis Pasteur: The Scientist Who Found the Cause of Infectious Disease and Invented Pasteurization* (Milwaukee: Gareth Stevens Children's Books, 1989), 50.

91 Vallery-Radot, *The Life of Pasteur*, trans. Devonshire (Garden City, New York: Doubleday, Page & Company, 1923), 107.

92 Ibid., 107–9.

not one proof that has stood the test of time. Yet it is still the humanist bible. Darwin said it, humanists blindly believe it, and that settles it in their minds—even though all evidence disproves it.

Charles Darwin is said to have been a shy man, who did not like public speaking. Thomas Huxley, grandfather of Sir Julian Huxley (previously quoted) was a close friend and public defender of Charles Darwin and his *Origin of Species*. So fervently did he promote Darwinian evolution that he earned the nickname "Darwin's Bulldog." Yet listen to Huxley's admission:

> To say ... in the admitted absence of evidence, that I have any belief as to the mode in which the existing forms of life have originated, would be using words in a wrong sense.
>
> But expectation is permissible where belief is not; and if it were given to me to look beyond the abyss of geologically recorded time to the still more remote period when the earth was passing through physical and chemical conditions which it can no more see again than man can recall his infancy, I should expect to be a witness of the evolution of living substance from non-living matter.... This is the expectation to which analogical reasoning leads me; but I beg you once more to recollect that I have no right to call my opinion anything but an act of philosophical faith.[93]

Huxley was one of the rare evolutionists who would admit that his belief in evolution was "an act of philosophical faith" in a theory for which there is complete "absence of evidence." Huxley revealed to us the naked truth: evolution is pagan religion, not science! It is superstition pure and simple. It really takes faith to believe in something for which there is not one shred of evidence! To this day, no one has ever—even once—witnessed dead matter give birth to life. If it ever happened, why isn't it still happening? Evolution is a monstrous lie! Think of the multitudes of people who died of infectious diseases because of this myth! Think of the millions now who are rejecting God and dooming themselves to Hell because of faith in this pagan religious fable!

The Strong Case Against Evolution

Not only is the root idea from which evolution springs wrong, but also all the other theories humanists submit as proofs of evolution are either obviously wrong or unprovable. Neither evolution nor the theories given to defend it are provable by the scientific method. In order for a theory to be tested by the scientific method, it must be repeatable under controlled conditions. Obviously the beginning of matter cannot be repeated. Nor can the conditions prevailing on earth when life began be duplicated or controlled. In the Bible God gives us an eye witness account of what happened; but if we reject what God says we are reduced to merely guessing about what happened.

While it is outside the scope of this book to give a detailed refutation of the theory of evolution, the following major points are easily made.

The Laws of Thermodynamics Disprove Evolution

The First and Second Laws of Thermodynamics directly contradict the Theory of Evolution. While the theory of evolution implies a continual creation of new species, the first law of thermodynamics states that although matter can change forms, it can neither be created or destroyed. The second law of thermodynamics states that in any real process, in a closed system, the entropy must increase. In other words, the universal tendency of all things is toward disintegration and decay. Things wear out and die. The complex reverts to the simple. Order degenerates into randomness. Evolution, however, teaches just the opposite, that there is a universal tendency for things to become better organized, more complex, more highly specialized, etc. Clearly, the Theory of Evolution contradicts these two scientific laws. If the first and second laws of thermodynamics be true, then the Theory of Evolution is not true. Consider that the first and second laws of thermodynamics have been tested innumerable times in virtually every field of natural science, and have been proven reliable without exception. Evolution, of course, has never been observed ever—not even once. The Theory of Evolution goes against all observable facts, and is therefore blind faith not science.

---

93 "The Origin of Life," 226–7.

Big Bangs Disprove Evolution

The Second Law of Thermodynamics also proves that the universe had a starting point. It is an observable fact that the universe is expanding—degenerating into randomness. The sun and stars are burning up energy at a terrific rate. Calculations indicate that they will some day burn out and die. Obviously, the universe had a beginning. This proves to be an embarrassment to humanists. How do they explain this beginning? The most popular explanation is the Big Bang Theory. Humanists speculate that before the beginning all the matter of the universe was compressed into a dot perhaps the size of this period: "." Then for some unknown reason there was an unbelievably huge non-explosion—some humanists insist it was not an explosion— in which all that matter violently expanded and formed itself into the planets, stars, etc., and also sparked life into being.

There is one very big problem with this theory. All big bangs that have ever been observed in history ***are*** explosions, and they do not ***create*** order and design—rather they ***destroy*** order and design. A bundle of dynamite big-banged under your home would not cause your home to evolve into a bigger and better one. Rather it would blow your home into thousands of unusable pieces. A nuclear bomb would do an even better job of disintegrating your home. Also, big bangs tend to kill, not create life. The atomic bombs dropped on Hiroshima and Nagasaki did not spark the dead matter in those cities into life. Instead those big bangs killed a multitude of people and an innumerable number of other living creatures. Every big bang ever observed tends to disintegrate, kill or maim everything nearby. The bigger the bang the more thorough the destruction. This is just the opposite of evolution. The so-called Big Bang Theory of the origin of the universe therefore goes against all observable facts, and is based wholly upon atheistic faith not upon scientific facts.

The Existence of Distinct Kinds Disproves Evolution

Were evolution true there would be no distinct kinds of living beings. Now we must be careful using the term "species," as that is a man-made term, not a Bible term, and therefore can mean whatever men want it to mean. The Bible uses the term "kind." Each kind differs in characteristics from other kinds as to make classification into distinct kinds possible. The distinct kinds can reproduce only after their own kind. That is, one kind can only produce babies by breeding with its own kind, and the babies produced will be of its same kind. While there might be what modern humans would call various species within a kind (for example the many types of dogs), and these species can interbreed with each other producing various breeds of dogs, their offspring are all obviously dogs. Dogs never give birth to cats or to cat-dogs. Even within a kind there is some restriction in breeding capabilities. Horses and donkeys are both of the same kind, and can breed, producing mules (still of the same kind). Mules, however, are sterile. Mules cannot reproduce, as would be the case if this were an example of evolution taking place.

The theory of evolution states that each modern specie has evolved from a common one-celled life-form by a painfully slow process of minute changes over a period of billions of years. Were this actually the case every birth would result in a slight change within a ***common*** kind, and all life would be able to interbreed, rendering division into ***distinct*** kinds impossible. The fossil records show that this is not the case. Instead specimens of every distinct kind found on earth today can also be found in the fossil records. Other distinct but extinct kinds are also found. But no kinds not found in the fossils can be observed alive today; that is, there are no ***new*** kinds coming into existence. The so-called "missing links" that the evolutionists of Darwin's day predicted would be found have not been found, and obviously never will be found. Since the evolving of one kind into another kind has never been observed happening ***even once*** since the beginning of history, we must conclude that evolution is not science at all, but mere faith in a theory of which there is no evidence of truthfulness whatsoever.

Sex Disproves Evolution

The necessity of having a male and female of each kind to make reproduction possible highlights the folly of life having evolved by random chance. For each of the millions of kinds of animals, a male and a female would have had to evolve at the same time so as to be able to reproduce themselves. For this to have happened goes far beyond the realm of chance. Such imaginative dreaming takes faith of the blindest sort!

Demography Disproves Evolution

The growth rate of the human population since the beginning of written history proves that man has only been here a few thousand years, not the millions required by the Theory of Evolution. The very same humanists who are preaching the Theory of Evolution as fact also preach that the world is experiencing a population explosion which threatens the survival of the human species. The birth rates and formulas humanists use to try to prove this mythical population explosion if applied backwards in time instead of forward, show the beginning of the human race to be a mere two or three thousand years ago! That is half the six thousand years or so the Bible indicates, and has the human race beginning after written history did! Obviously the humanists have inadvertently disproven at least one of their theories. Both of their theories cannot be true. Therefore at least one —probably both—of them is not scientific. My what faith these humanists have!

Sedimentary Rock Disproves Evolution

Humanists reason in a circle. If you ask them how they know that certain fossils are so many billions of years old, they will tell you that those fossils are so dated because they are found in a certain layer of rock. If you ask them how they know that rock layer is so old, they tell you that that rock layer is so dated because of the particular fossils found within it! Such circular reasoning flagrantly violates sound logic, and is invalid. Not only do humanists reason in a circle in this matter of the fossil record, they also ignore the fact that in reality the rock layers are not consistently found in the chronological order demanded by evolution, nor is a particular specie found only in a certain layer of rock, but is instead apt to be found in any layer of sedimentary rock. Furthermore, evolutionists reason that the rock layers must be billions of years old because at present rates of sediment build-up it would take that long for them to form. But they fail to point out that fossils are not presently being formed, and the reason is because plants and animals must be covered suddenly and deeply in order to become fossils—else they decay or are devoured before fossil formation is possible. Obviously, the fossils could have been—and probably were—formed as a result of the world being destroyed by the catastrophic flood during the days of Noah, and do not prove evolution.

The Complexity of DNA Disproves Evolution

Recent scientific advances have shown that "simple one-celled animals" are not so simple after all. In fact they are exceedingly complex and could not possibly have been formed by random chance. Dr. Charles McCombs, a Ph.D. organic chemist trained in the methods of scientific investigation, and a scientist who has 20 chemical patents, explains the significance of DNA as follows:

> Proteins and DNA are complicated chemical molecules that are present within our body. Cells which make up the living body contain DNA, the blueprint for all life, and proteins regulating biochemical processes, leading scientists to conclude these components are the cause of life. While it is true that all living bodies have proteins and DNA, so do dead bodies. These chemicals are necessary for life to exist, but they do not "create" life by their presence; they only "maintain" the life that is already present.... Let's take a closer look at proteins and DNA, and the problems of their synthesis by evolutionary processes. Proteins are long polymers of amino acids linked in a chain. There are thousands of proteins within the human body, and they all differ by the sequence of the amino acids on the polymer chain. DNA (deoxyribonucleic acid,) is a polymer of nucleotides. Nucleotides themselves are complicated chemical molecules consisting of a deoxyribose molecule and a phosphate chemically bonded to one of the following heterocycles: guanine, cytosine, thymine, and adenine. Although there are only four different heterocycles, the DNA chain contains billions of nucleotides connected together in a long precisely ordered chain. The sequence of the human DNA chain is so complicated, that even with the sophisticated scientific equipment available today, we still do not know the complete sequence. Proteins and

DNA contain a unique order of the individual components..... If the sequence is changed even slightly, the altered polymer is no longer capable of performing the same function as the natural protein or DNA. If these polymers were formed by evolution in some primordial soup, then we should be able to explain how natural chemical processes were responsible for forming the sequence of amino acids. Evolutionists would say that amino acids eventually combined to form proteins and the nucleotide molecules combined to form DNA, and from them, life. To someone not trained in chemistry, this might sound like a reasonable process, but this is not how chemical reactions work.

Chemists are trained to understand the mechanisms of how molecules react and how to activate molecules so they will react predictably and in a controlled fashion. If a chemist wanted to synthesize the polymer chain of proteins or DNA in the laboratory, the starting compounds must be first activated so that they will begin to react. The chemist must then control the reactivity and the selectivity of the reactants so that the desired product is formed.

The problem with life arising from chemicals is a three-fold problem: chemical stability, chemical reactivity, and chemical selectivity during the chain building process....

Chemical stability is a question of whether the components can even react at all. ... In order to make amino acids and nucleotides react to form a polymer, they must be chemically activated to react with other chemicals. But this chemical activation must be done in the absence of water because the activated compounds will react with water and break down. How could proteins and DNA be formed in a hypothetical primordial watery soup if the activated compounds required to form them cannot exist in water? ...

Chemical reactivity deals with how fast the components react in a given reaction. If life began in a primordial soup by natural chemical reactions, then the laws of chemistry should be able to predict the sequence of these chains. But when amino acids react chemically, they react according to their reactivity, and not in some specified order necessary for life. ... Since all of the amino acids have relatively similar structures, they all have similar reaction rates; they will all react at about the same rate making the precise sequence by random chemical reactions unthinkably unlikely. ...

Chemical selectivity is a problem of where the components react. Since the chain has two ends, the amino acids can add to either end of the chain. Even if by some magical process, a single amino acid "B" would react first as desired for the pre-determined life supporting sequence followed by a single amino acid "A," the product would be a mixture of at least four isomers because there are two ends to the chain. If there is an equal chance of amino acid "B" reacting in two different locations, then half will react at one end, half at the other end. The result of adding "B" will form two different products. When the addition of amino acid "A" occurs, it will react at both ends of the chain of both the products already present. ... The result is a mixture of several isomers of which the desired sequence seldom results, and this is the problem with only two amino acids reacting. As the third amino acid is added, it can react at both ends of four products, and so on, insuring randomness, not a precise sequence.

Since proteins may contain hundreds or thousands of amino acids in a sequence, imagine the huge number of undesired isomers that would be present if these large proteins were formed in a random process.... Evolutionists say that nature is blind, has no goal, and no purpose, and yet precise selection at each step is necessary....

The chemical control needed for the formation of a specific sequence in a polymer chain is just not possible in a random process. The synthesis of proteins and DNA in the laboratory requires the chemist to control the reaction conditions, to thoroughly understand the reactivity and selectivity of each component, and to carefully control the order of addition of the components as the chain is building in size. The successful formation of proteins and DNA in some primordial soup would require the same control of the reactivity and selectivity, and that would require the existence of a chemical controller.... Evolutionists have always been quick to claim that life came from chemicals, but their theory does not hold up to scientific scrutiny. Evolution claims that random chance natural processes formed life as we know it, but they fail to mention that their theory is anything but random or natural! This is the false logic of evolution. Evolutionists just hope you don't know chemistry![94]

We must conclude therefore that to teach children that the Theory of Evolution is scientific fact is to teach them a lie. The Theory of Evolution is a religious teaching which requires blind faith—and a lot of it—to be accepted.

But What About Theistic Evolution?

What confuses many people about the Theory of Evolution is the surprisingly strong support it receives from some religious leaders. These preachers call themselves "theistic" evolutionists, and claim that God created the earth alright, but using the process of evolution to do so. Some theistic evolutionists are no doubt sincere, but ignorant. As Professor Donald Symons said in a letter to *Free Inquiry* magazine:

Gardner's claim that modern Christianity "involves no dogmas that render any aspect of today's science impossible to accept" is tenable only if "dogmas" and "impossible" are defined so restrictively and legalistically as to sap Christianity of its pith, its essence, its very raison d'être. Nonfundamentalist Christians are able to accept Darwin evolution so easily because they do not fully understand its implications.[95]

---

[94] Charles McCombs, "Evolution Hopes You Don't Know Chemistry: The Problem of Control," *Impact* 374 (August 2004): i-iv, Http://www.icr.org/pdf/imp/imp-374.pdf.

[95] Donald Symons, letter to the editor in *The New Age---Notes of a Fringe Watcher*, collection of columns of Martin Gardner (Buffalo, New York: Prometheus Books, 1988), 61–4.

The two major implications of evolution, of course, are that (1) the Bible is not true, and that (2) there is no God. To accept evolution is to accept practical atheism whether a person realizes it or not.

The Gap Theory

Many theistic-evolutionists believe that between Genesis 1.1 and 1.2 there is a gap of billions of years, before which—or during which—evolution took place. This is called the Gap Theory. Those who believe in the Gap Theory believe that there were men living before Adam, but that they were destroyed in this assumed gap. The verse of Scripture they usually give to prove this theory is Jeremiah 4:23. However, a quick check of the context of this verse shows that it refers to God's judgment upon Israel, and that it has no connection to Genesis 1:1-2 whatsoever. Here it is so that you can see this for yourself (note especially verses 4:31 and 5:1):

> (4:23) I beheld the earth, and, lo, it was without form, and void; and the heavens, and they had no light. (4:24) I beheld the mountains, and, lo, they trembled, and all the hills moved lightly. (4:25) I beheld, and, lo, there was no man, and all the birds of the heavens were fled. (4:26) I beheld, and, lo, the fruitful place was a wilderness, and all the cities thereof were broken down at the presence of the LORD, and by his fierce anger. (4:27) For thus hath the LORD said, The whole land shall be desolate; yet will I not make a full end. (4:28) For this shall the earth mourn, and the heavens above be black: because I have spoken it, I have purposed it, and will not repent, neither will I turn back from it. (4:29) The whole city shall flee for the noise of the horsemen and bowmen; they shall go into thickets, and climb up upon the rocks: every city shall be forsaken, and not a man dwell therein. (4:30) And when thou art spoiled, what wilt thou do? Though thou clothest thyself with crimson, though thou deckest thee with ornaments of gold, though thou rentest thy face with painting, in vain shalt thou make thyself fair; thy lovers will despise thee, they will seek thy life. (4:31) For I have heard a voice as of a woman in travail, and the anguish as of her that bringeth forth her first child, the voice of the daughter of Zion, that bewaileth herself, that spreadeth her hands, saying, Woe is me now! for my soul is wearied because of murderers. (5:1) Run ye to and fro through the streets of Jerusalem, and see now, and know, and seek in the broad places thereof, if ye can find a man, if there be any that executeth judgment, that seeketh the truth; and I will pardon it.

There are also other problems with this theory that make it obviously wrong. For instance, 1 Cor. 15:45-47 tells us that Adam was the first man:

> And so it is written, The first man Adam was made a living soul; the last Adam was made a quickening spirit. Howbeit that was not first which is spiritual, but that which is natural; and afterward that which is spiritual. The first man is of the earth, earthy: the second man is the Lord from heaven.

Note that Jesus Christ is called the last Adam, but not the last man Adam. Adam, however, is called "the first man Adam." There were no humans before Adam. We did not originate from aliens or an earlier race of humans.

Another problem with the Gap Theory is that it implies that there was death before sin. Darwin's Theory of Evolution is based upon the survival of the fittest—the weak die, the strong survive. If God had created animals this way, then God would be a sadistic monster. But the Bible clearly implies that there was neither sin nor death among men until Adam: "Wherefore, as by one man sin entered into the world, and death by sin; and so death passed upon all men, for that all have sinned" (Rom. 5:12). This verse exposes a really major flaw in the Gap Theory, for it implies that death is not the result of sin; and if death is not the result of sin, then Christ's death on the cross for our sins would have accomplished nothing. No, God did not create death. God is not death but life. There is only ***one*** creation referred to in Genesis, not ***two*** creations. Before Adam's fall into sin animals and people alike ate vegetation, not meat. There was no survival of the fittest—all were fit—and there was no death.

Yet another problem with the Gap Theory is that it implies that a mother of one kind can give birth to babies of a different kind. That this is not so is emphasized nine times in Genesis chapter one by repeatedly stating that all living things reproduce "after their kind." They do not give birth to new kinds. See Genesis 1.11, 12, 21, 24, and 25.

Also, Exodus 20:11 says that "in six days the LORD made heaven and earth, the sea, and all that in them is, and rested the seventh day: wherefore the LORD blessed the sabbath day, and hallowed it." It does not say that in day one the LORD made the earth, then in the next five days recreated it. No gap is even hinted at here.

The Day-Age Theory

Other theistic-evolutionists believe that the six days of creation were not actually days but ages of billions of years each. This is called the Day-Age Theory. Advocates of this theory quote as their proof-text 2 Peter 3.8: "But, beloved, be not ignorant of this one thing, that one day is with the Lord as a thousand years, and a thousand years as one day."

Immediately we see a problem with this theory. Making each day only a thousand years does not help the theory of evolution, which evolutionists say took many billions of years. A thousand years is an insignificantly tiny drop in the bucket compared to billions.

Also, a quick look at the context of this verse shows that it does not refer to creation at all, but to the coming judgment.

> (3) Knowing this first, that there shall come in the last days scoffers, walking after their own lusts, (4) And saying, Where is the promise of his coming? for since the fathers fell asleep, all things continue as they were from the beginning of the creation. (5) For this they willingly are ignorant of, that by the word of God the heavens were of old, and the earth standing out of the water and in the water: (6) Whereby the world that then was, being overflowed with water, perished: (7) But the heavens and the earth, which are now, by the same word are kept in store, reserved unto fire against the day of judgment and perdition of ungodly men. (8) But, beloved, be not ignorant of this one thing, that one day is with the Lord as a thousand years, and a thousand years as one day. (9) The Lord is not slack concerning his promise, as some men count slackness; but is longsuffering to us-ward, not willing that any should perish, but that all should come to repentance. (10) But the day of the Lord will come as a thief in the night; in the which the heavens shall pass away with a great noise, and the elements shall melt with fervent heat, the earth also and the works that are therein shall be burned up. (2 Pet. 3:3-10)

Verse 8 is merely stating that God is not limited by time. The very next verse (verse 9) tells us that because God is not limited by time we should not interpret His delay in judging the world as slackness. Because God is not limited by time He can be—and has been—very patient toward us sinners, giving us opportunity to repent so that we do not perish in the coming judgment.

Anyway, if "one day is with the Lord as a thousand years" means what day-agers say it means, then "and a thousand years is as one day" cancels it out! A verse similar to 2 Pet. 3:8 is Psalms 90:4: "For a thousand years in thy sight are but as yesterday when it is past, and as a watch in the night." Were we to interpret this verse in the same manner Day-ager's interpret 2 Pet. 3:8, we would have the earth being only a few thousand ***days*** old! Actually, in both 2 Pet. 3:8 and Psalms 90:4 the words "day" and "year" have the ordinary meaning they always have. They are simply contrasted to show that God is not limited by time. Anyway, how do the day-ager's make a "thousand years" mean "age"? Obviously, they are trying to make the Bible conform to their theories, instead of making their theories conform to the Bible. That is simply unbelief.

Also, the fact that the days mentioned in Genesis chapter one are regular 24 hour days is emphasized 6 times by the use of the phrase "and the evening and the morning was the first [or second, or third, or forth, or fifth, or sixth] day."

Another Bible fact that refutes the Day Age Theory is the fact that vegetation was created on day three, and the sun not until day four. Vegetation can survive a day without the sun. Can vegetation survive a thousand years (or billions of years) without the sun? No.

Most theistic evolutionists are convinced that the fossil record proves evolution (which it does not, as has already been shown), but Noah's flood should make them reconsider. Why? Because the flood destroyed the earth and would have also destroyed the fossils, if, in fact, the fossils predated the flood. Gen 6:13: "And God said unto Noah, The end of all flesh is come before me; for the earth is filled with violence through them; and, behold, I will destroy them with the earth."

In summary, theistic evolution is really just unbelief—it is disguised atheism. It is believing Darwin's guessing more than God's Word. It is believing someone who was not there in the beginning more than God who was.

> ... the "light" of the religious evolutionists has not dawned upon our great educational centers. Our university professors and high school teachers have not been persuaded to teach evolution as "God's method of creation;" instead, they increasingly teach it as the proof and pillar of atheism. And as a result, atheism is rampantly on the increase among students as well as among professors. ... Dr. Leuba found that in a large

and progressive American college, ... in 1914, that 80 percent of the new students [freshmen] were believers. But in 1933 only 42 per cent were believers. Why? Because between 1914 and 1933 the teaching of evolution was WIDELY INTRODUCED INTO THE HIGH SCHOOLS! ... over 50 percent of our high school students are being converted into disbelievers before they graduate from secondary school and enter college! The religious evolutionists tell us that one can make evolutionists without making atheists, that evolution can be taught without destroying or disturbing [theistic] religious belief. But the evidence shows that our high school teachers have not been successful in doing this. The religious evolutionists should either SHOW THEM HOW or admit that it can't be done.

Is it not time for a "showdown"? Is it not time to demand of the "compromisers" and the "reconcilers" that they show something in the way of results for their efforts, their promises, and their boasts? Let them wrest evolution, as an intellectual weapon, from the atheists! Let them demonstrate their oft-repeated claim that evolution is the friend and not the foe of [theistic] religion! Let them make their widely-heralded "light" effective and penetrating where it is needed most—in secular educational circles! Let them refute the scholarly arguments of the atheist professor who use evolution as the foundation stone of their godless gospel! Let them do this—or confess their own futility and falsity. Let them do this—or STOP OPERATING AS FALSE PROPHETS WHO ARE GIVING AID AND ASSISTANCE TO THE ENEMIES OF [THEISTIC] RELIGION.[96] [Emphasis original.]

The Bitter Fruits of Evolution

It is absolutely amazing that most Americans are unaware that the Theory of Evolution is directly responsible for the deaths of millions of Americans and multiplied millions of other nationalities in World War II (started by Nazis and Fascists), the Korean War, the Viet Nam War, and a multitude of other wars (started by communists). Nazism, Fascism, and Communism are all based on and spring from Darwin's Theory of Evolution. This is not new knowledge. As far back as 1941 Dan Gilbert warned that Darwin's Theory of Evolution was subversive of true Americanism.

The [Darwinian] evolutionary philosophy produced the totalitarian ideologies [Nazism, Fascism, and Communism]. The second World War is the fruitage of Darwinism. ... Darwinism is subversive of true Americanism. It is the equivalent of treason that it should be taught in our educational institutions![97]

America could have surrendered to Japan or to Germany or to the Soviet Union. We could have avoided those bloody wars by simply becoming Nazis or Communists. Instead, we fought all those wars to protect our children from the evils of those wicked philosophies. How then can we be so stupid as to allow the very mother of those death philosophies to be taught to our children as true science?!

Who can reasonably defend the evolutionary dogma, even though it be attested by every scientist on earth, if it acts as the tap root from which has sprung the upas tree of atheist-communism? Who can honorably defend as true on "scientific" grounds a doctrine which proves itself false—on humanitarian and moral grounds—by poisoning human life and civilization with the lethal gases of communism and free-love?[98]

Friedrich Nietzsche developed a system of philosophy based upon Darwin's idea of the "survival of the fittest" as developed and preached by Darwin's close friend, Thomas H. Huxley.

Now, the fundamental principle of Nietzsche's philosophy is that man is an animal, "a beast of prey," that he has evolved into what he is now, the "beast of prey," because of his "superior" cunning and brutality; that if he is to evolve into a superman, a "better beast of prey," he must become more brutal and more ruthless. ... As he loved and glorified brutality and bestiality, so Nietzsche hated and despised humanity and humaneness—love, justice, kindness. And as bestiality and brutality have led to success in the evolutionary struggle, so "Christian" moral virtues lead to failure. That was the teaching of Nietzsche—and that was the lesson of evolution, according to Huxley. ... Nietzsche claimed that the practice of the Christian religion and of Christian morality leads to "decadence," to "reaction," to a cultural standstill, and that they stand in the way of the evolution of the superman. ... Nietzsche thought selfishness the highest goal and good and guide: "Blessed be selfishness!" he exulted. "Make thy law the desire of thy flesh.... Live on thy own account, and not for the sake others." Nietzsche loathed the very thought of the Golden Rule.[99] He thought it "monstrous" for the strong to be considerate of the weak. Huxley, too thought the practice of the Golden Rule "destructive" of the evolutionary progress of man in society.... The Golden Rule would tie the hands of the strong and prevent them from trampling under the weak; hence, if "strictly observed" it would bring an end to progress; it would constitute, in Huxley's words, "the refusal to continue the struggle for existence."... Nietzsche counseled potential supermen: "Be hard. ... Have no pity. ... Be cruel toward everything that grows old and weak."[100]

It is only fitting to let a former American Humanist Association president tell you about one of the evils that came out of Nietzsche's Darwinian-evolution-based philosophy. Wrote Corliss Lamont:

---

96 Dan Gilbert, *Evolution: The Root of All Isms* (San Diego, California: The Danielle Publishers, 1941), 126–28.

97 Ibid., xi.

98 Ibid., 19.

99 The Golden Rule is found in Mat. 7:12: "Therefore all things whatsoever ye would that men should do to you, do ye even so to them: for this is the law and the prophets."

100 Gilbert, *Root of Isms*, 24–30.

> In his most brilliant book, *Thus Spake Zarathustra*, Nietzsche wrote, "A good war halloweth any cause."
>
> This fierce philosophy, paradoxically enough produced by a constitutional invalid, later became a stimulus and inspiration for the German Nazis under Adolf Hitler.[101]

In other words, Darwin's Theory of Evolution caused World War II. Under the guidance of Nietzsche, Hitler took Darwin's Theory of Evolution to its logical conclusion when applied to politics and relations between nations. The result was the largest war in history.

Important Points Made In This Chapter

The main purpose of this chapter has been to make six important points: (1) the Theory of Evolution is not based on science, but is a religious teaching that one accepts by faith; (2) the Theory of Evolution is the most basic doctrine of atheism and of the humanist religion; (3) accepting the Theory of Evolution automatically makes a person a practicing humanist, whither he realizes it or not; (4) Humanism and Christianity are diametrically opposed to one another, and cannot long peacefully co-exist; (5) the teaching of evolution as truth in the schools of America is actually treason, for it attempts to make our children enemies of this country; and (6) the main reason Humanists are so intent that only the Theory of Evolution be taught to our children in public schools (to the exclusion of the Genesis account of creation) is because they want their evangelism efforts to convert our children into atheistic humanists to be without competition while funded by public taxes—they want to force us to pay for our own children's spiritual, emotional, and mental destruction!

The following quote from a high school textbook published by a major textbook publisher, and used in many public schools shows that Louis Pasture did not win his battle against abiogenesis (spontaneous generation) near as conclusively as he thought: "Today, however, the principle of biogenesis may have to be modified. When considering the origin of life on Earth, some scientists have hypothesized that the first cells arose from non-living materials."[102] Such silly statements in textbooks are indeed unbelievable giant-steps back to the Dark Ages for science—and for our children! Such is the dubious science of wizards and soothsayers. No wonder the Bible warns us to avoid "profane and vain babblings, and oppositions of science falsely so called: which some professing have erred concerning the faith" (I Tim 6.20-21). In no way does evolution fit the definition of science, but it fits the definition of superstition perfectly. Superstition, according to *Webster's New Twentieth Century Dictionary*, is "any belief or attitude that is inconsistent with the known laws of science." The Evolution superstition does not become science by being cloaked in scientific sounding terms. A lie by any other name stinks the same.

The First Amendment to the Constitution expressly forbids the state from making any laws regulating religion. The government is clearly violating the law every time it makes a law either for or against the teaching of either The Theory of Evolution or the Genesis account of creation in public schools. Both are religious teachings. Which religion's teachings are (or are not) taught to a child should be determined by that child's parents, not by the government. And the government has no right forbidding anyone, be he teacher or student or parent, from expressing his or her religious beliefs on any public property either verbally or in print. When the government banned the Genesis account of creation from the classroom, and ruled that only the Theory of Evolution may be taught, the government established a state religion—the religion of atheistic humanism.

---

[101] Corliss Lamont, *The Philosophy of Humanism*, reprint, 1949 (New York: The Wisdom Library, a division of Philosophical Library, 1957), 117.

[102] Harvey D. Goodman, *Biology* (Orlando: Harcourt Brace Jovanovich, 1989), 32 and 228–30.

Charles Darwin did not invent the theory of evolution, but merely took the religious dogma of pagan religions and made it look scientific. While Louis Pasteur's work showed scientists how to discover cures for infectious diseases, and thus saved many lives, Darwin's writings have been the basis for many social movements that have murdered countless numbers of people.

Louis Pasueur disproved abiogenesis, one of the root doctrines of evolution, and in so doing became the father of modern medicine. For this evolutionists hated him, and to this day still defame him.

Chapter 7

WHO MADE GOD?

Pondering What Existed BEFORE the Beginning

The author of this book once asked a humanist friend, "What are the odds that your car does not have a maker?" To this question, he answered:

> Analogies are fun when someone does not have a model. But I understand your model. My car has a maker. If you think this is a good analogy, then lets use it. There is a 100% chance my car has a maker. And then there is also a 100% [chance] the maker has a maker (Henry Ford's maker was your God in your eyes). Hence your maker also has a maker. So who made God? I hope you find that silly. I do too. You can use this model (analog) your way, and I can use it too. But that is silly, no?

Nobody made my car. There was this big explosion—no, I don't know the cause—and lo and behold this car landed in my driveway. And not a scratch on it!

The Significance of the Answer

Who made God? That is a good question, and it is not silly. Rather it is even more basic than the beginning of the universe. And like it or not, it is a question that all thinking men have to answer to their own satisfaction sometime in their lifetime. Whatever the answer, it will require faith, for there is no way to test it in a science laboratory. The answer a person accepts may very well determine that person's eternal destiny, so the wise man will be very careful in his choice.

Another Vital Question

Actually, there is another question that also must be answered. What existed ***before*** the beginning of the universe? The reason atheists came up with the Big Bang theory is because there is overwhelming evidence that this universe did indeed have a beginning, just like the Bible says. But the Big Bang theory does not solve the atheist's problem, for there is no way to avoid having to ultimately decide where all that matter that became the universe came from. The atheist's answer, of course, is that matter is eternal. Can the atheist prove this? No, he must accept it by faith—not by science. Science cannot prove that matter always existed. No. It is by faith that the atheist accepts the eternity of matter.

The Simple Answer

When an atheist asked the question, "Who made God?" He thinks he has asked a question for which there is no answer but a silly answer. But he is wrong. The answer, of course, is that God is eternal. Deut. 33:27 says, "The **eternal God** *is thy* refuge, and underneath *are* the everlasting arms." Why is this not a silly answer? Because if God is not eternal, then matter has to be. And if it is silly for the Christian to answer that God is eternal, then it is at least equally as silly for the atheist to answer that matter is eternal.

The Cause of the Amazing Design

So, the atheist is still not free from answering the question of why this universe has such amazing design. Were there no order in this universe—if we could not tell time by the movement of the sun, moon, stars, planets, etc., and if we could not see such marvelous design in plant and animal life and in our bodies, and if all matter were in random chaos—then perhaps it might be reasonable to believe that it just always existed. But there ***is*** order and there ***is*** design. Were there no beginning of the universe, the atheist might be able to say that there has ***always*** been order in the universe, but the evidence that the universe had a beginning is so overwhelming that the atheist cannot deny it. What is witnessed now is a deteriorating universe. The lifespan of man has dropped from up to 900 plus years to approximately 70 years, the sun is burning up, and the whole universe is returning to randomness. There is no evidence whatsoever that matter can organize itself without cause.

When you ask an atheist, "What are the odds that your car does not have a maker?" He is forced to answer, "Zero. The odds are 100% that my car ***does*** have a maker." Why is he forced to make that concession? Because he knows that the natural laws presently in effect in this universe do not allow matter to organize itself without an intelligent being making it happen. It would be silly for him to answer otherwise. People would laugh at him if he did not make this admission. But this concession leaves the atheist in a logical trap from which he cannot escape.

If under the present laws of nature random matter cannot organize itself, then what is to make us believe that it could organize itself in the past? Have the laws of nature changed? The atheist cannot admit that without also admitting the possibility of Noah's flood. So in the end, the atheist can only answer the Christian's questions with a question. But the Christian can answer that final atheist question with a logical answer.

The Trap

The law of nature which traps the evolutionist is the one known as the 2nd Law of Thermodynamics—that all natural processes irreversibly increase in entropy (a measure of disorder). There is no known exception to this law. It is one of the most basic laws known to science. In the Bible, this law is called the curse (Gen. 3:17-19). We can see today that God put the curse on the earth so that humans can realize that matter is not eternal, and that therefore God is the only answer to the question, "Where did we come from?"

> Whether rank-and-file evolutionists know it or not, this problem they have with entropy is thus "one of the most fundamental unsolved problems in biology." It is more than a problem in fact—it is a devastating denial of the evolution model itself. It will continue to be so until evolutionists can demonstrate that the vast imagined evolutionary continuum in space and time has both a program to guide it and an energy converter to empower it. Otherwise, the Second Law precludes it.[103]

The Only Logical Conclusion

The odds then that this universe has a maker are the same as that of my humanist friend's car having a maker: 100%.

[103] Henry M. Morris, "Entropy and Open Systems," *Impact*, no. 40 (1976) (Institute In Creation Research), Http://www.icr.org/pubs/imp/imp-040.htm.

Did the LORD God of the Bible make this or did Evolution, the imaginary god of the atheists, make it?

"Because that which may be known of God is manifest in them; for God hath shewed *it* unto them. For the invisible things of him from the creation of the world are clearly seen, being understood by the things that are made, *even* his eternal power and Godhead; so that they are without excuse." (Rom. 1:19-20)

Chapter 8

ARE GOD'S LIGHTS ON?

Checking To See If Anyone Is Home

Since atheism is so crucial to humanist dogma, humanists constantly ridicule and mock the existence of the creator God. The following words from Sir Julian Huxley are very typical humanist rhetoric:

> ***In the evolutionary pattern of thought there is no longer either need or room for the supernatural.*** The earth was not created: it evolved. So did all the animals and plants that inhabit it, including our human selves, mind and soul as well as brain and body. So did religion. Religions are organs of psychosocial man concerned with human destiny and with experiences of sacredness and transcendence. In their evolution, some (but by no means all) have given birth to the concept of gods as supernatural beings endowed with mental and spiritual properties and capable of intervening in the affairs of man. These theistic religions are organizations of human thought in its interactions with the puzzling, complex world with which it has to contend—the outer world of nature and the inner world of man's own nature. In this, they resemble other early organizations of human thought confronted with nature, like the doctrine of the Four Elements, earth, air, fire and water, or the Eastern concept of rebirth and reincarnation. Like these, they are destined to disappear in competition with other, truer, and more embracing thought-organizations which are handling the same range of raw or processed experience.
>
> Evolutionary man can no longer take refuge from his loneliness by creeping for shelter into the arms of a divinized father-figure ***whom he has himself created,*** nor escape from the responsibility of making decisions by sheltering under the umbrella of Divine Authority, nor absolve himself from the hard task of meeting his present problems and planning his future by relying on the will of an omniscient but unfortunately inscrutable Providence.[104] [Emphasis added]

So, according to the doctrine of humanism, God did not create man; instead man created God! Instead of God being the origin of the universe, He is just a myth created by imaginative men to explain facts of nature not yet understood by science. But notice: the above quotation from Huxley is just a statement of his faith. He offers no proof that what he says is so. The vital question is, ***Can humanists offer proof that there is no God?***

Prometheus Books (Buffalo, New York), the same publisher that publishes *Humanist Manifesto I and II* and numerous other books for the American Humanist Association, has published a little book by B.C. Johnson titled *Atheist Debater's Handbook* designed to "offer a concise set of rejoinders for use by atheists in their formal (and informal) debates with theists."[105] Since the American Humanist Association is the umbrella for all the other Humanist groups in the United States, I was very interested in reading this book. I have long desired to know what possible proofs against the existence of God an atheist could offer; I had never been able to think of any such proofs at all. So I sat down and read the whole book in one sitting. To my great amazement the book offered not one proof against the existence of God! I expected at least to find some phony proof, but Johnson offered no proof whatsoever! I was so surprised at this that I read the book a second time more slowly and carefully to see if I had missed something. Indeed, in the first chapter I had missed Johnson's foundational argument.

The Atheist's Foundational Argument

In the opening chapter of his book, Johnson sets forth the foundational argument that underlies all the following chapters. If this one argument can be disproven, the rest of Johnson's book falls like a house of cards built upon shifting sand. Here is Johnson's argument:

> It is incumbent upon the theist to provide reasons for his belief that God is the true explanation of the universe and morality. The atheist, for his part, does not necessarily offer an explanation; he simply does not accept the theist's explanation. Therefore, the atheist need only demonstrate that the theist has failed to justify his position.
>
> Another point to note is that the atheist believes in the existence of the universe and does not believe in anything which is more fundamental. The theist believes in the existence of the universe and—in addition—he believes in the existence of God. The theist, therefore,

---

[104] Julian Huxley, *The Humanist Frame*, 18–9.

[105] B.C. Johnson, *Atheist Debater's Handbook* (Buffalo, New York: Prometheus Books, 1983), 10.

believes in one more thing than the atheist. If all beliefs should be justified, then surely the more one believes, the more justification one must produce. Clearly, the theist must justify this extra belief to the atheist.[106] [Emphasis original]

There are three untruths in this foundation premise of atheism. The first untruth is that theists believe one thing more than an atheist. The second untruth is that atheists are not obligated to prove their position. The third untruth is that showing that theists have failed to prove their arguments proves atheism.

The Idol Named Evolution

It is not true that theists believe in one thing more than atheists. While theists worship a creator God who is separate from His creation, atheists worship an idol (self-made god) called evolution. Since they reject God as creator of the universe, they have replaced Him with an imaginary dead force, which (say they), is continuously forming simple things into complex ones.

It is true that ***God*** is the theist's "explanation of the universe and morality." But it is equally true that ***Evolution*** is the atheist's "explanation of the universe and morality." Therefore, if it is incumbent upon the theist to prove the existence of the living creator God, it is equally incumbent upon the atheist to prove the existence of the dead-force god he calls Evolution—an idol humanists have created with their own vain imaginations. If atheists cannot prove the existence of Evolution, they have lost their case, for the only alternative to Evolution is special creation, and special creation means that the creator God does exist.

If you do not believe that Evolution is a god, then consider carefully the following words from Julian Huxley:

> Religious concepts like God, incarnation, the soul, salvation, original sin, grace, atonement, all have a basis in man's experiences of phenomenal reality. It is necessary now to analyze that basis of reality into its component parts, and then to reassemble these elements, together with any new factors that have come to light, into concepts which correspond more closely to reality and are more relevant to present circumstances.
>
> Thus, if I may over-simplify the matter, God appears to be a semantic symbol denoting what Matthew Arnold called 'the power not ourselves,' or rather the various powers felt to be greater than our narrow selves, whether the forces of external nature or the forces imminent in our nature, all bound together in the concept of a personal or super-personal sacred being in some way capable of affecting or guiding or interfering in the course of events. The forces are real enough: what we have done is, quite illegitimately, to project the god concept into them. And in so doing we have distorted their true significance, and effectively altered the course of history.[107]

Huxley realized very clearly that evolution was a substitution for the creator God. Of course, he did not want the title "god" to be given to Evolution, because he wanted Evolution to be considered science. But a god (idol) by any other name smells the same. Evolution is an idol because it is a dead god and a human-created god. Evolutionary humanism with its militant pro-abortionism and pro-infanticide, is really just a new form of the ancient Baal worship with its burnt sacrifices of children. Like Buddhism or Taoism it is pantheistic, making the creation itself to be God.

The Burden of Proof

Since it is not true that theists believe one thing more than the atheist, it is also not true that atheists are not obligated to prove their position. To the contrary, they are even more obligated to prove their position than the theist is to prove his, for the atheist position is worse then just unscientific (as was shown in chapter 5), it also illogical, contradicting all observable natural processes. It is not good enough for the atheist to show that the theist has failed to demonstrate his position; the atheist must also demonstrate his position. Show us—even just one time—dead matter giving birth to a living being. This the atheist knows he cannot show. The reason Humanists do not want creationism to be taught alongside evolution in public schools is because they know that the theory of evolution cannot survive in the light of truth. Competition exposes and destroys the deceptions which make up the Evolution dogma. While it is true that even highly intelligent men often become irrational when they love the pleasures of sin, it is nevertheless also true that no rational, thinking person will believe the theory of Evolution, once he knows all the facts. Why? Because the theist

---

[106] Ibid., 12.

[107] Julian Huxley, *The Humanist Frame*, 43–44.

position—that life comes only from life of like kind—is demonstrated millions of times every day around the world.

Atheists Have No Proof There Is No God

Building on the false foundational premise just analyzed, the remaining chapters of Johnson's *Atheist Debater's Handbook* make no attempt whatsoever to prove that God does not exist. Instead, they use distorted facts, twisted logic, and cleaver double-talk to attempt to define (often misdefine) and then disprove what Johnson perceives to be the major arguments for the existence of God. The simple fact is that atheists offer no proof against the existence of God because they have no proof to offer! Atheism is based on faith not fact. Henry M. Morris, in his book *The Long War Against God: the History and Impact of the Creation/Evolution Conflict*, gives an amusing yet sad example of this:

God's lights are on! He is home! "The heavens declare the glory of God; and the firmament sheweth his handywork. Day unto day uttereth speech, and night unto night sheweth knowledge. There is no speech nor language, where their voice is not heard." (Psalms 19.1-3)

> That humanism is merely a more genteel term for atheism is confirmed by the current president of the American Humanist Association, Dr. Isaac Asimov, who is also probably the most prolific writer in the whole world of science, having authored approximately three hundred books, covering every scientific field. He says: "I am an atheist, out and out. It took me a long time to say it. I've been an atheist for years and years, but somehow I felt it was intellectually unrespectable to say one was an atheist, because it assumed knowledge that one didn't have. Somehow it was better to say one was a humanist or an agnostic. I finally decided that I'm a creature of emotion as well as of reason. Emotionally, I am an atheist. I don't have the evidence to prove that God doesn't exist, but I so strongly suspect he doesn't that I don't want to waste my time." ["An Interview with Isaac Asimov on Science and the Bible," Free Inquiry 2 (Spring 1982), page 9]
>
> One very significant admission appears in this statement of atheistic faith by Asimov. Not only does he acknowledge that humanism is essentially the same as atheism, but also that atheism is nothing but an emotional belief. In spite of the fact that he is one of the most knowledgeable scientists in the world, having written books on just about every branch of science in existence, he recognizes that he has no "evidence to prove God doesn't exist."
>
> If Asimov has no evidence against God, we can be sure nobody does! He believes in humanism/atheism simply because that is what he wants to believe! The same is true for every other devotee of this man-centered religion. Yet they commonly deride creationism because it requires faith! One naturally thinks of Psalms 53:12: "The fool hath said in his heart, There is no God."[108]

God's Lights Are On—He's Home!

Johnson ends chapter one of his book with the following illustration of how to apply his premise:

> Atheism can be more positively defended in the following way. We can properly claim to know that many things are not so if reasons have not been offered to support the claim that they are so. For example, I am able to claim that I know my friend Frank is not home precisely because there is no reason to believe that he is home. There is no noise coming from his house, the lights are out at a time when he is usually awake, his bed is empty, and so forth. Everything seems to count for my belief and nothing against it. I could discover that I was mistaken, but the possibility of error exists for virtually any knowledge claim one might make.

---

[108] Henry M. Morris, *The Long War Against God* (Grand Rapids, Michigan: Baker Book House, 1989), 114.

> The parallel between the belief that Frank is at home and the belief that God exists is an exact one. If Frank is at home, there will be evidence indicating this state of affairs. On the other hand, if there is no evidence that he is home, one can claim to know that he is not at home. Similarly, if God exists, there will be evidence of this; signs will emerge which point to such a conclusion. However, if there is no evidence that He exists, then one can claim to know that God does not exist.... If I am correct, then the claim that there is no God can be justified on the grounds that there is no reason to believe that he exists.[109]

The folly of Johnson's logic is apparent at once. I invite him and all his atheist friends to step outside and gaze up at the sun and stars in the heavens. ***God's lights are on—He's home!***

> The heavens declare the glory of God; and the firmament sheweth his handywork. Day unto day uttereth speech, and night unto night sheweth knowledge. There is no speech nor language, where their voice is not heard. (Psalms 19.1-3)

Not only is God home, He is also actively involved in this universe He created, holding it all together.

> For by him were all things created, that are in heaven, and that are in earth, visible and invisible, whether they be thrones, or dominions, or principalities, or powers: all things were created by him, and for him: and he is before all things, and by him all things consist. (Col. 1:16-17)

Not only is God "at home," and involved with the universe, but He is also involved with the people in the universe. People still feel guilt and anxiety when they do wrong; that is because God is still actively involved with His creatures, drawing—but not forcing—them back to Himself.

The Root of Atheism

Are there reasons to believe in God's existence? Of course there are (as was just demonstrated), but Johnson has already let us know that the atheist has chosen to not accept them even before he hears them. Writes Johnson, "The atheist, for his part, does not necessarily offer an explanation; he simply does not accept the theist's explanation." So no matter what evidence the theists gives, the atheist does not even give it serious consideration because he is "willingly ignorant" (2 Pet. 3:5). The important question is, Why does the atheist so desperately want to reject God as the explanation of the universe and morality?

People become atheists for one reason only: they love of vile sins which they know God says makes them worthy of receiving the death penalty. Most atheists are homosexuals or have indulged in other gross immoralities. At the least, there is some sin which they love and do not want to give up. Atheism is their attempt to free themselves from the awful guilt and fear resulting from such sins. If there is no God, they reason, then there is also no sin or judgment. The fact that when atheists want their speech to have great force they interlace their profanity with such Bible words as "God," "Jesus Christ," "Hell," and "Damn" shows that deep down inside they know God is. Oh, but how they hate Him! How they wish He would go away and quit bothering their consciences! How they want to drive His promise of eternal judgment from their minds!

> For the wrath of God is revealed from heaven against all ungodliness and unrighteousness of men, who hold the truth in unrighteousness. Because that which may be known of God is manifest in them; for God hath showed it unto them. For the invisible things of him from the creation of the world are clearly seen, being understood by the things that are made, even his eternal power and Godhead; so that they are without excuse: because that, when they knew God, they glorified him not as God, neither were thankful; but became vain in their imaginations, and their foolish heart was darkened. Professing themselves to be wise, they became fools, and changed the glory of the uncorruptible God into an image made like to corruptible man, and to birds, and fourfooted beasts, and creeping things. Wherefore God also gave them up to uncleanness through the lusts of their own hearts, to dishonour their own bodies between themselves: who changed the truth of God into a lie, and worshipped and served the creature more than the Creator, who is blessed for ever. Amen. For this cause God gave them up unto vile affections: for even their women did change the natural use into that which is against nature: and likewise also the men, leaving the natural use of the woman, burned in their lust one toward another; men with men working that which is unseemly, and receiving in themselves that recompense of their error which was meet. And even as they did not like to retain God in their knowledge, God gave them over to a reprobate mind, to do those things which are not convenient; being filled with all unrighteousness, fornication, wickedness, covetousness, maliciousness; full of envy, murder, debate, deceit, malignity; whisperers, backbiters, haters of God, despiteful, proud, boasters, inventors of evil things, disobedient to parents, without understanding, covenantbreakers, without natural affection, implacable, unmerciful: who knowing the judgment of God, that they which commit such things are worthy of death, not only do the same, but have pleasure in them that do them. (Rom. 1:19-32)

Why Atheists Are Fools

God says that a person who chooses not to believe in God is a fool: "The fool hath said in his heart, There is no God" (Psalms 14:1). Webster's Dictionary defines a fool as "a person with little or no judgment,

---

[109] Johnson, *Atheist Debater's Handbook*, 14–16.

common sense, wisdom, etc.; a silly person; a simpleton." A simpleton is "a person of weak intellect; someone who is easily fooled."

Atheists Reject the Key of Knowledge

Atheists are fools because they have rejected the only basis of knowing anything. They are not atheists because they are fools; rather, they are fools because they are atheists. When God calls atheists fools, He does not mean that they have low I.Q.'s or that they cannot learn facts. Why some of them hold doctorates from leading universities, and their heads are filled with megabytes of data. But their closed-minded refusal to even consider the possibility of God's existence, much less anything God has revealed to them in His Word, makes them incapable of logically and scientifically analyzing data so as to arrive at valid conclusions. They are "ever learning, and never able to come to the knowledge of the truth. … so do these also resist the truth: men of corrupt minds, reprobate concerning the faith" (2 Tim 3.7-8).

Please stop and consider the implications of this Bible verse: **"The fear of the LORD is the beginning of knowledge" (Proverbs 1.7)**. If this verse be true then how can we with good conscience allow our children to be taught that the Theory of Evolution with its atheistic implications is true? Since atheists don't even believe in God, much less fear Him, they have no beginning for knowledge. This fact is clearly seen in one of the atheist's basic principles—the contradictory idea that "the only absolute is that there are no absolutes." This idea (which is necessary if one is to reject the ***absolute*** God) is found over and over again in atheist writings. For example, "Humanism," says atheist/Humanist Sir Julian Huxley, "will have nothing to do with Absolutes, including absolute truth, absolute morality, absolute perfection and absolute authority."[110] Since the atheist believes nothing to be absolutely true, he has no firm foundation upon which to base knowledge. Look up the word knowledge in your dictionary and you will find that to know something is to be sure of it. The atheist believes one can not be absolutely sure of anything; therefore the atheist can know nothing for sure. Therefore, a humanist education—a know nothing education—is really no education at all.

Logically, there cannot be an absolute that there are no absolutes. However, even atheism's absurd principle that there are no absolutes proves atheism wrong. For if there are no absolute truths, then it must not be absolutely true that there is no God. Therefore God must be.

In chapter two of the *Atheist Debater's Handbook*, Johnson says, "Ignorance [of the natural causes of puzzling phenomena] is not a good reason to believe that God exists."[111] But Johnson fails to apply this same logic to himself: ignorance is not a good reason to believe God does not exist. Instead Johnson declares, "The atheist may claim to know that God does not exist because no good reason has been given to support the belief that He does" even though neither has good reason been given to support the belief that God does not exist! With this declaration Johnson has actually inadvertently admitted that the atheist presupposes that there is no God before examining the facts. He ***wants*** to interpret nature as disproving God, so he refuses to give the evidence its logical conclusion. Johnson's declaration also proves that atheists are dishonest, for they claim to "know" something for which they have no evidence whatsoever. An agnostic can at least be honored for admitting lack of knowledge, but atheists dishonestly claim to know something they do not know. Their lie is true, they think, simply because they want it to be true.

We should also point out to Johnson that if "Ignorance [of the natural causes of puzzling phenomena] is not a good reason to believe that God exists," then it is logically just as true that ignorance of the natural cause of puzzling phenomena is not a good reason to believe that Evolution exists. And we might also point out to Johnson that it is not the puzzling phenomena that causes Christians to believe in God, but rather the fact that all the evidence is in the Christian's favor.

---

[110] Julian Huxley, *The Humanist Frame*, 14.

[111] Johnson, *Atheist Debater's Handbook*, 23.

Atheists Confuse Faith With Science

Atheists are fools because they refuse to differentiate between faith and science. Specifically, they confuse the theory of Evolution with science, when it is in reality a faith doctrine of the Satan-designed religion called Humanism, and is without one shred of scientific proof. No one has ever observed dead matter spontaneously turn into living beings, yet atheists insist that this has happened. Science demands observation; so the idea of spontaneous generation is pure faith, not science. No one has ever observed non-human life birth a human baby, yet atheists insist that this has happened. Science demands observation, so the idea that humans evolved from non-humans is pure faith, not science. Atheists insist that the universe is evolving upward from the simple to the complex without the help of a designer of high intellect, yet such evolution has never been observed. Since the upward evolution claimed by atheists has never been observed and is just the opposite of what actually ***is*** observed, it must be recognized as an unscientific, blind faith of people who refuse to open their eyes to the plain facts of nature which are screaming at them from every corner.

Atheists Ignore Evidence of Divine Judgment

Atheists are fools because they willingly are ignorant of the evidences of Divine judgment upon past God-rejecters. Only a fool would scoff and laugh at He who gives to all creatures life and breath and takes it at His will. Only a fool mocks his Maker. Only a fool spits in the face of the Almighty God, who drowned every unbeliever on the face of the earth in the days of Noah, then cast their souls into eternal Hell. Only a fool can notice fossils inland and high upon mountains, massive layers of sedimentary rock everywhere, and huge glaciers slowly melting away without at least acknowledging that there might have been a universal flood!

> Knowing this first, that there shall come in the last days scoffers, walking after their own lusts, and saying, Where is the promise of his coming? for since the fathers fell asleep, all things continue as they were from the beginning of the creation. For this they willingly are ignorant of, that by the word of God the heavens were of old, and the earth standing out of the water and in the water: whereby the world that then was, being overflowed with water, perished: but the heavens and the earth, which are now, by the same word are kept in store, reserved unto fire against the day of judgment and perdition of ungodly men. But, beloved, be not ignorant of this one thing, that one day is with the Lord as a thousand years, and a thousand years as one day. The Lord is not slack concerning his promise, as some men count slackness; but is longsuffering to us-ward, not willing that any should perish, but that all should come to repentance. But the day of the Lord will come as a thief in the night; in the which the heavens shall pass away with a great noise, and the elements shall melt with fervent heat, the earth also and the works that are therein shall be burned up. (2 Pet. 3:3-10)

> For if God spared not the angels that sinned, but cast them down to hell, and delivered them into chains of darkness, to be reserved unto judgment; and spared not the old world, but saved Noah the eighth person, a preacher of righteousness, bringing in the flood upon the world of the ungodly; and turning the cities of Sodom and Gomorrah into ashes condemned them with an overthrow, making them an ensample unto those that after should live ungodly; and delivered just Lot, vexed with the filthy conversation of the wicked: (For that righteous man dwelling among them, in seeing and hearing, vexed his righteous soul from day to day with their unlawful deeds;) The Lord knoweth how to deliver the godly out of temptations, and to reserve the unjust unto the day of judgment to be punished. (2 Pet. 2:4-9)

How To Know the God That Is

All that atheism offers in the here and now is "the pleasures of sin for a season" (Heb. 11:25). It offers nothing for the hereafter except the prospect of eternal punishment in the Lake of Fire if it should be wrong—which it is.

Christianity, on the other hand, offers immediate knowledge that it is true. It is not only possible to know God is, it is also possible to know the God that is. In a prayer to God the Father, Jesus Christ said: "And this is life eternal, that they [believers] might know thee the only true God, and Jesus Christ, whom thou hast sent" (John 17:3). True Christianity is not just pie in the sky by and by when you die. True faith in the gospel of Jesus Christ results in immediate—***right now***— knowledge that the Bible is true, that God is, and in knowing God. Yes, faith must precede knowledge, "for he that cometh to God must believe that he is, and that he is a rewarder of them that diligently seek him" (Hebrews 11:6). But the promise of salvation, forgiveness, reconciliation, and everlasting life is fulfilled instantaneously at the moment we place our faith in the Lord Jesus Christ. At that moment a miraculous change called the "new birth" takes place in our inner man, and the Spirit of God "beareth witness with our spirit, that we are the children of God" (Rom. 8:16). At that moment we no longer just ***believe*** God is, we ***know*** He is!

"And God said, Let there be lights in the firmament of the heaven to divide the day from the night; and let them be for signs, and for seasons, and for days, and years: and let them be for lights in the firmament of the heaven to give light upon the earth: and it was so. " Gen. 1:14-15)

"And even as they did not like to retain God in *their* knowledge, God gave them over to a **reprobate mind**, to do those things which are not convenient..." (Romans 1:28)

Chapter 9

HOW IS LIFE WITHOUT GOD?

What It Is Like Living With an Atheist

Perhaps the most famous atheist of modern times is Madalyn Murray O'Hair, the woman responsible for removing Bible reading and prayer from public schools in 1963. Her eldest child, William J. Murray, was the plaintiff in that case. In 1977 William severed all connections with atheists and humanists after receiving Jesus Christ as his personal Lord and Savior. In 1982 he wrote a book, *My Life Without God*, describing what life was like being raised in an atheist home. This is an important book which every American should read. Especially, people considering becoming an atheist should read William's book, so that they can realize what they will be getting into. Since an atheist lifestyle is what humanists are trying to force upon our children, it will be wise for us to examine a few facts from William's book.

A Humanist Describes Her Atheist Lifestyle

According to a statement issued in 1960 by Madalyn Murray (she was not yet married to O'Hair):

> An atheist loves his fellowman instead of God. An atheist believes that heaven is something for which we should work now, here, on earth, for all men together to enjoy. An atheist believes that he can get no help through prayer, but that he must find in himself the inner conviction and the strength to meet life, to grapple with it, to subdue it, and to enjoy it. An atheist believes that only in a knowledge of himself and his fellow can he find the understanding that will help him in a life of fulfillment. He seeks to know himself and his fellowman rather than to know God. An atheist believes that a hospital should be built instead of a church. An atheist believes that a deed should be done instead of a prayer said. An atheist strives for involvement in life and not escape into death. He wants man to understand and love man: he wants an ethical way of life. He believes that we cannot rely on God, channel action into prayer, or hope for an end of troubles in a hereafter, that we are our brother's keeper, we are the keepers of our own lives, that we are responsible persons, that the job is here and the time is now.[112]

Now those words are really impressive—all that talk about love for fellow man instead of love for God. But William commented concerning them: "The ideas expressed sounded so lofty and noble, but from personal experience, I already knew the words were nothing but deceitful propaganda."[113] As we will see, Madalyn Murray O'Hair didn't have much love for anyone—not even for her own family.

Her Son Describes Her Atheist Lifestyle

What is it like in the privacy of an atheist's home? Just how much love is there, actually, and what lofty and noble deeds are really done?

Madalyn Murry O'Hair Hated Her Father

William says that when he was a child his mother threatened to kill her father. She threw dishes at him, cursed him, and once, in 1954, she even tried to stab him with a butcher knife because he voiced disapproval of her illegitimate pregnancy.[114]

Madalyn's cursing of her father grew continually worse. As he grew older and weaker he eventually reached a point where he could no longer endure it. To get away for it, he swore to never eat at the dinner table with Madalyn again, and he never did, not even for his own birthdays.[115]

---

[112] William J. Murray, *My Life Without God* (Nashville: Thomas Nelson Publishers, 1982), 70–71.

[113] Ibid., 70.

[114] Ibid., 7–8.

[115] Ibid., 69.

Through the next few years Madalyn talked openly with William about desiring to murder her father;[116] however, in the end this was not necessary. In 1963 Madalyn and her father had another argument which resulted in Madalyn screaming at him: "You old __________! I hope you drop dead. I'll dump your shriveled body in the trash for the niggers to pick up!" To Madalyn's joy, he died later that same day of a heart attack.[117]

Madalyn Murray O'Hair Hated Her Sons

The story of Madalyn's abusive treatment of William is sad indeed. As we contemplate it we can only shudder, knowing that this is the kind of lifestyle humanists are going to bring upon us all—if we allow it.

Because of her neglect of him, William did not realize clearly that Madalyn was his mother until he was in grade school. Learning that she was his mother, he says, was painful.

Madalyn Murray O'Hair with her sons, William and Jon Garth.

William felt that his mother subtly blamed him, and tried to make him feel guilty for, her not marrying the father of the illegitimate baby she was carrying. She didn't marry him, she told William, because he wanted her to dump William.[118]

After Garth was born, Madalyn ignored him just as she did William. Garth responded by butting his head against the headboard of his crib for hours. This continued for days without Madalyn even seeming to notice, much less ever picking Garth up to comfort him or to give him attention and love.[119]

William said that his mother had a "vicious and violent temper" which was quite unpredictable and therefore one of her more disruptive and troubling characteristics. In a fit of anger she once threw all his model airplanes to the floor and smashed them.[120] She cursed him, and called him brainless and stupid.[121] She called him a "stupid fool" and slapped him in the face.[122] Once she grabbed a cup of fruit cocktail and hurled its contents point blank into his face.[123] She once bit him so deeply on the arm that blood oozed from several puncture wounds, and his grandfather took him to get a tetanus shot.[124] William summed up his relationship with Madalyn by saying, "Although incidents like this were frustrating, I probably was hurt deepest by her basic lack of interest in me."[125]

---

[116] Ibid., 81.

[117] Ibid., 80–81.

[118] Ibid., 18.

[119] Ibid., 20–21.

[120] Ibid., 33.

[121] Ibid., 48–49.

[122] Ibid., 49.

[123] Ibid., 68.

[124] Ibid.

[125] Ibid., 33.

Madalyn Murray O'Hair Hated Her Employers

Madalyn could never keep a job for long. William believes that her inability to keep a job for more than six months is what drew her into radical politics in Baltimore. William says that Madalyn had no respect for her bosses, believed herself to be superior to them, felt that she should be allowed to run things, and since they would not do so, she would end up quitting.

William believes that while on these jobs Madalyn met other radical socialist discontents. When William was nine she began to have Socialist Labor Party meetings in the basement of her house and made William attend to learn how bad capitalism is.[126]

Madalyn Murray O'Hair Hated Her Country

William wrote of the above mentioned radical socialist meetings:

> I remember sitting at the edge of these meetings, fighting off sleep as I heard that the United States was bad because it had rich people. Rich people were bad because they did not work; instead they exploited the labor of others. Our nation was, in fact, an enormous fascist slave labor camp. We had been tricked into believing we were free. A dramatic Socialist revolution was needed to divest the rich of their wealth. Then the workers would control the means of production under the benevolent protection of a leftist dictatorship.... Heated discussions of this type—always seething with righteous indignation—would continue deep into the night.[127]

That Madalyn believed this Socialist propaganda is obvious from her actions. So deeply did she come to detest America that she eventually tried to defect to the Soviet Union.

In 1957, Madalyn became a follower of the communist party of Leon Trotsky. This militant group held anti war demonstrations, protested against the House Unamerican Activities Committee, and supported Castro. However, so strongly did Madalyn hate the U.S.A., this anti-America activity did not satisfy her. She began contemplating moving permanently to the Soviet Union.[128]

From that time Madalyn began filing papers with the embassy of the Soviet Union in Washington, D.C., requesting to be granted citizenship. Despite her repeated efforts over the process of many months, she was never given an answer. Finally, she grew impatient, and decided she would take her two boys to France to apply for Russian citizenship at the Soviet embassy in Paris. So certain was she of success that "she wrote to the U.S. State Department and formally renounced her American citizenship."[129] On August 24, 1960, they departed for France on the Queen Elizabeth.[130] In Paris they were in for bitter disappointment. The Russian Embassy refused to grant them visas because of Madalyn's poor work record and because she had two illegitimate sons. The embassy official told her:

> In looking at your work record, it would seem you would be working for the most part at half pay....Besides, you do not speak the mother tongue. More than likely your two fatherless boys would become wards of the state. Perhaps you and your children would be better off working for the revolution in your native land.[131]

Madalyn was forced to purchase the cheapest tickets available, and return to the United States immediately. It was while enrolling William back in school after this trip that Madalyn learned of the Bible reading and prayer that began each class day there. She became incised. Soon she was plotting how to stop this violation of her atheistic beliefs. This eventually led her to file lawsuits which in 1963 would bring her to the United State Supreme Court to hear the decision that she had won her case.

While Madalyn was waiting for her lawsuit to work its way to the Supreme Court, she became manager of a Communist party bookstore—the New Era Book Shop, 101 W. 22nd Street, in Baltimore.[132] Shortly after this, in 1962, an event transpired which illustrates clearly that humanism and communism are essentially

---

126 Ibid., 21–22.

127 Ibid., 22.

128 Ibid., 31.

129 Ibid., 43.

130 Ibid., 36.

131 Ibid., 41.

132 Ibid., 80.

the same thing. They differ in name, of course, but in goals they are virtually identical. Communists, in fact, are humanists, although not all humanists claim to be communists. The publisher of the *Free Humanist* magazine asked Madalyn if she would like to take over publication of the magazine at no cost to herself. She jumped at this opportunity to broadcast her radical views. The magazine came complete with a mailing list of 600 radical atheists like herself.[133]

This publication, was renamed the *American Atheist*, and its circulation grew greatly under Madalyn's leadership. The 1992 edition of the *Writer's Market* (Cincinnati: Writer's Digest Books, 1992) listed the circulation of the *American Atheist* at 50,000, and said that William's daughter, Robin, was the editor, and William's half brother, Garth, the managing editor.

William also reports that in 1964 his mother met in Hawaii with Gus Hall, who was chairman of the Communist Party of the U.S.A.[134]

Later, Madalyn, broke the law, and to keep from being jailed she tried (unsuccessfully) to defect to Cuba.[135] That after this second attempt to flee this country, she was freed by the court after being arrested trying to reenter the country, shows just how pro-traitor, pro-criminal, and anti-God some parts of our superior judicial system have become. Wrote William:

> Fred Weisgal, the ACLU attorney who had briefly helped Mother with the prayer and Bible-reading case, filed a motion in criminal court asking that all charges against Mother be dropped. The reason given was very ironic—even for the American justice system. The Maryland Court of Appeals had just declared that members of grand juries need not affirm that they believe in God, a statement which the swearing-in oath had long contained. Furthermore, the appeals court had ruled that actions taken by grand juries sworn in by this oath could be overturned.
>
> Sure enough, the grand jury that had indicted Mother had been sworn in by such an oath. The court resolved that my mother and others like her had been denied equal protection under the law. The timing of this series of events should have made even Mother believe an angel was watching over her affairs. On October 26, all charges against her were dropped. And the state's attorney decided not to try to reindict Mrs. O'Hair.[136]

Atheism Destroys Moral Foundation

Atheists/humanists love to talk about ethics. They pride themselves in being "ethical." But just how ethical can one be who believes (as atheists/humanists do) that right and wrong are determined from within by the individual himself rather than from without by God? People who accept such an idea feel immediately "liberated" from all moral restraints. That is simple fact. As already shown, Madalyn Murray O'Hair's whole life demonstrates that fact. Two more examples will now be given.

The Example of William J. Murray

As already discussed at length, William J. Murray is the illegitimate son of Madalyn Murray O'Hair. It was her atheism that caused her to give birth to two illegitimate sons. Instead of admitting that she had sinned in sleeping with men with whom she was not married, she called fornication "a beautiful story."[137] She taught such principles to William. William says virginity had no meaning to him since he had not been given any foundation of morality at home. Therefore, he went farther than just kissing Jennifer, his first serious girlfriend.[138]

William goes on to tell how Jennifer introduced him to Susan with whom he immediately had sex.[139] Susan's father was opposed to her relationship with William. Madalyn, rather than supporting Susan's dad, invited Susan into her home to share William's bed without even discussing it with William first.[140] William

---

133 Ibid., 78.

134 Ibid., 118.

135 Ibid., 123.

136 Ibid., 143–44.

137 Ibid., 20.

138 Ibid., 92.

139 Ibid.

140 Ibid., 96.

was only seventeen years old. Susan soon became pregnant out of wedlock.[141] This was just the first of many illicit affairs William experienced up to the point he found Christ.[142] During his life without God, William also stole,[143] abused alcohol,[144] faked an automobile accident in order to bilk an insurance company,[145] used drugs,[146] dabbled in the occult,[147] battered his girlfriend,[148] sold drugs,[149] deserted the army,[150] took bribes,[151] defrauded men at a cock fight,[152] and engaged in a gun battle.[153]

Life without God really sounds ethical, doesn't it?!

The Example of Gina Allen

Prometheus Books, publisher of *Humanist Manifesto I & II*, has published a book titled *The Best of Humanism.* This book, edited by Roger E. Greeley, is a compilation of quotations from prominent Humanists. These quotations supposedly represent the very best of humanism. In this book is a personal testimony by a woman named Gina Allen, concerning how becoming an atheist instantly removed her inner desire to refrain from tobacco, alcohol, and premarital sex. Writes Gina on pages 35-36:

> I first saw the light one night when I was sixteen years old. It was initially a very small light—the beam from the flashlight that enabled me to read under the bed covers when I was supposed to be sleeping. That night I was reading a Little Blue Book that had been given me by my boyfriend. It was Percy Bysshe Shelley's *The Necessity of Atheism*.
>
> I usually say that until the moment I opened the book I was a very religious young women, but I suppose I had actually been outgrowing my religion for a while. For one thing, my boyfriend, a freethinker, had been giving me books like this and had been making me defend my religious beliefs—which I had difficulty doing to his satisfaction, and my own.
>
> So I was prepared for Shelly and his atheism even though I didn't know it. And, as I read, the light got brighter and brighter. Not from the flashlight I was reading with but from my mind absorbing what I read. Shelley's logic shattered, in one memorable night, all the Sunday school lessons, Bible studies, and sermons I had been exposed to for years.
>
> My first reaction was fury, a fury so strong that I risked confronting my father the next morning at breakfast. "You can't possibly believe all that god stuff! Do you?" I demanded. "You're an intelligent, educated man. God is as much a hoax as Santa Claus and not nearly as much fun. And only kids believe in Santa."
>
> His response made me even angrier, This pillar of the religious community, this trustee of the local Presbyterian church, this man who supported the church financially and attended services every Sunday told me calmly that no, he didn't believe what the church taught. But he did believe that without the church there would be no morality in the world. Children learned right and wrong in the church, and adults lived righteous lives because they believed in God and heaven and hell.
>
> I have since learned that this attitude is not unusual among many who appear to be religious. They are no less concerned with their own spirituality than with the conduct of others. They see themselves as superior, able to understand their religion as mythology and still conduct their lives morally. But they don't think the ordinary person can do that, so they count on religion to keep the masses under control. Indeed, throughout history such "superior" men have used religion to regulate their slaves and subjugate women.
>
> In my first heady release from religion I too thought it was the only thing that had kept me "good." My life would change: I could sin. As a teenager, for me the three great sins were smoking, drinking, and premarital sex.
>
> I told my boyfriend that I had seen the light. He was glad. He said he thought I was too intelligent to stay caught up in religion forever. Then I told him that we could sin together. We could drink, and smoke, and have sex. He looked at me as if I were crazy. I could do those things if I wished, he said, but he was in training. As captain of the high-school football team, a star basketball player, and a Golden Gloves boxer, he was always in training.

---

[141] Ibid., 102.
[142] Ibid., 126, 152–53.
[143] Ibid., 148.
[144] Ibid., 218.
[145] Ibid., 150.
[146] Ibid., 126.
[147] Ibid., 119–20.
[148] Ibid., 169–70.
[149] Ibid., 192.
[150] Ibid.
[151] Ibid., 194.
[152] Ibid., 132–33.
[153] Ibid., 133–35.

> He wasn't "good" because he believed in a god but because he wanted to be an athlete. Slowly it dawned upon me that I hadn't been "good" because I believed in a god but because I loved my family and friends, enjoyed my studies and my music, and wanted to prepare myself for all life's possibilities.

How amazing is Gina's conclusion that God was not the basis of her morality before she became an atheist! If belief in God's existence had not kept Gina good, then why did she—immediately upon becoming an atheist—tell her boyfriend they "could sin together"?

As Gina very well knows, atheists do not even believe there is such a thing as sin, for sin is a transgression of God's law (1 John 3:4), and if there is no God, then no law can have issued from Him. So of course she cannot sin since (in her eyes) there is no such thing! Since according to atheist dogma there is no such thing as sin or immorality, Gina can feel herself to be good and moral no matter what she does! That Gina in fact is not "good" ("There is none good, no not one" according to Rom. 3:10), but sins (in spite of her claim to the contrary) is evident from her statement that theistic religion "spreads guilt instead of joy."[154] Gina seems to be talking from experience. Only those who do something they consider to be a sin against God feel guilt. So obviously it is the "joy" of committing what theists call sin to which Gina is referring. So, her atheism has not kept her good, but rather made her evil. Atheism has destroyed her moral foundation. She is now adrift upon the churning sea of situation ethics. Her life is without doubt a mess and she to be pitied.

Atheism is Pagan Religion

After William Murray turned from atheism to God, he went to Washington, D.C. to testify before a senate committee debating the Supreme Court Jurisdiction Act of 1979. Wrote William of his testimony: "I noted that by precluding all religions advocating faith in God from public schools, the Federal Government was in fact establishing a materialistic atheistic religion by default."[155] William made an exceedingly vital point. Atheism is pagan religion. It is worship of self, and worship of Satan. And it has, in fact, been established as the state church of the U.S.A.

William reports that Madalyn's atheism did not prevent her from believing in the forces of darkness, the spirit that now worketh in the children of disobedience. While hiding from the law in Hawaii, Madalyn helped arrange meetings for a psychic from Seattle to conduct seances.[156]

Why an Atheist Turned to God

Atheists take pride in calling themselves freethinkers. But a person is not really free whose mind is so chained in the bondage of sin that it cannot come to logical conclusions. The man who has never tasted alcohol (or drugs, or illicit sex, etc.) is free from its addiction. But the man who takes that first drink (or fix or fornication) often finds that he is not free to quit. And until his sin makes such a hell out of his life that he can no longer ignore it, his mind is no longer going to function properly. Even then it will take the grace of God to bring him to the truth. William Murray testifies that he came to believe in God as a result of seeing the extreme evil in his mother and in his employer at that time, Tom Evans. Says William, "One day while driving home from work the truth struck me. I thought, There has to be a God because there certainly is a devil. I have met him, talked to him, and touched him. He is the personification of evil. He is Tom Evans, my mother, and others like them I have met."[157] When William became a Christian, Madelyn cut him off with this vicious remark: "One could call this a postnatal abortion on the part of a mother, I guess; I repudiate him entirely and completely for now and all times...He is beyond human forgiveness."[158]

---

154 Roger E. Greeley, ed., *The Best of Humanism* (Buffalo, New York: Prometheus Books, 1988), 37.

155 Murray, *My Life Without God*, 250.

156 Ibid., 119.

157 Ibid., 232–33.

158 Lona Manning, "The Murder of Madalyn Murray O'Hair: America's Most Hated Woman," *Dunamai.Com*, Http://www.dunamai.com/articles/atheist/murder_of_ohair.htm.

The Bitter End of Atheism

Madalyn Murray O'Hair once bragged, saying, "I love a good fight...I guess fighting God and God's spokesmen is sort of the ultimate, isn't it?"[159] But such words lose their humor as one approaches death. "The Lord is not slack concerning his promise, as some men count slackness; but is longsuffering to us-ward, not willing that any should perish, but that all should come to repentance" (2 Pet 3.9). Therefore He may let even atheists live on for some time even while they fight against God and seemingly win a few battles. But the war they will lose. In the day of death, God will say unto them,

William J. Murray, raised an atheist, born again into the family of God, now a Baptist preacher—a trophy to the manifold mercy and grace of God!

> Because I have called, and ye refused; I have stretched out my hand, and no man regarded; but ye have set at naught all my counsel, and would none of my reproof: I also will laugh at your calamity; I will mock when your fear cometh; when your fear cometh as desolation, and your destruction cometh as a whirlwind; when distress and anguish cometh upon you. Then shall they call upon me, but I will not answer; they shall seek me early, but they shall not find me: for that they hated knowledge, and did not choose the fear of the LORD: they would none of my counsel: they despised all my reproof. Therefore shall they eat of the fruit of their own way, and be filled with their own devices. For the turning away of the simple shall slay them, and the prosperity of fools shall destroy them. But whoso hearkeneth unto me shall dwell safely, and shall be quiet from fear of evil. (Prov. 1:24-33)

The famous Voltaire spent his whole life in debauchery and opposition to theism, but on his death bed drank his own urine and ate his own excrement, and screamed in horror before dying in agony. It is folly to fight against God. God always wins. The wise man joins the winning side while he has the chance.

In August of 1995, Madalyn Murray O'Hair, William's brother, Jon Garth, and his daughter, Robin, disappeared. Madalyn was 77 years old at that time. For three years the national atheist organization Madalyn led claimed that she had left the country with a large amount of money—but that was not true. In the first half of 1999 evidence came to light that Madalyn, Garth, and Robin had been murdered on September 29, 1995, about 30 days after their kidnapping and disappearance. The murderers were three convicts: David Waters, Gary Karr, and Danny Fry. Madalyn had hired convicted murderer David Waters to be her office manager, William believes, because "she had found that employees who were convicted felons allowed her to work them harder and many times under pay them,"[160] and because "she got a sense of power out of having men in her employ who had taken human life."[161]

The evidence is strong that Madalyn was tortured before her death. Robin was repeatedly raped and tortured. After Madalyn, Robin, and Jon Garth were murdered, their bodies were dismembered, burnt, and then buried on a 5,000 acre ranch near Camp Wood, Texas.

Wrote William later:

> The media asked me if I would hold a funeral and if so would there be prayer. My answer was simple but Biblical and sort of surprised them I am sure. I said, "They are already either in heaven of hell, praying over them now will not make a difference."

---

159 Murray, *My Life Without God*, 98.

160 William J. Murray, "Update to William J. Murray's Statement on the Murder of His Mother as of January, 2000" (2000), Http://www.wjmurray.com/madalyn/update2000.htm.

161 William J. Murray, "May 1999 Statement of Evangelist William J. Murray on the Kidnapping and Murder of Family Members: My Mother, My Brother, and My Daughter Were Murdered!!" (1999), Http://www.wjmurray.com/madalyn/madayln.htm.

I made that statement knowing the torture they must have gone through the last thirty days of their lives. Did Robin pray to receive Christ as she was bound and gagged? Perhaps. Did my mother or brother cry out to the Lord just before they were murdered? I don't know.

Christ is there for the vilest offender. The serial killer whose prayer at the hour of his death is genuine is also forgiven. My mother, my brother and my daughter may well await me in heaven. On the other hand, they may have stood their ground defying God to the end, in which case they are now spending yet another day of eternity in hell. If that is the case I will never see them again.

The deaths of my mother, brother and daughter should make all too clear the need for Christ to others that proclaim atheism. But those who would follow my mother continue to fight against God and His authority. "Fools make a mock at sin... " Prov. 14:8[162]

O'hair demonstrating against God. Her sign shows that she did not know the meaning of true freedom.

Humanists mistake wantoness for liberty, and sin for freedom. Sin enslaves; it does not free. "Why do the heathen rage, and the people imagine a vain thing? The kings of the earth set themselves, and the rulers take counsel together, against the LORD, and against his anointed, *saying*, Let us break their bands asunder, and cast away their cords from us. He that sitteth in the heavens shall laugh: the Lord shall have them in derision. Then shall he speak unto them in his wrath, and vex them in his sore displeasure." (Psalms 2:1-4)

"Jesus answered them, Verily, verily, I say unto you, Whosoever committeth **sin** is the **servant** of **sin**. And the **servant** abideth not in the house for ever: but the Son abideth ever. If the Son therefore shall make you free, ye shall be free indeed." (John 8:34-36) God's law does not enslave, but rather frees: it is the "law of liberty" (James 1:25).

---

162 Ibid.

Chapter 10

IS THE BIBLE TRUE?

Yes! Hares Do Chew the Cud

How could the digestive process of the lowly hare become the object of an important educational, political and theological discussion? How hares digest their food is more interesting than one would first assume. The Bible says that the hare chews the cud, but a certain humanist book claims that the Bible is in error on this point. Furthermore, this humanist book claims that since the Bible contains this error, it is not the Word of God and cannot be taken seriously on any other points either. These are serious charges. On the other hand, if the humanists be wrong on this point, perhaps it is they whom we should not take seriously on any other points either.

So let's study the hare closely to see if the Bible is indeed wrong, or if it is these atheistic religious humanists who are wrong.

The Bible Says Hares Chew the Cud

These religious humanists are right about one thing: the Bible does teach that hares chew the cud.

> Nevertheless these ye shall not eat of them that chew the cud, or of them that divide the cloven hoof; as the camel, and the hare, and the coney: for they chew the cud, but divide not the hoof; therefore they are unclean unto you. (Deut. 14:7)

> And the hare, because he cheweth the cud, but divideth not the hoof; he is unclean unto you. (Lev. 11:6)

These two passages of Scripture very clearly state that the children of Israel were not to eat the hare because the hare chews the cud but does not have a divided hoof. (Some people believe that not all hares can be considered rabbits. However, everyone seems to agree that all rabbits are hares. So, for this article the two terms will be used interchangeably.) It is correct to say that the Bible does, indeed, teach that rabbits (hares) chew the cud.

Humanists Say Hares Do Not Chew the Cud

It cannot be said that *all* humanists teach that hares do not chew the cud, for we would have to question every humanist in the world to ascertain that. However, it can truthfully be said that some very well known ones do so say. Rod L. Evans and Irwin M. Berent have written a book titled *Fundamentalism: Hazard and Heartbreaks* which has a forward by Steve Allen and an introduction by Isaac Asimov. Allen and Asimov are big names in the Humanist movement. Asimov was one of the signers of *Humanist Manifesto II* and has written many books opposing Christianity and teaching humanism, and was till his death president of the American Humanist Association, so we can safely conclude that he would not have written the introduction to this book unless it was in accord with his humanistic views. This book is a collection of many of the excuses atheists have given over the years for rejecting God, the Bible, and Jesus Christ. Most of these excuses were proven erroneous years ago shortly after they were given, and only dishonest people would continue to use them. However, there was one excuse listed in this book that was new (at least to me). On page 86 of their book, Evans and Berent state:

> Evidently the belief in perfect Biblical accuracy is also a misconception. For Leviticus 11:6 states that "the hare...chews the cud...", which is a demonstrably false statement.[163]

Since Evans and Berent make this statement publicly in a book devoted totally to discrediting people "who believe that the Bible is infallible,"[164] it behooves us to see if these two atheistic religious humanists really base everything on conclusions reached by the scientific method, as they claim. Or are they simply spouting off some of the "profane and vain babblings, and oppositions of science falsely so called" we are warned about in 1 Tim 6.20?

What Are the Facts

Surprisingly little is known about hares. Until relatively recent times, few scientific studies were made of them. R.M. Lockley, a distinguished British biologist and field naturalist, is among the foremost hare experts. His book, *The Private Life of the Rabbit: An Account of the life and History and Social Behavior of the Wild Rabbit* (New York, Macmillan Publishing Co., Inc., 1964), details his fascinating research and provides an authoritative answer to our question.

Lockley spent most of his life studying rabbits. As a child he raised rabbits. When he was twenty he obtained the lease to "240-acre Skokholm island, five miles off the entrance to Milforn Haven."[165] His intention was to kill off the wild rabbit population on this island so that he could raise a more valuable strain of rabbit which had fur resembling that of the chinchillas. He preformed many experiments to try to control the wild rabbit population on this island. Says Lockley,

> Indirectly my experience in studying rabbit control methods at Skokholm led to an invitation from the Nature Conservancy to investigate on their behalf the progress of myxomatosis, when it broke out in England in 1953; and subsequently from 1954 to 1959 I was able to carry out a life-history study of the rabbit on my small estate of Orielton in Pembrokeshire.[166]

Lockley and his helpers built a special observatory where they could observe wild rabbits up close, both above ground and in their burrows, without disturbing the rabbits. From his careful and systematic observations in this unique observatory, Lockley became one of the foremost authorities on rabbits.

Chapter 10 of Lockley's book is titled "Reingestion." He begins this chapter by quoting Leviticus chapter 11, as we did at the beginning of this article. He then reports that rabbits do little underground except rest, sleep, and preen themselves. However, there is one exception to this relative lack of activity while underground. Writes Lockley:

> So long as we could watch the rabbits underground we had an ideal opportunity to study the phenomena of coprophagy or reingestion.
>
> The fact that rabbits ... and hares 'chew the cud' was recorded in the Bible. It is mentioned in Leviticus, Chapter 11, ... Also (the Jewish law of clean and unclean meats) in Deuteronomy XIV.... Later writers, even authorities on both wild and domestic rabbits, have seldom referred to this phenomenon. In general, textbooks on rabbit physiology and management ignore the subject, not because of its lowly theme but because the authors apparently were ignorant of it. Since its recent rediscovery it has been called 'reingestion,' a suitable term implying that it is a form of re-eating and redigestion of food.[167]

Lockley goes on to explain that rabbits chew their cuds differently than cows, goats or sheep, which

---

[163] Rod L. Evans and Irwin M. Berent, *Fundamentalism: Hazard and Heartbreaks*, foreword by Steve Allen, introd. by Issac Asimov (La Salle, Illinois: Open Court Publishing Company, 1988), 86.

[164] Ibid., xix.

[165] R.M. Lockley, *The Private Life of the Rabbit: An Account of the Life and History and Social Behavior of the Wild Rabbit*, introd. by Richard Adams (New York: Macmillan Publishing Co., Inc., 1964), 14.

[166] Ibid., 16.

[167] Ibid., 101–02.

regurgitate their food and rechew it. The rabbit, instead, eats its own excrement (faecal pellets), and thus redigests them. Usually this occurs during the daytime underground as the rabbit is resting. Occasionally this was observed above ground, but

> could easily be overlooked by the casual observer. A swift bending of the head during which the long ears almost touched the ground between the hind legs, then the rabbit's head would come up and the jaws work for a few seconds as the pellet was swallowed and the tongue licked around inside the mouth afterwards. In the rabbit there is a curious infolding of the lower lips over the space between the incisor and molar teeth which protects and hides the tongue. The observer could not see the faeces because of the masking action and the closed mouth.[168]

We are forced to conclude that simple faith in God's Word would have resulted long ago in scientists looking more specifically, and therefore seeing, rabbits chewing their cud. But unbelief kept them blinded to the facts.

But Do Hares Really "Chew" the Cud?

Lockley reports that researchers Mervyn Griffiths and David Davies in Australia have

> demonstrated that each soft pellet is separate and by the time it reaches the rectum is enveloped in a strong membrane.... These soft pellets pass down to the rectum in glossy clusters. They are swallowed whole by the rabbit, that is, without breaking the enveloping membranes. This in itself is a remarkable feat, as, although the rabbit (under observation in the open as well as in our artificial burrow) sometimes appears to chew this faecal 'cud' after collecting it from the anus, with movements of the jaws varying in time from one to over one hundred seconds, Griffiths and Davies assert that the soft pellets are found whole in the stomach and therefore must be swallowed whole. The movement of the jaws may therefore be solely a swallowing, followed by a cleaning action of the tongue, during which saliva is ingested along with the soft pellets and must aid in the digestive process.[169]

So, are the pellets (cud) chewed or not? It is perhaps impossible to ever observe what is actually going on inside the rabbit's mouth as it appears to chew the cud. I would suggest that since the Bible was right about the rabbit having a cud, it is also right about the rabbit chewing the cud. Perhaps the chewing is gentle enough so as to not break the membrane, but rough enough to crush its contents so as to make redigestion easier. This certainly seems possible as Lockley says that "the membrane is quite tough",[170] and would account for the fact that the rabbit spends from "one to over 100 seconds" doing something with its jaws that certainly appears to be chewing after taking the cud into its mouth. One thing for certain: God's Word has certainly proven to be more accurate than the speculation of unbelievers. Is it not significant that unbelieving "scientists" have not known about a rabbit's cud for thousands of years even though the fact of it is recorded in the oldest book on earth? It should be obvious to all that the Bible is no ordinary book to be set aside lightly.

Conclusion

Having proved humanists wrong on yet another point in which they contest the Bible, how can we trust anything they say any longer? All my life I have been examining the claims of unbelievers that there are errors in the Bible. In every case to date, after careful examination the Bible has proven to be correct and the men that questioned it have proven to be in error. God's Word has without exception proven itself fully qualified to correct men, while men have shown themselves to be totally unqualified to correct God's Word. The wise man will agree with the Bible: "Let God be true, but every man a liar" (Rom. 3:4).

Perhaps the most important lesson to be learned from this study about hares chewing the cud is this: had we gone to the library at an earlier point in history we may not have been able to find any books supporting the Bible position concerning this matter. However, the Bible would still have been true, and the men who disputed it would have been wrong. Sometimes direct research has to be done to confirm the accuracy of a questioned Bible verse, but the Bible is always proven to be true in the end.

The cud of a hare is just one example of proof that the so-called "science" of humanism is not actually science at all, but is mere philosophy—unproven opinions of men—superstition. A true scientist reports only what he observes. But no one has ever observed life come spontaneously from dead matter, or a non-

---

[168] Ibid., 103.

[169] Ibid., 105.

[170] Ibid., 106.

human give birth to a human. No one has ever observed an animal of one kind give birth to an animal of a different kind. These are the presuppositions of the religion of evolution. The fact that humanists claim such unscientific theories to be scientific shows that they are unable to look at anything without bias. The truth is that they approach all aspects of life with the fanatical belief that "the only absolute is that there are no absolutes." They have espoused such a silly idea because God claims to be absolute authority, and the Bible claims to be the absolute truth, and so they must reject both God and the Bible to keep from feeling guilty when they purposely break God's laws which are recorded in the Bible. Therefore, rejection of absolutes is inseparable from atheism.

The moment a person rejects absolutes that person declares war on God and Christianity, for if God is not absolute in holiness as the Bible of Christianity teaches, then there must be a better morality then God's, in which case the Christian teaching that Christian morality is perfect would be a great hindrance to progress and therefore a great evil. As Sir Julius Huxley, one of Humanism's most famous champions, states in *The Humanist Frame*,

> Humanism ... will have nothing to do with Absolutes, including absolute truth, absolute morality, absolute perfection and absolute authority.... any belief in supernatural creators, rulers, or influencers of natural or human process introduces an irreparable split into the universe, and prevents us from grasping its real unity. Any belief in Absolutes, whether the absolute validity of moral commandments, of authority of revelation, of inner certitude, or of divine inspiration, erects a formidable barrier against progress and the possibility of improvement, moral, rational, or religious.[171]

This rejection of absolutes is why humanists spend so much time, energy, and resources opposing Christianity.

Unfortunately, it is impossible to reason with most humanists. One cannot have a logical discussion with a person who believes one cannot be absolutely sure about anything, and that nothing matters except winning the argument. Since humanists ares not absolutely sure that what they themselvesf believe is true, they possess no solid, unchanging values. Thus it is impossible to find a mutually accepted foundation upon which to base logic so as to be able to persuade them of anything. The moment they sees that their challenger's argument is valid, they change their belief so as to make their challengers efforts to communicate with them fruitless.

A humanist can justify any evil behavior—even murder of unborn babies, robbery, rape, or sodomy—with a giddy "nothing is absolutely wrong." Having no clear concept of right and wrong, such a person constantly changes positions, and lies, sincerely believing that even lying is not absolutely wrong. Such a person therefore cannot be of high integrity or character, for he can never be trusted to tell the truth or to keep his promises.

Consider how stupid and illogical this foundational ideological belief of humanism actually is. If there are no absolutes, then it cannot be absolutely true that there are no absolutes. And if it is not absolutely true that there are no absolutes, then it must be absolutely false that the there are no absolutes. And if it be absolutely false that there are no absolutes, then it must be absolutely true that there are absolutes.

Obviously then when a person rejects absolutes he is intentionally closing his eyes to the light. He can't see because he won't see. This is why rejecting God and the Bible makes it impossible for a person to ever find truth.

> This know also, that in the last days perilous times shall come. For men shall be lovers of their own selves, covetous, boasters, proud, blasphemers, disobedient to parents, unthankful, unholy, without natural affection, trucebreakers, false accusers, incontinent, fierce, despisers of those that are good, traitors, heady, highminded, lovers of pleasures more than lovers of God; having a form of godliness, but denying the power thereof: from such turn away. For of this sort are they which creep into houses, and lead captive silly women laden with sins, led away with divers lusts, **ever learning, and never able to come to the knowledge of the truth.** (2 Tim. 3:1-7)
>
> **The fear of the LORD is the beginning of knowledge**: but fools despise wisdom and instruction. (Prov. 1:7)
>
> To the law and to the testimony: **if they speak not according to this word, it is because there is no light in them.** (Is. 8:20)
>
> **Beware lest any man spoil you through philosophy and vain deceit**, after the rudiments of the world, and not after Christ. For in him dwelleth all the fulness of the Godhead bodily" (Col. 2:8-9).

One is also reminded of Rom 1:28: "... as they did not like to retain God in their knowledge, God gave them

[171] Julian Huxley, *The Humanist Frame*, 14 and 40.

over to a reprobate mind." Webster's New World Dictionary, Second Edition, defines reprobate as "depraved, corrupt, unprincipled; rejected by God; excluded from salvation and lost in sin." Such is the humanist mind—a high price to pay for closing ones eyes to the plain facts of all true science.

UPDATE

This chapter is an edited version of an article written by the author years ago. Other Christian authors also pointed out these facts. All these articles showing the truth put the humanists on the defensive, and they began to publish articles defending what Evan and Berent had written and Allen and Asimov had endorsed. All of these humanist articles that the author has read can be summed as: The Bible is wrong in Lev. 11:6 and in Deut. 14:7 because what the word "cud" means in that verse is not what modern science says the word "cud" means. Interpretation of that humanist argument: humanists can win only by redefining words so that they no longer mean what they originally meant. That is intellectual dishonesty. Lenny Esposito is correct in saying,

> Now, we must also remember that artiodactyls were first defined as a separate order in 1847 by Richard Owen and the behavior of cecotropy was first recognized in 1882. Deuteronomy, however, was written approximately 1500 BC in an ancient Hebrew. It would be intellectually dishonest for someone to claim that a 3500 year old writing is contradictory because it doesn't match with a scientific classification invented only about a hundred years ago. Further, if the ancient Hebrews defined 'cud-chewing" as that process where half digested vegetation was re-chewed by an animal for easier re-digestion (and that is a very specific and scientific definition), I would say the hare fits here fine.[172]

---

[172] Lenny Esposito, "Does the Hare Really Chew Cud?" *ComeReason.Org* (2007), Http://www.comereason.org/bibl_cntr/con055.asp.

One atheist published this Photoshopped image to mock what the Bible says about hares chewing the cud. But actually the joke is on him. Atheists believe that new kinds of animals such as this can actually happen. According to them, their god, Evolution, is still making new kinds of animals like this even today! They've never seen it happen; but they have faith! They claim to have common ancestry with the apes. But Apes take that as an insult!

Chapter 11

ARE ALL HUMANISTS HUMANISTS?

Not Knowing the Difference Could Be Fatal

Humanists are masters of deception. One of their favorite techniques is to take words with good connotations and use them to name one of their wicked organizations. Even though their organizations may stand for the exact opposite of what the words means, most people's initial impression of those organizations will be favorable because they are unaware that the good words are used to deceive them.

Ancient humanists Were Not Like Modern humanists

The words *humanist* and *humanism* are good examples of this deceptive practice. Before modern Humanists hijacked these words for their own use these words had no atheistic implications.

Ancient humanists

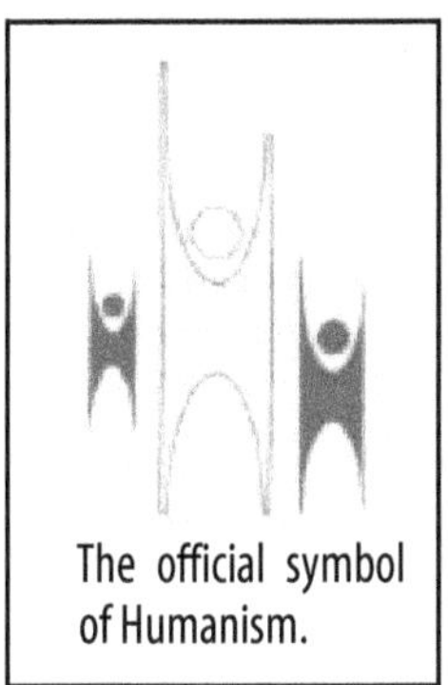
The official symbol of Humanism.

For instance, in the field of literature a humanist was a person that had passion humanities—the languages, history, art, the social sciences, etc.—, as opposed to someone whose passion was studying the natural sciences. During the Renaissance the word humanism referred to the revival of interest in studying the classical letters written in the Greek language, including the New Testament of the Bible. Erasmas, who produced the first printed edition of the Textus Receptus Greek New Testament, was this type of humanist. Humanism in those days was not a religion, and there was, of course, nothing wicked or dangerous about humanists such as those. Modern day humanism, however, is a religion, is based squarely on atheism, is organized into political action groups very similar to the Communist Party, and its leaders are wicked and dangerous in ideology and goals. Millions of American babies have already been murdered due to the efforts of these people to kill our soldiers before they are even born.

Modern humanists

The American Humanist Association describes modern day humanism as follows:

> MODERN HUMANISM, also called Naturalistic Humanism, Scientific Humanism, Ethical Humanism and Democratic Humanism is defined by one of its leading proponents, Corliss Lamont, as "a naturalistic philosophy that rejects all supernaturalism and relies primarily upon reason and science, democracy and human compassion." Modern Humanism has a dual origin, both secular and religious, and these constitute its sub-categories.
>
> SECULAR HUMANISM is an outgrowth of 18th century enlightenment rationalism and 19th century freethought. Many secular groups, such as the Council for Democratic and Secular Humanism and the American Rationalist Federation, and many otherwise unaffiliated academic philosophers and scientists, advocate this philosophy.
>
> RELIGIOUS HUMANISM emerged out of Ethical Culture, Unitarianism, and Universalism. Today, many Unitarian-Universalist congregations and all Ethical Culture societies describe themselves as humanist in the modern sense.[173]

Remember, calling something scientific, ethical or Democratic does not make it so. Just saying that an organization "relies primarily upon reason and science, democracy and human compassion" does not mean

[173] Edwords, "What is Humanism?"

that it actually does. We must not be naive, especially when we can see that the very opposite is the truth. Humanists are masters of deceit.

The one element of truth in the above definition is that modern humanism "rejects all supernaturalism." In other words, modern humanists reject—and are at war with—God.

Secular and Religious Humanism the Same

For all practical purposes, there is no difference between secular and religious humanists. As the American Humanist Association explains:

THE HUMANIST magazine is the most influencial of the many Humanist publications.

> The most critical irony in dealing with Modern Humanism is the inability of its advocates to agree on whether or not this worldview is religious. Those who see it as philosophy are the Secular Humanists while those who see it as religion are Religious Humanists. This dispute has been going on since the early years of this century when the secular and religious traditions converged and brought Modern Humanism into existence.
>
> **Secular and Religious Humanists both share the same worldview and the same basic principles.** This is made evident by the fact that both Secular and Religious Humanists were among the signers of Humanist Manifesto I in 1933 and Humanist Manifesto II in 1973. **From the standpoint of philosophy alone, there is no difference between the two.** It is only in the definition of religion and in the practice of the philosophy that Religious and Secular Humanists effectively disagree....while Secular Humanists may agree with much of what religious Humanists do, they deny that this activity is properly called "religious." This isn't a mere semantic debate. Secular Humanists maintain that there is so much in religion deserving of criticism that the good name of Humanism should not be tainted by connection with it.
>
> Secular Humanists often refer to Unitarian Universalists as "Humanists not yet out of the church habit." **But Unitarian-Universalists sometimes counter that a secular Humanist is simply an "unchurched Unitarian."**[174] [Emphasis added.]

Both those who call themselves secular humanists and those who call themselves religious humanists are members of the same American Humanist Association, and signed the same Humanist Manifesto I which established Humanism as a "frank religion." As its leaders all know, humanism is a religion whether some of its followers want to admit it or not.

Most Christians have been warned about "secular humanism," but have never heard of "religious humanism." That is most unfortunate, as understanding that Humanism is a religion is essential to ending its dominance of education in the USA.

The Difference Between humanists and Humanists

While there is no practical difference between secular humanists and religious humanists, there is a way to divide modern day humanists that does make a difference. The American Humanist Association distinguishes between humanists with a lower case h (people espousing humanist philosophy), and Humanists with a capital H (members of their association or of one or more of its front groups).[175]

---

[174] Ibid.

[175] Lebrun, "Humanism with a Capital H."

humanists with a lower case h

The vast majority of people who live their lives according to the principles of humanism are not members of any organized humanist movement. Many of them do not even realize that they are humanists. They are not conscious that humanism is a religion. They simply accepted the Theory of Evolution as scientific fact because they were taught humanist religious dogma in public school. They were just children at the time, and never really questioned what they were taught, but simply accepted it in blind faith, and based their whole idea-system upon it, just as their humanist or Humanist teachers hoped that they would.

Humanists With an Upper Case H

But there is another group of humanists which is highly organized into religious and political action subgroups. This group is the most dangerous one, for it has international goals of world conquest—with very detailed and well-thought-out plans for reaching those goals. Very similar—in fact, almost identical—to the communist party in philosophy and goals, these Humanists work through many front organizations which are careful not to include the words "humanism" or "humanist" in their names. The remainder of this book will expose several of the most important of these front groups. In the United States these Humanists are united under the umbrella of the American Humanist Association. Worldwide they are united under the umbrella of the International Humanist and Ethical Union (IHEU). This book refers to members of these groups not as "humanists" but as "Humanists" (with a capital H). They deserve this distinction for they are the ones working fervently toward clearly defined goals which are international in scope.

humanists contrasted with Humanists

Let us consider these two groups (humanists and Humanists) in more detail.

Characteristics of humanists–lower case h

The typical humanist in this group most likely does not know that he is a humanist. He may not even know what a humanist is. He may be a minister in a Christian church, or a teacher in a mosque. He may be a school teacher, a college student, or a worker in just about any occupation or profession. He is a humanist, not because he has joined any organization, but simply because he has accepted the Theory of Evolution as scientifically proven fact. His faith in the Genesis account of creation (and therefore in the whole Bible) has been greatly shaken or completely destroyed, and he therefore no longer lives his life in submission to the dictates of God's revealed Word. He now considers human reason at least equally authoritative with the Bible, or may consider the Bible to have no authority whatsoever. After all, if the very first chapter of the Bible cannot be believed literally, why should other parts of it be taken as literally true? He may still claim to be a Christian, but Christianity is no longer a vital influence in his life. In fact, deep inside, he doubts that there is really a God and he feels that Christianity restricts his personal freedom. He would probably never say this publicly because his parents and many of the people he grew up with still go to church and consider atheism a vile evil. But he secretly resents having some of his favorite pastimes called "sin." He has deep contempt for "Bible-quoting fundamentalists." Christianity is no longer a living influence to him, though he may still turn (rather resentfully) to Christianity when a ritual such as a wedding or funeral is needed. For all practical purposes his Christianity (if he claims any) is already dead—and beginning to stink.

> When religions decay, form generally outlasts substance: rituals continue to be observed, sometimes even intensified, but they move outside the lives of the people who practice them. In these circumstances, ritual is celebrated but no longer believed; it may even become embarrassing. Vital religions are different. Although the extent of ritual observance varies from one to another, all living religions are part of daily life and their central tenets are accepted as truths that need no further verification.

> Humanism is one of the vital religions, perhaps no longer growing but very much alive. It is the dominant religion of our time, a part of the lives of nearly everyone in the "developed" world and of all others who want to participate in a similar development. There is very little ritual in humanism, and most of its devout followers do not seem to be aware that they are humanists. Ask them for the name of their religion and they will deny having one, or, more commonly, name one of the traditional faiths. On the other hand, people who consider themselves humanists usually are—frequently, however, for reasons other than the ones they know and admit.
>
> Can a person unknowingly belong to one religion while under the impression that he or she is part of another? If that person believes in the dogma of the former and only celebrates the latter, why not?[176]

Some public school teachers fall within this group. And because they know about the second group, and are not a part of them, they deny being humanists. However, they are still teaching humanist doctrine, even if they do not realize it. And thereby they are helping the Humanist cause. They may not be Humanists, but they are nevertheless humanists.

The fact is, the vast majority of public school teachers are humanists, and many are active members of the American Humanist Association or one or more of its front groups, and are purposely and zealously using the public school system to brainwash our children in Humanist religious dogma.

Characteristics of Humanists–with an upper case H

The distinguishing mark of a Humanist (with a capital H) is that he has joined one or more of the organizations associated with the International Humanist and Ethical Union[177], and is working according to clearly laid out plans (*Humanist Manifesto I & II*) to change the culture, values, politics and religion of the country he lives in. Especially, he wants to destroy people's faith in the Bible and in God. As the following words from Humanist leader Edward L. Ericson show, Humanism is an international conspiracy against God:

> Whether individual Humanists, or particular groups of Humanists, prefer to consider Humanism as religious (the position taken here [in Ericson's book]), or as solely philosophical, Humanists generally are in agreement that human life is the outcome of an incalculably dynamic natural universe in its ongoing evolutionary progression. In this conception of reality there is no need to assume a supernatural intelligence presiding over the origin and destiny of life or the cosmos.
>
> While millions of people in the United States, and millions more around the world, subscribe to the concepts and attitudes expressed above as a purely personal philosophy, or faith, Ethical Humanism also exists as an organized religious and ethical movement. Founded more than a century ago in New York City as the Society for Ethical Culture, the movement has grown into a national federation of local societies known as the American Ethical Union. A European Ethical movement, headquartered in Switzerland, was organized soon after the American development.
>
> Individual societies may be known as Ethical societies, Ethical Culture societies, or Ethical Humanist societies, according to local preference. But regardless of variations in name, all member groups of the American Ethical Union share the same essential moral and spiritual faith that has come to be known as Ethical Humanism.
>
> Today Ethical Humanism is part of the global Humanist movement. In 1952 the American Ethical Union collaborated with the American Humanist Association and other Humanist and Ethical bodies in Britain, Western Europe and India to organize a worldwide alliance of Ethical Culture and Humanist groups named the International Humanist and Ethical Union (IHEU). Although each member association retains its independence and historic identity, all are linked in a worldwide community for the promotion of Ethical Humanist principles and ideals.[178]

The Humanists are the most dangerous humanists because they are so organized and influential. Because American Humanists have succeeded in gaining dominance in the US Supreme Court, in public

---

[176] David W. Ehrenfeld, *The Arrogance of Humanism* (Oxford: Oxford University Press, 1981), 4.

[177] The International Humanist and Ethical Union is present located at 1 Gower Street, London, WC1E 6HD, United Kingdom. "IHEU shares the premises with the British Humanist Association and the Rationalist Press Association." It is "located just behind the British Museum." (http://www.iheu.org/address)

[178] Ericson, *The Humanist Way: An Introduction to Ethical Humanist Religion*, 4.

education, and in the communications media, they pose a far greater threat to the United States of America than the communist party of the Soviet Union ever did.

Humanists contrasted with Communists

It must be pointed out again that communism is, in fact, a form of humanism. All communists are humanists. While not all humanists are communists, they are nevertheless of the same basic beliefs and goals. Humanist minister Ericson admits that

> **Communism** is at heart intensely **humanistic**, for it contains the central idea that rational planning can alter any pre-existing condition of man.[179] [Emphasis added.]

And Ehrenfield warns that

> the most openly and avowedly **humanistic** philosophies are the **liberal** group, which includes all forms of **communism, socialism**, and **moderate liberalism**. Classical **communism**, with Marx's dream of a classless society and a minimal government achieved by social engineering, is the most committed of these to the **humanistic assumptions**, and it is the one that has failed the most dramatically. First in Russia and now in China the **humanist dream** of a perfectible life has crumbled.... And in both these **humanistic countries** the vaunted freedom that the **humanists** admire has vanished without a trace. Each time a dream crumbles a new generation of believers is disillusioned, then makes excuses, then starts over again with the same dream in another country.... their good intentions have been overwhelmed by the falseness of their basic assumptions, and it is time for the morally just, the humane, and the ecologically sophisticated people of the twentieth century to admit this before any more damage is done.[180] [Emphasis added.]

The main difference between Humanists and Communists is that Communists believe in using guns to force their humanism upon a population, but Humanists realized that it is wiser to work through the communications media and the public school systems to brainwash people (especially children) so as to eventually take power through popular vote. As we saw with the election of humanist Bill Clinton to the presidency, and in the Gore versus Bush election, they had already achieved their objective only to lose it due to President Clinton committing adultery with Monica Lewinsky.

Especially in the USA, Humanists realize that humanism cannot be imposed upon the population by physical force due to the large segment of the US population which owns guns, and therefore could mount vigorous resistance. That is why they are working so hard to get gun-control legislation passed. Once guns have been taken away from the American citizens, we can expect Humanists to begin to use much harsher methods to force complete implementation of humanist principles. Meanwhile, expect continued lies, disinformation, and treasonous support of our enemies from the Humanist dominated news media.

Humanists Contrasted With Patriots

As avid internationalists, Humanists are loyal to the United Nations and not to the United States of America. As the American Humanist Association boasts:

> The United Nations is a specific example of Humanism at work. The first Director General of UNESCO, the UN organization promoting education, science, and culture, was the 1962 Humanist of the Year Julian Huxley, who practically drafted UNESCO'S charter by himself. The first Director-General of the World Health Organization was the 1959 Humanist of the Year Brock Chisholm.... And the first Director-General of the Food and Agricultural Organization was British Humanist John Boyd Orr.[181]

It is clear from the above quote why the UN opposes the USA on just about every issue. As the only remaining superpower, the USA stands directly in the way of the Humanist dream of Humanism being the government of the world. The American Humanist Association therefore has voiced its opposition to President George W. Bush's administration, as follows:

---

[179] Ehrenfeld, *The Arrogance of Humanism*, 152.

[180] Ibid., 249–50.

[181] Edwords, "What is Humanism?"

> The AHA has supported the work of the United Nations for decades. It has issued many strong resolutions in support of the vision of a global, inter-related world.... These resolutions include the dedication of the AHA to lobby our domestic government in support of United Nations and its treaties and conventions....
>
> However, the current climate of aggressive unilateralism pursued by the US has not only brought a cold chill to these many years of work, but left the United States in a lonely position in the world. While many new and emerging countries have embedded the International Declaration of Human Rights, ***a purely Humanist document***, in their new constitutions, and made concerted efforts to apply the standards of the United Nations conventions in the fields of women's rights, the environment, arms proliferation and social development, the U.S. has repeatedly repudiated and withdrawn from these agreements. And the US, of all nations the proponent of democracy, has opted out of the new International Criminal court.
>
> **As we continue to promote the cause of Humanism at the United Nations, we call for the renewed dedication of the AHA and its members, to "think globally and act locally."** And to renew our efforts to inform and urge Congress to act wisely, logically and heroically to restore the United States to the world stage in a position of leadership instead of one of belligerence and diplomatic isolation.[182] [Emphasis added.]

Why does the US "repudiate" or "withdraw" from these UN agreements? Because those UN agreements compromise or completely invalidate US sovereignty. Because they would rob US citizens of basic human rights.

Why has the US "opted out" of the new International Criminal Court? Because it would supersede and invalidate the US Supreme Court. Because US soldiers could be tried as war criminals before that UN "court" by foreign judges from the very countries which are promoting aggression against the USA and which our soldiers are fighting.

THE HUXLEYS were very important prophets of the modern Humanist religion. Thomas Huxley (left) was known as "Darwin's bulldog" because of his vigorous preaching of humanist theology. He was the first person to call himself an egnostic. The second picture shows his grandson, Julian on his lap. The third picture is of Julian as an adult. Julian was one of the signers of Humanist Manifesto I. He became the first head of UNESCO, and in that position made Humanism the religion of the United Nations. The last picture is of Aldus, Julian's younger brother. Aldus became a novelist and toured the USA visiting college campuses to introduce mind-altering drugs to students as a replacement for the Holy Spirit.

The Humanists groups support the UN in these matters because their loyalty is not to the USA but to the international Humanist movement. Humanists love the UN because it is a Humanist organization with a phony and "purely humanist" Declaration of Human Rights based squarely on atheism. No true Christian can support the United Nations. It is designed from its very foundation to be anti-God, anti-Christian and pro-Communist. It should not be allowed on U.S. soil.This avid loyalty to the United Nations is also why Humanists speak with such contempt for patriotism. Humanists consider people who put the interests of the USA above the interests of the United Nations to be their enemies. They hate our stars and strips flag.[183] They take the side of our enemies in every war.

Viet Nam veterans should take note that pro-Communist "Hanoi" Jane Fonda, the woman that went to Viet Nam during the Viet Nam War to demonstrate against our country, married the 1990 Humanist of the

[182] "AHA UN Office" (New York: American Humanist Association), 1, Http://www.americanhumanist.org/hsfamily/UNOffice.php#location.

[183] The American Civil Liberties Union (ACLU), a Humanist front organization, is notorious for defending what they call "the right" of people to desecrate the flag, under the guise of defending freedom of speech.

Year Ted Turner. Ted Turner is the man that donated one billion dollars to the United Nations. In the case of Ted Turner and Jane Fonda, the marriage between Humanists and Communists was more than just a marriage of common dogma and goals.[184]

Humanists Indirectly Advocate the Violent Overthrow of the United States Government

Humanists learned from the mistakes of the Communist Party USA. The Communists made the mistake of openly advocating the violent overthrow of the US government.

> In 1948, for the first time since the 1920's, the [Communist] Party found itself on the defensive when the Department of Justice initiated prosecution against its leaders. The twelve members of the Party's National Board were indicted under the Smith Act (enacted in 1940), which prohibits any conspiracy that advocates the overthrow of the United States government by force and violence. Previously, in 1941, the government had instituted prosecutions against members of the Socialist Workers Party (Trotskyites) under this statute. Other statutes since used by the government in the attack on the Party include the Internal Security Act of 1950 and the Communist Control Act of 1954.
>
> In a long trial, running through most of 1949, eleven members were convicted, the twelfth, William Z. Foster, having been severed from the trial because of illness. In June, 1951 the Supreme Court upheld these convictions, and the government subsequently took prosecutive action against additional Party leaders.
>
> This government prosecution was a strong disabling blow against the Party. Many of its top leaders were arrested and convicted. Others lived in fear of arrest. As a result the Party to a large extent went underground in the first large-scale underground operation since the early 1920's. Party officers were closed, top leaders went into hiding, records were destroyed. Courier systems were instituted and clubs broken up into small units, if not completely disbanded. For about four years, for mid-1951 to mid-1955, the Party in protecting itself spent energy, time, and money that otherwise would have gone into agitation and propaganda.[185]

Humanists determined not to make the same mistake. They are careful not to openly call for the violent overthrow of the US government. This has proven to be a very wise policy on their part, as it has enabled them to use the freedoms provided by the Bill of Rights to openly operate in opposition to our government in the news media, in courts of law, and in public schools.

However, the fact that Humanists are not openly calling for the violent overthrow of our government does not mean that they are not indirectly advocating it. Examples of Humanist sedition include them declaring war on President Bush instead of on Al Qaeda after 9/11, saying that President Bush lied about weapons of mass destruction in Iraq; blaming the results of Hurricane Katrina on President Bush; providing lawyers for terrorists that attacked us; ignoring the abuse of our soldiers and the Iraqi people by terrorists while publicizing the pictures of abuse at Abu Ghurayb prison world-wide so as to encourage Muslims everywhere to attack the USA; implying that that abuse was ordered by the Bush administration; sending Cindy Sheehan to camp in front of President Bush's ranch and accuse him of murdering her son; insinuating that President Bush is the behind the scenes cause of the high price of fuel; condemning the efforts of our government to prevent terrorists and others from illegally crossing the border from Mexico; distributing a petition to stop the Bush administration from preventing Iran from developing nuclear weapons; openly calling for the impeachment of President Bush. All of this activity encourages our enemies to keep fighting us, and results in more of our soldiers being killed in Afghanistan and Iraq.

---

[184] They have since divorced. During the stress leading up to this divorce, Fonda reportedly became a Christian. However, time has shown that her profession was false. She is still actively promoting abortion and other humanist causes.

[185] Hoover, *Masters of Deceit*, 68–69.

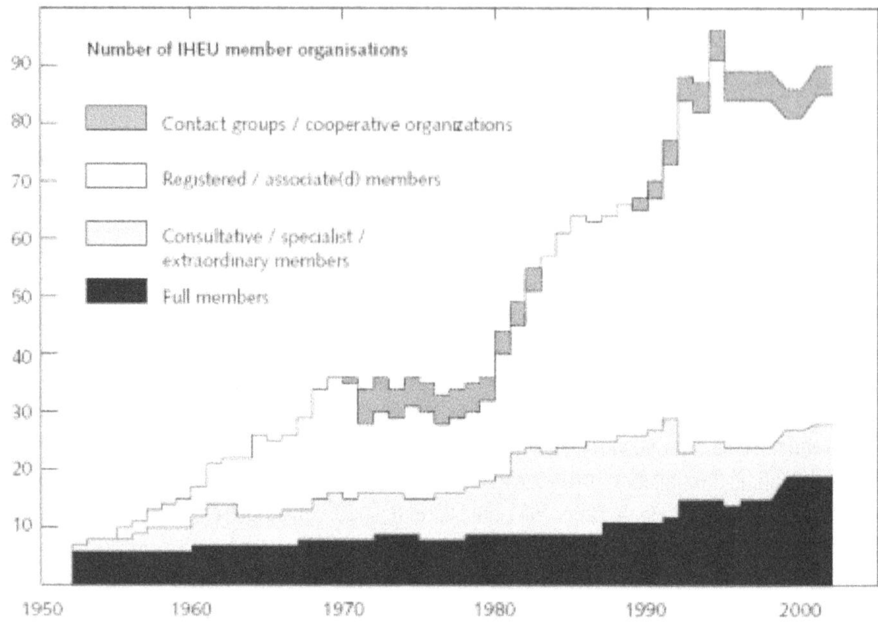

Number of IHEU member organizations, 1952-2002

(http://www.iheu.org/uploads/iheu%201952-2002%20ebook.pdf page 120)

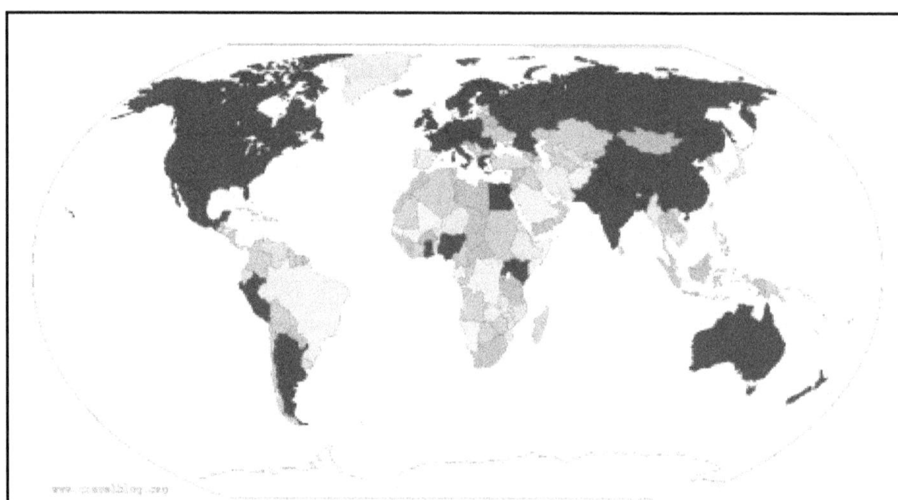

The darker the areas are on the above map the more Humanists organizations there are. "IHEU [International Humanist and Ethical Union] is a union of more than 100 organizations from 40 nations, with special consultative status with the United Nations in New York, Geneva and Vienna, and a general consultative status at UNICEF in New York and the Council of Europe in Strasbourg. IHEU also maintains operational relations with UNESCO in Paris." (http://www.humanistbioethics.org/).

Chapter 12

IS THE ACLU TRULY FOR LIBERTY?

No, It Works To Enslave Us

The American Civil Liberties Union (ACLU) was organized January 19, 1920 by Roger Baldwin and a large group of his radical left-wing friends.

It grew out of a predecessor group, The National Civil Liberties Bureau which in turn had grown out of the American Union Against Militarism, and a soiree that was held in New York City and attended by just about every radical from the thriving New York scene of the time. The founders numbered over 60 but the bulk of the work was assumed by the following core:

ROGER BALDWIN, founder and director of the ACLU until his death. He said, "Communism is the goal."

Roger Nash Baldwin—the founding, long time, director of ACLU. Born to wealth, at the time of the founding, he was deeply involved in the communist movement. As late as 1935, he gave a speech stating that his political vision was communist. . . .

Norman Thomas— a Presbyterian minister and radical socialist who advocated the total abolition of capitalism. He was also a eugenicist who warned against the excessive reproduction of undesirables. Thomas was a six time Socialist Party presidential candidate. Also a committed pacifist, he joined Charles Lindbergh's American First Committee to keep us out of World War II. . . .

John Haynes Holmes— a Unitarian minister, a pacifist, socialist and also a founder of The National Association for the Advancement of Colored People.

L. Hollingsworth Wood—a Quaker, pacifist and a co-founder of the Urban League. . . .

John Nevin Sayre—an ordained Episcopal minister, Sayre was a pacifist and believed that Jesus Christ was also. . . .

The following is a random selection of others who were among the founders:

Crystal Eastman— pacifist, socialist and feminist. She had been active as a supporter of the radical International Workers of the World (I.W.W.), a radical group with very strong ties to communism.

Helen Keller—a communist. . . .during the early 1920s, she wrote and spoke flatteringly about the two competing and emerging German variations of socialism, the national socialism of Adolf Hitler and international revolutionary socialism, or communism.

Radicalized at Radcliffe, she addressed others, as she was often addressed, as 'Comrade'. Ironically, under the eugenics of German National Socialism, Keller would likely have been judged as flawed and exterminated for having been so vulnerable to have been left damaged by her illness.

Elizabeth Flynn Gurley— a communist, she later became chairman of CPUSA [Communist Party, USA].

Felix Frankfurter—a social reformer, became interested in ACLU when pacifists and socialists were being harassed by the government. Frankfurter would later be appointed to the Supreme Court by Franklin Delano Roosevelt. . . .

John Dewey— radical socialist educator who believed that the function of the educational system was to train future agents for the goals of the state. His educational theories dominate our system today.

Clarence Darrow—lionized by Hollywood in 'Inherit The Wind' and the Left for defending teacher John Scopes for teaching evolution.... He was an agnostic.

Jane Addams—social activist, feminist, and pacifist. She was also a founder of the NAACP.

FELIX FRANKFURTER was later appointed to the US Supreme Court by Franklin D. Rosevelt.

Upton Sinclair—socialist and author of many novels. He began his career by writing ethnic full novel, was an expose of disgusting conditions in the Chicago meat packing industry. It led to the Pure Food and Drug Act which established the FDA....

A. J. Muste— at the time, a communist who was committed to revolutionary politics. He later became a Christian pacifist after a trip to the Soviet Union and a meeting with Leon Trotsky. Many associates maintained though that he never completely abandoned his attachment to Marxism.

Harry F. Ward— a lifetime communist, he authored *Soviet Democracy* and *Soviet Spirit*, two pro-Communist books.

Albert DeSilver—radical socialist attorney who had worked with the I.W.W. He willed his entire fortune to ACLU.[186]

JOHN DEWEY is called the Father of Humanist Philosophy. Through his teachers schools he influenced public education in America more than any other man.

Roger Baldwin (1884-1981), was one of the most important leaders in the humanist movement. As founder and director of the ACLU he organized humanist lawyers into a fantastically influential legal force dedicated to opposing Christianity and promoting the Humanist religion in the USA. The crowning achievement of the ACLU has been its success in so manipulating courts of law as to unofficially but very effectively establish humanism as the established state religion of the USA. It is because of the ACLU that evolution must be taught in public schools, and the teaching of creation by God is forbidden. The ACLU achieved this incredible victory by redefining the meaning of the phrase "separation of church and state" to mean separation of God and state, and by carefully hiding from the American public the fact that humanism itself is a religion. This deceptive redefining (actually misdefining) of phrases and words is very typical of humanism. Humanists are also very clever at giving their front organizations names which identify them as advocating the very opposite of what they actually advocate. The name American Civil Liberties Union is a good example of this; it would be more accurate to call it the Anti-America Uncivil Enslavem Union, for it has done more to deprive Americans of liberty than any other organization in history. As will be shown in this chapter, an even more accurate name would be Anti-America Communist Lawyers Union. After all, several of the founders of the ACLU were communists, and, as you will see in this chapter, the ACLU has a long history of aiding and abetting communism. To understand the true nature of the ACLU we must look past its deceptive name to the beliefs and principles of its founders.

In this chapter we will examine the religious beliefs and ambitions of Roger Baldwin, the main founder and long time director of the ACLU.

---

[186] Roderick T. Beaman, "THE AMERICAN CIVIL LIBERTIES UNION: Uncomfortable Truths About the Origins," *Ether Zone*, 1916 September 2004, Http://www.etherzone.com/2004/beam091604.shtml.

In college I pursued these leads and by researching the library discovered a magazine called *The Humanist*, edited by a Unitarian minister, Edwin H. Wilson, who also served as the director of the American Humanist Association. I corresponded with Dr. Wilson and later followed his footsteps into the Unitarian ministry, where I spent eight years in preparation and service. At about the same time that I encountered The Humanist, I chanced upon a copy of *The Standard*, then the official journal, now unfortunately discontinued, of the Ethical Culture movement. An inquiry to the headquarters of the American Ethical Union in New York brought me information and introductory books. In Ethical Culture I found my religious ideals most fully and satisfyingly expressed. Even after I had entered the ministry as a **Humanist Unitarian**, I continued to look toward Ethical Culture as the flagship of religious Humanism. When the unexpected invitation came, I entered the professional leadership in 1959 as leader of the Ethical society in Washington, D.C.[189] [Emphasis added.]

It is important to note that approximately half of the signers of *Humanist Manifesto I & II* were Unitarian Ministers.

The point is that by establishing that a person (Roger Baldwin in this case) is a Unitarian, we have established that he is a humanist. Humanism, I repeat, is simply the doctrines of the Unitarian-Universalist Church.

Baldwin's Sex Life

Peggy Lamson talked with Baldwin a great deal about his friendships with many different older women. Says Lamson, "I again commented on how many such relationships he had had. Answered Baldwin, 'Yes, I had a good many. Very affectionate they were, but sexless.' He grinned. 'And you know the Freudian implications of all that.'" "I nodded knowingly," writes Lamson, "but did not speculate. To be sure homosexuality came to mind, but there is no evidence to support that particular Freudian implication." She obviously was embarrassed to directly ask him if that is what he meant, but the fact that she included this conversation in her book indicates that she believed it was.

One thing for sure, *Humanist Manifest II* teaches that homosexuality and other sexual perversions are not wrong:

In the area of sexuality, we believe that intolerant attitudes, often cultivated by orthodox religions and puritanical cultures, unduly repress sexual conduct. The right to birth control, abortion, and divorce should be recognized. While we do not approve of exploitive, denigrating forms of sexual expression, neither do we wish to prohibit, by law or social sanction, sexual behavior between consenting adults. The many varieties of sexual exploration should not in themselves be considered "evil." Without countenancing mindless permissiveness or unbridled promiscuity, a civilized society should be a tolerant one. Short of harming others or compelling them to do likewise, individuals should be permitted to express their sexual proclivities and pursue their life-styles as they desire.[190]

That Baldwin was a thoroughly immoral man by Bible standards there is no doubt. Commented Lamson:

I asked him [Baldwin] for his reaction to the morals of today's young. Did he object to everyone sleeping with everyone else. No, emphatically, he did not object, his only reservation being that he thought boys and girls living together in the same college dormitory was a mistake. "You go to college to learn something. You don't go to college to make love."[191]

Baldwin's Contempt of Marriage

People who know they are humanists and know why they are humanists do not believe in marriage. The institution of marriage is based on belief that there is a creator God. If there is no creator God, then humans

---

[189] Ericson, *The Humanist Way: An Introduction to Ethical Humanist Religion*, 7–9.

[190] Kurtz, *Humanist Manifestos I & II*, 18–19.

[191] Lamson, *Roger Baldwin: Founder of the American Civil Liberties Union*, 289.

were not created in God's image. And if human's were not created in God's image, then they are just animals like all the other animals. And if humans are just animals, why should they limit themselves to sex with just one individual? After all, dogs have sex with an unrestricted number of partners. Why, humanists reason, should humans have less sexual freedom then dogs?[192] In his wedding vow to Madeleine Doty on August 8, 1919, shortly after his release from prison for refusal to report for the draft, Baldwin made the following statement:

Baldwin should be remembered always for writing this: "I am for socialism, disarmament and ultimately for abolishing the state itself.... Communism is the goal."

> To us who passionately cherish the vision of a free human society, the present institution of marriage among us is a grim mockery of essential freedom. Here we have the most intimate, most sacred, the most creative relationship shackled in the deadening grip of private property and essentially holding the woman subservient to the man....We deny without reservation the moral right of state or church to bind by force of law a relationship that cannot be maintained by the power of love alone. We submit to the form of law only because it seems a matter of too little importance to resist or ignore.[193]

Madeleine soon learned that a man who can so easily reject God can also easily reject God's command that a husband love his wife (Eph. 5:25-33). Baldwin was openly unfaithful to her and eventually divorced her. Just how little love he ever had for her (or anyone else) is evident from this quote from a letter he wrote to her a few years after their wedding: "Much love Maddy—all I've got to spare from loving myself which is my first duty! (how's that for a husband?) Roger."[194]

Baldwin's Communism

Repeatedly in the preceding chapters Humanism has been shown to be virtually identical to communism. Each time a quote has been given to prove that this is not being said without reason. In *Thirty Years Later*, a publication of the Harvard Class of 1905, Baldwin made the following declaration:

> I am for socialism, disarmament and ultimately for abolishing the state itself as an instrument of violence and compulsion. I seek social ownership of property, the abolition of the propertied class and sole control by those that produce wealth. **Communism is the goal.** It all sums up into one single purpose—the abolition of the system of dog-eat-dog under which we live.[195] [Emphasis added.]

Later, when it became obvious that to publicly espouse communism would be detrimental to his humanist cause, Baldwin repudiated communism, and even fired a communist from the board of directors of the ACLU. A Unitarian historian tells it like this:

> Baldwin became increasingly disturbed by events in the Soviet Union, where purge trials were being undertaken, and by politically troublesome accusations leveled at the ACLU by the House Committee on un-American Activities.

---

[192] That is the twisted kind of reasoning that people have who believe that freedom is *to* sin instead of *from* sin. Are people free if criminals are allowed to rob them on the streets? No. The criminals might call that freedom, but if people must fear to leave their homes they are enslaved. Is a man free if another man is allowed to commit adultery with his wife—thus destroying his family—and get away with it? No, true freedom is to do right, not to do wrong. True freedom is having opportunity to do what God has commanded without someone being allowed to prevent you from doing it. If you are allowed to study God's word, and pray, and tell others what God says, then you are free. Otherwise, you are enslaved. If you are allowed to be born and to grow up to serve the Lord, then you are free. If your mother is allowed to murder you before you are even born, then you are enslaved. You have to be alive to be free.

[193] Lamson, *Roger Baldwin: Founder of the American Civil Liberties Union*, 115.

[194] Ibid., 151.

[195] Ibid., 192.

> Baldwin became less happy with the Popular Front approach and concerned about the very existence of the ACLU after the announcement of the Nazi-Soviet Non-Aggression Pact in August 1939. The following spring, in an effort to stave off criticisms of the organization and the cause he had devoted much of his adulthood to, Baldwin orchestrated a campaign to revise the ACLU charter. Henceforth, those affiliated with totalitarian organizations would not be allowed to serve on the ACLU board. The immediate target was the former-Wobbly and present Communist Party member, Elizabeth Gurley Flynn.[196]

But time has proven that his philosophy and goals never changed. And why was Flynn on the Board of Directors of the ACLU anyway? Years before this, in 1916, Flynn responded to the question "Do You Believe in Patriotism?" by saying,

> What an odd question to ask revolutionists! Might it not be better put, "American Socialists, have you the courage of your principles? Shall it be 'America First' or 'Workers of the World, Unite!'"
>
> Count m for Labor First. This country is not "our" country. Then why should the toilers love it or fight for it? Why sanction the title deeds of our masters in the blood of our fellow-slaves? Let those who own the country, who are howling for and profiting by preparedness, fight to defend their property. . . . I cannot work myself into a frenzy of patriotism wherever a contraband ship is sunk and we lose a few prominent citizens.
>
> I save my concern for. . . the innumerable victims of the class war. . . . The train on which I write rushes by factories where murder instruments are made for gold. I would be ashamed to be patriotic of such a country. In the black smoke belched from their chimneys, I see the ghostly faces of dead workers—our poor, deluded slain brothers. I re-affirm my faith, "It is better to be a traitor to your country than a traitor to your class!"[197]

Baldwin no doubt knew about Flynn's words; Flynn was Baldwin's kind of girl! She was not fired because she was communist. They parted for one reason only: the sake of the Communist Party and of the ACLU. She was about to be arrested and go to prison for advocating the overthrow of the US government, and they both knew it. Outwardly, Baldwin appeared to have changed, but inwardly communism was still the goal.

It is interesting to note that the Communist Party USA web site (as of April 6, 2006) lists the ACLU at the top of its list of "groups and resources for deepening and protecting civil rights,"[198] which in communist talk means other radical, left-wing, God haters, working to divide, defeat, and enslave the American people in whatever way possible. So the Communist Party USA obviously still considers the ACLU its comrade in its long war against God.

Baldwin's View of Freedom

Humanists constantly talk about freedom. They portray themselves to the world as champions of liberty. Yet in every country in which they gain total control freedom vanishes. The reason for this is that humanists do not desire true freedom (that is, unrestricted opportunity to worship and obey God), but rather humanists desire licentiousness (disregard of God-given moral laws). Peggy Lamson points out that in the September 1934 issue of *Soviet Russia Today*, Baldwin wrote an article entitled "Freedom In the USA and the USSR" in which he rhetorically stated the question most frequently—and justifiably—asked of phony civil libertarians (especially humanists): ***How can you consistently fight to support free speech and free dissent in capitalist countries and at the same time defend a dictatorship that permits no dissent at all against its rule?*** He then proceeded to answer the question:

---

196 Robert C. Cattrill, "Roger Baldwin: Founder, American Civil Liberties Union," *Harvard Square Library*, Http://www.harvardsquarelibrary.org/unitarians/baldwin.html.

197 Elizabeth Gurley Flynn, "Do You Believe in Patriotism?" *The Masses*, March 1916, Http://www.marxists.org/subject/women/authors/flynn/1916/patriotism.htm.

198 http://www.cpusa.org/link/category/22/

Our critics are in error in denying us a class position.... All my associates in the struggle for civil liberties take a class position, though many don't know it.... I too take a class position. It is anti-capitalist and pro-revolutionary.... I champion civil liberty as the best of the nonviolent means of building the power on which worker's rule must be based. If I aid the reactionaries to get free speech now and then, if I go outside the class struggle to fight against censorship, it is only because those liberties help to create a more hospitable atmosphere for working-class liberties. *The class struggle* is the central conflict of the world; all others are incidental.

When that power of the working class is once achieved, as it has been only in the Soviet Union, I am for maintaining it by any means whatever.[199] [Emphasis original!]

Please consider the implications of the above quotation very carefully, and remember it next time you see a representative from the ACLU speaking on television. Remember, Humanists will fight for freedoms in the short run only if those freedoms will help them achieve dictatorship in the long run. Once that dictatorship is established it will be maintained by "any means whatever."

Never forget that the American Civil Liberties Union was established by an anti-capitalist, pro-revolutionary, pro-Soviet Union, draft-dodging, marriage-hating, God-defying Humanist activist who lived by the principle that "communism is the goal."

Humanists have a plan, and that plan is to rule the world. The sedition taking place in public schools is all being carried out according to well-thought-out plans. It is on purpose. America must be destroyed in order for the Humanist one-world government to be established.

The United Nation is promoting Humanism as the new world religion, as a result of the work of Humanist leader Sir Julian Huxley being the first head of UNESCO.

How the ACLU Helps America's Enemies

The following rather boring quote from the cover jacket for a book by Corliss Lamont becomes more interesting once one realizes that it establishes the fact that Humanists help Communists in their subversion of the United States of America:

Born in Englewood, New Jersey in 1902, Dr. Lamont graduated first from Phillips Exeter Academy in 1920, then magna cum laude from Harvard University in 1924. He did graduate work at Oxford and at Columbia, where he received his Ph.D. in philosophy in 1932. He was a director of the American Civil Liberties Union from 1932 to 1954, and is currently chairman of the National Emergency Civil Liberties Committee. A leading proponent of the individual's rights under the Constitution, he has won famous court decisions over Senator Joseph McCarthy, the CIA, and in 1965 a Supreme Court ruling against censorship of incoming mail by the U.S. Postmaster General. Dr. Lamont has long been associated with Humanism, and authored the standard text on the subject, *The Philosophy of Humanism*, in 1949. He taught at Columbia, Cornell, and Harvard Universities, and at the New School for Social Research. Corliss Lamont is currently honory president of the American Humanist Association.[200]

The above about-the-author quote reveals much more information than immediately meets the eye, and gives us a better understanding of how Humanists work to subvert the USA.

ACLU Lawyers Are Not Loyal To America

The ACLU is not an organization of loyal American lawyers who are fighting for basic human rights as they claim. They are Humanist internationalists who are working to abolish the sovereignty of the USA in order to set up a one-world government. As the twelfth theses of *Humanist Manifesto II* states:

---

199 Lamson, *Roger Baldwin: Founder of the American Civil Liberties Union*, 190–91.

200 Corliss Lamont, *The Illusion of Immortality*, John Dewey, reprint, 1935, Half-Moon Foundation, Inc. (New York: The Continuum Publishing Company, 1990), Cover jacket.

We deplore the division of humankind on nationalistic grounds. We have reached a turning point in human history where the best option is to transcend the limits of national sovereignty and to move toward the building of a world community in which all sectors of the human family can participate. Thus we look to the development of a system of world law and a world order based upon transnational federal government.

The ACLU and the AHA Are Basically the Same People

Note that Lamont was "director of the American Civil Liberties Union from 1932 to 1954," and when the copy for the above cover jacket was written Lamont was the "honory president of the American Humanist Association." These two organizations are led by the same people. Actually, this should not surprise us when we remember that one of the founders of the ACLU, John Dewey, was also one of the founders of the American Humanist Association.

This graphic is displayed on the web site of the Tulsa, Oklahoma branch of the American Humanist Association. This would be considered treason in just about any other country in the world. Humanists are always against America and for our enemies.

The AHA Has Many Front Organizations Just Like Communism

The American Civil Liberties Union and the National Emergency Civil Liberties Committee are just fronts for the American Humanist Association. They have many fronts like this, many of which were started and led by the exact same people. By doing this they appear to be many different and unrelated groups representing a large number of people, when in fact they are all Humanists and represent a rather small segment of the population.

The AHA Defends America's Enemies and Villanifies Patriots

Note that Lamont is claimed to be "a leading proponent of the individual's rights under the Constitution, he has won famous court decisions over Senator Joseph McCarthy, the CIA, and in 1965 a Supreme Court ruling against censorship of incoming mail by the U.S. Postmaster General." That is a very deceptive statement. Humanists are working constantly to undermine individual human rights. They are the people responsible for removing the Ten Commandments, which is the very foundation of individual human rights, from court rooms and school rooms. And Humanists do not honor the U.S. Constitution at all except when they can use it to defend our enemies.

Most people know nothing about Senator Joseph McCarthy, yet they have heard his name mentioned so often in a negative way by the Humanist-controlled news media that they think he must have been a exceedingly evil man like Hitler or Osama bin Laden. They have no idea that Joseph McCarthy was an American hero who exposed Communist spies which had infiltrated our government—it is very likely that our country would have been taken over by Communism were it not for Joseph McCarthy. Nor do they realize that the ACLU and other Humanist front groups and humanist journalists defended the spies and villanified Senator McCarthy by falsely accusing him of falsely accusing the spies. "Former ACLU President Norman Dorsen....was co-counsel with Joseph Welch during the U.S. Army-Joseph McCarthy hearings."[201]

Ann Coulter has written an excellent book documenting how liberals (humanists) always take the side of the enemy, and giving the history of how the term "McCarthyism" was invented and is used by liberals. Liberals are all humanists even though not all liberals are members of the American Humanist Association or one of its front groups. Sadly, the Democrat Party should now be called the Liberal Humanist Party, for it is promoting humanism in every aspect of its platform, as are also a few humanists such as Rudy Giuliani and Mitt Romney which have infiltrated the Republican party. Coulter correctly writes:

---

201 "Celebrate 50 Years of Defending Freedom at the ICLU," *Indiana Civil Liberties Union* (2003, 17 October), Http://www.iclu.org/news/news_article.asp?ID=71.

Liberals have a preternatural gift for striking a position on the side of treason....Everyone says liberals love America, too. No they don't. Whenever the nation is under attack, from within or without, liberals side with the enemy.... If anyone has the gaucherie to point out the left's nearly unblemished record of rooting against America, liberals turn around and scream "McCarthyism!"

Liberals invented the myth of McCarthyism to delegitimize impertinent questions about their own patriotism. They boast (lyingly) about their superior stance on civil rights. But somehow their loyalty to the United States is off-limits as a subject of political debate.... Liberals demand that the nation treat enemies like friends and friends like enemies.... The ACLU responded to the 9-11 terrorist attack by threatening to sue schools that hung GOD BLESS AMERICA signs.... Liberals want to be able to attack America without anyone making an issue of it.... Liberals relentlessly oppose the military, the Pledge of Allegiance, the flag, and national defense. But if anyone calls them on it, they say he's a kook and a nut. Citing the unpatriotic positions of liberals constitutes "McCarthyism".[202]

Sen. Joseph McCarthy was a great American hero. By pointing out evidence that communists spies had infiltrated our government, he prevented them from enslaving us under communism and its godless humanist religion. For this he was (and still is) mercilessly slandered by humanists world wide to prevent people from believing his warnings.

As FBI director J.Edgar Hoover said, in March 1947 there were only about one million Americans registered to vote with the Communist Party, but that was more than there were in Russia in 1917 [when the Communists overthrew the Russian government]. What held the Communist left to the madrasahs of the Ivy League was Joe McCarthy. Sneering at McCarty today because the only people who call themselves Communists are harmless cranks is like sneering at the Sabin vaccine since, really, almost no one gets polio anymore. The big argument against McCarthy is that the whole notion of Communist subversion was a joke. It was not a joke. It was real. And the Democrats didn't care.

In the twentieth century, nearly million people were murdered in the name of Communism. Stalin held his monstrous Soviet show trials, committed genocide against the Kulaks, and created a forced famine for the Ukrainians when they resisted collectivization. There was Mao's "Great Leap Forward" murdering tens of millions of people. There was the Khmer Rouge's massacre of one quarter of the entire Cambodian population. Communist mass murder not only predated the Nazi variety but far surpassed it. Wherever there was Communism, there was repression, torture, and mass murder.

It is a fact that hundreds of agents of this blood-soaked ideology became top advisers to Democratic presidents, worked on the Manhattan Project, infiltrated every segment of the United States government. Stalin's agents held top positions in the White House, the State Department, the Treasury Department, the Army, and the OSS. Because of Democrat incompetence and moral infirmity, all Americans lived under the threat of nuclear annihilation for half a century. As Soviet spies passed nuclear technology to Stalin, President Roosevelt gave strict orders that the OSS engage in no espionage against the country ruled by his pal, Uncle Joe.

When it could have been stopped, when, days after the Hitler-Stalin Pact was signed, an ex-Communist came to the United States government and informed on [Communist spy] Hiss, as well as dozens of other Soviet spies in the government, President Roosevelt had laughed. McCarthy punched back so hard, liberals are still reeling.[203]

By simply drawing public attention to the mounting evidence that numerous communist spies had infiltrated the US government, McCarthy set back the Communist-Humanist agenda for years.

However, the Humanists were eventually able to stop McCarthy by mounting an unrelenting ferocious attack upon his character. The numerous Humanist front groups and humanist journalists and humanist television anchormen all began attacking him at once and without letup. Over and over and over again, they falsely accused McCarthy of the very things of which they themselves were guilty: slander, homosexuality,

---

202 Ann Coulter, *TREASON: Liberal Treachery from the Cold War to the War on Terrorism* (New York, New York: Three Rivers Press, 2003), 1–3.

203 Ibid., 34.

demogaguery. To draw attention away from the Communist spies McCarthy was exposing in his investigations, the Humanists along with their liberal friends began screaming that McCarthy himself be investigated.

> In 1954, when liberal loathing of McCarthy had reached a fever pitch, CBS ran a vicious, deceptive hatchet piece on him viewed by millions of Americans. It was produced by Edward R. Murrow, friend of Soviet spy Laurence Duggan. Other organs of establishmentarian followed suit. The Senate voted to hold hearings on a censure resolution against McCarthy.
>
> Among the grounds being considered for censure were McCarthy's remarks about Senator Ralph Flanders (R-Vt.). In a fire-breathing diatribe on the Senate floor, Flanders had called McCarthy a homosexual and compared him to Hitler. In response, McCarthy said, "I think they should get a man with a net and take him to a good quiet place." For this the Democrats thought McCarthy should be censured. It is intemperate for Republicans to respond to vicious abuse by the Democrats. In the end, that particular censure count was rejected, but McCarthy was censured on two similarly absurd counts: statements he made in defiance of senators investigating him. Senators were free to defame and abuse McCarthy, but it was considered a grave violation of the dignity of the Senate if he criticized them back. McCarthy said Senator Flanders had to be "taken out of mothballs" to pursue the censure resolution. He called one of his inquisitors, Senator Robert Hendrickson (D-Md.), "a living miracle...the only man in the world who had lived so long with neither brains nor guts." For these statements, McCarthy was censured by a body that, fifty years later, would do nothing about a president who committed felonies to obstruct a sexual harassment lawsuit.[204]
>
> The wolf pack had caught the scent. The [liberal] news media would not relent. The unending attacks finally wore down McCarthy. Most painfully for him, the attacks wore down his supporters. The cheering crowds and widespread support he had enjoyed through so many battles began to evaporate. As Roy Cohn said, "He had taken more punishment than a normal man could be expected to absorb.... Never have so much vituperation and defamation been directed toward a person in public life."
>
> At the age of forty-eight McCarthy died broken and defamed. The [liberal-humanist] *New York Times* did not mention McCarthy's death in an editorial out of pure hatred.[205]

So that is how the term "McCarthyism" originated. By simply telling the same lies about McCarthy hundreds of times the humanists succeeded in convincing the public that the lies were true.

However, McCarthy was even more right than he realized. The passing of time has proven that McCarthy knew of only a small part of the Soviet espionage that was actually taking place. There was an abundance of evidence available at the time (sworn testimony by ex-Communists, confessions of arrested spies, and the arrest of spy Judith Coplon when caught in the very act of handing a U.S. counterintelligence file to a KGB officer), so the humanists were without excuse in defending Communist traitors. But on July 11, 1995 decrypted Soviet cables of that era were declassified and made public. These cables prove that

> McCarthy was absolutely right in his paramount charge: The U.S. government had a major Communist infestation problem. It is treated as a mere truism [by liberals] that McCarthy was reckless, made mistakes, and was careless with his facts. It can now be said that McCarthy's gravest error was in underestimating the problem of Communist subversion.
>
> The scale of the conspiracy was unprecedented. Hundreds of Soviet spies honeycombed the U.S. government throughout the forties and fifties. America had been invaded by a civilian army loyal to a hostile power. There was no room for denying it. Soviet operatives were stealing technical information from atomic, military, radar, aerospace, and rocket programs. The cables revealed the code names of the spies, the technical espionage, and the secret transmission of highly sensitive diplomatic and strategic policies.

---

[204] Ibid., 120.

[205] Ibid., 122–23.

McCarthy was accused of labeling "anyone with liberal views" a Communist. As we now know, that wouldn't have been a half-bad system. Contrary to Caute's preposterous claim that Communists were innocent idealists, the American Communist Party was linked to Stalin like an al-Qaeda training camp to Osama bin Laden.[206]

Since it was the ACLU that defended many of these Communists spies in court, it is about time for loyal Americans to demand that the ACLU and its lawyers be investigated and its subversive activities be fully exposed, and that all ACLU lawyers who have engaged in treason be brought to justice. As Michel Savage points out,

Ruth Ginsburg is not a just judge. She does not believe in the U.S. Constitution, but bases her decisions on United Nations and foreign nations' law. Our demands that she be impeached for this should be relentless.

> Among *all* internal enemies...the ACLU has done the greatest damage to our nation. My heart breaks when I see this dangerous pack of maniacs tearing at the heart and soul of freedom. Books have been written on their outrageous litigation. As far as I'm concerned, the ACLU is the KKK on the Left. While they don't wear hoods or burn crosses, they are more dangerous. They don't need to wear hoods because they no longer fear being found out....While many well-meaning American citizens support civil liberties groups like the ACLU and the National Lawyers Guild, they're doing so not understanding the true agenda and nature of these organizations. To be redundant, they are using the courts to advance their internationalist, anti-God, anti-traditional family, and hate-America ideals.[207]

Why ACLU Lawyers Win So Many Court Cases

Humanists have gained influence beyond their numbers by helping each other get into positions which allow them to do the most damage to the USA. After the presidency, the judicial branch of government allows Humanists opportunity to do the most damage to America. A Humanist president can do more damage than an activist humanist judge only by appointing Humanist judges to the Supreme Court where they remain for life overriding the will of the citizens of this country by redefining the Constitution. This redefining—actually, changing—of the Constitution generally takes place under the guise of the Constitution being a "living Constitution." A warning flag should go up in our mind when we hear someone preaching a "living Constitution." Those are the words of judges who do not like what the Constitution says and want to change it to suit their own political aims. Those are the words of traitors.

> It's almost impossible to read much commentary about the role of the courts without stumbling across arguments for more judge-made law, often couched in fancy rhetoric about "a living Constitution" or the alleged need to read the Constitution "in the light of societal needs and evolving legal policy." (U.S. liberals aren't unique: In approving gay marriage, Canada's Supreme Court said, "Our Constitution is a living tree, which, by way of progressive interpretation, accommodates and addresses the realities of life.")
>
> In part, relying on judges for political decision is the result of a conscious strategy within the Democratic Party, as political analyst William Galston of the University of Maryland said last week. Galston, a former aide to President Bill Clinton, says his party "convinced itself that, especially on social issues, the principle vehicle of advance would be the court." It's easier to find a judge or two to rule your way than to go through the drudgery of building a majority for normal democratic decision making, particularly if you are pushing liberal agenda in a conservative age.

---

206 Ibid., 37.

207 Michel Savage, *The Enemy Within: Saving America from the Liberal Assault on Our Schools, Faith, and Military* (Nashville, Tennessee: Nelson Current, 2003), 41–42.

The dependence on judges has been accelerated by the rise of groups that have little interest in majoritarian politics. The gay movement, the primary example, spends almost all its energy hoping to win from judges what a large majority of American oppose. ...The rise of the lawmaking judge and the conversion of the Supreme Court into a sort of superlegislature make the political system less democratic.... on major issues of the culture war the courts have heavily favored the left and attempted to settle controversial issues that should have been left to politics—most obviously abortion and affirmative action. On church and state, the courts have generally imposed the views of the secular elites, converting the Founding Father's ban on federal establishment of a church into a broad program for eradication religion from the public square. Even the recent baffling and apparently contradictory 5-to-4 decisions on the display of the Ten Commandments seem narrowly political. They bar new displays of the commandments, as in Kentucky, while allowing a token old one in Texas, probably so that the public won't get too inflamed about the plain meaning of the Kentucky decision.[208]

Since there are only nine Supreme Court judges, it takes only five judges voting pro-humanist to do a lot of damage. It is easy for ACLU lawyers to win cases before unjust ACLU judges. And that is the reason that

the most important thing to do is to take back the judiciary. Why? This assault on the Bible belt by the Libel Belt was energized when Ruth Ginsburg was put on the Supreme Court in 1993 by Bill Clinton....Ginsburg is possibly the most radical lawyer in the history of the United States of America!...When Clinton appointed her to the highest court in the land, she was chief counsel for the ACLU—that ultra-leftist group which believes, among other things, that virtual child porn is protected speech....so today we have a Supreme Court that has slowly but surely come under her control.[209]

Even before Ginsburg the Supreme Court was dominated by humanists appointed by Democrat presidents. The decisions to ban Bible reading and prayer in public schools were before Ginsburg. So was the decision making the murder of unborn children a woman's right. But with Ginsburg the court has become more anti-family and anti-country than ever. The survival of our freedom depends on removing her and the other humanist judges from the bench before the destruction of our country reaches the point of no return.

As of this writing, President Bush has appointed a conservative, John G. Roberts, Jr., to the bench to replace William H. Rehnquist, who was also a conservative. He then appointed another conservative, Samuel Anthony Alito, Jr., to replace humanist-leaning justice Sandra Day O'Connor. This already may have tipped the balance against atheism in the Supreme Court; only time will tell. President Bush may have opportunity to replace another Supreme Court justice before his term of office expires. If that happens he could possibly tip the balance of power decisively away from the humanists. Much is at stake!

Naturally, the humanists vowed to do everything in their power to prevent President Bush from appointing conservative justices—and they did do everything in their power. They searched through the records of President Bush's nominees looking for the slightest thing they could use against them. They even stooped so low as to demand that the papers concerning the adoption of justice Robert's children be released, so that perhaps they could find some infraction there.

The ACLU sent the following letter to each senator in the US Senate:

Dear Senator:

The American Civil Liberties Union strongly urges you to vote "NO" on cloture on the nomination of Judge Samuel A. Alito, Jr. to replace retiring Justice Sandra Day O'Connor on the Supreme Court. This vote is critical to protecting the Supreme Court as a guardian of civil liberties and civil rights.

The ACLU does not make the decision to oppose Alito lightly. Only twice in the ACLU's 86 year history has our Board voted to oppose Supreme Court nominees – that of Chief Justice William Rehnquist, in his initial nomination to the Court, and Judge Robert Bork. But this is a momentous time in history, and Alito's confirmation to the Supreme Court would have significant impact on the American people. A nominee with Alito's history of deference to executive authority and support for government power would

[208] John Leo, "A Judge with no Agenda," *U.S. News and World Report* 139, no. 2 (18 July 2005): 66.

[209] Savage, *The Enemy Within*, 169–70.

Baldwin's Religion

Roger Baldwin was raised a Unitarian, and he was very proud of this fact, as the following statement he made to his biographer, Peggy Lamson, shows. "We Unitarians," he said, "knew we were very advanced people and that the other churches were backward. They believed things we Unitarians knew were not so."[187] Lamson probed deeply into Baldwin's Unitarian beliefs concerning Jesus Christ with the following question: "But you and Mr. Emerson and Mr. Thoreau and most of the people who influenced you when you were growing up didn't believe in Jesus as the Son of God sent to redeem you?" Baldwin's answer: "Oh, no, of course not, although there was quite a lot more of Jesus in the Unitarianism of my time than there is today. So I got to revere Jesus, not as a divine figure but for what he said. And I still think it's great stuff."[188]

CLARENCE DARROW, the son of a Humanist minister, became famous for making Christianity look unscientific at the Scoops Monkey Trial. This man was very good at defending criminals.

It is important at this point to show that by proving that Roger Baldwin was a Unitarian we have also proven that he was a humanist. And it is even more important to understand that ***humanism is simply the doctrines of the Unitarian-Universalist church***. To establish this fact, let us refer once again to *The Humanist Way* by Humanist minister Edward L. Ericson. After explaining that he had been raised in a conservative Protestant religion, Ericson says he came to question its teachings, and therefore began to search for a more suitable religion:

> I discovered that the Unitarians and Universalists came even closer to my spiritual ideal [than the Quakers] with their rejection of orthodox Christian doctrine and their emphasis on a religion of character, reason, and practical philanthropy—beliefs that prefigured Humanism. But I knew that I was not a unitarian (note the lower case) in the historic dictionary definition: one who rejects the doctrine of the trinity and, the deity of Christ, but who retains belief in a unitary (one) God. In truth I no longer believed in any kind of supernatural, personal deity, whether defined as the Christian trinity or simply as "God the creator." But my interest in the Unitarians revived when my dictionary—even then a well-worn copy as old as I was—gave one the surprising information that "the [Unitarian] denomination now includes in its ministry and membership a number of nontheistic humanists. See HUMANISM."
>
> I pursued the reference to Humanism and learned that among other meanings, it was defined as a religion "that substitutes faith in man for faith in God," (a definition that despite its scholarly source, I recognized as oversimplified). Still, I was assured that I was not alone in supposing it possible to have a religion without belief in a deity. The thought passed through my mind that some day I might become a Humanist minister.
>
> Many questions still required answers. What would a religion without a doctrine of God teach? The answer necessarily pointed to ethics. So, with no available library books on the subject, I turned back to my large dictionary and carefully studied every entry on ethics. My attention quickened when I came upon the following:
>
> ethical culture. A religious movement that asserts the "supreme importance of the ethical factor in all relations of life," and avoids formal creeds or ritual. See AMERICAN ETHICAL UNION; SOCIETY FOR ETHICAL CULTURE. —Webster's New International Dictionary, Second Edition.

---

[187] Peggy Lamson, *Roger Baldwin: Founder of the American Civil Liberties Union* (Boston: Houghton Mifflin Company, 1976), 2.

[188] Ibid., 6.

> strike a blow to basic freedoms. In this high-stakes climate for civil liberties and civil rights, the Supreme Court must be a bulwark against incursions on our fundamental freedoms. If confirmed as the next Associate Justice of the Supreme Court, Alito could dramatically change the direction of the Supreme Court by tipping the balance from the moderate position of Justice O'Connor, whom he would be replacing, to a position hostile to civil liberties and civil rights. He could thereby change the country for years to come.
>
> We are witnesses to an extraordinary time in history when our executive branch is trying to centralize power and bypass other branches of government. At a time when our President has claimed unprecedented authority to spy on our own people and jail people indefinitely without trial, America needs a Supreme Court justice who will uphold our precious civil liberties, staying true to the balance of powers envisioned by our Founders. But confirming Alito, someone with a proven record of undue deference to executive powers, could dangerously upset that balance of powers.[210]

Their letter went on to give the real reason they oppose judge Alito:

> Perhaps the best description of Alito's overall philosophy in these critical areas was provided by Alito himself in 1985, when he submitted a now well-publicized letter to the Reagan Administration seeking a position with the Justice Department's Office of Legal Counsel. "I am and always have been a conservative and an adherent to the same philosophical views that I believe are central to this Administration," he wrote. Alito then went on to explain that he had been inspired to attend law school by his disagreement with the decisions of the Warren Court, "particularly in the areas of criminal procedure, the Establishment Clause, and reapportionment."

Older readers will remember the "Impeach Chief Justice Earl Warren" signs that were posted across America by conservatives during the Warren court era. The Warren court almost always sided with criminals and enemies of the USA, and with atheists and humanists seeking to kick God out of public schools. The anti-God rulings of the Warren court are the cause of many of the problems in the USA today.

We can expect to see humanists continue to use nasty tactics to prevent conservatives from being appointed to the Supreme Court. The humanists will be screaming, slandering, and trying to terrorize people with scare tactics. Just like the Muslim terrorists, the humanists have learned that if they get emotional enough, repeat their lies often enough, slander their opponents viciously enough, and terrorize the public deeply enough, they can often get their way. They will try to destroy every person that stands in their way, just like they destroyed Senator McCarthy and are now trying to destroy Ann Coulter, Rush Limbaugh, and Sean Hannity. Expect humanist sodomites to hypocritically accuse their conservative opponents of being homosexuals. Expect minor molehill infractions of obscure laws by conservatives to be blown into major felonies by the humanist news media to try to make conservatives look like criminals. Expect the ACLU to file lawsuits against conservatives. It will be an extremely nasty and unpleasant test of wills. Atheists against theists. Humanism against theism. Evil against good. Wrong against right. Darkness against light. Enslavement against freedom. Satan's ministers will present themselves as angles of light—although in reality they are demons of darkness. Every time the ACLU lyingly claims to be fighting for civil liberties, remember the words of their founder:

> Communism is the goal....If I aid the reactionaries to get free speech now and then, if I go outside the class struggle to fight against censorship, it is only because those liberties help to create a more hospitable atmosphere for working-class liberties. *The class struggle* is the central conflict of the world; all others are incidental.
>
> *When that power of the working class is once achieved, as it has been only in the Soviet Union, I am for maintaining it by any means whatever.*

---

[210] "ACLU Letter to the Senate Urging Opposition to Cloture Motion on Nomination of Judge Samuel Alito," *ACLU Web Site*, 1927 January 2006, Http://www.aclu.org/scotus/2005/23964leg20060127.html.

Humanists go by many different names: liberal, left-wing, Unitarian, skeptic, socialist, communist, progressive, do-gooder, Democrat, libertarian, Ethical Union member, secularist. Since they believe lying is ok if it achieves their goals, some of them may even claim to be conservative, right-wing, Christian, Baptist, Bible-believer, capitalist, anti-communist, Republican, etc. They especially like to call themselves moderates, when in reality they are insanely radical, left-wing, atheist nut cases in total rebellion against God. Whatever they call themselves, their basic beliefs and goals remain the same. You can know them by their fruits.

The ACLU's Radical Pro-Sodomy Agenda

The most scary thing presently happening in public schools is the promotion of sodomy as an acceptable alternate lifestyle, and the advocacy of "gay rights." The ACLU is the leader and pusher of this movement, and the result has been hundreds of thousands of young people being convinced that they were born gay, and thereby being seduced into very dangerously unhealthy sodomite practices.

The Sodomites' Champion

The present Executive Director of the American Civil Liberties Union is Anthony D. Romero. According to the ACLU website,

Anthony D. Romeo

> He took the helm of the 87-year-old organization just four days before the September 11, 2001 attacks. Shortly afterward, the ACLU launched its national Safe and Free campaign to protect basic freedoms during a time of crisis. Under Romero's leadership, the ACLU gained court victories on the Patriot Act filed landmark litigation on the torture and abuse of detainees in U.S. custody, and filed the first successful legal challenge to the Bush administration's illegal NSA spying program.
>
> Romero, an attorney with a history of public-interest activism, has presided over the most successful membership growth in the ACLU's history and more than doubled national staff and tripled the budget of the organization since he began his tenure. This unprecedented growth has allowed the ACLU to expand its nationwide litigation, lobbying and public education efforts, including new initiatives focused on racial justice, religious freedom, privacy, reproductive freedom and **lesbian and gay rights**.
>
> Romero is the ACLU's sixth executive director, and the first Latino and **openly gay** man to serve in that capacity. In 2005, Romero was named one of Time Magazine's 25 Most Influential Hispanics in America,[211] [Boldface emphasis added.]

Notice that not only is Romeo is an open sodomite—bragging about it to the world on the ACLU website—, but also that he is leading the ACLU in an aggressive and highly successful campaign to start Gay Straight Alliance (GSA) clubs in every public school in America to promote "gay rights" and "gay marriage." Obviously speaking about these clubs, he said,

> The ACLU is working to promote a new generation of committed civil libertarians and civil rights activists who want to devote their free time and resources to protecting freedoms. We have many energetic and committed student clubs and chapters in high schools and colleges across America that continually impress us with their creative endeavors to recruit new members. At our first national membership conference in 2003, 33 percent of attendees were between the ages of 18 and 34.

A large section of the ACLU website is devoted to starting these GSA sodomite clubs.

In his effort to promote sodomy, Romero has stopped at nothing. He has even "hired deposed Georgia Congressman Bob Barr as a consultant—the same Bob Barr who co-authored the Defense of Marriage Act."[212] It turns out that many conservatives are actually liberals. In an interview with AlterNet, Romero said,

---

[211] "Anthony D. Romero, Executive Director," *ACLU.Org*, Http://www.aclu.org/about/staff/13279res20030205.html.

[212] Ta-Nehisi Paul Coates, "Anthony Romero," *Time*, 1913 August 2005, Http://www.time.com/time/nation/article/0,8599,1093634,00.html.

We're now fighting to secure marriage equality for lesbians and gays, reproductive choice for women, and fair and secure voting systems that enfranchise minority voters. I'm incredibly proud of the way we have responded to the additional challenges of 9/11 while maintaining our vigilance and effectiveness in areas such as women's rights, racial justice and lesbian and gay rights.

Other interesting facts:

Romero sits on several not-for-profit boards, including serving as the Chairman of the Center of Disability and Advocacy Rights, and as Vice Chairman of the New World Foundation's Board of Directors. <u>He is also a member of the Council on Foreign Relations</u>, the New York State Bar Association and Hispanics in Philanthropy. His previous volunteer experiences include serving as Vice Chairman of the <u>White House Internship Advisory Committee</u> and as Co-Chairman of the Funders' Committee for Citizen Participation.[28] [Underline emphasis added].

Romero is a blogger for The Huffington Post website (www.huffingtonpost.com), which is an ultra-liberal, humanist website, and he is a very persuasive writer. There is no doubt that he is very smart at using our legal system to defeat Christians.

According to Time magazine, Romero is the son of illegal immigrants.[29] He is also working hard to defend the "rights" of illegal immigrants. Just think: if his parents hadn't been allowed to stay in the U.S.A. illegally, he most likely wouldn't be here promoting atheism and sodomy in our schools, and defending our enemies in court.

Lesbian Gay Bisexual Transgender and AIDS Project

The Lesbian Gay Bisexual Transgender and AIDS Project is not new. It is now 22 years old, and has expericence phenomenal success. According to the ACLU website,

Founded in 1986, the Lesbian Gay Bisexual Transgender & AIDS Project are a combined division in the national headquarters of the American Civil Liberties Union. The Project staff are experts in constitutional law and civil rights, specializing in sexual orientation, gender identity, and HIV.

The ACLU's national network of affiliates allows the Project to broadly advocate for fairness and equality in every community and the federal government. Today, the ACLU brings more sexual orientation cases and advocacy initiatives than any other national civil rights organization. As part of the broad civil liberties mission of the ACLU, the Project brings together the LGBT and AIDS communities with other social change movements in order to achieve a just society for all.

What We Do

The Project brings impact lawsuits in state and federal courts throughout the country, cases designed to have a significant effect on the lives of LGBT people and those with HIV/AIDS. In coalition with other civil rights groups, we also lobby in Congress and support grassroots advocacy from local school boards to state legislatures. Our legal strategies are built on the idea that fighting for civil rights means not just persuading judges but ultimately changing society for the better. As we litigate for change, we implement targeted media, online, and outreach campaigns and provide advocacy tools to help people take action in their community.

Most of the large public school districts in the US are administrated by humanists, and so the establishment of GSA clubs is actively pushed from the top. However, there are still a few public schools, especially in the heartland of America, that are resisting the Humanist agenda. But all it takes is one or two humanist students and the ACLU to break the resistance of most such schools. The ACLU deals with such fights on a daily basis, and has its battle plan down to a science.

The material below is taken directly from a page on the ACLU website titled "What's Your Problem?" It is for gay students, and after listing common problems gay students face in promoting their agenda, gives legal

---

[28] "Anthony Romeo," *Pbs.Org*, Http://www.pbs.org/now/politics/romero.html.

[29] Coates, "Anthony Romero."

advice on how to overcome those problems. You should note that this material repeatedly encourages gay students to phone the ACLU for help if they meet any resistance from their school's administration.

How the Law Looks at Your Problem

These are usually considered Equal Access Act issues:

* My school won't let me start a GSA

* My school won't let our GSA meet on school grounds

* My school lets other clubs do things that it doesn't let our GSA do

* My school says we can't start a GSA unless we have a sponsor and we can't find one

* My school says we have to have a parent's permission to join the GSA

The federal Equal Access Act is a law that was passed in 1984 that protects the right of students to form clubs at public high schools. The Equal Access Act defines two types of school clubs: curricular and non-curricular clubs. Curricular clubs are clubs that relate directly to classes taught at a school - for example, math club or Spanish club. Non-curricular clubs are anything else, like chess club or anime club. GSA's are almost always defined as non-curricular clubs.

The Equal Access Act says that if a public high school allows students to form one non-curricular club, then it can't say no to any other students who want to form any other type of non-curricular club. So if your school allows ANY non-curricular clubs at all, it's illegal for the school to deny your application to start a GSA.

The Equal Access Act also says that schools that have non-curricular clubs must treat all of those clubs the same. So if the school allows some clubs to make announcements about meeting over the P.A. system or post signs in the hallways about their activities, it can't then say any other clubs can't do those things. Also, schools can't require students to have parental permission to join a GSA unless they also require that for all other clubs.

The flipside of this is that you have to satisfy any rules your schools set up for clubs - so, for example, if the school requires all clubs to have a faculty sponsor, you will have to find one for your GSA to be recognized. Find out exactly what the rules are to start a club at your school and follow them carefully.

Some of these issues may also be overlap with other areas of the law, like equal protection or free speech.

If your school isn't allowing you to start a GSA or is treating your GSA differently from other clubs, we may be able to help. Please contact us. You can find out more information and resources on the "Library" page.

These are usually considered free speech/free expression issues:

* My school told me I shouldn't talk about being gay at school

* My school told me I couldn't wear my gay pride t-shirt

* My school won't let us publish an article about gay rights in the school newspaper

* My school won't let me wear makeup or a skirt because I'm a guy

* My school is won't let me wear a tux in my senior yearbook photo or to graduation because I'm a girl

The First Amendment of the U.S. Constitution protects your right to free speech and expression, and forbids the government from violating that right. Since public schools are considered part of the government, it is illegal for a public school to tell you what you can and can't talk about or who you can be out to, as long as you don't do it during class time. So don't climb up on your desk in the middle of social studies class to tell everyone you're gay, but if you talk to a friend at lunch about being gay that's perfectly okay.

> That right to expression usually extends to things like t-shirts, as long as the school treats all students the same. Schools can enforce dress codes, but they have to enforce the dress code equally for all students. For example, if your school allows other students to wear t-shirts that express their political or social beliefs, then the school shouldn't tell you not to wear a gay pride t-shirt. But if your school doesn't allow t-shirts at all, then it's probably legal for them to tell you not to wear yours.
>
> The right to take a same-sex date to a school dance is usually considered to be a matter of free expression too. We can usually persuade schools to let students bring a same-sex date to the prom or homecoming, so if this is happening to you, contact us!
>
> Things like what you wear for pictures or graduation and what you can publish in the school newspaper are a little different. What you wear for graduation or pictures is an area of the law that isn't entirely clear. And the school newspaper is usually considered the school's speech, not yours, because the school pays for and publishes it - although there are state laws that give student journalists more rights in certain states.
>
> If you have questions about your free speech/free expression rights as a lesbian, gay, bisexual, or transgender student, or as a student who wants to be able to speak out at school on those topics, please contact us. You can find more information and resources on the "Library" page.
>
> These are usually considered privacy issues:
>
> * My school told my parents that I'm gay without my permission
>
> Some federal courts have ruled that schools shouldn't reveal a minor's sexual orientation to their parents or anyone else without the student's permission. Your school should not do this to you, even if you're open about your sexual orientation or gender identity among friends or staff at your school. If your school is threatening to do this to you and you're afraid of the consequences at home, call us at 212-549-2673 immediately. If you have questions about your privacy rights, please contact us. You can find more information and resources on the "Library" page.[215]

In the above quote, the ACLU has made its intentions and goals clear: sodomite clubs are going to be started in every public school in the USA no matter how many people are against it. They are going to seduce as many children into sodomy as they can. And "call us at 212-549-2673 immediately" they say to students, if a teacher or other school official try to inform your parents. The implication is, We won't let the school get parents involved to try to prevent the seduction into sodomy. Note the threat implied toward anyone interfering with their agenda. They even provide a letter that gay students can download to give to their school administrators. The ACLU website describes this letter as "an open letter to school administrators about why they must allow students to form GSA's. You can print this out and give a copy to your school when you turn in your application to start your club."[216] The letter is long, and is a threatening letter any way you look at it. It details lawsuit after lawsuit that the ACLU has filed against school districts and won. The threat is, Don't buck us, or we will file a lawsuit against your school district too.

Notice the mention of the "Library" page in the above quotes. There is so much pro-sodomy material on the ACLU website that the average person would never have enough time to read it all. Nevertheless, on the Library page there are links to 38 other sodomite organizations—all with information on how to fight for the legalization of sodomy and the breaking down of morality in every level of society, but especially in public schools. Sodom and Gomorrah would be amazed at the phenomenal organization and zeal the ACLU is putting into their Lesbian Gay Bisexual Transgender and AIDS Project.

---

[215] "What's Your Problem?" *ACLU*, 2007, 3 January 2007, Http://www.aclu.org/lgbt/youth/28754res20070301.html#4.

[216] http://www.aclu.org/lgbt/youth/28943res20070301.html

This is one of the publications linked to by the ACLU website. This 48 page manual instructs transvestites how to fight for their "right" to enter bathrooms of the opposite sex. In some states like California and New York transvestites already have this "right." In the other states, they are instructed by this manual how to fight to get the proper legislation passed so they will have this "right." So, when your wife or daughter enter an empty woman's restroom alone at night, and a male dressed as a woman follows her in, that means just the two of them are in there alone. How safe is she? Does she have a right to privacy? or do only sodomites have rights? Does she have a right to be safe from being raped? or do only sodomites have rights? Humanists have been made insane by their unnatural lusts. A thief can't have the right to rob, and you have the right to own property. A transvestite can't have the right to enter the other sex's bathroom, and straight people have the right to privacy and safety. If criminals prevail good people suffer.

Chapter 13

WHO IS THE MOST EVIL WOMAN OF ALL TIME?

The Woman Rebel

On October the 10th 1991 the author of this book heard that a female teacher held a full-sized plastic model of a male sex organ in one hand, pointing to it and touching it with the other, as she taught a co-ed class at N.W. Classen High School in Oklahoma City. Needless to say this was the talk of the school.

The next school day I visited N.W. Classen High to see and hear for myself what teachings my tax dollars were funding. The school principal said content of this course was determined by central administration for all Oklahoma City schools. The female teacher I had heard about was not teaching that hour, but I was nevertheless allowed to sit in on the first hour "life skills" (sex-ed) class, taught by a male teacher who wore earrings and several bead necklaces. He used very explicit language, which embarrassed most of the co-ed students so much they could not look up from their desks. A student asked if it was better to have sex before or after marriage. Teacher: "The best time to have sex is after you have experienced life a little more. But if you do have sex, use a condom." Another student asked, "Shouldn't you wait until after marriage to have sex?" Teacher: "That is ok if you believe that." Anal intercourse was discussed at length—how to do it without getting AIDS; never was it suggested to be wrong. A color film was shown of a young woman's unshaved pelvic area as she gave birth. Later a portion of this film flashed on the screen repeatedly, "AIDS is hard to get, AIDS is hard to get, AIDS is hard to get." After class the teacher showed me the soft, life-like and life-size models of male and female sex organs used in teaching the class.

Later I learned that the above mentioned teacher was from Planned Parenthood Federation of America, a Humanist front organization founded by Margaret Sanger—the Woman Rebel.

A Rebel's Upbringing

To properly understand the true nature of Planned Parenthood Federation of America it is needful to examine the life and beliefs of its founder, Margaret Sanger. Why is she called—indeed, why did she call herself—the Woman Rebel?

Margaret Louisa Higgins was born September 14, 1879 in Corning, New York to Michael Higgins and the former Anne Purcell. Anne was a devout Catholic, but Michael was a socialist and an atheist, who taught Margaret from an early age to rebel against God and against morality. Ellen Chesler, in her biography of Sanger titled *WOMAN OF VALOR: Margaret Sanger and the Birth Control Movement in America*, implies that Margaret had her first sexual experience with her father.[217] From her early teenage years Margaret became obsessed with sex. There is evidence that she had both heterosexual and homosexual sex during her high school years.[218]

A Rebel's Marriage

August 18, 1902 she married a young architect, Bill Sanger, having known him for less than six months. After several years of a rather ordinary married life, during which three children were born, Bill built Margaret a new house, but it partially burned only a few days after they moved into it. To restore the house, Bill overextended himself financially. Margaret never forgave him for this.[219] Desperatxe for cash Bill sold

---

[217] Ellen Chesler, *Woman of Valor: Margaret Sanger and the Birth Control Movement in America* (New York: Simon & Schuster, 1992), 28.

[218] Ibid., 30.

[219] Ibid., 54.

the property in 1910, and moved his family to New York. Margaret was forced to take a job as a visiting nurse and midwife to supplement the income. The Sangers joined Socialist Party Local 5. Being both young and attractive, the Sangers were very popular with the leaders among the young rebels and scoffers of that time such as Bill Haywood, International Worker of the World organizer, and his lover Jessie Ashley, John Reed, Walt Lippmann, anarchist Alexander Berkman, fresh out of 14 years in prison for attempting to murder industrialist Henry Clay Frick, and Emma Goldman, an anarchist and an outspoken opponent of the institution of marriage.[220] Goldman introduced Margaret to NeoMalthusian ideology and advocated the use of contraceptives as a political tool. Margaret became a radical activist. "Despairing of conventional political processes, Margaret drifted toward the party's left wing and radical tactics of direct action in support of labor."[221] Margaret began to write articles for a socialist publication named *The Call*. She became a close friend of IWW's favorite female agitator, Elizabeth Gurley Flynn, the "Rebel Girl", and her lover Carlo Tresca who had abandoned his Italian wife and daughter.[222] Margaret began to spend a great deal of time away from home with Haywood, Tresca, Reed, and other immoral atheists, causing Bill to become increasingly jealous.[223] In 1913 Bill quit his job to become an artist. "Margaret never forgave him this decision—as she never excused the insolvency of his earlier real estate dealings....The lesson Margaret took from childhood was that men were worthy only as providers, and she seems to have quickly punished her husband's profligacy with sexual infidelity."[224] Mabel Dodge's famous and fashionable salon in the Village became a popular socialist meeting place. "Here Margaret encountered a world of new and unconventional ideas. There was discussion of Nietzsche, whose attack on established religion and morality had just been translated and was embraced uncritically, while his less tasteful views about racial supremacy and female inferiority were apparently ignored."[225] Nietzsche, of course, was the German philosopher who applied Darwin's theory of evolution to politics. Adolf Hitler later put Nietzsche's philosophy into action with his Nazi party. There were also "lectures by the young Will Durant on the pathbreaking research of the British sexual psychologist, Havelock Ellis, into the diversity and range of human sexual expression. In sum,

THE WOMAN REBEL

NO GODS NO MASTERS

HUMBLE PIE

MAN'S LAW

Sangers newspaper was the most radical, blasphemously anti-God publication the USA had ever seen. Sanger was the Madalyn Murray O'Hair of her day. She lived in rebellion against God all her life. She said that children are a curse. She taught and practiced sexual perversions. Through her Planned Parenthood Federation of America she is the all-time queen of mass murderers—the blood of tens of millions of victims drip from her hands.

220 Ibid., 37.
221 Ibid., 75.
222 Ibid., 76.
223 Ibid., 81.
224 Ibid., 89–90.
225 Ibid., 91.

there was an unapologetic celebration of freedom in love."[226] Bill wrote to Margaret, "Madame Pompadeau Dodge's—her salon—Oh! Gosh! how nauseating!....a hellhole of free love, promiscuity, and prostitution masquerading under the mantle of revolution....saturnalia of sexualism, deceit, fraud and Jesuitism let loose."[227] Mabel Dodge later wrote that Margaret was "the first person I ever knew who was so openly an ardent propagandist for the joys of the flesh.... [Margaret] told us all about the possibilities in the body for 'sex expression'; and as she sat there, serene and quiet, and unfolded the mysteries and mightiness of physical love it seemed to us we had never known it before as a sacred and at same time scientific reality."[228]

According to Margaret's son, Grant, Margaret's daughter, Peggy, came down with polio during this time, and Margaret would not admit the severity of Peggy's sickness.[229]

> Bill prevailed upon Margaret to accompany him to Paris, where he hoped to restore their relationship and pursue his painting in an atmosphere free of the corrosive immorality of New York. But his efforts were futile. In Europe Margaret met other socialists who shared her obsession with sex and encouraged her in her crusade to separate sexual pleasure from sexual responsibility. After approximately a year in Europe, she and the children took a steam ship back to New York where she immediately renewed her sexual relationship with a man named Walter Roberts and demanded of Bill to be released from her wedding vows. "As her own commitment to the new relationship developed, Margaret tried to enlist Bill's understanding and encourage his own sexual experimentation in the belief that their marriage might survive, if their infidelities were mutual. She told him that their future together depended upon the shattering of old habits, but the more consumed she became with issues of her own autonomy and satisfaction, the more intensely he communicated a paramount sense of emotional obligation to their shared past and to their children's future. He literally begged her to consider her children.[230]

But his pleas were to no avail; their marriage was over.

A Rebel's Newspaper

While aboard the ship coming back from France, Margaret decided to start a magazine to promote her views on sex. The purpose of this magazine, which she named *The Woman Rebel*, would be to purposely challenge the Comstock Obscenity Law which forbade the dissemination of contraceptive information and devices. Most people today do not realize that it was once against the law in the United States to use or distribute birth control information or devices. Birth control was considered immoral because it springs from atheism's radical denial of the Bible teachings concerning sex. "She gathered a group of radicals one evening in the cheap flat she had rented way uptown, and on that historic occasion a young friend by the name of Otto Bobsein coined the term 'birth control' to identify the social and economic objectives of the campaign Margaret planned to launch."[231]

Actually, the complete name of Margaret's newspaper was *The Woman Rebel—No Gods, No Masters*. It was truly a suitable name, as her newspaper was probably the most anti-God, anti-government, anti-family newspaper ever published.

Before we continue with the story of Margaret's life, let us examine some of the contents of Margaret's newspaper so that we can learn what Margaret believed. The eleven issues of The Woman Rebel have since been compiled and photographically reprinted in book form, along with a short history of Margaret Sanger. The quotes of Margaret in the following paragraphs are taken from that book (Alex Baskin, ed., *Margaret Sanger, the Woman Rebel and the Rise of the Birth Control Movement in the United States*). While Sanger did not actually author all of these quotes, she believed their contents and therefore chose to print them. As Alex Baskin put it, "Though she invited others to contribute articles to the *Woman Rebel*, she assumed full responsibility for determining editorial policy and determining the format of the paper." These quotes reveal the doctrinal foundation upon which Margaret later built Planned Parenthood Federation of America. Each quote will be listed under a title describing one of Margaret's beliefs. Please notice, however, that several other of her rebellious beliefs will also be revealed in each of these very significant quotations.

---

[226] Ibid.

[227] Ibid.

[228] Ibid., 96.

[229] Ibid., 93.

[230] Ibid., 95.

[231] Ibid., 97.

Sanger Rebelled Against God

Margaret based her whole life on belief that there is no God. She loathed Jesus Christ. As already mentioned, the masthead of *The Woman Rebel* declared, "No Gods No Masters." The following quotes reveal her as a militant, anti-Christian atheist:

> The Savior. O—I am sick of you [Christ]!...All men are cruel that make us think you real.... But today I have broken the image of Christ, There is joy in my life, I am free.[232]

> Alas, brethren, that God whom I created was man's work and man's madness, like all gods.[233]

> I have been true to my higher self—my only god and master.

Sanger Rebelled Against Church

Margaret despised Christian churches of all kinds. She especially hated churches that claimed authority over moral behavior, or that believed the Bible has authority over moral behavior, as the following quotes show:

> Compared with the diseased, perverted, hypocritical ghouls of American "civilization," cannibals strike you as simple, healthy people who live in an earthly Utopia.... They do not use the charred skulls and skeletons of women and children as the foundation of institutions that will hide the cries and shrieks of the tortured, or attempt to kill the nauseating stench of their bloody breath by vomiting forth the perfumed hypocrisies of the Baptist Church—words of peace on earth and goodwill toward men.... Have we workers been inoculated with this foul pollution of the spirit? Certainly we have if we do not boycott the Baptist Church and its allies.... Certainly we have been if we remain silent or inactive in the campaign against the poison of the "religion" that is weakening and killing the spirit of the American workers.... They want to inculcate in you the stupid spirit of submission to their mastery. They want to feed you upon the vapid innocuities of religion. They want to make you keep books with their God.[234]

> The day a woman becomes a mother at will she will not be far from complete emancipation. Only a ridiculous idea of love and of the act of reproduction, an idea handed down from the infamous Christian religion, could have led women to forget that she alone has the right to decide.[235]

Sanger Rebelled Against Moral Absolutes

Margaret resented being told that anything she wanted to do was wrong. She didn't want anyone telling her something was wrong—not even God. However, she did not mind telling others they were wrong—not even God. As she stated in the first issue of the *Woman Rebel*:

> It will also be the aim of this paper to circulate among those women who work in prostitution; to voice their wrongs; to expose the police persecution which hovers over them and to give them free expression to their thoughts, hopes and opinions.[236]

> The Rebel Women claim:
> The Right to be lazy.
> The Right to be an unmarried mother.
> The Right to destroy.[237]

> A Woman's Duty
> To look the whole world in the face with a go-to-hell look in her eyes; to have an ideal; to speak and act in defiance of convention.[238]

---

[232] *Margaret Sanger, the Woman Rebel and the Rise of the Birth Control Movement in the United States*, ed. Alex Baskin (New York: Stony Brook, Archives of Social History, State University of New York, 1976), 45.

[233] Ibid., 40.

[234] Ibid., 17.

[235] Ibid., 10.

[236] Ibid., 1.

[237] Ibid., 3.

[238] Ibid., 8.

Every girl who works for a master should build a class-conscious militant character within herself, differing from the teachings of the Church and present day morality.[239]

Ellen Key's ideal of erotic love is a monogamic relation "so perfect and consummate" to quote her own words "that it can be given to only one and only once in a lifetime." But there are woman souls as great as Ellen Key's who have an ideal of erotic love so perfect and consummate that it can be given to as many during a lifetime as circumstances bring within its glorious sunlike range, and even to more than one at a time.[240]

The Feminist movement is an organized attempt by women of today to extricate themselves from the "moral" standards that originated in the benighted past.[241]

Sanger Rebelled Against Marriage

Margaret began the birth control movement to undermine the institution of marriage. She hated monogamy. She hated the responsibility of marriage. And she hated the pleasures of sex being confined to the marriage bed:

ET TU? Beatrice Forbes-Robertson Hale said at a debate on feminism that she knew of only two feminists who advocated free love and unmarried motherhood, and that they were not suffragists, but anarchists. What a limited knowledge of women Mrs. Hale has! Perhaps after all self respect and morality are confined to the anarchist women![242]

Marriage, which is a personal agreement between a man and a woman, should be no concern of the State or of the Church. Never have either of these institutions interested themselves in the happiness or health of the individual. Never have they concerned themselves that children be born in healthy and clean surroundings, which might insure their highest development. The Church has been and anxious only if a child be trained Catholic, Baptist, Methodist and so forth. The state and church are concerned only in maintaining and perpetuating themselves even to the detriment and sacrifice of the human race. In the willingness to accept without protest or question the indignities imposed through the barbarities of the Law, together with the stupid superstitions of the Church, can be traced a great proportion of the world's misery.... Marriage laws abrogate the freedom of women by enforcing upon her a continuous sexual slavery and a compulsory motherhood.

Marriage laws have been dictated and dominated by the Church always and ever upon the unquestionable grounds of the wisdom of the Bible.

A man and woman who under a natural condition avow their love for each other should be immediately qualified by this to give expression to their love or to perpetuate the race without the necessity of a public declaration.... The marriage institution viewed from the light of human experience and the demands of the individual has proved a failure.[243]

Sanger Rebelled Against Civil Government

Margaret believed that the ends justified the means. Therefore she never hesitated to break the law if she thought that would help her reach her goals. Birth control, she rightly believed, would weaken the foundations of church, state, and employers, as the following quotes clearly show:

Stupidity and Ignorance and Slavery are the foundations of Church, State and Business.... the Government realizes that once the women of the United States are awakened to the value of birth control, these institutions—Church, State, Big Business—will be struck such a blow that they will be able only to beg for mercy from the workers.[244]

In the July 1914 issue of *The Woman Rebel* Sanger published an article entitled "A Defense of Assassination" in which assassination of government officials as a method to achieve social reform was advocated. One characteristic of humanists is that when their methods fail, they say it is not the method that is wrong, but the fact that the method has not be applied persistently enough. Thus the following statement is found in this article: "If assassination has failed to achieve very much in the way of reform, it may be not because the method is wrong, but because it has not been practiced persistently enough." From that statement it should be obvious to anyone that humanists will not stop at just murdering unborn babies to

---

239 Ibid., 28.

240 Ibid., 18.

241 Ibid., 35.

242 Ibid., 11.

243 Ibid., 16.

244 Ibid., 35.

achieve their goals. Adults also will be targets of assassination if humanists believe that will help them bring about "reform."

Sanger Rebelled Against Her Husband

Margaret refused to submit to any authority, whether it be the authority of God, of church, or of state. But especially she refused to submit to her husband's authority. Said Sanger:

> Woman can give suffrage or the ballot no new quality, nor can she receive anything from it that will enhance her own quality. Her development, her freedom, her independence, must come from and through herself. First, by asserting herself as a personality and not as a sex commodity. Second, by refusing the right to anyone over her body; by refusing to bear children, unless she wants them; by refusing to be a servant to God, the State, society, the husband, the family, etc.

Commenting on the Biblical texts of Col. 3:18, 1 Tim. 2:11-15, 1 Tim. 5:11-14 and 1 Cor. 14:34 which instructs a woman to be in subjection to her husband, Sanger sent forth in printed form the following bitter sarcasm:

> SUBMISSION, SILENCE, and SUBJECTION are the chief tenets of the system of religious ethics that has been imposed upon suffering women for nearly 2,000 years. "Saint" Paul, officially canonized by "Holy Church," was that truly great and good man who started out with the ambition of massacring the bodies of a handful of Christians; became converted and massacred the intellects, their individual liberties and their opportunities for social, industrial, and spiritual progress instead. Filled with the spirit of God he deprived women of the comparative freedom and equality which she enjoyed under the patriarchal system, and imposed upon her the infamous serfdom of sexual, intellectual, personal and spiritual bondage which has deprived the world of the results which should have accrued from the free and proper development of her divine potentialities, for upwards of twenty centuries.[245]

Sanger Rebelled Against Motherhood

Sanger hated the responsibility brought upon her by motherhood. She wanted to be able to come and go as she pleased without regard for some little people to whom she had just happened to give birth. She loved the pleasures of sex, but despised the consequences of sex. She spent all her life trying to maximize the pleasure while eliminating the consequences. She believed motherhood to be slavery:

> It will also be the aim of the WOMAN REBEL to advocate the prevention of conception and to impart such knowledge in the columns of this paper.
>
> Other subjects, including the slavery through motherhood; through things, the home, public opinion and so forth, will be dwelt with.[246]

> Why the Woman Rebel?
>
> Because I believe that deep down in woman's nature lies slumbering the spirit of revolt.
>
> Because I believe that woman is enslaved by the world machine, by sex conventions, by motherhood and its present necessary child-rearing, by wage-slavery, by middle-class morality, by customs, laws and superstitions.[247]

> A child is a curse, a curse to them [its poor parents] and to itself.[248]

It should be obvious to everyone that people who believe like Margaret Sanger do not love children. It is hypocrisy for a person to talk about loving children when he or she considers a child a "curse," tries to prevent its conception, tries to murder it before birth, and if having failed in all that believes it right to simply kill it after birth. Yes, Margaret Sanger even advocated killing babies ***after*** birth!

Sanger Rebelled Against Life

Margaret Sanger not only advocated birth control and abortion, but she also advocated infanticide:

---

245 Ibid., 20.

246 Ibid., 1.

247 Ibid., 8.

248 Ibid., 5.

> It is worth while to point out that Christianity and the Church first inaugmented these taboos, not only against the prevention of conception, but against "criminal" abortion and infanticide.[249]

Infanticide is a logical position for a humanist to take. Humanist leader Joseph Fletcher says, "It is reasonable, indeed, to describe infanticide as postnatal abortion."[250] Humanists, then, know that killing a baby before birth is no different then killing the baby after birth. If infanticide is murder then so is abortion. In this same book *(Infanticide and the Value of Life)* Arval A. Morris submits "Proposed Legislation" which states:

> Section 1. Authorization of euthanasia. Subject to the provisions of this Act it shall be lawful for a qualified physician, or his professional medical agent, as authorized by a qualified physician's written statement, to administer euthanasia to a qualified child for whom the child's parent or guardian previously has made a written declaration voluntarily requesting euthanasia for the qualified child and which declaration is lawfully in force at the time of administering euthanasia.[251]

Only 11 issues of The Woman Rebel were published before Margaret had to flee the USA with a forged passport to keep from being jailed for violating the Comstock Obscenity Laws. After the very first issue of her paper, the Post Office warned her that she was violating the law. Finally, on August of 1914, she was arrested and charged with four criminal acts punishable with a maximum sentence of forty-five years in prison.[252] Margaret knew that if she stayed in the United States she was almost certain to be convicted, for she was also a teacher at the Ferrer Center Association (also known as the Modern School). This socialist humanist school advocated the radical educational theories of such humanists as John Dewey. "In New York especially, the Ferrer Center established itself as a local forum for labor and cultural radicalism. In addition to its program for children, the school featured evening courses for adults with Goldman and Berkman, Tresca and Flynn, Jack London, Upton Sinclair, and Rose Pastor Stokes speaking on Socialist theory. The realist painter George Bellows and the young modernist Man Ray gave art lessons. Eugene O'Neill and Theodore Dreiser taught writing, and Margaret lectured on sexuality and family limitation."[253] The reason this was a problem for Margaret was that

> Sometime in June at the Ferrer Center, a conspiracy was launched by Alexander Berkman and a group of young militants to blow up the Rockefeller home....On July 4, ...a bomb accidentally exploded in a Harlem tenement, killing three young men and a woman. The dead were immediately identified with the Ferrer movement, and the plot on the Rockefellers was uncovered. A dramatic memorial service in Union Square the following week attracted an estimated crowd of 15,000 to 20,000, many of them wearing red and black revolutionary armbands and singing the Internationale.[254]

All of this violence and radicalism was sensationalized by the newspapers, dramatizing the dangerous nature of the Ferrer Center; and since Margaret was a teacher at the Ferrer Center this cast her in an extremely bad light. Pondering all this as she awaited trail she realized that if she went to court she would surely also go to jail, which would keep her from accomplishing her goals. Therefore, she carefully plotted her strategy.

First, she would break the law again. She sat down and wrote a pamphlet entitled *Family Limitation* which showed how to use all the birth control methods available at that time. The pamphlet also gave pro-contraceptive political arguments. Then she arranged for a radical printer, Bill Shatoff of New Jersey, to print 100,000 copies. These were addressed and bundled for clandestine distribution as soon as Margaret was out of the country.

Then, without even saying goodbye to her children, she deserted them, and "boarded a mid-night train for Canada, where contacts in the radical community falsified papers that provided her passage to Europe under an alias."[255]

---

[249] Ibid., 10.

[250] Fletcher, *Religioethical Issues*, 17.

[251] Arval A. Morris, "Infanticide and the Value of Life," in *Religioethical Issues*, ed. Marvin Kohl (Buffalo, New York: Prometheus Books, 1978), 17.

[252] Chesler, *Woman of Valor: Margaret Sanger and the Birth Control Movement in America*, 99.

[253] Ibid., 101.

[254] Ibid., 102.

[255] Ibid., 103.

A Rebel's Exile In Sex

Disembarking in Liverpool, Sanger immediately made her way to the Clarion Café, a gathering place of activists and radicals, arriving

> just in time for an informative Fabian lecture on the war. An enthusiastic rendering of Nietzsche later restored her own rebellious conviction and purpose. She reveled in the poetry, if not the often elusive meaning of the text, and copied down the aphorism since recited by legions of kindred rebel spirits: "Men and women must be Gods unto themselves and stop worshipping at the shrine of other egos."[256]

HAVELOCK ELLIS, a sexologist who strongly promoted sexual perversions of all kinds, became Sanger's mentor and one of her many illicit lovers.

She became acquainted with a Spanish socialist radical named Lorenzo Portet, who always carried a gun. Portet was a married man but that did not concern Margaret. She immediately began an extended adulterous affair with him. This ended the next year, however, when Portet died of tuberculosis.

From the time of her arrival in Europe, Margaret began to be more careful of her public image. Hoping to be able someday to return to the U.S.A., Margaret became cautious to hide her licentious conduct. Most of her shameful sexual deviations were not known until her journals were made available after her death.

Margaret lived a profoundly unconventional life, but unlike the more comfortably flamboyant Emma Goldman, traditional social sanctions always governed the public image she projected, if not her actual behavior. Beyond a small group of intimates that did not include her family, she carefully cultivated an outward appearance of propriety.[257]

Margaret did not at all confine her love making to one man. During her time of fornication with Portet, she also had found another lover. In December of 1914, Margaret visited the home of Henry Havelock Ellis, the famous sex psychologist. Margaret immediate fell in love with this man, accepting his sex theories with enthusiasm and without question. "Unlike Freud, Ellis did not demand that his patients change their habits, whatever they might be, only that they accept them.... Ellis, in fact, celebrated deviation from conventional coital sexuality as a laudable, inventive and distinctively human phenomenon."[258] Ellis demanded legal and political protection for homosexuality and even sanctioned fetishism, sadism, and masochism.[259] "He endorsed premarital and extramarital sexuality...on the grounds that most couples would benefit from a diversity of experience".[260] Ellis was married to a lesbian named Edith Lees. She and he both had affairs with other women by mutual agreement.[261] Ellis, though obsessed with sex just like Margaret Sanger, was impotent. Though he was 56 at the time, and she only 35, within a week he and Margaret were involved in a torrid adulterous relationship.

> After the failure of her first marriage, Margaret never again demanded that any one man be all things to her, or she to him. In this regard her own oedipal disappointments may have cast a shadow, but she used Ellis' teachings to license her behavior. Often she went to bed with men like Ellis who enriched her thinking and advanced her work. She perceived herself as fully liberated in her personal and sexual life and never

---

256 Ibid., 107.

257 Ibid., 110.

258 Ibid., 114.

259 Ibid., 113–14.

260 Ibid., 116.

261 Ibid., 117.

willingly tolerated control by any man. If she ever again yearned for the integrity of a single enduring relationship with one individual, she did not admit it.

> Margaret's intimacy with Ellis may never have been entirely satisfactory, but there is no doubt of the profound intellectual impression he made. She did not always welcome his advances, but she became nonetheless one of his most devoted disciples, and through the essays and commentaries, he produced with remarkable frequency for the remainder of his life, he continued to shape and educate her mature world-view.[262]

Meanwhile, back in the United States, Margaret's husband, Bill Sanger, was arrested for handing out a copy of *Family Limitation*. Nevertheless, Margaret's radical friends were working relentlessly to sway public opinion in her favor. They did this by widely distributing her *Family Limitation* brochure, by defending her in their publications, and by persuading other publications to do the same. The *New Republic* was one of the first to take up her cause. Then between April and November *Harper's Weekly* ran a series of articles advocating birth control. Bill's arrest made it all the easier to portray Margaret as a modern heroine. *The New York Times* now gave Margaret favorable press coverage. There had been only three articles on birth control in 1914. There were fourteen in 1915, and in the following two years a total of ninety.[263]

Margaret's radical friends were also working behind the scenes to obtain promise of more favorable treatment for her in the courts.

On September 10, 1915, Bill Sanger was brought to trial and sentenced to $.00 or 30 days in jail. Said the judge:

> Your crime is not only a violation of the laws of man, but of the law of God as well, in your scheme to prevent motherhood. Too many persons have the idea that it is wrong to have children. Some women are so selfish that they do not want to be bothered with them. If some persons would go around and urge Christian women to bear children, instead of wasting their time on woman's suffrage, this city and society would be better off.[264]

The hundred or so supporters of Margaret who had crowded into the courtroom, and another hundred or so outside, broke into raucous protest upon hearing the judges verdict and opinion. In an apparent attempt to regain Margaret's heart, Bill Sanger chose to go to jail rather than pay the fine. The judge's remark about woman's suffrage combined with Bill's decision to jail rather than pay the fine gave Margaret's radical friends cause for celebration. They felt they could use these things to make Margaret look even more of a martyr in the eyes of the public.

Then two weeks after the trial something happened to really cause Margaret to rejoice: Anthony Comstock, the author and driving force behind the Comstock Obscenity Law, died of pneumonia at the age of seventy-six. Probably sensing that events were swinging in her favor, Margaret returned home in October 1915 to stand trial herself.

A Rebel's Triumphant Return

Arriving in Manhattan, Margaret found that numerous woman's suffrage groups had rallied around her cause. Not realizing Margaret's atheism and hatred of Christianity, and not understanding the implications of her birth control cause, these groups rallied around her to protest the remark made by Bill Sanger's judge. "By martyring herself and creating a dramatic new public controversy, Margaret compelled women who were already politically mobilized [by the woman's suffrage movement] to deal frankly and openly with the issue of sexuality and contraception for the first time. She gave them a new cause."[265] Unfortunately, most of them had no idea that they were endorsing a cause rooted deeply in atheism and rebellion against God and against the morality taught in the Bible.

Having very little income, Margaret concealed her radical past, and from this point on devoted herself to just one radical cause: birth control. By dressing very conservatively, and by carefully choosing her words so as to make her speeches and articles appear logical and scientific instead of radical, she hoped to appeal to the masses.

---

[262] Ibid., 121.

[263] Ibid., 130.

[264] Ibid., 127.

[265] Ibid., 130.

Bill's reward for trying to regain Margaret's favor by going to jail for her birth control cause was that Margaret never even bothered to visit him in jail, or to even let him know that she had returned to New York. When finally they met again, Bill was bitterly disappointed to find that Margaret no longer had any affection for him whatsoever. Their estrangement became irreparable on November 6, 1915 when their daughter, Peggy, died. Peggy, who had been weakened by polio, and had never recovered from a broken heart at being deserted by her mother, died of pneumonia in Margaret's arms about one month after Margaret returned home. For years after this Bill and Margaret's relationship was marked by open mutual contempt.[266]

A Rebel's Occultism

Margaret was never able to rid herself of the guilt she rightly felt because of Peggy's death. Often she suffered nightmares of Peggy in emotional agony needing her. For months she suffered heighten anxiety "as she felt herself overcome by the certainty that the dead child's pattering footsteps continued to follow her around".[267] Humanism is really Satanism, as the following quote reveals.

> Seeking comfort, she embraced a set of mystical beliefs that provided spiritual solace and emotional relief that she had since rejected.... Desperate to hold on to some dimension of the child, Margaret began to study Rosicrucianism, then a fashionable mystical cult among British intellectuals to which Havelock Ellis introduced her in London. The Rosicrucians advanced an oriental regimen of private meditation intended to connect the individual to powers within the self that derive from a supreme higher force, a "god within," as she paraphrased Nietzsche.... Never troubling herself with intricacies of theological speculation, she simply accepted uncritically the Rosicrucian notion that every individual possesses "a spark of divinity," which determines the potential to express oneself in a constructive and meaningful way. This gave a spiritual dimension to the doctrine of self-reliance she absorbed from such icons of secular American culture as Ralph Waldo Emerson and her father's hero, Robert Ingersoll.[268]

Thus it is demonstrated why the New Age Movement is so readily accepted into Humanist-controlled public schools, while Christianity is vigorously rejected. From this point on, Margaret's

> dabbling in spiritualism helped strengthen private doubts and misgivings for which neither political ideology, nor the objective world of science and medicine, provided meaningful solutions. She sometimes "talked" to Peggy and encouraged close friends to do the same with deceased loved ones of their own.[269]

Margaret was motivated and guided by an evil spirit, and nothing would now stop her.

> Publicly, she identified herself with the increasingly rationalized world of science and medicine, but privately she maintained a fascination with the spiritual and the occult, frequently stopping between appointments to consult psychics, astrologers, and others who offered specious, but generally comforting, explanations of events and behavior she could not objectively explain.[270]

Neglecting her two remaining sons again just as she had before, she plunged herself into her birth control campaign.

A Rebel's Trial

Early in 1916 as Margaret's trial date approached, she prepared her defenses. She refused to plead guilty. With the help of her radical socialist friends and her new found woman's suffrage friends, Margaret "orchestrated a forceful lobbying and publicity campaign. Hundreds of sympathetic letters deluged judges, legislators, and other prominent political figures."[271]

For her publicity campaign a photograph was needed. For this photograph, Margaret planned to wear a black skirt, with a white shirt and tie—very manish and arrogant for that time. John Reed persuaded her instead to wear a feminine, delicate, lace-collared dress. Also, she was posed with her young sons. The resulting photograph portrayed her to be a gentle mother and housewife and lady. Judging from the photograph alone, it was hard to believe that she was actually a hardened atheist, adulterer, fornicator, sex pervert

---

266 Ibid., 133.

267 Ibid., 135.

268 Ibid.

269 Ibid., 136.

270 Ibid., 221`.

271 Ibid., 138–39.

and child deserter. This photograph was printed in newspapers throughout the United States, and did much to make American woman believe that birth control was not the radical, immoral act that they had been taught it was. Indeed, so favorable was the response from American women, that Margaret later described the resulting situation as, a "prosecutor loath to prosecute and a defendant anxious to be tried."[272]

Though still identified in newspapers as a "Socialist leader," Margaret was clearly courting an elite constituency, undoubtedly hoping to avoid prosecution. Conscious of the broadening of her support she said in her speech at the Brevoort: "I realize that many...cannot sympathize with or countenance the methods I have followed in my attempt to arouse working women to the fact that bringing a child into the world is the greatest responsibility. They tell me that *The Woman Rebel* was badly written; that it was crude; that it was emotional and hysterical; that it mixed issues; that it was defiant, and too radical. Well, to all of these indictments I plead guilty." But she quickly defended herself, proclaiming that, "there is nothing new, nothing radical in birth control. Aristotle advocated it; Plato advocated it; all our modern thinkers have advocated it!"

Of course, Margaret neglected to mention that Plato also believed children to be property of the state. Nor did she mention that all the modern thinkers she was referring to were atheists and humanists. She was appealing to ordinary housewives, and all the press coverage Margaret was receiving substantially strengthened the rationale of her defense on free speech grounds. Who would be willing to punish her for initiating a debate that had since been discussed with impunity in major newspapers and magazines throughout the country? Uncertain of just how to proceed, the prosecutor, Harod Content, foolishly arranged to have the trial date postponed twice, allowing each adjournment to enhanced Sanger's public profile and add more suspense to the drama of her persecution. She became a celebrity, with newspapers interested not only in what she said but in what she wore....Finally, having failed to structure a settlement, Content, on February 14, 1916, dropped all charges against her. Margaret Sanger, fugitive from the law for more than a year, was once again free.[273]

Margaret and her supporters were jubilant. In a rally held several nights later she lauded a "victor." She immediately took opportunity from all the fame she received from the press to book speaking engagements all across America, giving her canned speech hundred of times, often to large audiences. Always, she was careful to advocate no socialist causes except birth control. She would not dilute her effectiveness by embracing any other cause. And always she hid birth control's radical implications.

Publicly courting a broad base of public support, Margaret nevertheless continued to receive enthusiastic support from her radical socialist friends. One of them, a radical lesbian-feminist physician in Portland, Oregon named Marie Equi, wrote to Margaret, saying,

My Sweet, sweet girl. I love you with an ecstasy and understanding of Spirit that you alone have imparted to me thru the very brightness & flow of your intellect....My arms are around you. I kiss your sweet mouth in absolute surrender.[274]

Also, staying true to her radical socialist training, Margaret refused to obey laws she did not believe in, and refused to confine her activities to legislative reform alone. Rather her mode of action was "agitate, educate, organize, and legislate."[275]

A Rebel's Judicial Victory

Upon her return to America from exile in Europe, Margaret had allied herself with an organization organized in her absence, The National Birth Control League. However, she had personal conflict with the leader of that organization, Mary Ware Dennett. Mary did not share Margaret's vision of a socialized health care system patterned after the birth control clinics of the Netherlands, which Margaret had visited while in Europe. To this end Margaret sought and obtained the support of prominent physicians. Among those who publicly endorsed Margaret's plan were Herman Biggs, commissioner of the New York State Board of Health; S. Adolphus Knopf, M.D., who addressed the American Public Health Association in her behalf in October of 1916; Abraham Jacobi, who later became president of the American Medical Association; and Dr. William J. Robinson, who had long advocated birth control. Dr Robinson advised Margaret that the New York medical society was unlikely to interfere with her plan to open such a clinic, provided she staffed it with a licensed physician.

Suggesting that she make a direct challenge on First Amendment grounds to the state's Comstock prohibitions on contraception, he reminded her of New York's "venereal disease" clause, the amendment to the state's original Comstock act that exempted doctor's from prosecution for

272 Ibid., 139.

273 Ibid., 140.

274 Ibid., 142.

275 Ibid., 145.

prescribing condoms to prevent the spread of disease. This in his view, presented the possibility of a judicial reinterpretation that would sanction the prescription of contraceptives on broader medical grounds.[276]

Encouraged by this advice, Margaret rented space for a clinic in Brooklyn. On October 16, 1916, in intentional violation of the law, Margaret opened the first birth control clinic in America. For this Margaret and her sister, Ethel Byrne, were arrested, and first Ethel then Margaret were sentenced to one month in jail.

An appeal was filed, even though Margaret was self-evidently guilty and had already served her jail sentence. The saga of the Brownville clinic continued through January 8, 1918, when a verdict was rendered by Judge Frederick Crane of the Court of Appeals of the State of New York. Crane upheld Sanger's conviction under Section 1142 of the state's obscenity law and thereby affirmed the state's right to prohibit laymen and women from distributing contraceptive information. His opinion, however, offered an interpretation of Section 1145 of the law that granted specific license to physicians to prescribe contraception not just to prevent or cure venereal disease, but on more broadly defined medical grounds. The decision offered protection from risk of prosecution to doctors and to pharmacists acting on medical orders.

Just as Margaret's friend Dr. William Robinson had anticipated, the court provided a legal rationale for building a system of contraceptive service delivery with doctors in charge, the constraint under which Margaret subsequently built the birth control movement.[277]

A Rebel's Anti-USA Activities

In the spring of 1917 America entered World War I. Many of Margaret's radical friends, including Bill Haywood, Eugene Debs, Emma Goldman and Alexander Berkman, were convicted of criminal activity or outright treason, and were imprisoned or forced to leave the country. Margaret joined the League for Amnesty of Political Prisoners to protest some of these arrests. She continued to vote for the Socialist Party presidential candidate until she died.

In a successful attempt to maintain her leadership of the birth control movement, Margaret became founding editor of a magazine named *Birth Control Review*. In this magazine she defended pacifism and mocked the war effort.[278] She also continued to violate the law by "using her office as an informal clinic to instruct from twenty to forty women a week in the use of pessaries."[279] [Pessaries are contraceptive diaphragms.]

A Rebel's Friends

Margaret was kept financially afloat during this period by generous donations from wealthy leftist friends, including Gertrude Pinchot, Dorothy Whitney Straight, publisher of *The New Republic*, and Juliet Rublee. Juliet Rublee was wife of George Rublee, who served on the Federal Trade Commission, and her social clot did much to help Margaret succeed.[280]

By the early months of 1919, however, Margaret was under pressure to earn money and embarked on an extended lecture through the South. Not feeling well, she then extended her leave of absence to write her book *Woman and the New Race* and placed another old friend in charge, the rebellious journalist and self-styled revolutionary, Agnes Smedley.

Smedley was newly released from jail, where she had been held until the war's end, charged under the Sedition Act with abetting the Germans.[281]

Throughout this time Margaret was very lonely and renewed her adulterous affair with Walter Roberts. Soon, however, Margaret's editor, Billy Williams, replaced Roberts as Margaret's lover. Williams died suddenly of kidney disease in 1920.[282]

Having finished the manuscript for her book, Sanger went to London to visit her socialist friends and to renew her vision. Immediately she renewed her erotic relationship with Havilock Ellis. Margaret also began an extended adulterous affair with Hugh de Selincourt. At de Selincourt's Wantley countryside estate, Margaret participated in group sex orgies. Margaret experienced a lesbian encounter with de Selincourt's

---

[276] Ibid., 149.

[277] Ibid., 159–60.

[278] Ibid., 165–66.

[279] Ibid., 168.

[280] Ibid., 167.

[281] Ibid., 168–69.

[282] Ibid., 173.

wife, Janet, and in a letter to Juliet Rublee confided that she and Janet had "an embrace beyond any earthly experience." Margaret also introduced Juliet Rublee to Hugh de Selincourt, and while Juliet and Hugh de Selincourt were committing adultery, Margaret fornicated with Harold Child, Janet de Selincourt's illicit lover. During this six month visit to London, Margaret also began an extended adulterous affair with the well known novelist and Fabian socialist H.G. Wells.[283]

H.G. WELLS, a novalist and radical Fabian socialist, was one of Sanger's many sex partners. He was a married man, but had at least four other lovers in addition to Sanger. Sexual infidelity is a characteristic of humanism.

Sometime during this period, Margaret also began work on another book, *The Pivot of Civilization* (New York: Brentano's Publishers, 1922). Writing the introduction to this book, H.G. Wells correctly observed that there can be little doubt that birth control

> has become a test issue between two widely different interpretations of the word civilization, and of what is good in life and conduct. The way in which men and women range themselves in this controversy is more simply and directly indicative of their general intellectual quality than any other single indication.... We are living not in a simple and complete civilization, but in a conflict of at least two civilizations, based on entirely different fundamental ideas, pursuing different methods and with different aims and ends.[284]

Wells goes on to explain that the two conflicting civilizations are the Traditional or Authoritative Civilization in which morality is based upon the dictates of God, and the so-called New or Creative or Progressive Civilization in which morality is supposedly based upon the findings of science. Actually, Wells and other humanists are deceitfully renaming philosophy as science. The root idea upon which birth control is based is the idea that morals are not absolute but relative—that right and wrong should be determined by the elite among men rather than by omniscient God. There is nothing scientific about that idea at all. Birth control is simply the result of applying the philosophy of humanism to human reproduction.

But while Wells is wrong to call humanism science, he is right that the humanist philosophy and Christianity are in a war in which there can be no compromise. Wells is totally correct when he writes:

> It is a conflict from which it is almost impossible to abstain. Our acts, our way of living, our social tolerance, our very silences will count in this crucial decision between the old and the new.... Mrs. Margaret Sanger sets out the case of the new order against the old.[285]

Through her elite friends, Margaret gained access to many wealthy contributors. Among the most notable was multi-millionaire Noah Slee, founder of the 3 in 1 Oil Company. Upon meeting Margaret at a party hosted by Juliet Rublee, Noah deserted his wife of more than 30 years, and pursued Margaret. Margaret had just recently finally obtained a divorce from Bill Sanger.

Following the death of Billy Williams and the marriage of Jonah Goldstein, she had been without a reliable companion in New York. Nevertheless, her calender for 1920 and 1921 notes occasional evenings and holidays in the company of the still devoted Harold Hersey and others, including [Bill] Sanger himself, with whom relations seem to have eased somewhat, once her independence from him was made official. Marriage made "not a whit of difference" to her she confided in a letter to Hugh de Selincourt after the divorce was final. Earlier she had vowed that if she ever married again, it would be for money alone, and then, only so that she could come and live nearby him in England. She was "no fit person for love or home or children or friends or anything which needs attention or consideration," she admitted candidly in still a third letter, this one mentioning Noah Slee directly, though not by name. She referred to him only as "the millionaire."[286]

---

283 Ibid., 179–91.

284 H.G. Wells, *The Pivot of Civilization* (New York: Brentano, 1922), ix-xvii.

285 Ibid., xvii.

286 Chesler, *Woman of Valor: Margaret Sanger and the Birth Control Movement in America*, 244.

Slee bought her expensive gifts and accompanied her on a trip to Japan, China, Hong Kong, Singapore, Ceylon, Egypt, then to Venice, Milan, Paris and London, apparently picking up the tab. In London Margaret was a speaker at the Fifth International Neo-Malthusian Conference. While there she spent some private time with both H.G. Wells and Hugh de Selincourt, apparently while Slee was busy obtaining a

> French divorce from his American wife on the obviously specious grounds that she had refused to follow him to Paris. Then quite suddenly, on September 18, 1922, James Henry Noah Slee and Margaret Higgins Sanger were secretly wed by the registrar of marriages for the district of St. Giles, in Bloomsbury, London.[287]

This was four days after Margaret's forty-third birthday. Slee was sixty-three.

According to Margaret, Slee agreed in writing at their wedding that they would maintain separate residences with separate keys in New York, that she would keep her own name professionally, that, in all respects, she would maintain her freedom.[288]

As the deal turned out, Margaret got money and prestige rather permanently, while Noah got sex sporadically. Margaret was home only enough to keep the money flowing.

> Repeated assurances that she desired him, for example, quite clearly pandered to his insecurity in the relationship. This was particularly apparent when they spent the second anniversary apart in 1924. She wrote from London that she missed him deeply and yearned for his embraces, even as she was carrying on again with Wells and had begun a torrid new love affair with Harold Child.[289]

A Rebel's Humanism

It is beyond the scope of this book to give the history of how Margaret Sanger lobbied congress to change laws in her favor; how she constantly broke laws she disagreed with, then used her ties with radical left-wing journalists to obtain favorable press coverage so as to get those laws changed; how she used the newly made loopholes in the law to open birth control clinics, which eventually resulted in the founding of Planned Parenthood Federation of America. Rather, the purpose of this chapter is threefold: (1) to show the evilness and wickedness of Margaret Sanger's character; (2) to show that her character was so evil because she was a humanist; and (3) to show that Planned Parenthood Federation of America is a Humanist organization, and is an atheist, anti-US, anti-Christian, anti-children, anti-God organization.

Her Humanism Shown By ACLU Association

Margaret was defended in court by the American Civil Liberties Union.[290] At one time, Roger Baldwin himself, the founder of the ACLU, defended Margaret.

Her Humanism Shown By UNESCO Association

In 1930, when Noah Slee purchased an elegant five-story townhouse in Manhattan to house Margaret's Birth Control Clinical Research Bureau, Margaret chose Sir Julian Huxley, head of United Nations Educational, Social, and Cultural Organization (UNESCO), signer of *Humanist Manifesto II*, and one of the leading champions of humanism, to give the inaugural speech.[291]

Her Humanism Shown by AHA Affiliations

Several months after Margaret's book, *My Fight for Birth Control* came out, she held a dinner for 500 paying guests at the new Waldorf-Astoria Hotel in New York. Chairman of this dinner was John Dewey, co-founder of the ACLU, and founder of the American Humanist Association.[292]

---

[287] Ibid., 247.

[288] Ibid., 248.

[289] Ibid., 251.

[290] Ibid., 203.

[291] Ibid., 292.

[292] Ibid., 315.

According to March/April 1992 issue of *The Humanist* (page 4), Margaret Sanger, was awarded the Humanist of the Year award in 1957.

Alan F. Guttmacher, who became president of Planned Parenthood Federation of America several years after Margaret Sanger, was a signer of *Humanist Manifesto II*.

Closely associated with Planned Parenthood Federation of America is SIECUS [Sex Information and Education Council of the United States] another Humanist front organization whose sex education films and books are used in most public schools. One of the Humanist contributors to *Humanist Ethics—Dialogue on Basics*, published by Prometheus Books (the publisher of Humanist Manifesto I & II) is "Lester A. Kirkendall—Professor Emeritus of Family Life, Oregon State University, Co-founder of SIECUS. Author of *Premarital Intercourse and Interpersonal Relationships*; *The New Sexual Revolution*; *The New Bill of Sexual Rights and Responsibilities*; and other books" (p. 302). Mary Caldrone, the other co-founder of SIECUS, is featured in a "Humanist Profile" inside the front cover of the March/April 1993 issue of *The Humanist* magazine. According to that profile, "Her work began in 1953, when she was appointed medical director of Planned Parenthood Federation of America....she has received over 15 awards, including the 1968 Woman of Conscience Award from the National Council of Women, the 1980 Margaret Sanger Award from the Planned Parenthood Federation, and the 1974 Humanist of the Year Award from the AHA [American Humanist Association]."

Faye Wattleton, the president of Planned Parenthood Federation before Pamela Maraldo, was awarded the Humanist of the Year Award in 1986.[293]

Planned Parenthood Federation and SIECUS are virtually one and the same in teachings and goals, relentlessly preaching humanist "situation ethics" to our children.

> Humanists who control SIECUS and Planned Parenthood (organizations that frequently provide lecturers for schools) and a large percentage of the curriculum designers are evolutionists. Many are also atheists. Why is that important? Because an atheistic evolutionist considers man an animal that does not possess an innate conscience and is not responsible to God for his behavior. He rejects moral absolutes, insisting that each generation establish his own judgments of right and wrong. In fact, modern education repeatedly affirms that "there are no rights and wrongs." Nowhere is that false notion more harmful than in the classroom...Teaching sex education in mixed classes to hot-blooded teenagers without benefit of moral values is like pouring gasoline on emotional fires. An explosion is inevitable....Sex education in the schools was promoted to parents as a means of solving social problems. However, the obsession with sex created by such classes has more than doubled the problems they promised to solve—which is typical of godless humanism's solutions to anything. It solves nothing but instead compounds the dilemma.
>
> Children are born with two parents who are responsible to teach them about sex. The parents should never delegate that responsibility to a stranger, particularly one who teaches in an environment hostile to religion and moral values.[294]

Planned Parenthood and SIECUS obviously cannot be trusted to teach sex education without doing so from the Humanist viewpoint. Since Humanists do not believe in marriage, and believe premarital, extra-marital, and even homosexual sex is ok, we can only guess how much illicit sexual activity these Planned Parenthood taught sex-ed classes have stimulated.

One thing for sure: the same school year the author of this book attended the sex-ed class mentioned in the first paragraph of this chapter, one male student at Northwest Classen High School was so stirred up sexually that he couldn't even wait to get off the school grounds to rape a female student. By so doing he robbed this girl of her fundamental human right to keep her own body pure—to remain a virgin until marriage.

A Rebel's Murder Machine

Carol Everett had an abortion in 1973, then opened and ran her own abortion clinic until 1983 when she experienced a religious conversion. This is what she says about Margaret Sanger's organization, Planned Parenthood Federation of America:

---

293 *The Humanist*, November/December 1991, 4.

294 Tim LaHaye, "Sex Education Belongs in the Home," in *Teenage Sexuality: Opposing Viewpoints*, ed. David Bender, Bruno Leone, Neal Bernards, and Lynn Hall, Opposing Viewpoints (St. Paul, Minnesota: Greenhaven Press, 1988), 58–60.

Planned Parenthood is the largest abortion provider in the nation. They have a hidden agenda to get our kids sexually active as early as possible because they know that sex education sells abortions.

They create their market by telling the safe sex lie. They know that when they give out contraceptives in school-based clinics the pregnancy rate goes right up, the birth rate goes down, and the abortion rate goes up.

They know, like I did, that if I could get a girl in the fifth or sixth grade sexually active, we could get 3-5 abortions from her between the ages of 13 and 18. That was our agenda, and we knew that telling them about safe sex was a waste of energy.[295]

Through her promotion of abortion as birth control, Margaret Sanger has been responsible for the murder of more innocent people than any other person in history. January 2003 marked 30 years since abortion was legalized in all 50 states. During those 30 years, [over] 40 million abortions have been performed in America.[296] This does not count the abortions in other countries. Wm. Robert Johnston estimates that from the year 1920 to 2000 527,000,000 to 836,000,000 babies were aborted. Estimated current global monthly average is 1,524,000 abortions.[297] Sanger's application of humanism to human sexuality has already massacred—AT LEAST—half a billion innocent human beings! That is well over twice the population of the entire United States, and the true figure could possibly be almost four times the US population!

Forty million unborn American soldiers and unborn American mothers since Roe versus Wade—many fold more people than we lost in all of our nation's wars put together—have been slaughtered in cold blood. Do you realize that 134 of the nations of this earth do not have a population amounting to even 28 million people? Yet because of Margaret Sanger's instigation over 40 million innocent American babies have been murdered with no more concern than one would have when exterminating rats. If these 40 million aborted babies were put in tiny coffins one meter long, and those coffins put end to end with no space in between, approximately 9 rows of those coffins would extend the 4,497 kilometers (2,795 miles) from Los Angeles to New York City! The world-wide abortion total from 1920 to 2000 would create 117 to 185 rows of such tiny coffins! But because we are never allowed to see the bodies, the enormous carnage Humanists are dealing us fails to alarm us. Mark well that anyone who can cold-bloodedly butcher innocent, unborn babies alive will have no qualms whatsoever about murdering adults who stand in their way, if the "situation" makes murdering us a way to obtain, or retain, total Humanist victory. The atrocities of Stalin and Hitler, and the killing fields of Cambodia are insignificant compared to the sea of blood on Margaret Sanger's hands from the multiplied millions of babies that her Planned Parenthood Federation of America and its sister organizations world-wide have slaughtered in cold-blooded, precalculated murder. Margaret Sanger is without any shadow of doubt the most immoral, evil, and effective mass murderer that has ever walked upon the face of the earth. No one else even comes close to the numbers she has murdered—and every day the blood of more and more innocent babies flows from her wicked hands.

A Rebel's Pathetic End

Margaret Sanger suffered extreme guilt feelings all her life from the death of her little daughter, Peggy. She eventually became addicted to alcohol and the drug Demerol.[298] She became even deeper involved in spiritism by enrolling in a Rosicrucian mail-order course on self-realization.[299] Her health deteriorated, and she became senile. Her son, Steward, put her in a nursing home in Tucson, then moved his family to Mexico, deserting her in her old age just as she had deserted him in his youth.[300] In this nursing home Margaret received few visitors. She died on September 6, 1966, just a few days short of her eighty-eighth birthday. She remained to the end a sexoholic in rebellion against God and against God's moral laws. Contraceptives were

---

[295] Carol Everett, "Interview With the Scarlet Lady," *Rutherford* 2, no. 4 (April 1993): 8.

[296] "30 Years of Abortion and Its Impact on Women---National Symposia," *Americans United for Life Website* (2003), Http://unitedforlife.org/30_year_symposia/symposia.htm.

[297] Wm. Robert Johnston, "Summary of Registered Abortions Worldwide, Through 2000," *Johnston's Archive* (2001), Http://www.johnstonsarchive.net/policy/abortion/wrjp333sd.html.

[298] Chesler, *Woman of Valor: Margaret Sanger and the Birth Control Movement in America*, 417–18.

[299] Ibid., 418.

[300] Ibid., 463.

her methods of enjoying the pleasures of fornication, adultery, and sodomy without suffering the consequences.

Thus lived and believed the founder of Planned Parenthood Federation of America—the Humanist organization which is called in to encourage our children to engage in illicit sex in almost every public school in America. Perhaps by now you are beginning to understand why attending public school is hell on earth for your children. The extreme peer pressure on young people to sin against God is created on purpose by ministers of the Satanic religion deceptively called "humanism.".

MARGARET SANGER, founder of Planned Parenthood Federation of America, is the most evil woman that ever walked upon the face of the earth. She lived in rebellion against God all her life. She said that children are a curse. She taught and practiced sexual perversions. Through her Planned Parenthood Federation of America she is the all-time queen of mass murderers—the blood of tens of millions of victims drip from her hands.

Chapter 14

IS THE POPULATION EXPLODING?

No, Don't Fear the Fear-mongers

The public school system is constantly drilling into our children the idea of a "population explosion." One of the main reasons humanists give for promoting birth control, homosexuality, abortion, infanticide, suicide and euthanasia is that they believe that unless the population is reduced, or at least controlled, the Earth will rapidly become overpopulated and everyone will starve to death. People who espouse this population explosion idea are called Neo-Malthusians.

Neo-Malthusianism

Thomas Robert Malthus (1766-1834) was an English economist and demographer who theorized that population always tends to increase faster than production. This was—and still remains—an unproven theory. Charles Darwin's theory of natural selection was based on his belief in Malthusianism. In the mid-1800s, socialists used Malthus' theory as a basis to advocate birth-control for the poor. They founded the Malthusian League in 1877, and called themselves Neo-Malthusians. At least some of these people believed that the non-white races evolved separately from the white race and are not really human. They advocated birth-control (forced if necessary) for these races, which they considered inferior. Such ideas were, in fact, quite popular among humanists in both the United States and Europe right up until Hitler put them in practice in Germany by exterminating Jews.

Thomas Robert Malthus

Margaret Sanger was a Neo-Malthusian, as are almost all Humanists. In her old age, Margaret Sanger said the following in an interview given to Lloyd Shearer of *Parade Magazine*:

> Fifty years ago I realized what was coming—the population explosion we hear so much about today, women having more and more babies until there's neither food nor room for them on earth. And I tried to do something about it. Now I have thousands of people all over the world aware of that problem and its only possible solutions—family limitation and planned parenthood.[301]

This alarmist idea—that the earth is going to overpopulate and we are all going to starve to death if we don't use birth-control—is one of the most fundamental doctrines of humanism. In virtually every issue of *The Humanist* magazine there is a full-column ad encouraging people to contact and help the following seven population control organizations: International Planned Parenthood Federation—Western Hemisphere; Pathfinder Fund; Association for Voluntary Surgical Contraception; The Population Institute; Population Communications International; Imagine a World of Wanted Children; and Zero Population Growth. And there are other humanist population control organizations besides these. Take serious note: the Humanists are expending great energy and huge amounts of money to convince the American people that America and the world are in a terrible population crisis. Birth control is not a Christian idea; it is a humanist idea designed to undermine Christianity.

---

[301] Chesler, *Woman of Valor: Margaret Sanger and the Birth Control Movement in America*, 462.

The Humanist Neo-Malthusian Agenda

Since Humanists make such a big deal out of needing to control the population, it is important that we understand just how they intend to control it. I could not help but get a little emotional when I read the following materials which were taught to my son as part of a required college course he took at Oklahoma City University in the Fall of 1992. This material is from the book *Living In the Environment* by G. Tyler Miller, Jr. Promotional material for the book reveals that since 1975 Miller's books have been the most widely used textbooks for environmental science in the United States and throughout the world. They had already been used by more than 2 million students at that time. *Living In the Environment* reveals where humanism plans to take us:

APPROACHES TO POPULATION CONTROL

Basic Voluntary Family Planning

Strictly speaking, basic family planning is not a population control policy, because its goal is to help parents have the number of children they want when they want them.

Extended Voluntary Family Planning

1.Open access to contraceptive information, devices, and counseling, regardless of age, marital status, or economic situation.

2. Open access to voluntary abortion and sterilization.

3. Intensive education campaigns using schools and media to alter cultural values and to inform and convince people to practice contraception, to have fewer children, to see reproduction (not the sex act) as having important social and ecological consequences, and to avoid migration from rural to urban areas where jobs are not available.

4. Changes in school institutions by increasing the choices open to people. Goals include elimination of narrow stereotyped roles (especially of women as mother and of male machismo or virility), instituting women's rights and unbiased work opportunities, encouraging women to work, encouraging changes in family structure that would reduce the number of children desired, and promoting later marriages.

Economic Motivation: Incentives and Deterrents

1. Further extension of voluntary programs by using economic inducements of penalties to increase an individual's motivation for reducing fertility.

2. Possible incentives include direct cash payments, tax breaks, savings certificates, transistor radios (an incentive used in India), and providing free or low-cost contraceptives, abortion, sterilization, maternity care, and child care. Other methods include health plans, old-age pensions, and education for individuals or couples who agree to use contraceptives, to delay marriage or childbearing, to limit their number of children, to become sterilized, or to move from crowded urban areas to rural areas.

3. Possible deterrents include elimination of income tax deductions for some or all children; elimination of welfare, health, and maternity benefits after two children; limitations on government housing, scholarships, and loans for families with more than the allowed number of children; and taxes on marriage, children, and child-related goods and services.

Involuntary Population Control

1. Limiting couples to one or two children.

2. Licenses or certificate, which can be sold, that allocate the number of children a couple can have.

3. Compulsory reversible sterilization for all. A time capsule contraceptive could be implanted at birth or after a couple had the allotted number of children, or reversible sterilants could be added in the drinking water or to staple foods. Sterilization could be reversed by physicians so that couples could have their allotment of children.

4. Compulsory abortion for women exceeding the allotted number of children.

5. Reducing or eliminating immigration.

6. Limiting food rations so that a family can eat adequately with three or four members but not with five or more.

7. Banning, restriction, or forcing movement within a country in order to obtain a more favorable population distribution.

8. Death control by euthanasia (mercy killing) and infanticide.

Political, Scientific, and Administrative Support for all Methods

1. Population stabilization as an official national and world goal.

2. Private and governmental population planning and control agencies at local, national, and world levels.

3. Population control as a condition for foreign aid.

4. Improvement of health standards so that parents need fewer children to aid them in their old age.

5. Expanded basic research in human reproduction and applied research to improve contraceptive methods.

6. Increased social and psychological research on the relation of population to other problems; on the consequences of various population control policies; and on methods to increase the motivation to have fewer children, to move from urban areas, and to adjust to a society with a stabilized population.[302]

Now the above ideas are downright wicked and scary! Even if there really were a population explosion all true Christians should and would oppose such tyranny. But in spite of all the hype from the humanists, THERE IS NO POPULATION EXPLOSION! The whole idea is a hoax. As is their standard working procedure, humanist alarmists are simply trying to scare us with tales of doom so that they can persuade us to allow them to implement their radical, anti-God, social experiments. Humanists have made a science out of scaring people out of their way so they can get on with their dirty deeds.

Proofs There Is No Population Explosion

The only reason the public has swallowed the population explosion lie is because they have been passively accepting instead of actively observing.

The Proof of Empty Space

If a person does any traveling at all, all he has to do is open his eyes as he drives along to see that the vast majority of this Earth is virtually empty of human life.

Recently, I made a 2,000 mile trip from Oklahoma City to Cincinnati to western Kentucky back to Cincinnati to Chicago to Sioux Falls, South Dakota to Kansas City to Oklahoma City. Except while passing through these cities, I hardly saw any people at all—few people walking, few houses, not even very many animals.

Even more recently, two of my sons and I drove to Albuquerque, New Mexico and back—1,100 miles round trip. This trip was even more barren than the one mentioned above. Outside of ducks returning to the north, and a few cows, we saw no native animate life. The only people we saw were in cars. We hardly even

302 G. Tyler Miller, Jr., *Living in the Environment: Problems, Connections and Solutions* (Stamford, Connecticut: Wadsworth Publishing Co., 1994), 144–51.

saw any houses. Most of the few farm houses we did see were vacant and caving in. We even saw a small ghost town. The people have all moved to easier life in some city. And this brings up another point: if dense population is so bad, and country life so wonderful, why aren't people flocking to these desolate areas? No one is making them stay in the cities. People in the USA are free to live where they want. So how come country youth all flock to those awful cities?

Indonesia is often cited as a country with a serious over-population problem. Indeed, the island of Java has one of the densest populations in the world. But that is not true of the other islands of Indonesia, and Indonesia has 17,508 islands! Of these 17,508 islands, only about 6,000 are inhabited! I have traveled to many of Indonesia's larger islands, and except for Java they are sparsely populated. As just stated, most of the smaller islands have no population at all. Why is this? Because everyone who can moves to Java. Why? Because life is generally easier and better there and more opportunity exists to improve financially. The larger number of people on Java means that the provision of daily needs can be divided and specialized, which means a higher standard of living for everybody. More people also means a greater market for the goods of entrepreneurs. Large populations are not bad; they are good.

The Proof of Census Data

It takes a True Fertility Rate (TFR) of 2.1 to maintain a constant population size. In other words, the average woman must bear 2.1 children just to keep the population constant. The .1 is to compensate for the barrenness of some women and for infant mortality. The TFR in the United States has been below 2.1 since 1951, and was 1.84 in 1986. For over 40 years now the parents in this country have not produced enough children to maintain the population.

> If two parents (on average) don't bear and raise two children to reproductive age, then—over a period of time and with all other things being equal—a population will decline. Two parents must be replaced by two children. That is not my law. It is (depending on your preference) God's law, a law of nature, or a law of arithmetic. Two must yield two, whether you are a believer or an atheist.[303]

In 1790 the TFR in the USA was about 7.0. In 1988 the TFR was 1.93. That is a drop of 360 percent! The United States is not experiencing a population explosion, but a population implosion—a birth dearth of horrendous consequences.

> Demography, at its mathematical root, is a science that deals with multiplying and dividing more than with adding and subtracting. It deals with geometric progressions rather than arithmetic progressions. That point was made early on by the patron saint of doomsayers, Thomas Malthus.
>
> The idea is obvious on a small scale. Consider: If two parents have four children, they have doubled their number in a single generation. Then suppose each of the children, in turn, takes a spouse and each new couple continues to begat four children. At that rate, after only nine generations, there will be 1,024 offspring!
>
> That is geometric growth; we don't add, we multiply. And so, demographers, thinking geometrically, often talk of the "doubling" time of a population. Such calculations can yield big numbers quickly and the big numbers lend themselves easily to horrific metaphors like "population explosion" or "population bomb."
>
> Now, however, there is talk in the demographic community of "halving" times. A population trend that is losing numbers because of a below-replacement fertility also proceeds geometrically, not arithmetically. Suppose we choose a model that (for simplicity's sake) deals with two parents who produce only one child. That population has been halved in a single generation. Work that backward. Start with 1,024 adults, divided into 512 couples. After nine generation, with the TFR at 1.0 (not that far away from the present West German rate), the population of 1024 people is reduced to two people! On the Malthusian downside, we don't subtract, we divide.
>
> The moral of this particular demographic tale is clear: Once they get started, things can move very quickly. In our current Birth Dearth situation, the "momentum" effect...will begin to change direction, yielding, at least in theory, not a geometric population explosion, but a geometric population implosion....Western population will drop, with growing speed, by about 200 million souls if present fertility continues through the next century. In abstract theory if one turns the crank for another few centuries, you could end up with hardly any people at all—yielding not ZPG (Zero Population Growth), but ZP (Zero Population).[304]

---

[303] Ben J. Wattenberg, *The Birth Dearth* (New York: Pharos Books, 1987), 21. This book is one of the most important books written in the last 50 years. In the first edition of this book Wattenberg correctly predicted the fall of the Soviet Union based on census information. Every American should read his predictions for the USA.

[304] Wattenberg, *The Birth Dearth*, 37–38.

Conflict With Evolution Theory

Either the Population Explosion theory is wrong or the Theory of Evolution is wrong; or both theories are wrong (as I maintain). But it is not possible for both of them to be right, for they are contradictory.

When my son brought home the "APPROACHES TO POPULATION CONTROL" material quoted above, I gave him a math assignment. "Take the birth rate information they use to figure the population explosion," I told him, "but figure backward in time, instead of forward, to see how long it has been since Adam and Eve." Now my son's major was math, so this was no problem for him to do. Using the fertility rate of 2 percent given by his humanist teacher, and starting with today's world population of approximately 5 billion people, my son calculated that the first human couple lived only 1,092.8 years ago! How interesting. That means that evolution—which requires literally billions of years—could not possibly have happened. Either that, or else this whole population explosion business is a big fraud. In fact, both theories are frauds. The Bible indicates that the world was created from nothing—and Adam and Eve lived—about 6,000 years ago.

When my son challenged his teacher with this the next day, his teacher said that fertility rates were once much lower than they are today. To that I answer, Wow! If that be the case, then the best path to population control would be for the world to quit using all these modern contraceptives and abortion methods so that the fertility rate might go back to its previous snail-slow pace. After all, without birth- control and abortion it took multiplied millions of years for earth's population to reach its present level, according the humanist's root doctrine—the theory of evolution.

Here is the paper and calculations my son handed his teacher:

P = population at any given time.
Pn= population n years later.
r= proportional annual increase in population.
n= time.

Given the annual increase of 2% in the population and that we now have approximately 5 billion people on earth, how long ago was it when there were only 2 people on earth?

Pn= P(1+r)n
Pn/P = (1+r)n
ln(Pn/P) = n * ln(1+r)
ln(Pn/P) / ln(1+r) = n
n = 1,092.8 years

According to the Bible, after the flood there were only 8 people (they were in the ark and so didn't drown). This was about 4,000 years ago. What is the rate of annual increase according to the Bible?

Pn = P(1+r)
Pn/P = (1+r)n
ln(Pn/P) = n * ln(1+r)
1/n * ln(Pn/P)1/n = ln(1+r)
ln (Pn/P)1/n = ln(1+r)
(Pn/P)1/n = 1+r
(Pn/P)1/n - 1 = r
r = .0051

That is a MUCH slower growth rate than the .02 rate my son's teacher claimed. Nevertheless, using even this much lower rate of annual increase, how long will it be before there are 50 billion people on the earth? My son's paper continues:

ln((5 * 1010) / (5 * 109)) / ln(1+.0051) = n
n = 455 years.

Are you sure the human species has been around for 200,000 years as it says in our textbook (*Science Matters*, p.257)?

Of course, humanists don't believe in absolutes, so they aren't absolutely sure about anything, except that they don't believe in absolutes.

The Bitter Fruits of Birth Control

The command to be "fruitful and multiply" (Gen 1.27) was God's first commandment to humankind. It is foolish for men to believe that they can violate this commandment without suffering dire consequences. Humans do not know better than God, although many of them think that they do. Demographer Ben Wattenberg's book, *The Birth Dearth*, explains what the effects of birth control are going to be upon the USA. Most of the following is summarized from his book.

The US Economy Will Decline

Less people means smaller market. Smaller market means less profit. This should be obvious, for if there were no population there would be no market and zero profit.

Unemployment Will Increase

Population growth produces more new jobs, while population decline produces unemployment. This also should be obvious, for if the population declined to zero there would be no jobs left at all.

Humanists of course say that we have unemployment now. According to them, we don't have enough jobs for the workers we already have. Therefore, they say, fewer workers in the years to come, will mean less unemployment. Of course they are right. If there were zero population there would be no unemployment at all. Nor would there be any employment.

The Percentage of Old People Will Go Up

If the present trend continues, the median age in the USA will increase from 28 in 1970 to 42 in 2025[305] Now I have nothing against the elderly. I am becoming elderly myself. But as people get older their health begins to break down, and eventually they can no longer work. They retire and take pensions. The cannot support others, but rather become dependent upon others.

The Percentage of Young People Will Go Down

Babies must be born for a country to replenish its supply of young people, for young people turn into old people with age.

In 1985, there were 145 million people for 29 million elderly. That's a ratio of five producers for one retiree. But in 2035, as the Baby Boomers retire and the Baby Busters fill the labor force, the ratio will be only two-and-a-half producers to one retiree.[306]

The Social Security Administration Will Go Broke

Social Security is socialism, and like all socialist programs will not work for the long run. Socialism is built on greed: wanting something for nothing; and "there ain't no such thing as a free lunch."

There is a popular conception among Americans that our federal Social Security pensions are paid for by our very own contributions that have been put into an earmarked fund that is just waiting for us when we reach retirement age. Wrong. That is not how government pay-as-you-go social security programs typically work.

Let this be understood clearly: *Typically, we don't put money into the Social Security program for our own pensions. We put in babies.*

---

[305] Ibid., 67.

[306] Ibid., 68.

Thus, as a rule, most of our money doesn't pay for our own pension with our own dollars. It pays for our *parent's* pensions and our *grandparents'* pensions. But who will pay for our pensions if we don't have children, or more precisely if we as a population have ever-fewer children?[307]

Baby Boomers, aged 29-49 in 1994, especially should be asking that question, as they see a much smaller sized generation coming up behind them.

Socialism is always unfair. Socialism always takes from the good and diligent and gives to the greedy and lazy. Social Security is no exception.

The dollars young and middle-aged workers put in to Social Security go to their parents and grandparents or people in those generations. The money we receive when we are at retirement age comes from our children and our grandchildren—or from someone else's. Such is the nature of "pay as you go" social security plans.

Consequently, people who have no children, or perhaps only one child, are in a sense, cheating the system. The are "free riders." They end up drawing full pensions paid for by children who were raised and reared—at a large expense—by other people.

That's not fair. Couples without children have extra discretionary income while they are young, which they can invest for their retirement. That is not the case for many couples rearing young children at a time when schooling and housing are felt to be particularly costly. Yet childless people get full Social Security benefits when they are older, paid for by other people's children, raised by parents who were almost always short of money.[308]

Of course, in the end socialism brings total destruction. "Sooner or later, under a 1.8 or a 1.6 TFR, Social Security 'goes broke' unless something changes."[309] The grandchildren of those on Social Security pensions today will most likely receive no pensions. Perhaps that is what some older people are drawing attention to when they put bumper stickers on their cars stating: WE ARE SPENDING OUR GRANDCHILDREN'S INHERITANCE. Or perhaps they are bragging about their greed and lack of concern for their offspring.

People Will Be Alone In Old Age

Even now there are thousands of elderly people in state run nursing homes, who are immensely lonely because they failed to have any children. No one ever visits them. They are totally dependent upon the state, even though they may have been highly opposed to welfare in their younger years.

Our Culture Will Continue to Degenerate

There is something basically wrong with a husband or wife who does not love his or her mate enough to want to see him or her reproduced. A person is materialistic indeed if he doesn't want to share his life and resources with children. A person certainly lacks valid priorities if he or she considers a new car or corporate status more valuable than children.

The degeneration in our culture will further erode our economy.

In considering economies, then, we must consider spirit and culture as well. This relationship can be seen by looking around the world; one culture produces wealth, another poverty. Spirit and culture drive economies. Even some economists understand this. An innovative, optimistic, forward-looking society will likely be a prosperous one. Those are typically the features of youth.

The Birth Dearth circumstance, by definition, yields us an ever-aging society. What kind of spirit is there in a society that doesn't even have the gumption or interest to reproduce itself ?[310]

Our National IQ will Go Down

The birth control movement in the USA is actually serving as a selective breeding program in which only the poor and ignorant reproduce. Assuming that the more educated and more wealthy are more apt to also be more intelligent, the conclusion is unavoidable: birth control is lowering our national IQ. Why do I say this? Because

---

[307] Ibid., 67.

[308] Ibid., 154.

[309] Ibid., 68.

[310] Ibid., 75.

> the age-adjusted estimated CPS data show Americans with less than $10,000 family income had a 2.2 TFR. Americans earning between $20-25,000 have a TFR of 1.7. And Americans with incomes over $35,000 have a TFR of 1.3. That's the West German rate, too—the lowest in the world. Accordingly, let it be noted, *the Birth Dearth is due to low fertility among the middle and upper class!*[311] [Emphasis original]

The hard working, intelligent people are thinning themselves right out of existence, while the people lacking character and ambition are encouraged to reproduce so as to get larger handouts from our socialist welfare system. Generally these people are not even married, and therefore have no business giving birth to children at all.

Our Military Will Become Weaker

The enemy does not have to shoot soldiers that are never born. And numbers do make a difference in military strength. Ben J. Wattenberg, the demographer I have been quoting throughout this chapter, puts it like this:

> Question: Would the United States be a world power, the "leader of the free world," if our current population were still 4 million people, as it was in 1790? Or 62 million, as it was in 1890? We shall come to an answer: No.[312]

Humanists Anne and Paul Ehrlich, writing in The AMICUS JOURNAL (Winter/'88), criticize Wattenberg as follows:

> Besides the obvious questions today—how many able-bodied, healthy young men are required to push a few buttons?—Wattenberg apparently has failed to notice that, in modern armies and navies, only 10 percent of the personnel are combat troops and that women increasingly have joined men in virtually all other roles. Moreover, most jobs performed by members of the armed services these days could be done just as easily, if not better, by people over 35. The personnel needs of modern, technologically sophisticated armed forces are more different from those of World War II than the latter's were from the army of Julius Caesar. What counts today is quality (in training and ability to understand and use modern weapons), not quantity.[313]

To those arguments, Wattenberg points out the obvious:

> The Ehrlichs reveal a stunning ignorance of modern warfare when they ask, "How many able-bodied, healthy young men are required to push a few buttons?"
>
> What buttons? Buttons to fire anti-aircraft missiles from an aircraft carrier? But how many people, how large a tax base, does it take to build a dozen aircraft carrier battle groups? Or what kind of large specialized economy does it take to build thousands of tanks, smart missiles, and indeed, nuclear warheads?
>
> The answers are: lots of people in big modern economies.[314]

Without "lots of people" we will become weak, and weak nations fall prey to the strong.

Not only is birth control weakening our military by keeping soldiers from being born, but also by polluting our morals. The most effective birth control method of all is homosexuality, which humanists are teaching to our public school children with a zeal. Homosexuality not only keeps soldiers from being born, but effectively kills (by means of AIDS and other sexually transmitted diseases) at an early age what few are born. Homosexuality also demoralizes the troops which are trying to live upright, moral lives.

So, once again we see how humanism is actually treason, for it seeks to destroy our nation's ability and will to defend itself.

Some Very Personal Conclusions

You say you are a conservative, that you love our Christian heritage, that you believe in God and marriage and family values. Do you really? Do you love your heritage enough to raise a large family—trusting God to know how large—, thereby preserving that heritage and multiplying what you believe in your children. There is a way we can free ourselves from the present humanist tyranny. We can become more and mightier than our adversaries. Read Exodus chapter 1 for an inspiring example of a nation freed from tyranny because they obeyed God's command to "be fruitful and multiply." It's what you do in the privacy of your bedroom that shows how much you really believe what you say you believe, and that proves what you really

---

311 Ibid., 77.

312 Ibid., 79.

313 Ibid., 181.

314 Ibid.

are. As Wattenberg wisely points out, sex is a very private act, but it has very public consequences. The choices you make in the bedroom are going to affect the whole world for the rest of eternity.

UPDATE: The Threat of Radical Islam

The atheism and birth control of humanism have so paralyzed America that the prospect of her defeat by radical Islam is very real. The brutal fact is that Muslims are willing to have babies to promote what they believe, but humanism-influenced Christians are too materialistic and selfish to do so. While the populations of western countries are rapidly decreasing, Muslims are having as many babies as possible.

> Which brings us to the threat of radical Islam. "You are decadent and hedonistic. We on the other hand are willing to die for what we believe, and we are a billion strong. You cannot kill all of us, so you will have to accede to what we demand." That, in a nutshell, constitutes the Islamist challenge to the West.
>
> Neither the demographic shift toward Muslim immigrants nor meretricious self-interest explains Western Europe's appeasement of Islam, but rather the terrifying logic of the numbers. That is why President Bush has thrown his prestige behind the rickety prospect of an Israeli-Palestinian peace. And that is why Islamism has only lost a battle in Iraq, but well might win the war.
>
> Not a single Western strategist has proposed an ideological response to the religious challenge of Islam. On the contrary: the Vatican, the guardian-of-last-resort of the Western heritage, has placed itself squarely in the camp of appeasement. Except for a few born-again Christians in the United States, no Western voice is raised in criticism of Islam itself. The trouble is that Islam believes in its divine mission, while the United States has only a fuzzy recollection of what it once believed, and therefore has neither the aptitude nor the inclination for ideological warfare.[15]

A hedonist is one who regards pleasure as the chief good. A hedonist lives just for himself, and so is not willing to sacrifice or suffer for the good of others or for the glory of God. Humanism makes people into hedonists. That is why humanists are against the war against Islamist terrorists. They are living just for pleasure. War disrupts that pleasure. They would rather just submit to Islam and start having fun with four wives. Of course, it wouldn't be quite that simple for them, but they are too caught up in pleasures of sin to think that far ahead. Since they are using birth control to prevent being bothered with children, they aren't concerned about preserving the freedoms they enjoy for their decendents (since there aren't any), or what few there are are "mistakes" (the birth control method the hedonists used didn't work) which they wish hadn't happened. Sodomy is so popular with humanists because it is "only for pleasure," and as a birth control method always works.

Perhaps the most unbelievable election in the history of mankind took place in Spain only a few days after al-Qaeda terrorists bombed the train station and trains in Madrid. After hundreds of people being killed or wounded, it was expected that the people of Spain would take up arms in mass to fight Muslims. But that is not what happened. Instead, they voted out the government that had sent troops to Iraq to aid the U.S.A. fight al Qaeda, and voted in a pro-Islamic government! It was insane, and the Bush administration was stunned. Why would the people of Spain do something so crazy?

The answer is very simple. Spain has the lowest fertility rate in the world—only 1.12 live births per female. Without muslim immigrants paying into Spain's pension system, it would soon go bankrupt. The choice was, Would you rather be Christian or have a pension? Spain chose a pension.

> By 2050 Spain will have lost a quarter of its population. ... Half a millennium after the Reconquista, when Spanish Catholicism expelled the country's Muslims and Jews, Spain has no choice but to ask the Muslims to return and take possession of its land by stages.
>
> Every Spanish worker in 2050 will support one pensioner, which is to say that the pension system will be bankrupt. According to one academic study, 5 million additional immmigrants must be working in Spain in 2050 to save the pension system, out of a projected population of 37 million - and that assumes an immediate recovery in the fertility rate to 1.5. At this point, it hardly matters what future fertility rate Spanish demographers might project. The demographic catastrophe of the past 30 years puts the pension system on a crash course toward bankruptcy, unless Spain attracts an army of immigrants.
>
> Except for a trickle of immigrants from Latin America, North Africa provides most of Spain's immigrants at present. Two hundred thousand Muslims now reside in Spain, and they have built 100 new mosques in the past 10 years. Unless Spain were, most improbably, to attempt a recolonization from Latin America, it cannot do without more Muslims.
>
> Socialist voters may not have worked out the arithmetic; Jose Zapatero's supporter in the street simply does not want to be burdened with America's distant wars, especially if they draw fire at home. It all amounts to the same thing. Countries too lazy to produce their next generation will not fight. Who will lay down his life for future generations when the future generations simply will not be there?

---

[15] Spengler, "Why Radical Islam Might Defeat the West," *Asian Times Online*, 1909 July 2003, Http://www.atimes.com/atimes/Middle_East/EG08Ak02.html.

Like other former strongholds of Catholicism, Spain has made an abrupt and terrible shift away from traditional family life toward egregious hedonism.[316]

Guess what? The severely negative effect of birth control on our pension system is exactly why humanist politicians want to let illegal aliens become citizens of the USA; that is the only way to cover up their failure to address the horrendous problems they know are coming upon our Social Security system. Due to our lax immigration policy, Islam has grown by leaps and bounds in the USA, and there is abundant evidence that Barak Obama is a Muslim. Much of his family is Muslim. He was schooled in a radical Muslim school in Indonesia. The humanist church where he is a member praises Louis Farrakhan, the leader of the Nation of Islam, as being a great spiritual leader. A page on the Nation of Islam website shows that they support Obama for president.[317] Is America about to follow Spain into submission to Islam? Let us hope not. But frankly it looks like it might happen.

"Lo, children are an heritage of the LORD: and the fruit of the womb is his reward. As arrows are in the hand of a mighty man; so are children of the youth. Happy is the man that hath his quiver full of them: they shall not be ashamed, but they shall speak with the enemies in the gate" Psalms 127:3-5. Humanists believe this verse is a lie. Do you?

---

[316] Spengler, "Spain's Elections Show Why Radical Islam Can Win," *Asia Times Online*, 1916 March 2004, Http://www.atimes.com/atimes/Front_Page/FC16Aa01.html.

[317] http://www.finalcall.com/artman/publish/article_4285.shtml

Chapter 15

ARE ETHICS AUTONOMOUS AND SITUATIONAL?

Determining Right From Wrong

Even in school a child must make moral decisions. How does one determine right from wrong? The answer to this question which a student learns from his teacher will determine that child's "worldview" and how he will live his life. That answer divides the righteous from the wicked, and the free from the enslaved.

Humanist Manifesto II, which is the statement of faith of the atheistic religion called Humanism, answers our question as follows:

> We affirm that moral values derive their source from human experience. Ethics is autonomous and situational, needing no theological or ideological sanction. Ethics stems from human need and interest.[318]

In other words, the Humanist religion teaches that the Word of God, the Bible, is not the authority for differentiating between good and evil, but rather humans are their own authority—each individual, not God, decides for himself what is right and what is wrong.

One very clear example of the Humanist religion's situational ethics being taught in public schools can be seen in sex education. It is best seen if contrasted with Christianity. The Bible—the foundation of true Christianity—very clearly forbids sexual activity outside of the husband/wife marriage:

> Marriage is honourable in all, and the bed undefiled: but whoremongers and adulterers God will judge. (Heb 13.4)
>
> Thou shalt not lie with mankind, as with womankind: it is abomination. Neither shalt thou lie with any beast to defile thyself therewith: neither shall any woman stand before a beast to lie down thereto: it is confusion. Defile not ye yourselves in any of these things: for in all these the nations are defiled which I cast out before you: And the land is defiled: therefore I do visit the iniquity thereof upon it, and the land itself vomiteth out her inhabitants. (Lev 18.22-25)
>
> If a man also lie with mankind, as he lieth with a woman, both of them have committed an abomination: they shall surely be put to death; their blood shall be upon them. (Lev 20.13)

However Humanist Manifest II very expressly rejects both God and the Bible as the basis of morality, stating:

> We believe... that traditional dogmatic or authoritarian religions that place revelation, God, ritual, or creed above human needs and experience do a disservice to the human species.... In the area of sexuality, we believe that intolerant attitudes, often cultivated by orthodox religions and puritanical cultures, unduly repress sexual conduct.... neither do we wish to prohibit, by law or social sanction, sexual behavior between consenting adults. The many varieties of sexual exploration should not be considered "evil".... individuals should be permitted to express their sexual proclivities.[319]

Humanists wrongly define freedom as the liberty to do whatever one wants to do, even if one wants to do things God said are wrong. Such is not true liberty, but licentiousness—the very opposite of freedom. When wicked people are allowed to rob, murder, and indulge in immorality without meaningful punishment, then good people have lost their fundamental rights to life, liberty and property. Therefore a country ruled by humanism is not free, but enslaved.

Because humanism encourages sin, it also enslaves the will. Jesus said: "If ye continue in my word [the Bible], then are ye my disciples indeed; and ye shall know the truth, and the truth shall make you free " (John 8.31-31). But Jesus added: "Whosoever committeth sin is the servant of sin" (John 8.34). Drug abusers, alcoholics, fornicators, homosexuals, liars, thieves, and even murderers become addicted to their sins; they can't quit without outside help. They are slaves to their sins, and serve them faithfully they will.

---

318 Kurtz, *Humanist Manifestos I & II*, 16.

319 Ibid., 15.

If men reject God as the moral authority, and exalt themselves to that authority, anarchy results, for men are of many contradictory opinions concerning what is right and what is wrong. Humanist ethical systems, therefore, require a dictator to determine and enforce a system of state mandated behavior. Slavery is the direct result.

Hitler's Nazi Germany is a good example of what humanist situational ethics do to freedom. Nazism was based on Darwin's Theory of Evolution. Exterminating Jews will speed up the evolution of the human race, the Nazi reasoned, so how could it be wrong? American Humanists are no better, demanding "freedom of choice" to murder 1.6 million unborn children every year.

The following amazing admission that humanism is the religion upon which Marxist Communism is built in Humanist Manifesto II page 14:

> Many kinds of humanism exist in the contemporary world. The varieties and emphases of naturalistic humanism include "scientific," "ethical," "democratic," "religious," and "Marxist" humanism. Free thought, atheism, agnosticism, skepticism, deism, rationalism, ethical culture, and liberal religion all claim to be heir to the humanist tradition.

Humanism is thus revealed to be the core of every Satanic political system, every Satanic philosophy, and every Satanic religion. It underlies every dictatorship and police state.

True freedom is having opportunity to do all that God said is right to do. True freedom implies having government protection from those who would deny us this fundamental human right. No man has authority to deny others their right to live by the laws and precepts of God: "We ought to obey God rather than men" (Acts 5.29). The Bible explains true freedom in Romans 6.6-23:

> Knowing this, that our old man is crucified with him, that the body of sin might be destroyed, that henceforth we should not serve sin. For he that is dead is freed from sin. Now if we be dead with Christ, we believe that we shall also live with him: Knowing that Christ being raised from the dead dieth no more; death hath no more dominion over him. For in that he died, he died unto sin once: but in that he liveth, he liveth unto God. Likewise reckon ye also yourselves to be dead indeed unto sin, but alive unto God through Jesus Christ our Lord. Let not sin therefore reign in your mortal body, that ye should obey it in the lusts thereof. Neither yield ye your members as instruments of unrighteousness unto sin: but yield yourselves unto God, as those that are alive from the dead, and your members as instruments of righteousness unto God. For sin shall not have dominion over you: for ye are not under the law, but under grace. What then? shall we sin, because we are not under the law, but under grace? God forbid. Know ye not, that to whom ye yield yourselves servants to obey, his servants ye are to whom ye obey; whether of sin unto death, or of obedience unto righteousness? But God be thanked, that ye were the servants of sin, but ye have obeyed from the heart that form of doctrine which was delivered you. Being then made free from sin, ye became the servants of righteousness. I speak after the manner of men because of the infirmity of your flesh: for as ye have yielded your members servants to uncleanness and to iniquity unto iniquity; even so now yield your members servants to righteousness unto holiness. For when ye were the servants of sin, ye were free from righteousness. What fruit had ye then in those things whereof ye are now ashamed? for the end of those things is death. But now being made free from sin, and become servants to God, ye have your fruit unto holiness, and the end everlasting life. For the wages of sin is death; but the gift of God is eternal life through Jesus Christ our Lord.

Humanism is not new. As admitted in the preface to Humanist Manifesto I and II, "Humanism is a philosophical, religious, and moral point of view as old as human civilization itself." In fact, it originated with Satan in the Garden of Eden. God had clearly told Adam and Eve what was not sin and what was sin:

> The LORD God commanded the man, saying, Of every tree of the garden thou mayest freely eat: but of the tree of the knowledge of good and evil, thou shalt not eat of it: for in the day that thou eatest thereof thou shalt surely die. (Gen 2.16-18)

God knew that man could not know the danger of this one particular tree unless God told him. So God did tell him, and God never lies. This one tree would, and did, cause death. To eat of this one tree was therefore sin. Modern man likewise cannot know the difference between good and evil, except he accept the morality God reveals in the Bible. Of course, a humanist may even claim to believe the Bible while actually rejecting it. Satan did so when he used God's Word to persuade Eve to accept humanism in the Garden of Eden:

> Now the serpent was more subtle than any beast of the field which the LORD God had made. And he said unto the woman, Yea, hath God said, Ye shall not eat of every tree of the garden?.... Ye shall not surely die... your eyes shall be opened, and ye shall be

as gods, knowing good and evil (Gen 3.1-5).

It was a question of interpretation: What does the term "knowledge of good and evil" mean? The Bible tells us that "No prophesy of the Scripture is of any private interpretation" (1 Pet 1.20); it is always important to let the Bible interpret itself—interpretation must be in accordance with the context. God had already explained in Gen 2. 16-18 that "the knowledge of good and evil" was not desirable, but rather meant something bad. It meant that if they ate of the fruit of the forbidden tree they would come to know sorrow, suffering, and the agony of death. And if God says something it is absolute truth, whither we believe it or not.

Humanists deny it, but it is true nevertheless that Hitler was a humanist. He fervently believed in and based his whole life on the theory of Evolution. Just like with Margaret Sanger, it made him into a mass murderer. However, he didn't even come close to murdering as many people as Sanger. Humanism also made him into a racist.

The allegorical method of interpreting the Bible which underlies liberal theology is simply veiled humanism. The allegorical method simply creates a new, different meaning to replace the obviously intended meaning. The proper interpretation of the term "the knowledge of good and evil," Satan lyingly said, is that by eating of the forbidden fruit one would "not die" but rather become "wise" as a god—able to decide for one's self what is right and what is wrong, in spite of what God had clearly said about the matter. This was a false interpretation, and when Eve and Adam ate of the forbidden fruit they did not become wise at all, but rather became fools—even less able to determine right from wrong than before.

There is only one way to know right from wrong, and that is by studying the Bible in faith. If God's Word says something is wrong, it is wrong, no matter how persuasively men may argue otherwise. And if God's Word says something is right, it is right, and men who argue otherwise are wrong every time. There are no errors in the Bible, and in points where men say there are errors in the Bible those men are themselves in those points in error. Unlike men, God makes no mistakes.

In conclusion, even in public schools it is necessary to determine right from wrong. Therefore it is impossible to separate religion from education. Humanism, presently taught in public schools, is an oppressive, pagan, atheistic religion, ruled by Darwinian fundamentalists (that is, they believe and preach the fundamental lie taught in Darwin's *Origin of Species*, which is that the universe and all the creatures in it came into being without God). Either we adults willingly accept and defend God's perfect morality, or else an evil humanist dictator will force upon us his perverted morality, as is already happening to our children in public schools. When God was kicked out of public school classrooms, public schools exposed themselves as the humanist brainwashing camps they have been from their very beginning. Therefore it is vital that all government officials which espouse humanist principles be removed. Actually, action even more basic than this is needed.

In this time of moral crisis, it is immoral not to vote. Are you registered to vote? If not, please register immediately!

Hitler's religious belief in Evolution caused him to attempt to exterminate the whole Jewish nationality. He believed he could help speed up the evolution of the human race by killing those he considered to be weak and inferior. Most Humanists are elitists. Reasoning that their is no God, they conclude that humans are the highest life form, and that therefore they are gods. And of course THEY are the Most High gods. This picture shows how they reason with anyone that disagrees with them—lovers of freedom and free speech that they are. Fight them with all your might now while you can do it at the ballot box.

American Humanists say they are not like Hitler. True! They are thousands of times worse! Witness now their holocaust to eliminate Americans. If you can look at these pictures without realizing that abortion is murder, then you are probably a humanist yourself.

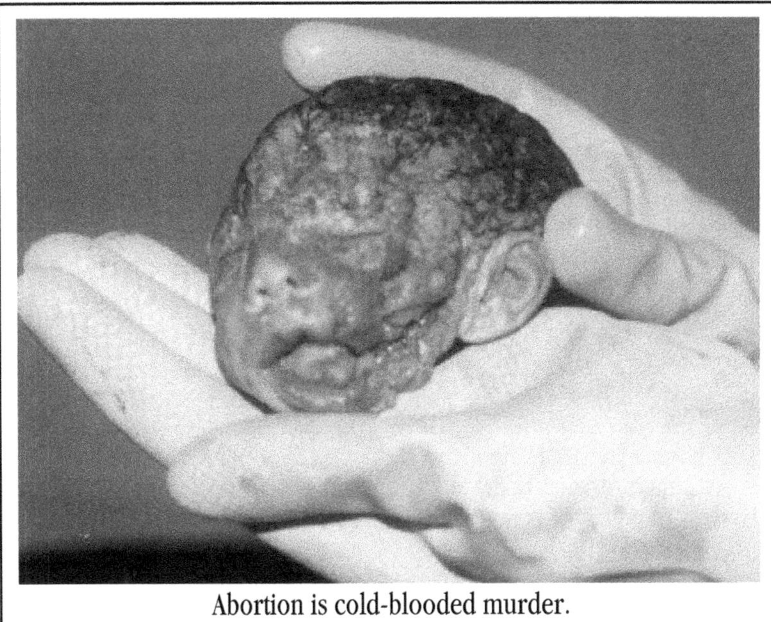

Abortion is cold-blooded murder.

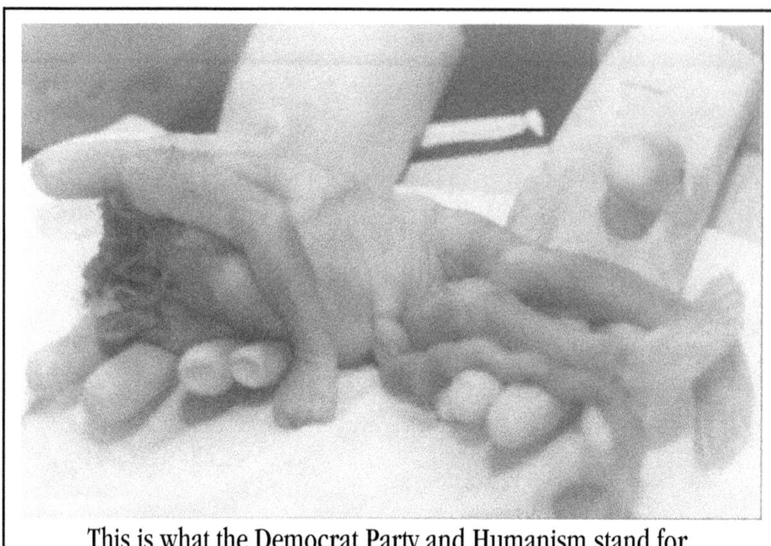

This is what the Democrat Party and Humanism stand for.

This is why you must fight the Democrat Party and Humanism with every ounce of your being until there is not one of them left in any level of our government. Millions of women have been tricked into having an abortion, not knowing what abortion actually is. If you are one of these women, don't just keep defending your sin. Repent and help fight these wicked deceivers hell-bent on slaughtering our youngest and most innocent. No judge who can approve this is just.

Chapter 16

DO HUMANISTS EVER TELL THE TRUTH?

Seldom, Usually They Lie

Do we want liars to teach our children? A teacher should be a role model—an example of what we want our children to become. Do we want our children to become liars? This is an extremely important question, because humanism considers lying a virtuous way of life. Humanists live in a shadowy way of darkness and lies. They lie to get your vote. They lie to get you off their case. They lie to cover up their lies. They lie even when they don't need to, just out of habit. It is vital to your health when dealing with humanists to realize that absolutely nothing they say can be believed without reservation. Not only do humanists lie as a means to obtain their goals, but they also greatly reward their own for lying—thus encouraging them to tell more and more lies.

The Cooney Example

A good example of a humanist lying to achieve an end, and then being rewarded by other humanists for doing so, is seen in the life of Timothy J. Cooney, the author of *Telling Right From Wrong: What Is Moral, What Is Immoral, and What Is Neither One Nor the Other* (Buffalo, New York: Prometheus Books, 1985). Prometheus Books is the publisher for the American Humanist Association that publishes *Humanist Manifesto I & II*, and hundreds of other humanist books. It is important to remember the name of this publisher.

Cooney begins his book by admitting that up to his own time "hard pressed, philosophers came up with solutions to the problem of morality without God, only to have them knocked down by other philosophers."[320] Cooney nevertheless attempts to offer a solution to the problem himself. To emphasize the fact that he rejects God as the basis of morality, Cooney makes such statements as, "But what a tragic answer God was to the basic metaethical question [of what is morality],"[321] and "Religion [Christianity] is to get us through dark nights; it is not for instruction on how to behave."[322]

The important question is, What did Cooney's humanist philosophy of morality do for Cooney? The answer to this question is very enlightening.

It seems that Cooney was having trouble finding a publisher willing to read his book. In a "Publisher's Note" at the beginning of Cooney's book, Paul Kurtz, well-known Humanist writer and editor at Prometheus Books which eventually published Cooney's book tells what Cooney did to overcome these problems:

> Acting out of desperation and in the hope of gaining entrance to the publishing world, Cooney wrote a letter extolling the virtues of his manuscript and signed the name of Robert Nozick, a well-known American philosopher.
>
> Prior to this forgery, however, and quite independent of it, an editor at Random House expressed interest in seeing the manuscript on the basis of reading the introduction and an outline of the book, which Cooney had submitted. The editor had heard of the endorsement and requested to see it as well. Cooney then forwarded the remainder of his manuscript accompanied by the falsified letter. Soon thereafter a contract was issued and the process of publication began. However, the editor eventually learned the facts of the forgery, and Random House decided to withdraw publication of the book.

In an afterward to his book Cooney comments rather half-heartedly on the morality of what he did:

---

320 Timothy J. Cooney, *Telling Right From Wrong: What Is Moral, What is Immoral, and What Is Neither One Nor the Other* (Buffalo, New York: Prometheus Books, 1985), 14–15.

321 Ibid., 124.

322 Ibid., 148.

> The publication of this book has had, to say the least, an unusual history, a history that has raised serious doubts in the minds of more than a few people about my qualifications for saying anything at all about morality.... Many people assumed that what I did was immoral because it involved a lie, but ***lying is not necessarily immoral and, indeed, in certain situations it can be the moral thing to do***, e.g., telling an axe murderer the axe is in the basement when in fact it is in the attic. Nevertheless, what I did was immoral—it was an act of stealing.[323]

Obviously, Cooney did not actually believe that what he did was immoral, but simply said this because he felt forced to in order to get his book published. After all, "lying is not necessarily immoral" to a humanist. As Joseph Fletcher, author of *Situation Ethics*, said, "It is precisely the end sought [in this case to get a book published] which justifies the means employed [forgery and lying]."

If a Christian author had done something like this the dominate humanist news media would have deplored the immorality of it continuously for years, and no publisher would have touched it. Why then did Prometheus Books publish Cooney's book? Said Paul Kurtz,

> The central issue was the relative merit of the work itself. Was it worthy of publication, notwithstanding the moral transgressions of the author? Our answer to that question was yes.... No doubt it will be perplexing to the reader to learn that an author who writes so eloquently on moral philosophy should violate his own principles. In spite of this, we firmly believe that *Telling Right From Wrong* is an insightful, thought-provoking, and controversial book that deserves to be published.

But Cooney ***didn't*** violate his own principles! He lived by them, as Paul Kurtz well knows. The real reason the editors at Prometheus Books published Cooney's book is because they share Cooney's principles. Perhaps by publishing Cooney's book they felt they could demonstrate that humanist ethics do indeed work. After all, Cooney's forgery and lying did generate a lot of publicity for his book, and it did therefore get published. So publishing Cooney's book was their way of saying, See! evil does accomplish good!

Let the public therefore be aware that humanists can never be trusted. To humanists, lying is simply a tool to accomplish their agenda. Nothing they say or promise can be believed. By their own confession they do not believe lying to be immoral. This fact should help us understand the Clintons and the Democrat Party a little better.

In closing, it is interesting to note what humanist ethics imply. If unrighteousness and lies could actually accomplish good, then evil would not be evil, but good. Evil conduct should therefore be praised, not punished. To denounce evil would then be evil, for you would be keeping someone from accomplishing good. Humanism thus turns true morality upside down and inside out. Good people are considered criminals, and criminals are considered righteous. This is the present situation in the United States.

> Woe unto them that call evil good, and good evil; that put darkness for light, and light for darkness; that put bitter for sweet, and sweet for bitter! Woe unto *them that are* wise in their own eyes, and prudent in their own sight! Woe unto *them that are mighty to drink wine, and men of strength to mingle strong drink: Which justify the wicked for reward, and take away the righteousness of the righteous from him! Therefore as the fire devoureth the stubble, and the flame consumeth the chaff, so* their root shall be as rottenness, and their blossom shall go up as dust: because they have cast away the law of the LORD of hosts, and despised the word of the Holy One of Israel. (Isaiah 5:20-24)

Considering all this, are humanists the kind of people we want to teach our children and lead our nation? If not, then why are we letting them teach and lead?

Important Facts About Lies and Liars

Liars want to believe a lie: *"A wicked doer giveth heed to false lips; and a liar giveth ear to a naughty tongue." (Proverbs 17:4)*

---

[323] Ibid., 147 and 156.

Liars are inferior people: "... *a poor man is better than a liar." (Proverbs 19:22)*

It is stupid for a person to think he or she knows better than God: *"Every word of God is pure: he is a shield unto them that put their trust in him. Add thou not unto his words, lest he reprove thee, and thou be found a liar." (Proverbs 30:6)*

Humanists don't want to believe this, but lies are not true: "... *no lie is of the truth." (1 John 2:21)*

This is what Jesus said to people that rejected the truths taught in the Bible: *"Ye are of your father the devil, and the lusts of your father ye will do. He was a murderer from the beginning, and abode not in the truth, because there is no truth in him. When he speaketh a lie, he speaketh of his own: for he is a liar, and the father of it. And because I tell you the truth, ye believe me not."*

People who deny that Jesus is the Messiah (the Christ) are liars: *"Who is a liar but he that denieth that Jesus is the Christ? He is antichrist, that denieth the Father and the Son." (1 John 2:22)*

Christians are commanded not to lie, but to speak the truth: "... *putting away lying, speak every man truth with his neighbour: for we are members one of another." (Eph. 4:25)*

Liars will not be allowed into Heaven: *"Blessed are they that do his commandments, that they may have right to the tree of life, and may enter in through the gates into the city. For without are dogs, and sorcerers, and whoremongers, and murderers, and idolaters, and whosoever loveth and maketh a lie." (Rev. 22: 14-15)*

Liars will spend eternity in the Lake of Fire: *"But the fearful, and unbelieving, and the abominable, and murderers, and whoremongers, and sorcerers, and idolaters, and all liars, shall have their part in the lake which burneth with fire and brimstone: which is the second death." (Rev. 21:8)*

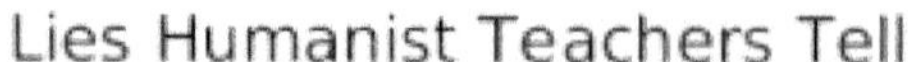
Lies Humanist Teachers Tell

Humanist Sex Ed Class
--- Sex before marriage is not wrong.
--- Adultery is not wrong.
--- Abstinence won't work; use a condom.
--- You are born gay, lesbian, transvestite.
--- You are gay and need to "come out"
--- AIDS is hard to get if you use a con
--- Anal sex is normal.
--- Gays and Lesbians have "right" to marry.
--- It's fun to be a transvestite like me!
--- Don't believe your ignorant parents.
--- Christianity is a "hate crime" religion.

Chapter 17

DO THE ENDS JUSTIFY THE MEANS?

No, But Humanists Think So

Is it right to lie, steal, deceive, compromise our morality, etc., in order to reach noble objectives? Graduating from school with good grades is good, is it not? Is it, therefore, ok to cheat on tests in order to get those good grades, thereby achieving that good end? If your children were to be asked this question, what would they answer?

"Cheating and Succeeding"

Most parents want to think that their children would not cheat. However,

> a nationwide study conducted in 1995 by Bowling Green State University revealed that 70 percent of undergraduate students surveyed admitted to cheating in class[324]

And in 1998 Who's Who Among American High School Students surveyed "3,123 high-achieving 16 to 18-year-old students, all of whom have an "A" or "B" average, and 97 percent of whom plan to attend college after high school graduation." The results were startling:

> Four out of five teens at the top of their classes say they got there the easy way, according to this year's poll of students honored in *Who's Who Among American High School Students*. A full 80 percent admit to having cheated during their impressive academic careers, the highest percentage in the 29-year history of the survey. Most students seem blasé about their own ethical slips (53 percent say it was "no big deal") and virtually all (95%) avoided getting caught. Even so, nearly two times as many students this year than last year (46% versus 25%) point to "declining social and moral values" as the biggest problem facing their generation today.[325]

Where did these students learn such ethics? Probably not at their church. Probably not in their home. Most likely they learned such ethics from humanist teachers in their public school. Humanist teachers set the example by cheating themselves.

> "When test scores are all that matter in terms of state aid, sometimes in media rankings or rewards and punishment from states, then educators try to get scores they need by hook or by crook," said Robert Schaeffer, public education director for FairTest, a Massachusetts-based organization critical of test use.
>
> "Being human, some of them (educators) cross the ethical line, sometimes quite far," he said.
>
> During the past week, dozens of teachers and principals from 32 different New York City schools were accused of cheating over a four-year period.
>
> Some of the educators have been fired and more could lose their jobs as a result of the one-year investigation, which alleges they helped students cheat on standardized exams.[326]

---

[324] Stephanie Coms, "Recent Survey Says Most College Students Cheat," *Arizona Daily Wildcat*, 1921 September 1998, Http://wildcat.arizona.edu/papers/92/20/01_2_m.html.

[325] *Cheating and Succeeding: Record Number of Top High School Students Take Ethical Shortcuts* (Lake Forest, IL: Who's Who Among American High School Students, 2000), Http://www.eci-whoswho.com/highschool/frame.html.

[326] Gilbert Gallegos, "Pressure Can Provide Incentive to Cheat," *The Albuquerque Tribune*, 1920 December 2002, Http://www.abqtrib.com/extras/education/121899_playing. shtml.

"Let Us Do Evil That Good May Come"

The Apostle Paul wrote of those who "slanderously reported" that he had said "Let us do evil that good may come." Paul described those slanderers as those "whose damnation is just" (Romans 3:8). Paul did not believe that the ends justify the means. It is never right to do wrong—no matter what the goal.

But cheating on tests, lying, violence, murder, indeed *any* wickedness, can be justified by Humanist ethics, as the following quote from Humanist Joseph Fletcher reveals:

> There are no "absolute" rights, just as there are no absolute duties (obligations). Always it depends on the situation. . . . When we make moral judgments or value choices—decisions as to right and wrong, good and bad, desirable and undesirable—we are consciously or not following one or the other of two alternative ethical modes. One is rule ethics and the other is situation ethics. Humanist are situationists. No genuine humanist would ever act out of what Kant called a "sense of duty" to any general principle of conduct. . . . Humanist ethics, in a word, is goal oriented, not rule bound.
>
> In rule ethics what we ought to do is decided *a priori*, by some predetermined precept of categorical imperative. It is decided abstractly, not on the facts. Variables are ignored or downgraded. Such rules might be "No abortion," or "No lying," or "No violence." This ethical modality means that some things may or may not be done regardless of the consequences. "Right is right," they say, acknowledging the circularity of their ethical reasoning. This also means that effectually conscience" is eliminated; responsible decision making is set aside. If you follow a rule that dictates your deeds, conscience is preempted and irrelevant. The moral agent is a null whenever a rule is relevant; he is passive and amoral.
>
> Situation ethics (philosophers commonly call it "act ethics") function, in contrast, with responsible moral agents—agents who judge what is best in the circumstances and in view of the foreseeable consequences. Like science, it is *a posteriori*, after or according to the facts, not *a priori*. You choose the course of action offering the greatest benefit, if need be even violation of a generally sound normative principle ("rule") if in the particular case more good can be done.
>
> "The end does not justifies the means" is a common but nonsensical saying. It is precisely the end sought (the consequences) which justifies the means employed. . . . A humanist is morally bound to say, for example, "It is better to end this pregnancy than to bear a baby with Tay-Sachs disease." The humanist cannot say, "That's too bad, but abortion is wrong."[327]

Fletcher makes abortion sound good—even righteous. Let's reword what he says, and see how it sounds: "Murder is better than compassion. Selfishness is better than love for others. Wickedness is better than righteousness." That is what Fletcher's words actually mean.

"Situation Ethics"

Before discussing the consequences of humanist morality, it needs to be pointed out that it is generally a mistake to use humanist terminology without close scrutiny. The term "situation ethics" as used by humanists is deceptive. Since humanism is the opposite of Christianity, using the term "situation ethics" in describing humanist morality implies, for example, that Christianity gives no consideration whatsoever to the situation. That is exactly the implication humanists intend; but it is, of course, not true. Rather, the Bible teaches that within the marriage *situation* sex is righteous, but that outside the marriage *situation* sex is wicked (see Heb 13.4). The Bible therefore condemns fornication (sex outside the marriage situation) always and absolutely. Humanism, on the other hand, concocts a *man-made* rule that condones or even encourages fornication is some *humanly defined* situations, and condemns marriage in some *humanly defined* situations. (For instance, humanist Ellen Key in the May 1914 issue of *The Woman Rebel*, page 2, says, "Love is moral even without legal marriage, but marriage is immoral without love.") In both Christian and Humanist ethics morality depends on the situation. But in Christianity God defines the situation, while in humanism man defines the situation. Humanism thus denies the depravity of man, saying that men are "responsible moral agents." We must ask the humanists, however, why, if humans are "responsible moral

---

[327] Joseph Fletcher, "Humanist Ethics: The Groundwork," in *Humanist Ethics* (Buffalo, New York: Prometheus Books, c1980), 258–59.

agents," do they murder, rape, rob, cheat, lie, etc.? The very fact that civil governments are necessary to prevent anarchy shows that unregenerate men are not by nature "responsible moral agents," and that they are not capable of defining the situations in which an action becomes wrong.

"The End Sought"

The humanist says, "It is precisely the end sought (the consequences) which justifies the means employed." The problem is that the ends humanists seek are often actually what they claim are only the means. For example, the murder of an innocent unborn baby to make possible a selfish and immoral lifestyle is portrayed as concern for freedom of choice. The baby, of course, is given no choice.

Another example: the humanists' fight to protect themselves from punishment for their crimes by banning capital punishment is called the fight to protect the sanctity of human life. Thus the sanctity of the human life of unborn babies is ignored while the sanctity of the inhuman life of criminals is hypocritically made a noble cause.

Another example: the legalization of robbery by the state (socialism) for the enrichment of—usually already very rich—humanists is called the fight to protect the poor.

Another example: the desire to commit sodomy without legal consequences is termed the fight for human rights.

Another sodomy example: the protection of pedophiles by the law branch of the American Humanist Association—the American Civil Liberties Union (ACLU)—so that pedophiles can continue to advocate on their web site the rape of little boys is termed protecting the First Amendment.

> BOSTON -- The American Civil Liberties Union will represent a group that advocates sex between men and boys in a lawsuit brought by the family of a slain 10-year-old.
>
> The family of Jeffrey Curley of Cambridge said the North American Man/Boy Love Association and its website which is now offline incited the attempted molestation and murder of the boy on Oct. 1, 1997.
>
> One of two men convicted in the killing, Charles Jaynes, 25, reportedly viewed the group's website shortly before the killing, and also had in his possession some of NAMBLA's publications. Also convicted in the killing was 24-year-old Salvatore Sicari.
>
> "For us, it is a fundamental First Amendment case," John Roberts, executive director of the Massachusetts branch of the ACLU, told *Boston Globe* Wednesday. "It has to do with communications on a website, and material that does not promote any kind of criminal behavior whatsoever".[328]

What is their true goal?

> According to the Globe, NAMBLA officials in the past have said their main goal is the abolition of age-of-consent laws that classify sex with children as rape.[329]

What is the specific crime these pedophiles are alleged to have committed?

> At two separate trials last year, prosecutors said Jaynes and Sicari were sexually obsessed with the boy, lured him from his Cambridge neighborhood with the promise of a new bike, and then smothered him with a gasoline-soaked rag when he resisted their sexual advances. They then stuffed him into a concrete-filled container and dumped it into a Maine river.[330]

By the way, as of this writing, the NAMBLA web site is back on-line.[331]

Another example of a hypocritical humanist end: the hateful crime of attempting to rob Christians of freedom of speech in order to stop them from preaching what the Bible says about sodomy is called the fight against...hate crimes! NAMBLA can publicly publish material advocating men to rape little boys, and according to humanist ethics that is not promoting "any kind of criminal behavior whatsoever," and is protected by the First Amendment. But for Christians to expose NAMBLA's hypocrisy is promotion of hate crimes, and not protected!

---

328 Associated Press, "ACLU to Defend Pedophile Group," *Wired News*, 1931 August 2000, Http://www.wired.com/news/politics/0,1283,38540,00.html.

329 Ibid.

330 Ibid.

331 A check on December 3, 2007 before sending this book out for publication found the Nambla web site still up.

Therefore, the true consequence of situation ethics is that right becomes wrong and wrong becomes right; the criminals are declared righteous, and the righteous are declared criminals. Isaiah 5:20-24 (the verses quoted in the last chapter) need now be quoted again—the Bible is so true!

> Woe unto them that call evil good, and good evil; that put darkness for light, and light for darkness; that put bitter for sweet, and sweet for bitter! Woe unto them that are wise in their own eyes, and prudent in their own sight! Woe unto them that are mighty to drink wine, and men of strength to mingle strong drink: which justify the wicked for reward, and take away the righteousness of the righteous from him! Therefore as the fire devoureth the stubble, and the flame consumeth the chaff, so their root shall be as rottenness, and their blossom shall go up as dust: because they have cast away the law of the LORD of hosts, and despised the word of the Holy One of Israel.

A NAMBLA parade. The NAMBLA web site says, "NAMBLA is strongly opposed to age-of-consent laws and all other restrictions which deny men and boys the full enjoyment of their bodies and control over their own lives....We call for fundamental reform of the laws regarding relations between youths and adults." The ACLU defends NAMBLA humanists RIGHT to advocate sodomy with underage boys, but works to enact laws to deny Christians the right to say such behavior is wrong. That is the Humanist idea of "free" speech—sin is right and right is sin.

Chapter 18

WHAT'S WRONG WITH SOCIALISM?

Government Fains To Be God

As Senator Robert F. Taft pointed out in 1949, "We have long had socialized primary and secondary education in the United States. The Government provides all education without cost to the student and supports the expense by taxation. Nearly a million teachers are on the public pay roll."[332] And therein lies the problem.

Most Christians have heard many bad things about socialism, and therefore if questioned will respond that they are against socialism. However, in reality they do not even know what socialism is, and in their ignorance they lend their willing support to socialism every day. For instance, most Christians do not realize that "public education" is simply a more socially acceptable way of saying "socialized education." The fact is, most Christians believe in, and support, socialized education. And since public education itself is, in fact, socialism, it should not be surprising that socialism is being promoted in our public school systems as the "politically correct" economic system. Our children are being taught that capitalism is wrong and socialism is right. The questions of the hour are, Should we be alarmed at that our children are being taught socialism? and, Should Christians support socialism?

Socialism Defined

Socialism is "any of various theories or systems of the ownership and operation of the means of production and distribution by society or the community rather than by private individuals, with all members of society or the community sharing in the work and the products" (Webster's New World Dictionary). In other words, under socialism the government owns all natural resources and businesses, and the government decides who gets the profits.

Government's Only Legitimate Purposes

"The powers that be are ordained of God" (Rom. 13:1). Government is ordained of God, and is the "minister of God" (Rom. 13:4), but government is not God, nor can government do for us what only God can do. For example, government cannot produce prosperity. There is a widely held misconception that all government has to do is pass a law to raise the minimum wage and instantly the poor will be lifted out of poverty. But if raising the minimum wage will bring prosperity, why raise it only a dollar or two an hour? Why not raise it $50.00 per hour? Better yet, why not make the minimum wage $500,000.00 per hour so that every American can live like a multi-millionaire? Raising the minimum wage never works because it forces businesses to increase the cost of their products to cover the extra labor expenses. The minimum wage earner then finds that the increased prices of the products he needs to live have increased at least as much as—and perhaps much more than— the increase in the minimum wage.

It is God that gives us the power to get wealth; government cannot do it. Therefore, it is foolish—even dangerous—to place one's trust in government instead of God for the provision of food, clothes, shelter and jobs. Here is what God says:

> When thou hast eaten and art full, then thou shalt bless the LORD thy God for the good land which he hath given thee. Beware that thou forget not the LORD thy God, in not keeping his commandments, and his judgments, and his statutes, which I command thee

---

[332] Senator Robert A. Taft, "Congress Should not Enact a National Compulsory Medical Insurance Law," *Congressional Digest* xxvii (March 1949): 79, 81 As Reprinted in Materials on American National Government (New York: Oxford University Press, *1952, pp. 522, 1949).*

> this day: lest *when* thou hast eaten and art full, and hast built goodly houses, and dwelt *therein*; and *when* thy herds and thy flocks multiply, and thy silver and thy gold is multiplied, and all that thou hast is multiplied; then thine heart be lifted up, and thou forget the LORD thy God, which brought thee forth out of the land of Egypt, from the house of bondage; who led thee through that great and terrible wilderness, *wherein were* fiery serpents, and scorpions, and drought, where *there was* no water; who brought thee forth water out of the rock of flint; who fed thee in the wilderness with manna, which thy fathers knew not, that he might humble thee, and that he might prove thee, to do thee good at thy latter end; and thou say in thine heart, My power and the might of *mine* hand hath gotten me this wealth. ***But thou shalt remember the LORD thy God: for it is he that giveth thee power to get wealth***, that he may establish his covenant which he sware unto thy fathers, as *it is* this day. And it shall be, if thou do at all forget the LORD thy God, and walk after other gods, and serve them, and worship them, I testify against you this day that ye shall surely perish. As the nations which the LORD destroyeth before your face, so shall ye perish; because ye would not be obedient unto the voice of the LORD your God. (Deut. 8:10-20)

When a nation turns its back upon God that nation is asking to become poor, and no politician will be able to save that nation from the poverty it deserves. Government is good for mankind provided it does not get out of its place and try to usurp the authority, throne, and position of God. Let it be repeated that government is not God, and cannot do the things that only God can do.

Consider for a moment that the only reason government is needed is because humans are inclined to sin against each other. Were humans only kind and good to each other, always treating each other fairly and honestly, no government would be necessary. Consider also that becoming a politician does not suddenly turn a person into a saint—in fact, just the opposite is often the case. Government officials are sinners just like everyone else. But because of their government positions they are sinners with the power of deadly force. In this lies the danger of government. It is a horrible thing indeed when criminals can rob and rape legally because they have been elected to be the government. This is why the citizens of a country must be very careful to pick only men of high character to lead their government; all men are sinners, but some men are more sinful—and some less sinful—then others. We must pick only the men of highest moral integrity to lead us, realizing that even they are imperfect men, and therefore even their powers over our lives must be limited.

Our founding fathers realized that the only legitimate purpose of government is to terrorize evil doers. This principle is based on the teachings of the Bible of Christianity. The God-given purpose and authority of government is clearly explained in the Bible as follows:

> Let every soul be subject unto the higher powers. For there is no power but of God: the powers that be are ordained of God. Whosoever therefore resisteth the power, resisteth the ordinance of God: and they that resist shall receive to themselves damnation. For rulers are not a terror to good works, but to the evil. Wilt thou then not be afraid of the power? do that which is good, and thou shalt have praise of the same: For he is the minister of God to thee for good. But if thou do that which is evil, be afraid; for he beareth not the sword in vain: for he is the minister of God, a revenger to *execute* wrath upon him that doeth evil. Wherefore *ye* must needs be subject, not only for wrath, but also for conscience sake. For for this cause pay ye tribute also: for they are God's ministers, attending continually upon this very thing. (Rom 13.1-6)-

To fulfill this purpose of terrorizing evil doers, our *federal* government should provide a military to protect us from attack from without; and *local* government should provide a police force and judicial system to protect us from criminals within. The legislative branch of government should see to it that all laws passed do not step out of these bounds. All branches of government should confine themselves to supporting these two simple tasks, else it meddles in business not its own.

Free Enterprise Versus Socialism

The United States of America was founded upon the principle of free enterprise—that is, a majority of our founding fathers believed that God had so designed things that individuals and private companies are to produce the products needed for life (such as food, clothing, health care, charity, education, etc.) and that government is not to involve itself in such matters.

When government assumes tasks other than providing an army and enforcing justice it goes into direct competition with the private businesses of its citizens (generally destroying those businesses) and becomes socialist. Socialism, therefore, is the exact opposite of free enterprise, and socialism and free enterprise are mutually exclusive—an aspect of life cannot be both free and enslaved at the same time.

Socialism is based on the idea that there is no God, and that, therefore, the Bible is not true. Socialism endeavors to replace trust in God with trust in government. The logical conclusion of such thinking is that government should take a role in all aspects of life. Under socialism, punishing people who do bad things is considered unimportant. Since there is no God, socialists reason, then who is to say what is good or what is bad, anyway? So under socialism, instead of enforcing justice, the government gets into the trash business, the electric and gas business, the communications business, the automobile business, the farming business, the charity business, the health-care business, and every other kind of business, including the school business. It is the socializing of our government which has caused the skyrocketing crime in this country. It is because of socialism that many American youth feel they must carry weapons and join gangs to protect themselves. Punishing bad people protects good people. Since the socialist public school administrators—we must not forget that public school administrators and teachers are government employees—will not protect well-behaved students by administering effective discipline to unruly students, the well-behaved students are forced to protect themselves.

Socialism Stifles Initiative

Socialism says, Take from the rich and give to the poor. Yet in socialist countries the poor always get poorer, while a few corrupt government officials and their friends get unbelievably rich. Why? Because in order for socialist governments to provide social services, they must levy extremely heavy taxes. Remember, government can only give what it has first taken; and socialist governments always subtracts high administrative costs before returning anything. Socialist governments cuts off the citizens' arms, eat the meat, then give the citizens back their own bones, expecting appreciation and thanks.

Socialism is legalized robbery. The Bible says, "Thou shalt not steal" (Ex. 20:15), thus establishing the right to personally own property. Socialism, on the other hand, is based on the idea that all property belongs to the state. Even though you work hard for your money, socialism says that lazy people deserve to live equally as well as you. Therefore socialism takes from the diligent and gives to the sloths, so that everybody can be equal. Socialism sounds great to lazy and greedy people and to politicians who are thieves; but honest, hard-working people hate it.

Socialism Is a Humanist Religious Doctrine

That socialism is a doctrine of the Humanist religion cannot be denied, for *Humanist Manifesto I & II* says:

> The humanists are firmly convinced that existing acquisitive and profit-motivated society has shown itself to be inadequate and that a radical change in methods, controls, and motives must be instituted. A socialized and cooperative economic order must be established to the end that the equitable distribution of the means of life be possible. The goal of humanism is a free and universal society in which people voluntarily and intelligently cooperate for the common good. Humanists demand a shared life in a shared world.[333]

That all sounds great, but it is based on a wrong doctrine about the nature of man. Humanists believe that man is basically good, and that man will do good unless the environment makes it impossible. Of course, no government at all would be needed if that were true, but socialists ignore that obvious truth, vainly trying to create a "free and universal society in which people voluntarily and intelligently cooperate for the common good" by being forced by the government to do so. The problem with this is that in reality man is depraved

---

[333] Kurtz, *Humanist Manifestos I & II*, 10.

and will not voluntarily cooperate for the common good. In fact, without a profit motivation man will not believe that he is working even for his own good, much less for the common good.

Socialism Never Works

Socialism has been tried repeatedly in countries around the world without success. Socialism is the economic system that underlies Nazism and Communism. Nazi is short for "National **Socialist** German Workers' Party." The letters U.S.S.R. stood for the "Union of Soviet **Socialist** Republics." History shows without any shadow of doubt that socialism never works. One of the reasons the Soviet Union fell was because it was a socialist government, and therefore prevented the growth of private enterprise—which alone can provide for the needs of the people. Any time government attempts to provide any services other than military and police forces, the costs of those services skyrockets, while the quality of those services nose dives. Under the Nazis, Germany became a hell on earth.

For the sake of this book, let it be stated clearly that ***socialized education never works***. Wherever it has been tried throughout the world, socialized education is more costly than private education, yet is far inferior to it. Even socialists like former President and Mrs. Bill Clinton realize this, and put their own children in private schools. Socialized education is what is wrong with education today, and until Americans take steps to desocialize education it is going to continue to be the greatest social problem Americans face. As Henry David Thoreau wrote many years ago,

> this government never of itself furthered any enterprise, but by the alacrity with which it got out of its way. It does not keep the country free.... *It does not educate*. The character inherent in the American people has done all that has been accomplished; and it would be somewhat more, if the government had not sometimes got in its way.[334] [Emphasis added.]

Socialism Is Not a Christian Practice

There is no end to the lies that Humanists will tell to try to promote socialism. Consider, for example, this quote from Patrick McCallister in the July/August1995 issue of *Socialist*, the voice of the Socialist Party USA:

> No leader in the conservative Christian churches would deny that the Christians of the 1st century lived cooperatively, according to Acts IV....But when challenged to justify their embrace of capitalism with this Biblical example of the socialist model, they resort to theological contortions instead of truly examining the relationship between Christianity and socialism. Paul, in the 6th chapter of his letter to Timothy emphatically states that "The love of money is the root of all kinds of evil...."[335] The love of money is better know today as "economic incentive." In the famous parable about the rich man (Luke 16) Jesus warned of the negative effects of wealth accumulation, and the hardened attitudes towards the less fortunate it can cause. But capitalism has a declared need for enough wealth seekers to keep the economy working. There is in fact no defense of capitalism's premises to be found in the Bible. Capitalism promotes the pursuit of personal wealth, but the Bible states that "The earth is the Lord's and the fullness thereof." (First Corinthians) The idea that the earth and its resources can be subject to personal ambitions cannot be made to fit with the Bible. Perhaps someday this will be understood by the conservative Christian community, and they will join with the rest of us Christian Socialists in the struggle for economic justice.[336]

If what McCallister said above were true—that socialism is taught by the Bible and is "economic justice"—, then I would want to be a socialist. In his article, McCallister also refers to Acts 4:32-35 as proof that the Bible teaches socialism. However, does the Bible really teach what McCallister says it teaches? Here is Acts 4:32-35 so we can examine it for ourselves:

> And the multitude of them that believed were of one heart and of one soul: neither said any of them that ought of the things which he possessed was his own; but they had all things common. And with great power gave the apostles witness of the resur-

---

334 Jonathan Messerli, *Horace Mann: A Biography* (New York: Alfred A. Knopf, 1972), 280.

335 McCallister misquotes this verse. It actually says, "the love of money is the root of all evil." The words "kinds of" are not in the verse and give a slightly different meaning.

336 Patrick McCallister, "Answering the Biblical Right with Biblical Socialism," *Socialist*, no. July/August (1995): 12.

rection of the Lord Jesus: and great grace was upon them all. Neither was there any among them that lacked: for as many as were possessors of lands or houses sold them, and brought the prices of the things that were sold, and laid them down at the apostles' feet: and distribution was made unto every man according as he had need. (Acts 4:32-35)

Some liberal theologians even claim that these verses teach communism (which is a particularly radical form of socialism). However, the context of these verses reveal some truths that are very much the opposite of socialist ideas.

Government Didn't Force This Benevolence

The first glaring difference between socialism and what the church at Jerusalem practiced is that the members of the church at Jerusalem were willingly, out of the goodness of their hearts, sharing all that they had with fellow Christians whom they personally knew and who were of like beliefs, practices and goals. Socialism, on the other hand, forces people against their will (by taxation backed up by gun-toting police and soldiers) to give their hard-earned money to strangers whose beliefs, practices and goals are often very offensive. For instance, under the present socialist welfare system of the United States, hard-working, god-fearing people are being forced to support drug addicts and prostitutes. Furthermore, they are being forced to support the anti-God doctrines of the Unitarian Universalist church (commonly called Humanism) in public (socialist) schools.

These Christians Owned Property

In verse 34 (quoted above), and also in verses 35-37, we read of people selling their land and other possessions, and donating the proceeds to be used as the church saw fit. This would not be possible under socialism, for under socialism the government owns all property, and private ownership of property is banned. Furthermore, in Acts 5:1-11, we read of a couple named Ananias and Sapphira who sold a possession, kept part of the price for themselves, then donated the rest as though it were the full price, thus lying. For this lie God killed them both (which shows what God thinks about lying). Peter's final words to Ananias before Ananias fell down dead were:

Ananias, why hath Satan filled thine heart to lie to the Holy Ghost, and to keep back part of the price of the land? Whiles it remained, was it not thine own? and after it was sold, was it not in thine own power? why hast thou conceived this thing in thine heart? thou hast not lied unto men, but unto God. (Acts 5.3-4)

Note that Peter said that "while it remained," that is, before Ananias sold the land, it was his "own." This is not true under socialism where the government owns the land. Note also that Peter said that after they sold the land it was in their "own power." In other words, the money they received as the price of the land was also their own property, and they alone had the power to decide how to use (to give or not give) that money. Their sin was in lying about how much they had given, not in refusing to be a socialist. Since the other members in that church had sold everything and had given all to be shared in common, Ananias and Sapphira were also being thieves by partaking of the commonly shared goods without contributing their fair share. Socialism, on the other hand, teaches that wealth should be distributed to everyone equally—even to those too lazy to work and who therefore contribute nothing to society. Thus we see that there was no socialism practiced in the church at Jerusalem at all—just Christian charity.

This Church Rejected Equal Wealth For the Lazy

The Apostle Peter taught that people who will not work do not deserve any wealth whatsoever, not even wealth in the form of food.

For even when we were with you, this we commanded you, that if any would not work, neither should he eat. For we hear that there are some which walk among you disorderly, working not at all, but are busybodies. Now them that are such we command and exhort by our Lord Jesus Christ, that with quietness they work, and eat their own bread. (1 Thes. 3.10-12)

How totally different this is from socialism which advocates all the welfare programs in this country which are feeding the lazy at the expense of the diligent.

"Economic Incentive" Isn't "The Love of Money"

The Bible does not teach that "economic incentive" is synonymous with "the love of money." If I put in 40 hours working for an employer, I want to be paid for my efforts. This does not mean that I love money. It is simply recognition of the fact that I must have money to feed my family. My incentive for working for an employer is to obtain the money I need for my family. There is nothing wrong with such an incentive. "For the workman is worthy of his meat" (Mat. 10:10), and the "labourer is worth of his hire" (Luke 10:7). Even if a man starts his own business, he still is working for someone else, even if he himself has employees. He provides a product or service in exchange for economic compensation. It is unreasonable to expect someone to provide for free a product or service to people he does not even know or for people he knows are lazy. Economic incentive is not "the love of money" and is not wrong. As has been pointed out by so many Bible scholars before me, money itself is not the root of all evil; it is the "love of" money that is the root of all evil. Money rightly used is a marvelous servant. But money loved before God and neighbor becomes a wicked and fearful master.

> No man can serve two masters: for either he will hate the one, and love the other; or else he will hold to the one, and despise the other. Ye cannot serve God and mammon. Therefore I say unto you, Take no thought for your life, what ye shall eat, or what ye shall drink; nor yet for your body, what ye shall put on. Is not the life more than meat, and the body than raiment? Behold the fowls of the air: for they sow not, neither do they reap, nor gather into barns; yet your heavenly Father feedeth them. Are ye not much better than they? Which of you by taking thought can add one cubit unto his stature? And why take ye thought for raiment? Consider the lilies of the field, how they grow; they toil not, neither do they spin: And yet I say unto you, That even Solomon in all his glory was not arrayed like one of these. Wherefore, if God so clothe the grass of the field, which to day is, and to morrow is cast into the oven, shall he not much more clothe you, O ye of little faith? Therefore take no thought, saying, What shall we eat? or, What shall we drink? or, Wherewithal shall we be clothed? (For after all these things do the Gentiles seek:) for your heavenly Father knoweth that ye have need of all these things. But seek ye first the kingdom of God, and his righteousness; and all these things shall be added unto you. Take therefore no thought for the morrow: for the morrow shall take thought for the things of itself. Sufficient unto the day is the evil thereof. (Mat 6.24-34)

It Is Socialism That Is the Love of Money!

Socialists politicians obtain the votes of the lazy and the greedy by promising them a share in the booty they will rob from the minority by unjust taxation once they get into office. They teach people that it is the government that gives them the power to get wealth, in opposition to the Bible principle that it is God that gives the power to get wealth (Deut 8.18). This putting money before God and neighbor is at one and the same time a love of money and a hatred of God and humanity. Socialism is legalized robbery, and is therefore a sin against both God and man. A person that votes for socialism, whither it be in the form of socialized education, socialized medicine, socialized charity, or some other form of socialism, is participating in the crime of robbery. He is attempting to use the government officials as armed robbers to forcefully take money from other people against their will to pay for his own expenditures.

Socialism Enslaves Employees

Socialism robs employees of protection against unjust employers. The purpose of government is to enforce justice, that is, to punish those that misuse liberty to abuse (rob, steal, cheat, deceive, etc.) others. If an employer refuses to pay an employee his due wages, that employee should have the right to sue said employer, thereby forcing the employer to pay the employee that which is justly his. Under socialism the government itself becomes the employer, against whom there is no recourse. History has shown that in every country where socialism becomes the economic system, it is corrupt businessmen who become the behind-the-scenes political leaders. In their positions of power, they become the only "legal" employers, stamping out all competition from their competitors. Their employees then become their slaves. These slave employees have no one to turn to in time of grievance. They can no longer quit to go to work for a more fair employer, for there are no longer any other employers. They cannot buy products made by other employers' companies, for all other companies are now out of business. It is under socialism that corrupt businessmen political leaders get richer and richer while the masses are stomped underfoot. We have only to look to any communist country to see that this is so. Poor working people need to realize that socialist leaders are not really on the side of the working man. To the contrary they are robbers who want to become our political leaders so that they can enact laws to force working people to hold still while they rape and rob them. After they cut off our right arms to eat for their own dinner, they will throw into our dinner plate our own bones, and expect us, like dumb dogs, to lick their hands in gratitude.

The Bible Condemns Class Warfare

While socialism calls workers to a class war against employers, thereby causing division in society, the Bible calls for employers and employees to unite in cooperation for the common good of all men. Contrary to what socialists would have us believe, neither the status of employer nor employee is sinful. Employees should remember that they may someday become employers, and employers are merely employees of their customers. Employees and employers need each other, and are together servants of God and of their fellow man. As Lord (Boss) over all, God has the authority to—and does in fact—tell both employer and employees how to act toward each other.

Servants, be subject to your masters with all fear; not only to the good and gentle, but also to the froward. (1 Pet. 2:18)

Let as many servants as are under the yoke count their own masters worthy of all honour, that the name of God and his doctrine be not blasphemed. And they that have believing masters, let them not despise them, because they are brethren; but rather do them service, because they are faithful and beloved, partakers of the benefit. These things teach and exhort. If any man teach otherwise, and consent not to wholesome words, even the words of our Lord Jesus Christ, and to the doctrine which is according to godliness; He is proud, knowing nothing, but doting about questions and strifes of words, whereof cometh envy, strife, railings, evil surmisings, perverse disputings of men of corrupt minds, and destitute of the truth, supposing that gain is godliness: from such withdraw thyself. But godliness with contentment is great gain. For we brought nothing into this world, and it is certain we can carry nothing out. And having food and raiment let us be therewith content. But they that will be rich fall into temptation and a snare, and into many foolish and hurtful lusts, which drown men in destruction and perdition. For the love of money is the root of all evil: which while some coveted after, they have erred from the faith, and pierced themselves through with many sorrows. (1 Tim 6.1-10)

Servants, obey in all things your masters according to the flesh; not with eyeservice, as menpleasers; but in singleness of heart, fearing God: and whatsoever ye do, do it heartily, as to the Lord, and not unto men; knowing that of the Lord ye shall receive the reward of the inheritance: for ye serve the Lord Christ. But he that doeth wrong shall receive for the wrong which he hath done: and there is no respect of persons. Masters, give unto your servants that which is just and equal; knowing that ye also have a Master in heaven. (Col 3.22-4.1)

Servants, be obedient to them that are your masters according to the flesh, with fear and trembling, in singleness of your heart, as unto Christ; not with eyeservice, as menpleasers; but as the servants of Christ, doing the will of God from the heart; with good will doing service, as to the Lord, and not to men: knowing that whatsoever good thing any man doeth, the same shall he receive of the Lord, whether he be bond or free. And, ye masters, do the same things unto them, forbearing threatening: knowing that your Master also is in heaven; neither is there respect of persons with him. (Eph 6.5-9)

Exhort servants to be obedient unto their own masters, and to please them well in all things; not answering again; not purloining, but showing all good fidelity; that they may adorn the doctrine of God our Saviour in all things. For the grace of God that bringeth salvation hath appeared to all men, teaching us that, denying ungodliness and worldly lusts, we should live soberly, righteously, and godly, in this present world; looking for that blessed hope, and the glorious appearing of the great God and our Saviour Jesus Christ; who gave himself for us, that he might redeem us from all iniquity, and purify unto himself a peculiar people, zealous of good works. (Titus 2.9-14).

The Bible Says Man's Nature Is Depraved

The Bible disagrees with socialists concerning the nature of man. The Bible teaches that God created perfect humans, but that they sinned of their own free choice, thereby bringing a curse upon the earth and passing a nature inclined to sin on to their offspring (us). Therefore, people left to themselves will lazy around on the job, steal from their employer, and if they become the employer will defraud their employees out of their wages, subject them to unsafe working conditions, and abuse them in many other ways. There is only one cure to this sin problem, and that cure is the Lord Jesus Christ. To rescue us from the consequences of sin (death and Hell), God sent His only begotten son, Jesus, to die on the cross in our place for our sins. His promise is that whosoever shall trust in the Gospel of Jesus Christ shall be born again (permanently changed by becoming a child of God) and saved from Hell. The free enterprise economic system (commonly known as capitalism) which made America the most wealthy nation on earth, acknowledges the depraved nature of man by confirming the right to private ownership of property ("Thou shalt not steal," Ex. 20:15), and by rewarding the diligent for their hard work:

> For the scripture saith, Thou shalt not muzzle the ox that treadeth out the corn. And, The labourer is worthy of his reward. (1 Tim 5.18)

Furthermore, the free enterprise system punishes the sin of laziness by letting the lazy go hungry, thereby motivating them to work.

Would you trust strangers with your checkbook? If you would you are a fool, and a fool and his money are soon parted. Realizing that governments are made up of depraved men just like other men, the free enterprise system refuses to allow the government access to the peoples' checkbooks. Socialism, on the other hand, denies the depraved nature of man, and claims instead that the only reason men do wrong is because of their environment. If only people were properly educated, socialists believe, they would always do right. (Of course, socialists close their eyes to the fact that many criminals are highly educated people.) Furthermore, the hypocrisy of socialism is evident from the fact that socialists are generally also elitists. That is, they believe that they are by birth intellectually superior to others, and that therefore only they are capable of making decisions. Ordinary folk, socialists believe, do not even have enough sense to choose a doctor, or to chose a school for their children, or to decide if a street person is worthy of help or is just a lazy bum. No, they will chose a doctor for us. They will decide for us what school our children will attend and what they will be taught. They will force us to support that lazy, alcoholic, drug addict bum better than we support even our own family. After all, socialists say, it is society's fault that he is the way he is.

Conclusion

Socialism is not Christian; it is Satanic. It is exactly the opposite of what the Bible teaches. McCallister did (almost) make one true statement in his article:

> Most conservative Christians believe that they are living today in the "end times"; they see socialists, and other progressives such as feminists and environmentalists, as being in league with the Devil himself, and themselves as the last vestiges of "God's Army" resisting the diabolical plot against God and themselves.

We conservative Christians do believe that this is the end time. While we realize that most of the followers in the socialist, phony feminist, and phony environmentalist movements do not know what evil they are espousing, we do believe that their leaders are in league with the Devil himself, and that they are conspirators in a diabolical plot against God and against Christians. However, we must point out that robbers aren't truly social, lesbians certainly aren't feminine, and worshipping the environment makes one an idolater not a true environmentalist. Furthermore, robbery, sodomy and idolatry represent moral putrefaction not progress. Socialists are not progressives; they are regressives. Giving their organizations deceptively grand-sounding names is typical of socialists; but it cannot mask the stench of their immorality. Socialism is falsely called "politically correct," but truly called Satanically incorrect. Isaiah 5:20-24 gives socialists good warning:

> Woe unto them that call evil good, and good evil; that put darkness for light, and light for darkness; that put bitter for sweet, and sweet for bitter! Woe unto them that are wise in their own eyes, and prudent in their own sight! Woe unto them that are mighty to drink wine, and men of strength to mingle strong drink: Which justify the wicked for reward, and take away the righteousness of the righteous from him! Therefore as the fire devoureth the stubble, and the flame consumeth the chaff, so their root shall be as rottenness, and their blossom shall go up as dust: because they have cast away the law of the LORD of hosts, and despised the word of the Holy One of Israel.

I am quoting this verse over and over again on purpose—because it fits Humanists perfectly.

A picture of the Socialist International council which met in Geneva, Switzerland on June 29-30, 2007. "The Socialist International is the worldwide organisation of social democratic, socialist and labour parties. It currently brings together 159 political parties and organisations [including communists] from all continents. The Socialist International, whose origins go back to the early international organisations of the labour movement, has existed in its present form since 1951, when it was re-established at the Frankfurt Congress. Since then it has been increasingly active and grown considerably in membership, particularly in recent years doubling the number of its members during the 1990s. Labour, social democratic and socialist parties are now a major political force in democracies around the world. Numerous member parties of the International, in all continents, are currently leading governments or are the main opposition force"(http://www.socialistinternational.org). http://www.michaelmoore.com links to the Democratic Socialists of America, which links to the Socialist International. Michael Moore also links to the People's Weekly World, which is the official paper of the Communist Party USA. He also links to the ACLU, NOW, NAACP, and many other humanist groups. All these groups are of the humanist religion, and work together toward their goal of setting up a "New World Order" based on the humanist religion.

Chapter 19

WHAT WILL BE THE OUTCOME OF OBE?

An Unpleasant Surprise

What will be the outcome of Outcome Based Education? Are you ever in for a surprise! Most likely you send your children to school to be ***taught***. You know from practical experience that nothing facilitates learning like good ***teaching***. Hard experience has taught you that experience may be a good teacher, but she is too slow and painful; it is simply not wise to "reinvent the wheel" every time we do something new. You don't want your children to have to learn everything in the school of hard knocks. That is why you pay big bucks in taxes to hire ***teachers*** to teach your children. And you think the public schools are in agreement with you—that they are actually trying to ***teach*** your children how to succeed in an increasingly technical workplace. Are you ever in for a surprise!

The Teacher of Our Children's Teachers

Perhaps the most amazing quote in the annals of history is from Carl Rogers, one of the humanist authors of Outcome Based Education—the new philosophy of education which is being implemented in public schools all across the USA under various names (when opposition to it arises, humanist educators simply change the name of the program, and continue on as before). This quote is found in *The Carl Rogers Reader* (Boston, Houghton Mifflin Company), 1989, pages 301-303, in a chapter entitled "Personal Thoughts on Teaching and Learning" in the Education section of the book. As you read the following words, keep in mind that this is one of the men whose philosophical ideas about teaching are being taught (or already have been taught) to the teachers who are (or will be) teaching your children or grandchildren. This quote is rather long, so I will interrupt it with my comments as appropriate so as to point out the significance of what Rogers says. You will find it interesting to note that the emphasis in this quote is all original to Rogers. Admits Carl Rogers:

> I find it very troubling to *think*, particularly when I think about my own experiences and try to extract from those experience the meaning that seems genuinely inherent in them. At first such thinking is very satisfying, because it seems to discover sense and pattern in a whole host of discrete events. But then it very often becomes dismaying, because I realize how ridiculous these thoughts, which have so much value to me, would seem to most people. My impression is that if I try to find the meaning of my own experience it leads me, nearly always, in directions regarded as absurd.
>
> So in the next few minutes, I will try to digest some of the meanings which have come to me from my classroom experience and the experience I have had in individual therapy and group experience....

Rogers finds it "very troubling to ***think***." His thinking even "becomes dismaying" to him because he realizes how "ridiculous" and "absurd" most parents of students would consider his conclusions. In fact, after carefully studying the implications of Carl Roger's conclusions, most parents will be even more troubled by Roger's thinking than he is. But remember Carl Rogers is writing to teachers, not to parents. He is trying to influence young college students who want to become teachers. He continues:

> I will put each idea or meaning in a separate lettered paragraph, not because they are in any particular logical order, but because each meaning is separately important to me.
>
> *a.* I may as well start with this one in view of the purposes of this conference. *My experience has been that I cannot teach another person how to teach.* To attempt it is for me, in the long run, futile.

Rogers cannot teach others how to teach! He admits that for him teaching is "futile." Why then was he made a teacher of our children's teachers?!!!

Mr. Rogers continues:

> *b.* *It seems to me that anything that can be taught to another is relatively inconsequential and has little or no significant influence on behavior.* That sounds so ridiculous I can't help but question it at the same time I present it.

This sounds ridiculous to Mr. Rogers because it is ridiculous. Thinking people also cannot help but question it, for it is obviously wrong.

Rogers continues:

> *c.* *I realize increasingly that I am only interested in learnings which significantly influence behavior.* Quite possibly this is simply a personal idiosyncrasy.
>
> *d.* *I have come to feel that the only learning which significantly influences behavior is self-discovered, self-appropriated learning.*
>
> *e.* *Such self-discovered learning, truth that has been personally appropriated and assimilated in experience, cannot be directly communicated to another.* As soon as an individual tries to communicate such experience directly, often with a quite natural enthusiasm, it becomes teaching, and its results are inconsequential....
>
> *f.* As a consequence of the above, *I realize that I have lost interest in being a teacher.*
>
> *g.* When I try to teach, as I do sometimes, I am appalled by the results, which seem a little more than inconsequential, because sometimes the teaching appears to succeed. When this happens I find that the results are damaging. It seems to cause the individual to distrust his own experience, and to stifle significant learning. *Hence I have come to feel that the outcomes of teaching are either unimportant or hurtful.*

Now these are indeed amazing conclusions! Rogers is advocating the abolishment of teaching! He says he has "lost interest in being a teacher." He says that teaching is "damaging," "unimportant," and "hurtful." He admits that as a result of his past teaching "damage was done," but he seems oblivious to the fact that it was the *content* of his teaching that caused the damage, not teaching itself. He thinks that it is *the act* of teaching that damaged his students instead of the *incorrect philosophies* he taught them. Therefore, rather than repenting of his perverse philosophies, he opposes the whole concept of teaching! Notice the use of the word "outcomes" in his last sentence above. Note that the outcomes of the educational system he proposes are not to be brought about by teaching but by the lack of it. How could such outcomes possibly be what we want for our children?

Notice in paragraph g above the importance Rogers puts on a student trusting his own experiences. This is very significant. Humanists exalt personal experience above Divine revelation. The problem with this is that personal experience can be very misleading. Things are not always as they appear to be. For example, it appeared to Anaximander (611-547 B.C.) that eels and other aquatic forms are produced directly from lifeless matter, but he was wrong. It appeared to Anaximenes (588-524 B.C.) that primordial terrestrial slime, under the influence of the sun's heat, produced plants, animals and human beings directly in the abiogenetic fashion—but he was wrong. They thought they experienced seeing something, but in fact they were misinterpreting their experiences. And the younger a child the more apt he or she is to misinterpret experiences. That is why children need teachers.

Also, some things cannot be learned by experience since we were not there when they happened (and therefore did not experience them), and since the events will never be repeated. Such things cannot be submitted to the scientific method. We must, therefore, accept them by faith. Personal experience cannot reveal to us how humans came into existence, why we are here, or where we will go upon death. That is why God gave us the Bible.

Rogers continues:

> *h.* When I look back at the results of my past teaching, the real results seem the same—either damage was done—or nothing significant occurred. This is frankly troubling.
>
> *i.* As a consequence, *I realize that I am only interested in being a learner, preferably learning things that matter, that have some significant influence on my own behavior.*
>
> *j.* *I find it very rewarding to learn,* in groups, in relationships with one person as in therapy, or by myself.

k. I find that one of the best, but most difficult, ways for me to learn is to drop my own defensiveness, at least temporarily, and to try to understand the way in which his experience seems and feels to the other person.

l. I find that another way of learning for me is to state my own uncertainities, to try to clarify my puzzlements, and thus get closer to the meaning that my experience actually seems to have.

m. This whole train of experiencing, and the meanings that I have thus far discovered in it, seem to have launched me on a process which is both fascinating and at times a little frightening. *It seems to mean letting my experiences carry me on, in a direction which appears to be forward, toward goals that I can but dimly define, as I try to understand at least the current meaning of that experience.* The sensation is that of floating with a complex stream of experience, with the fascinating possibilities of trying to comprehend its ever-changing complexity.

I am almost afraid I may seem to have gotten away from any discussion of learning, as well as of teaching. Let me again introduce a practical note by saying that by themselves these interpretations of my experience may sound queer and aberrant, but not particularly shocking. It is when I realize the *implications* that I shudder a bit at the distance I have come from the commonsense world that everyone knows is right.

Rogers's interpretations of his experiences are indeed queer and aberrant. In fact, they are so obviously wrong as to be shocking! But when any thinking parent realizes the implications, he or she will shudder more than a little bit.

Rogers proceeds to list these implications:

I can best illustrate this by saying that if the experiences of others had been the same as mine, and if they had discovered similar meanings in it, many consequences would be implied:

a. Such experience would imply that we would do away with teaching. People would get together if they wished to learn.

b. We would do away with examinations. They measure only the inconsequential type of learning.

c. We would do away with degrees as a measure of competence partly for the same reason. Another reason is that a degree marks an end or a conclusion of something, and a learner is only interested in the continuing process of learning.

d. We would do away with the exposition of conclusions, for we would realize that no one learns significantly from conclusions.

I think I had better stop there. I do not want to become too fantastic.[337]

Did you catch what Rogers said? He said that if we accept his philosophy of education ***"we would do away with teaching."*** It is obvious in Outcome Based Education that humanist educators want to do away with examinations. But did you realized they intend to do away with *teaching*! The outcome of no teaching will be little or no learning. Furthermore, if humanists get their way, what little learning takes place will not be measured, so will not be known. The fact that there is little teaching done is why they don't want examinations to measure it!

Isn't this a very, very, very, *bad* surprise?! And these people want us to think that they love our children and are concerned about their welfare. How can any sane parent leave his or her children in the public school system under the care of humanist teachers for even a minute?!!

The Union of Our Children's Teachers

The National Education Association (NEA) is one of the main reasons that reform of the public school system is impossible The radical left-wing nature of the NEA assures that the outcome is always going to be based on humanism.

The National Education Association (NEA) is the largest labor union in the United States, representing public school teachers and other support personnel, faculty and staffers at colleges and universities, retired educators, and college students preparing to become teachers. The NEA has 3.2 million members and is headquartered in Washington DC. It employs over 550 staff and had a budget of more than $307 million for the 2006-2007 fiscal year. Reg Weaver, a graduate of Roosevelt University, is the NEA's current president. NEA is both a professional association and a labor union (though it is not a member of the AFL-CIO or other trade

---

[337] Carl Rogers, "Personal Thoughts on Teaching and Learning," in *The Carl Rogers Reader* (Boston: Houghton Mifflin Company, 1989), 301–3.

union federations).

Because of its size, the NEA has a lot of clot, and it uses that clot to promote the humanist religion and to make Democrat voters and sodomites out of our children. USA Today reports that

> . . . the union has never endorsed a Republican for president and typically spends $9 out of every $10 it raises on Democrats.[338]

And OpinionJournal, a web site of the Wall Street Journal, reports that

> Under new federal rules pushed through by Secretary of Labor Elaine Chao, large unions must now disclose in much more detail how they spend members' dues money. Big Labor fought hard (if unsuccessfully) against the new accountability standards, and even a cursory glance at the NEA's recent filings--the first under the new rules--helps explain why. They expose the union as a honey pot for left-wing political causes that have nothing to do with teachers, much less students.[339]

For instance, in 2005 the NEA gave

> more than $65 million last year to Jesse Jackson's Rainbow PUSH Coalition, the Gay and Lesbian Alliance Against Defamation, Amnesty International, AIDS Walk Washington and dozens of other such advocacy groups. . . . The NEA gave $15,000 to the Human Rights Campaign, which lobbies for "lesbian, gay, bisexual and transgender equal rights." The National Women's Law Center, whose Web site currently features a "pocket guide" to opposing Supreme Court nominee Sam Alito, received $5,000. . . . The partisans at People for the American Way got a $51,000 NEA contribution; PFAW happens to be vehemently anti-voucher. . . . According to the latest filing, member dues accounted for $295 million of the NEA's $341 million in total receipts last year. But the union spent $25 million of that on "political activities and lobbying" and another $65.5 million on "contributions, gifts and grants" that seemed designed to further those hyper-liberal political goals."[340]

There are two very important facts to notice in this quote. First of all,

The NEA Promotes Teaching Sodomy

The teaching of sodomy in the public school system is the number one danger facing American families today. With the public school teachers giving millions to promote sodomy, it is obvious that they are to a very large extent the cause of the problem. Not that all of the public school teachers are humanists; there are some good people teaching in public schools. But the vast majority of public school teachers are humanists, and electing a new president for the USA, or even succeeding in passing a new amendment to the Constitution to define marriage as heterosexual, will not change these teachers. Humanism is their religion, and they are not going to stop teaching what their humanist religion says about sex or what it says about anything else.

> In1997 there were approximately 100 gay-straight alliances (GSAs)--clubs for gay and gay-friendly kids--on U.S. high school campuses. Today there are at least 3,000 GSAs--nearly 1 in 10 high schools has one--according to the Gay Lesbian Straight Education Network (GLSEN, say "glisten"), which registers and advises GSAs. In the 2004-05 academic year, GSAs were established at U.S. schools at the rate of three per day.
>
> The appearance of so many gay adolescents has, predictably, worried social conservatives, but it has also surprised gay activists, who for years did little to help the few teenagers who were coming out. ***Both sides sense high stakes.*** "Same-sex marriage--that's out there. But something going on in a more fierce and insidious way, under the radar, is what's happening in our schools," says Mathew Staver, president of Liberty Counsel, an influential conservative litigation group that earlier this year won a court order blocking a Montgomery County, Md., teachers' guide that disparaged Evangelicals for their views on gays. ***"They"--gay activists--"know if they make enough inroads into [schools], the same-sex-marriage battle will be moot."***[341]

The war in Iraq is just a minor skirmish compared to the all-out war being waged against us in the public school system of America. Social conservatives in America are in for certain defeat if the teachers of the NEA

---

338 "NEA Endorses Kerry for President," *USA Today*, 2005 July 2004, Http://www.usatoday.com/news/politicselections/nation/president/2004–07–05-nea-kerry_x.htm.

339 "'Teachers' Pets: The NEA Gave $65 Million in Its Members' Dues to Left-Liberal **Groups Last Year,"** ***OpinionJournal*, 2006, 1 March 2006, Http://www.opinionjournal.com/editorial/feature.html?id=110007761.**

340 Ibid.

341 Cloud, "The Battle Over Gay Teens."

and their radical, humanist friends are allowed to continue to teach America's children. Recent history shows that most children seduced into becoming sodomites are going become adults who vote pro-sodomy.

The NEA Produces Democrat Voters

Conservative Republican parents and Republican leaders need to wake up the fact that the teachers in the public school system are hell bent on making radical, socialist, humanist Democrat voters out of our children, and they are being extremely successful. As OpinionJournal puts it: "It's well understood that the NEA is an arm of the Democratic National Committee."[342] So,

> the trend is clear: according to Kevin Jennings, who in 1990 founded a gay-teacher group that later morphed into GLSEN [Gay, Lesbian, Straight Education Network] many of the kids who start GSAs identify themselves as straight. Some will later come out, of course, but Jennings believes a majority of GSA members are heterosexuals who find anti-gay rhetoric as offensive as racism. ***"We're gonna win," says Jennings, speaking expansively of the gay movement, "because of what's happening in high schools right now ... This is the generation that gets it."***[343] [Emphasis added.]

Children only find anti-gay rhetoric offensive if they are deceived about sodomy. The whole purpose of the "gay bash" claims is deception.

Federal law prohibits unions from using dues money or other assets to contribute to or otherwise assist federal candidates or political parties, in accordance with their tax-exempt status,"[344] but the NEA violates this law openly every election. Why are our Republican congressmen allowing this? Why are theists everywhere not rising up against the unholy public school of sodomy?

The Lawyers of Our Children's Teachers

The ACLU is assisting the NEA in assuring that the outcome of public education furthers the humanist plan to conquer America. The rapid establishment of the thousands of Gay Straight Alliances mentioned above was not spontaneous, but took place with zealous guidance and encouragement by the ACLU. The ACLU web site has a special section titled "Lesbian Gay Bisexual Transgender Project—Youth and Schools." The page starts out like this:

> The LGBT Project's Youth & Schools program has a ton of online information for students, but also for parents, teachers, and school administrators. Here's how to get around:
>
> "What's Your Problem?" contains information to help you better understand your rights, what steps you should take to fight back, and how we might be able to help
>
> * "Change Your School" gives you the tools you need to make your school a safer, more welcoming place for lesbian, gay, bisexual, and transgender students
> * "Library" is a huge collection of information about schools issues for LGBT youth and links to handouts, letters, and legal briefs from both the ACLU's website and elsewhere on the web
> * "Get Help" tells you how to contact us with questions about experiencing anti-gay discrimination in your school and how to find out what your rights are under the law[345]

Just as promised, the ACLU website gives "ton of information" to persuade children that they legally can and should start such clubs to protect their gay friends. A rather threatening letter from the ACLU to the school administrator is provided just in case he or she is against sodomy. A link is provided to the Gay Lesbian Straight Education Network website[346] where the student finds *The GLSEN Jump-Start Guide for Gay-Straight Alliances*, which is actually eight booklets giving detailed, step-by-step instructions concerning how to start and attract members into one of these homosexual clubs.

---

342 "'Teachers' Pets: The NEA Gave $65 Million in Its Members' Dues to Left-Liberal **Groups Last Year."**

343 Cloud, "The Battle Over Gay Teens."

344 "National Education Association," *Wikipedia*, Http://en.wikipedia.org/wiki/National_Education_Association.

345 "Lesbian Gay Bisexual Transgender Project—Schools & Youth," *ACLU*, Http://www.aclu.org/lgbt/youth/index.html.

346 "The GLSEN Jump-Start Guide for Gay-Straight Alliances," *GLSEN*, Http://www.glsen.org/cgi-bin/iowa/all/news/record/2226.html.

Folks, there is no way this Humanist sodomite movement can be stopped except by disbanding public education, and returning education to the private sector where it belongs.

Chapter 20

IS SECULAR EDUCATION POSSIBLE?

No! All Education Is Religious

Is it really possible to have non-religious, secular education? Are there actually non-religious aspects to life? Publicly and in courts of law humanists insist that schools can be completely non-religious if only theistic religion can be kept out of them. But actually they know that this is a lie—a very BIG lie. Please carefully study the following quote taken from the *Humanist Manifesto I*, for this is what Humanists actually believe:

> Religion consists of those actions, purposes, and experiences which are humanly significant. ***Nothing human is alien to the religious.*** It includes labor, art, science, philosophy, love, friendship, recreation—all that is in its degree expressive of intelligently satisfying human living. ***The distinction between the sacred and the secular can no longer be maintained.***[347] [Emphasis added.]

The founders of the American Humanist Association clearly recognized that every aspect of life is religious. So strongly did they believe this that they made it a part of their articles of faith. They declared: "Nothing human is alien to the religious." Education is human. Therefore education is religious. "The distinction between the sacred and the secular can no longer be maintained." Therefore the distinction between sacred education and secular education can no longer be maintained. The Humanists very well know that there is no such thing as secular education if by secular one means non-religious. Education can only be secular with the meaning "God is excluded." Why then do Humanists lie about it?

From the very beginning of the American Humanist Association the Humanists have intended to take over public education and use it to teach their own religious doctrines concerning God, the genesis of the universe, and the nature and origin of man. This is obvious from theses number eleven of *Humanist Manifesto I*:

> Man will learn to face the crises of life in terms of his knowledge of their naturalness and probability. ***Reasonable and manly attitudes will be fostered by education and supported by custom.*** We assume that humanism will take the path of social and mental hygiene and discourage sentimental and unreal hopes and wishful thinking.[348] [Emphasis added]

Of course what Humanists consider "reasonable and manly attitudes" cannot be fostered by education unless Humanists control the content of that education. This control they intended to capture, and in fact *have* captured. The thirteenth theses of *Humanist Manifesto I* states their goal like this:

> Religious humanism maintains that ***all*** associations and institutions exist for the fulfillment of human life. ***The intelligent evaluation, transformation, control, and direction of such associations and institutions with a view to the enhancement of human life is the purpose and program of humanism.*** Certainly religious institutions, their ritualistic forms, ecclesiastical methods, and communal activities must be reconstituted as rapidly as experience allows, in order to function effectively in the modern world.[349] [Emphasis added]

We are clearly told here that the "control" and "direction" of "all association and institutions" is "the purpose and program of humanism." That means that Humanists are working to either seize or retain control of schools, churches, government agencies, and all other institutions.

John Dewey was an atheist. He did not believe in the true and living creator God. However, he realized that he was part of a distinct minority in this regards. He knew that if he too often revealed his atheism the

---

[347] Kurtz, *Humanist Manifestos I & II*, 9.

[348] Ibid.

[349] Ibid., 9–10.

public would reject both him and his humanist philosophy of education. So in his public writings when he referred to the natural dead creation force of evolution he substituted instead the word "God." His fellow humanists knew that he actually meant "Evolution" when he wrote God, but the public was deceived. Keeping this in mind, consider the following statements Dewey made in "My Pedigodic Creed":

> I Believe that
>
> —education is the fundamental method of social progress and reform.
>
> ***
>
> —the teacher is engaged, not simply in the training of individuals, but in the formation of the proper social life.
>
> —every teacher should realize the dignity of his calling; that he is a social servant set apart for the maintenance of proper social order and the securing of the right social growth.
>
> —in this way the teacher alway is the prophet of the true God and the usherer in of the true kingdom of God.[350]

What did Dewey mean by the last amazing paragraph above? I remind you that Dewey was the first President of the American Humanist Association. His name is found on page 11 of the *Humanist Manifestos I & II* as a singer of *Humanist Manifesto I*. It is *Humanist Manifesto I* that declares,

> Religious humanists regard the universe as self-existing and not created....We are convinced that the time has passed for theism....In place of the old attitudes involved in worship and prayer the humanist finds his religious emotions expressed in a heightened sense of personal life and in a cooperative effort to promote social well-being....It follows that there will be no uniquely religious emotions and attitudes of the kind hitherto associated with belief in the supernatural.[351]

The Humanist public school teacher regards himself as a religious prophet, preaching the gospel of evolution, in order to bring in a new world order—a man-made Utopia and one-world government—based upon atheism. As *Humanist Manifesto II* puts it:

> But we can discover no divine purpose or providence for the human species. While there is much that we do not know, humans are responsible for what we are or will become. No deity will save us; we must save ourselves....We deplore the division of humankind on nationalistic grounds. We have reached a turning point in human history where the best option is to *transcend the limits of national sovereignty* and to move toward the building of a world community in which all sectors of the human family can Participate. Thus we look to the development of a system of world law and a world order based upon transnational federal government. This would appreciate cultural pluralism and diversity. It would not exclude pride in national origins and accomplishments nor the handling of regional problems on a regional basis. Human progress, however, can no longer be achieved by focusing on one section of the world, Western or Eastern, developed or underdeveloped. For the first time in human history, no part of humankind can be isolated from any other. Each person's future is in some way linked to all. We thus reaffirm a commitment to the building of world community, at the same time recognizing that this commits us to some hard choices.[352]

It is exceedingly clear, then, that the "true kingdom of God" to which Dewey referred is the very anti-thesis of the Kingdom of God referred to in the Bible. But it is also exceedingly clear that Dewey's so-called "true kingdom of God" is to be a religious kingdom, not a secular one, except in the sense of excluding the true God. It is to be a one-world atheistic religious kingdom based on the principles of Darwin's Theory of Evolution and will be ruled by a Humanist dictator. Those espousing this kingdom cannot be loyal to the USA, for their loyalty is to a different kingdom. This is another reason why Humanists are anti-patriotic and on the side of our enemies in every war.

We are forced to conclude, therefore, that there is no such thing as non-religious education. Every teacher advocates either the true and living creator God or else a pagan god. Humanists advocate a pagan god called Evolution. Evolution is what Dewey meant when he referred to "the true God." Our public schools are religious schools, and are secular only in the sense of excluding God from their classrooms. They are fiercely religious seminaries for the training of our youth in the Humanist religion. Americans had better realize and never forget this sobering fact.

---

350 John Dewey, "My Pedigodic Creed," in *John Dewey on Education*, editor Reginald D. Archamoault (New York: Random House, 1964), 437–39.

351 Kurtz, *Humanist Manifestos I & II*, 8–9.

352 Ibid., 16–21.

Chapter 21

IS SPANKING CHILD ABUSE?

No, Humanist Discipline Is Child Abuse

Another example of Religious Humanist doctrines being taught and practiced in public schools is in the field of discipline. It can best be seen if humanist discipline is contrasted with the teachings of Christianity concerning discipline.

The Word of God, the Bible, clearly states that spanking is a right and necessary form of disciplining children:

He that spareth his rod hateth his son: but he that loveth him chasteneth him betimes" (Prov 13.24).

Foolishness is bound in the heart of a child; but the rod of correction shall drive it far from him (Prov 22.15).

Withhold not correction from the child: for *if* thou beatest him with the rod, he shall not die. Thou shalt beat him with the rod, and shalt deliver his soul from hell (Prov 23.13-14).

The rod and reproof give wisdom: but a child left *to himself* bringeth his mother to shame (Prov 29.15).

Humanism says that God's Word is wrong concerning spanking. Spanking, humanists say, is child abuse. But is it really? Let us think this issue through very carefully.

Discipline Is Vital To Learning

Discipline cannot simply be ignored. Discipline is necessary in a school for learning to be able to take place. For a short time one of our children was enrolled in Moon Middle School in Oklahoma City, a school in which spanking was banned, and humanist disciplinary methods were used. The children in our child's classes were so out of control and made so much noise while the teachers were trying to teach that our child could not hear what the teachers were saying. His time spent in those classes was totally wasted. Discipline is a must for learning to take place. If we decide that God is wrong about spanking children, then some other method of discipline must be invented to take its place, and that other method will be a religious humanist method.

Humanist Discipline Is Stupid

Let's assume that a school bully has just busted your child in the face and knocked out a tooth. Let us also assume that your child is a student in the Oklahoma City school district or some other school district where "Lee Cantor's Assertive Discipline Program" is being practiced instead of God's discipline program. How is the teacher going to discipline the child that just knocked your child's tooth out? Amazingly, the teacher is not allowed to use any physical discipline whatsoever. In fact, virtually no meaningful discipline of any kind may be used by the teacher. At the very most the teacher can refer the bully to the principle to be temporally expelled—most likely to the bully's glee, since he doesn't like school anyway. What kind of justice is that!

To show you just how stupid humanist child discipline can be we need merely to examine a humanist child discipline program. Since I am most familiar with Oklahoma City public schools, we will examine Lee Cantor's Assertive Discipline Program just mentioned above, the humanist plan used in the Oklahoma City Public School District, as an example. This plan is called "Assertive Discipline" for short. I submitted the following expose of the Assertive Discipline program to all the state legislatures several years ago, shortly before a vote was to be taken on a bill which had been introduced to remove corporal punishment from public schools statewide. I also submitted this expose to several Oklahoma newspapers, thus the "Dear Editor."

Dear Editor:

For the last two years my wife and I have become increasingly alarmed at the increasing violence in the Oklahoma City public schools. Recently within a two week period our children were attacked and battered in the face by bullies in five different incidence. It just wasn't like this when we were in school, so we know it doesn't have to be this way now. Therefore, we began checking into the problem.

After talking to several teachers, three different principals, and officials at the Oklahoma City Public Schools Administrative Building at 900 N. Klien, Oklahoma City, OK 73106, we found the root of the violence to be a new discipline policy called "Assertive Discipline," which is based on principles which are clearly untrue. This policy is clearly written out in *Nanaiikana*, Vol. III, No. 6, dated January 1991 (hereafter referred to as *Nanai*), which is the school administration's newsletter to teachers. "More than a program, though, assertive discipline is an attitude, a philosophy of discipline" (*Nanai*, page 1). "Assertive Discipline is the formal district-wide discipline approach in Oklahoma City Public Schools. Two school years ago, the district established a task force on alternatives to corporal punishment.... As a result of the task force's work, corporal punishment was banned in the district" (*Nanai*, page 2). Many principals and teachers thoroughly disagree with this policy as it has tied their hands so they cannot effectively discipline disobedient students. As parents, we are concerned that "Assertive Discipline" is an atheistic approach to discipline, which will do nothing less then encourage minor offenders to continue on a road of crime. When I pointed out to one official of the Oklahoma City Public Schools Administration that the principles of "Assertive Discipline" diametrically oppose the discipline principles found in the Bible, she answered that she knew this, but because people of all faiths attend public schools Christian principles could not be used. However, such an answer is illogical, for the same principles found in the Bible and used by Christians are also found in other major religions. These are universal truths which are not the exclusive property of any one religion. Our children have to be taught according to some set of values and principles, so we may as well adopt true values and true principles, rather than atheistic ones. Benjamin Franklin's "Spare the rod and spoil the child" is as American as apple pie.

Numerous untrue principles are found in the "Assertive Discipline" plan; indeed, some statements made in that plan are absolutely absurd.

For example consider the following absurd statement: "Myth: Behavior problems are other than just symptoms.... Students who 'act up' are not a problem.... What you call problems are the results of gaps in your teaching" (*Nanai*, page 8). The fact is, students who act up are a problem, and if the teacher cannot get them under control, he or she may never have a chance to teach enough to fill in any gaps.

Another absurd statement: "Myth: There is no such thing as a trouble-maker.... Each person makes the best possible choice, 100% of the time—given the context, the perceived choices available, and the outcome desired" (*Nanai*, page 8). This is an outright denial of the concept of sin. If this is true then nothing is wrong, and thieves, rapists, and murderers are not trouble-makers and should not be punished. The truth is that "Foolishness is bound in the heart of a child; but the rod of correction shall drive it far from him" (Proverbs 22:15).

Another absurd statement: "Myth: A quiet class is a well-behaved one" (*Nanai*, page 8). In other words, a well-behaved class is noisy. The fact is that as a result of this policy some Oklahoma City public school class rooms are so noisy that students sitting toward the back of the room cannot hear what the teacher is saying. Quietness is a universally recognized virtue: "Study to be quiet, and to do your own business, and to work with your own hands, as we commanded you" (1 Thessalonians 4:11).

Another absurd statement: "If the framework you [the teacher] operate from is that it's not you, but the students, who are the cause of problems, nothing will be resolved" (*Nanai*, page 9). If this be true, than when a student hits another student in the face, it is the teacher's fault, and so the teacher should be blamed instead of the offender. Indeed, this is exactly what happens in the Oklahoma City public schools! It is the height of unfairness for a teacher or principal to punished for the evil deeds of a student they are not allowed to effectively discipline.

Another absurd statement: "Myth: Some students are out to get you. In this case 'to get you' means to annoy, pester, or foul up your class. This is absolutely false" (*Nanai*, page 9). The truth is that this statement is a spit in the face of common sense. Anyone who has ever been to school knows that there are some students who devote themselves with a stubborn and rebellious will to annoying, pestering, and fouling up every class in which they are allowed to do so.

Another absurd statement: "If your discipline is based on fear or obedience, it isn't a positive environment for your classroom" (*Nanai*, pages 5 and 6). In other words, under "Assertive Discipline" children are not taught to obey, nor are they taught to fear punishment if they disobey. Thus "Assertive Discipline" encourages rebellion and anarchy. Obedience and fear of sin's penalties are universally recognized virtues. "Obey them that have the rule over you, and submit yourselves: for they watch for your souls, as they that must give account, that they may do it with joy, and not with grief: for that *is* unprofitable for you" (Hebrews 13:17). "Wherefore now let the fear of the LORD be upon you; take heed and do *it*: for *there is* no iniquity with the LORD our God, nor respect of persons, nor taking of gifts" (2 Chronicles 19:7).

Another absurd statement: "Children will learn to internalize positive behavior choices without any kind of reinforcement" (*Nanai*, page 6). The truth is that without any kind of reinforcement children will learn to internalize *negative* behavior choices. "The rod and reproof give wisdom: but a child left *to himself* bringeth his mother to shame" (Proverbs 29:15).

It is needful to point out that "Assertive Discipline" confuses corporal punishment with abuse: "Hitting, spanking, does not teach. It humiliates" (*Nanai*, page 6). Corporal punishment is spanking on the buttocks; it's purpose is to infllct pain but not harm, so as to correct wrong, harmful behavior. Corporal punishment inflicts physical pain, so as to avoid inflicting spiritual damage; administered in love without anger (Proverbs 22.8 indicates that a rod of anger will fail), it stings the rear, instead of marring the soul; it breaks the will instead of the spirit. "Withhold not correction from the child: for *if* thou beatest him with the rod, he shall not die. Thou shalt beat him with the rod, and shalt deliver his soul from hell" (Proverbs 23.13).

To abuse is to "use with bad motives or to wrong purposes" (Webster's Dictionary). Twisting a child's ear, slapping in the face or head, twisting an arm, putting a child in a dark closet, slamming a child against lockers, hitting a child with a fist, and other such acts of violence are clearly child abuse, as they could easily cause permanent damage, both to body and soul. *Not spanking a disobedient child is another clear case of child abuse.* By not spanking a disobedient child, the parent or teacher of that child show that they do not care for—indeed even hate—that child. "He that spareth his rod hateth his son: but he that loveth him chasteneth him betimes[353]" (Proverbs 13.24).

Actual examples of how "Assertive Discipline" equals child abuse in Oklahoma City public schools will now be discussed. Since corporal punishment is banned by "Assertive Discipline," principals in Oklahoma City public schools have no effective means of disciplining children who commit acts of violence. Virtually the only means of stopping such behavior from disrupting the whole school is to expel the offender. In one school the offense of fighting (if the victim fights back) results in a 5 day suspension. Amazingly, the victim who defends himself also gets 5 days suspension! If the victim does not defend himself, the offender is suspended for 6 whole months! The principle of this school told me that he has already administered 6 months suspensions to 75 students so far this school year. This is child abuse on a grand scale! Six months education lost for 75 students, when all that they really needed was to have the board of education applied to the seat of knowledge. Six months suspension means they will surely suffer the humiliation of failing and having to repeat a class. This is child abuse in the extreme, is exceedingly unfair, and most likely will permanently damage these children's self-esteem. With six months to brood over the unfairness of this punishment and the loss of dignity involved, these students are likely to get both mad (angry) and even (revenge) by becoming professional criminals. "Provoke not your children to anger, lest they be discouraged" (Colossians 3:21). Ending up some day in jail, they will get revenge on their principal (and other taxpayers) by forcing him (and them) to pay their room and board, etc., while they lie in bed all day watching TV. The parent who does not love his child enough to discipline him with the rod, his child shall become a rod which will be used to discipline the parent. "He that spareth his rod hateth his son: but he that loveth him chasteneth him betimes" (Proverbs 13.24).

It should be pointed out that spanking is most effective on younger children. It becomes less effective as a child ages. Very light swats are generally very effective on a young child. Therefore it is a major mistake to make Kindergarten and Elementary children exempt from spankings. "Chasten thy son while there is hope, and let not thy soul spare for his crying" (Proverbs 19:18).

Of course, even corporal punishment could become child abuse if administered with a four foot long 2" x 4" board, or with a steel bar. The purpose is to break stubborn, rebellious wills, not to break bones or spirits. However, inappropriate administration of corporal punishment is not even close to as dangerous as the child abuse which results when the rod is spared. The vast majority of teachers and principals down through the years have administered the rod with genuine love and care, because they wanted to help children be successful in life. I know of not one case of a child dying or being maimed, or even suffering more than minor bruises as a result of true corporal punishment. If there ever have been such cases, they were certainly few and far between.

Experience teaches that corporal punishment works. In our parents' and grandparents' days, when corporal punishment was practiced in the home as well as the school, the schools were a safe place to be; most offenses known during those days were

---

353 Betimes means early. Discipline must be taught to a child early in his life. Once the child approaches adulthood discipline becomes more and more difficult and eventually is well neigh impossible.

in the category of throwing spit wads, or dipping a girls pig tail in the ink well. Children caught fighting were soundly spanked and put right back into class getting an education. Suspension was considered extremely severe, and was only used as a very last resort. The Oklahoma City public schools, having banned corporal punishment only two years ago, are already becoming places of violence. Because minor offenses are not punished in a manner that changes behavior, offenders proceed on to more major crimes. Students have raped and murdered in the Oklahoma City public schools during the last two years. The people who banned corporal punishment from our schools must bear the blame of our schools degenerating so.

An attempt is being made to ban corporal punishment in all schools throughout the state of Oklahoma. The state house of representatives will vote on this subject this Tuesday. The "Assertive Discipline" program presently used in the Oklahoma City schools to replace spanking is a failure, and will be a failure in other school districts as well. If spanking can be banned in schools, will it next be banned in homes? Godly people everywhere, whatever their faith be, should recognize this attempt to ban corporal punishment as an atheistic affront to values based on belief in a holy and just God who declares some things to be wrong, who demands obedience to His laws, and who punishes sinners.

It is extremely important that you phone your state representative now and express your concern that he or she vote Tuesday in support of corporal punishment. Also, it should be expressed to your representative that major moral issues like this should not be voted on by representatives, but rather should be brought to a vote of the people.

Sincerely,
Louis A. Turk

Humanist Discipline Is Child Abuse

I repeat that it is the Humanist methods of discipline that are child abuse, for their methods produce children with no self-control, and who therefore beat, murder, rob, and rape—brutally abusing others. Therefore, humanist methods of child discipline are abusive in two ways: (1) the child who misbehaves is abused by being encouraged to continue on in behavior which will surely lead him into a life of violence and/or other crimes, thus destroying his own life; and (2) innocent children are abused by being victimized by the children which are encouraged to misbehave by the knowledge that they will in no way receive physical punishment for their actions.

Dr. John Dewey, a signer of *Humanist Manifesto I* who established extremely influential teacher schools at the University of Chicago and Columbia University, was the major architect of the so-called "progressive education" which has dominated public education for decades. Dewey developed an educational philosophy based totally and unashamedly on Charles Darwin's atheistic Theory of Evolution, therefore totally rejecting God and God's plan of disciplining children. From the very beginning of Dewey's program to "reform" education wise men opposed it, as the following criticism, written in 1953, illustrates:

> It was only natural that Dewey's philosophy would be attacked by those committed to the traditional approach in education. Perhaps the most frequent criticism of progressive education has been that it placed too much emphasis upon freedom and self-expression and failed to provide the discipline necessary for the development of mind and character. The graduates of progressive schools have been widely pictured as thoroughly undisciplined and uninhibited individuals who not only do not know how to read, spell, or do mathematics, but who also do not know how to behave themselves. The children of parents who believed in Dewey's philosophy of education have been portrayed as not only a social nuisance but a real liability because of their tendency to destroy anything within reach.[354]

The Humanist systems of discipline provide no sane way to correct children for their sins against others. A thug can physically beat another child to a pulp, smashing his face and leaving him bloody and bruised, yet no physical punishment whatsoever may be administered to the thug, not even a few stinging swats on the rear. At most he will be expelled from school (which will probably make him most happy), and he will then prey on children on their way to and from school. Therefore good children are left without adult protection

---

[354] Robert F. Davidson, *Philosophies Men Live By* (New York: Dryden Press, 1953), 282.

against the violence of wicked children. And since the wicked children are not punished they are encouraged to be even more wicked. Thus our children feel forced to join gangs for their own protection. Some children bring guns to school for protection. Our schools have turned into places of terror and tyranny. All true freedom is crushed. The Humanist way of discipline is a stupid and insane path of rebellion against God.

Hooking Children on Drugs Is Child Abuse

Since banning corporal punishment from public schools, the discipline in classrooms disintegrated to such an extent that something had to be done to restore some degree of order. Did the humanists then admit that perhaps they were wrong about spanking after all? No, instead they decided to gain control over our children by drugging them. Their favorite drugs for this purpose are Ritalin and Prozac, but there are other similar drugs with the same effects—child abuse by prescription. Multiplied thousands of school children across America have been forced—often against their parents wishes—to take these very dangerous drugs.

Ritalin

Ritalin is an addictive, mood-altering drug manufactured by CIBA Pharmaceutical Company, 556 Morris Avenue, Summit, NJ 07901. Police departments will not hire anyone who has used Ritalin because of its addictive nature, and because it has the same effect as methamphetamine on adults. Thousands of children have already died as a result of using this drug. Before allowing your child to be put on Ritalin consider carefully these words from Lawrence Smith, founder of National Alliance against Mandated Mental Health Screening & Psychiatric Drugging of Children:

Mathew Smith and many other children have died from taking Ritalin. Humanists know this, yet use it insanely as a replacement for spanking. Humanists are the ultimate child abusers.

> Our fourteen year old son Matthew suddenly died on March 21, 2000. The cause of death was determined to be from the long-term (age 7-14) use of Methylphenidate, a drug commonly known as Ritalin.
>
> According to Dr. Ljuba Dragovic, the Chief Pathologist of Oakland County, Michigan, upon autopsy, Matthew's heart showed clear signs of small vessel damage caused from the use of Methylphenidate (Ritalin).
>
> *The certificate of death reads: "Death caused from Long Term Use of Methylphenidate, (Ritalin)."
>
> I was told by one of the medical examiners that a full-grown man's heart weighs about 350 grams and that Matthew's heart's weight was about 402 grams. Dr. Dragovic said this type of heart damage is smoldering and not easily detected with the standard test done for prescription refills. The standard test usually consists of blood work, listening to the heart, and questions about school behaviors, sleeping and eating habits.
>
> *What is important to note here is that Matthew did not have any pre-existing heart condition or defect.
>
> Matthew's story started in a small town within Berkley, Michigan. While in first grade Matthew was evaluated by the school, who believed he had ADHD. The school social worker kept calling us in for meetings. One morning at one of these meetings while waiting for the others to arrive, Monica told us that if we refused to take Matthew to the doctor and get him on Ritalin, child protective services could charge us for neglecting his educational and emotional needs. My wife and I were intimidated and scared. We believed that there was a very real possibility of losing our children if we did not comply with the school's threats.
>
> Monica further explained ADHD to us, stating that it was a real brain disorder. She also went on to tell us that the Methylphenidate (Ritalin) was a very mild medication and would stimulate the brain stem and help Matthew focus.

We gave into the schools pressure and took our son to a pediatrician that they recommended. His name was Dr. John Dorsey of Birmingham, Michigan. While visiting Dr. Dorsey with the schools recommendation for Methylphenidate (Ritalin) in hand, I noted that he seemed frustrated with the school. He asked us to remind the school that he was not a pharmacy. I can only conclude from his comment that we were not the first parents sent to him by this school. Dr. John Dorsey officially diagnosed Matthew with ADHD. The test used for the diagnosis was a five minute pencil twirling trick, resulting in Matthew being diagnosed with ADHD.

*It is important to note that the schools insistence and role in our son's drugging was documented in a letter written by Monica to the pediatrician stating: "We would have hoped you would have started Matthew on a trial of medication by now".

At no time were my wife and I ever told significant facts regarding the issue of ADHD and the drugs used to "treat it". These significant facts withheld from us inevitably would have changed the road that we were headed down by ultimately altering the decisions we would have made.

We were not told that The Drug Enforcement Administration had classified Methylphenidate (Ritalin) as a Schedule II drug, comparable to Cocaine.

We were not told that Methylphenidate is also one of the top ten abused prescription drugs.

At no time were we informed of the unscientific nature of the disorder.

We were not told that there was widespread controversy among the medical establishment in regards to the validity of the disorder.

Furthermore, we were not provided with information involving the dangers of using Methylphenidate (Ritalin) as "treatment" for Attention Deficit Hyperactivity Disorder. One of these dangers includes the fact that Methylphenidate, Ritalin causes constriction of veins and arteries, causing the heart to work overtime and inevitably leading to damage to the organ itself.

We were not made aware of the large number of children's deaths, that have been linked with these types of drugs used as "treatment".

While Matthew was taking Methylphenidate (Ritalin), at no time, were we informed of any test: echo-cardiogram, MRI. These types of tests could have detected the damage done to his heart. These test are not considered "standard" in monitoring "treatment" of ADHD they are usually never administered to children. Sadly death is inevitable without the possibility of detection.

*I want to ask every parent to ask themselves these important questions:

How different would your decisions be if information was withheld from you? How different would your decisions be if you receive only distorted data?

I, myself, know that our families and Matthews outcome would have been quite different had we received all information. If I had known certain facts I would have acted differently and my son would be alive today. This I am sure of.

Informed Consent, "which states in part a person's agreement to allow something to happen (such as surgery) that is based on a full disclosure of the facts needed to make the decision intelligently; i.e. knowledge of risks involved, alternatives etc" and "the probable risks against the probable benefits."

The violation of parent's rights is when they are not told of the unscientific nature of so-called disorders such as ADHD or the risks of the treatments involving drugs like Ritalin, and they certainly are not told of alternatives to their child's behavior such as undiagnosed allergies or food sensitivities, which could manifest with the symptoms of what psychiatry calls ADHD.

*Here are some facts that are being withheld from parents that could possibly alter their life decisions and outcomes.

Did you know that schools receive additional money from state and federal government for every child labeled and drugged? This clearly demonstrates a possible "financial incentive" for schools to label and drug children. It also backs up the alarming rise/increase in the labeling and drugging that has taken place in the last decade within our schools.

Did you know that parents receiving welfare money from the government can get additional funds for every child that they have labeled and drugged? In this way, many lower socio-economic parents (many times single mothers) are reeled into the drugging by these financial incentives waved in front of them in hard times, making lifestyle changes possible.

Did you know that by labeling your child with ADHD, you are actually labeling them with a mental illness listed in the DSM-IV, the unscientific billing bible for psychiatry?

Did you know that a child taking a psycho-tropic, psycho-stimulant drugs like Ritalin after the age of 12 is ineligible for military service?

Did you know that the subjective checklists that are being used as criteria for diagnosis are very similar to the checklists used to determine Gifted and Talented Children? These two checklists are almost identical.

The Drug Enforcement Administration clearly states in their report on Methylphenidate: "However, contrary to popular belief, stimulants like methylphenidate will affect normal children and adults in the same manner that they affect ADHD children. Behavioral or attentional improvements with methylphenidate treatment therefore is not diagnostic of ADHD." (p.11) This statement thoroughly contradicts what is being told to many parents by the many "professionals" that have a vested stake in the diagnosis itself.

The DEA further states that: "Of particular concern is that most of the ADHD literature prepared for public consumption by CHADD and other groups and available to parents, does not address the abuse potential or actual abuse of methylphenidate. Instead, methylphenidate (usually referred to as Ritalin by these groups) is routinely portrayed as a benign, mild substance that is not associated with abuse or serious side effects. In reality, however, there is an abundance of scientific literature which indicates that methylphenidate shares the same abuse potential as other Schedule II stimulants." (p.4)

Did you know that groups like CHADD and others available to parents are being supported financially by pharmaceutical companies? This is a red flag and demonstrates a conflict of interest in the role that these groups have regarding our children's health and well-being.

Did you know that there are studies such as the Berkeley Study that contends that Ritalin and other stimulants further raise the risk of drug abuse? From the Wall Street Journal, Monday, May 17, 1999 by Marilyn Chase: "Nadine Lambert, a professor of education, followed almost 500 children for 26 years. She argues that exposure to Ritalin makes the brain more susceptible to the addictive power of cocaine and doubles the risk of abuse." This study seems to never make it into the hands of parents because it doesn't support the theories of those using the diagnosis to profit off of our children. What does seem to make it into many parents' hands is research indicating that if children go "untreated", which corresponds with "unmedicated" they will "self-medicate" or end up as juvenile delinquents. Sadly many of these parents are not aware that many of this biased and unproven research (one such is the Beiderman study) infiltrating our schools are actually being distributed by pharmaceutical companies, such as Novartis. This in itself is another red flag and conflict of interest surrounding our children's health.

I leave you with this question: How many more 11 year old Stephanie Hall's, 14 year old Matthew Smith's and 10 year old Shaina Dunkle's need to die before we realize what is happening and speak out and act to put an end to it? One toy might be recalled if 1 or 2 children die from it. How many children have to die from these drugs before we realize and put an end to this horror. Why should hundreds or thousands have to die before we are outraged and act? Is the profit of so many, worth more than our children's safety and lives? Sadly the deaths of these children have remained unexposed and suppressed for so long because there is a tremendous amount of money and profit at stake for so many.[355]

If we really love children we will take action now to prevent humanists from continuing to abuse them.

Prozac

BusinessWeek magazine quotes Thomas J. Moore, author of ***PRESCRIPTION FOR DISASTER: the Hidden Dangers in Your Medicine Cabinet*** as warning that Prozac "was associated with more hospitalizations, deaths, or other serious adverse reactions reported to the FDA than any other drug in America."[356] Did you catch that? Prozac is perhaps the most dangerous prescription drug there is! And humanists want to give it to your child. Doesn't that alarm you?

According to the official Prozac web site maintained by Eli Lilly and Company, the makers of Prozac,

> PROZAC contains fluoxetine hydrochloride, the same ingredient as found in Prozac® Weekly™, Sarafem®, and generic versions of PROZAC. . . . In clinical studies, antidepressants increased the risk of suicidal thinking and behavior in children and adolescents with depression and other psychiatric disorders. Anyone considering the use of PROZAC or any other antidepressant in a child or adolescent must balance this risk with the clinical need. Patients who are starting therapy should be observed closely. Families and caregivers should discuss with the doctor any observations of worsening depression symptoms, suicidal thinking and behavior, or unusal changes in behavior. . . . Some people experience side effects like nausea, difficulty sleeping, drowsiness, anxiety, nervous-

---

[355] Lawrence Smith, "Our 14-Year-Old Son Died from Ritalin Use," *National Alliance Against Mandated Mental Health Screening & Psychiatric Drugging of Children*, Http://www.ritalindeath.com/index.htm.

[356] Naomi Freundlich, "When the Cure May Make You Sicker," *BusinessWeek Online*, 1916 March 1998, 14, Http://www.businessweek.com/archives/1998/b3569025.arc.htm?campaign_id=search.

ness, weakness, loss of appetite, tremors, dry mouth, sweating, decreased sex drive, impotence, or yawning. ... PROZAC can cause changes in sexual desire or satisfaction. Do not drive a car or operate dangerous machinery until you know what effects PROZAC may have on you. Contact your doctor or healthcare professional if you get a rash or hives, or other side effects that concern you while taking PROZAC.[357]

The fact that this extremely dangerous drug is given to children who need nothing more than a simple spanking shows just how insane and abusive humanist forms of discipline are.

Spanking Works

That spanking works is easily seen by going back in history to the time when spanking was the principle method of discipline. Spanking produced men and women of high self-discipline and character. Rape and murder were virtually unheard of in the schools of that time. God's method is a historically proven method. God's method works.

Spanking Is a Religious Method of Discipline

In 1989, after much lobbying by humanist groups, the school board of the Oklahoma City Public School District voted to ban corporal punishment. Immediately the violence skyrocketed. My children were repeatedly being beaten by bullies and by gangs. When I approached the administration of the Oklahoma City school district to protest the lack of physical discipline in our schools (and thus lack of protection for my children), they said they could not practice corporal punishment because that was a Christian practice, and was therefore a violation of the principle of separation of church and state.

That spanking is taught by the Bible—and is therefore a religious teaching and practice—is obviously true. But since some religion's discipline method will be practiced, the best method should be chosen.

Non-Spanking Discipline Is Also Religious

If spanking violates the concept of separation of church and state, then so do humanist methods of discipline. By using non-spanking methods of discipline, the public schools are practicing the disciplinary methods of the Unitarian-Universalist Church.

Most people in the US claim to be Christian. But the public schools are practicing the disciplinary methods of a non-Christian pagan religion on our children. Thus, what we teach and practice in our homes is being contradicted in the schools. This is highly offensive to Christians who hold the Bible to be the Word of God, for it is forcing non-Christian religious practices upon our children—practices which most certainly are child abuse. To paraphrase the Bible, schools that spare the rod hate children.

One More Major Problem

Having said all the above, there is one other major issue which needs to be discussed. This discipline problem is even more complicated than it first appears, for many things have changed in the USA.

Due to the influence of Humanist administrators, many public schools are giving sodomites first choice of teaching jobs. This has resulted in the skyrocketing of sexual molestation of students by teachers.

Such teachers are not of the proper character to be disciplining our children, for they could easily use the threat of discipline to force defenseless students into immorality with them. For example a pedophile teacher could use the threat of spanking to intimidate a child into allowing himself to be raped.

Also, a teacher that will drug a child to discipline him does not have the character needed to properly administer corporal punishment or any other form of discipline.

So it is not wise to let just anyone spank our children or grandchildren. Naughty children sometimes need to be spanked, but we parents should not delegate that responsibility to wicked pagans who might misuse spanking to abuse our children. There is only one solution to this dilemma, and it will be discussed later on in this book.

Chapter 22

WHAT IS SEPARATION OF CHURCH AND STATE?

The Answer Is the Key To Victory!

This is the most important chapter in this book because understanding the truth about separation of church and state reveals the key—the ONLY key—to disempowering humanism. Humanism can certainly be removed from control of education in this country if theists understand the truth about separation of church and state, and then act upon that truth. There is tremendous confusion concerning this subject, so please read this chapter carefully several times. This long chapter, shows how humanists used misconceptions about separation of church and state to gain and retain control of education in America.

The First Amendment

The First Amendment makes it possible for people of different religions to live together in peace. Its purpose is to assure absolute freedom of religion for people of ***all*** religions. The forty-five vital words all Americans must understand if they want their children to inherit freedom are:

> Congress shall make no law respecting an establishment of religion, or prohibiting the free exercise thereof; or abridging the freedom of speech, or of the press; or the right of the people peaceably to assemble, and to petition the government for a redress of grievances.

The First Amendment is like a coin—it has two sides—, but those two sides are inseparable. You cannot have one side without having the other. The two sides or aspects of this freedom-giving amendment are:

Congress Shall Make No Law Respecting an Establishment of Religion

"Congress shall make **no law** respecting an establishment of religion" means just that. Congress is forbidden to make any "law"—not even one law is allowed—pertaining to an establishment of religion. This means that the government has no authority to determine which religion or church is the true religion or church, because to do that a "law" would have to be made. The government is forbidden to establish or recognize one church or religion as the state church or religion, because that also would require making a "law." The government may not financially support any religion, because that would require a "law" being made to authorize spending the money. The government may not tax any religion, because that would require making a tax "law."

The purpose of this clause of the First Amendment was to prevent the religious oppression that minority religions suffered at the hands of the state religions in England and Europe, and even in the colonies at their beginnings. A church or religion may not become the civil government; for then it would have armed soldiers at its command to force its beliefs upon people of other religions against their will.

It is important to understand that First Amendment originally applied only to the federal government. Most of the states still had an established religion. Congress was not allowed to make any law pertainging to those established state religions. It could not take sides. It could not regulate them in any way. It could not stop them from influences politics.

One other important point about the establishment clause needs to be noticed. "Congress shall make no law respecting **an establishment** of religion." Congress does have authority to make laws respecting religion; just not laws respecting **an establishment** of religion." In fact, every law is a religious law. Even the Humanists acknowledged this in section seven of their Humanist Manifesto I:

> Nothing human is alien to the religious. It includes labor, art, science, philosophy, love, friendship, recreation -- all that is in its degree expressive of intelligently satisfying human living. The distinction between the sacred and the secular can no longer be maintained.[1]

Of course, Humanists deny that this is true when they are trying to influence the courts. Then they say that only that which pertains to belief in God is religious, and that beliefs based on atheism are "science." Sure! Their beliefs are science like Scientology and Christian Science are science. They are scientists like Anaximander (611-547 B.C.) was a scientist. He believed that eels and various other aquatic animals were produced without parents from lifeless matter in the abiogenetic fashion. If you want to call superstition science, then humanism fits that definition well. But in truth, Humanism is a religion, and is not true science. However, even true science is religious; everything has religious significance.

Government May Not Prohibit the Free Exercise of Any Religion

This means that government may not tax religions, for by taxing them they would be prohibited from free exercise. Church funds are to be totally separate from government funds, not combined into government funds.

This also means that the government may not financially support religions, for whatever the government supports the government of necessity controls; the government cannot pass out money without restriction. Qualifications have to be set, and those qualifications would prevent the free exercise of all religions that would not qualify. The members of these religions would be taxed, but their religion excluded from benefiting from those taxes. Therefore, whoever determines what qualifications must be met would determine the official religion for the state.

Freedom of speech, freedom to distribute printed matter, freedom to assemble, and freedom to tell the government you don't like what it is doing are all necessary for people to freely exercise their religious beliefs.

There is an exception to this free exercise clause, however. A religion that requires the violent overthrow of the government as part of its free exercise or that requires its advocates to exercise violence against people of other religions in order to prevent free exercise of those religions has declared war against freedom and against civilization and must bear the consequences of its actions. The government must intervene to protect its citizens. That is governments reason for existing.

> For rulers are not a terror to good works, but to the evil. Wilt thou then not be afraid of the power? do that which is good, and thou shalt have praise of the same: for he is the minister of God to thee for good. But if thou do that which is evil, be afraid; for he beareth not the sword in vain: for he is the minister of God, a revenger to execute wrath upon him that doeth evil. (Romans 13:3)

It is the business and duty of government to terrorize terrorists. Churches should not have to protect themselves from terrorists. That is the duty of civil government.

Public Schools Violate the First Amendment

The free exercise of religion is prohibited in public schools—Bible reading and prayer are prohibited. Freedom of speech is abridged—evolution must be taught, but its fallacies may not be pointed out, nor may creation by God be taught. There is no freedom of the press in public schools: religious pamphlets that honor God are prohibited from being distributed even in the halls, and even when purchased with private funds; but materials that teach the atheistic doctrines of the humanist religion are bought at taxpayer

---

1 Kurtz, *Humanist Manifestos I & II.*

expense and used as curriculum. Freedom is dead in public schools. The First Amendment is ignored and violated. Our government has ruled that the unproven religious teachings of the Humanist religion are not religious but are in fact science and must be taught as fact, but the teachings of Christianity are not science and can only be taught as myths. The Unitarian-Universalist/Humanist Church is established in public schools, and is using powers of state to force its teachings upon our children in total disregard to the wishes of parents and children alike. Billions of dollars of tax money are being used to teach our children religious lies. The Humanist minority rules over us with a rod of iron.

Phony Separation of Church and State

Humanists advocate a ***phony*** separation of church and state which denies freedom of speech to all religions except their own. They have defined the word "church" in separation of church and state to include only churches that worship God. They exclude from their definition pagan churches such as the Unitarian-Universalist Church and the Humanist Ethical Unions and other humanist churches (no matter what their names) which worship man (and, in reality, Satan) instead of God.

An example of this phoniness: on Thursday evening April the 15th 1993 the author of this book heard talk show host Dave Marshall on Oklahoma City's KTOK News Radio 1000 interview Barry Lynn of Americans United for Separation of Church and State. Both Marshall and Lynn vigorously promoted the idea that prayer should be banned from all public school events because it violated the principle of church and state. Lynn said that the founding fathers of this country intended for religion to be excluded from state affairs. Many Christians called in to protest Lynn's position. One man pointed out to Lynn that even our money bears the motto "In God We Trust." Nevertheless, Lynn was able to make most of the Christian callers look wrong and foolish. He made them look like oppressors of minority religions—like they were trying to *force* their Christianity upon non-Christians—***when in fact humanists themselves are forcing their atheistic humanist religion on everyone else in the public school system of America***. That was years ago, but up to now the Humanists continue to successfully use Christians' ignorance of the concept of separation of church and state to the advantage of humanism.

What is so ironic about this is that Americans United for Separation of Church and State is a Humanist organization, and its main purpose is to assure that the Humanist religion remains the state church of the USA so that Humanists can continue to receive billions of tax dollars to teach their wicked religion in public schools.

Is Separation of Church and State a Myth?

The very arguments Humanists use to keep Christian principles out of public schools could be used against the Humanists to disempower them—if only Christians understood the truth about Humanism and the truth about separation of church and state. What then prevents Christians from using these arguments to free themselves from Humanist tyranny? The sad fact is that many Christian writers have been denying that the First Amendment means separation of church and state. These writers teach that it is alright for the church to be combined with the state as long as that church is their ecumenical brand of Christianity. These writers declare that the principle of separation of church and state is a myth created by the humanist movement to keep God out of government and out of public schools. Here is a quote from such a writer:

> Anytime religion is mentioned within the confines of government today people cry, "Separation of Church and State". Many people think this statement appears in the first amendment of the U.S. Constitution and therefore must be strictly enforced. However, the words: "separation", "church", and "state" do not even appear in the first amendment. . . .
>
> The reason Jefferson choose the expression "separation of church and state" was because he was addressing a Baptist congregation; a denomination of which he was not a member. Jefferson wanted to remove all fears that the state would make dictates to

the church. He was establishing common ground with the Baptists by borrowing the words of Roger Williams, one of the Baptist's own prominent preachers. Williams had said:

"When they have opened a gap in the hedge or wall of separation between the garden of the Church and the wilderness of the world, God hath ever broke down the wall itself, removed the candlestick, and made his garden a wilderness, as at this day. And that there fore if He will eer please to restore His garden and paradise again, it must of necessity be walled in peculiarly unto Himself from the world..."

The "wall" was understood as one-directional; its purpose was to protect the church from the state. The world was not to corrupt the church, yet the church was free to teach the people Biblical values.

The American people knew what would happen if the State established the Church like in England. . . . England went so far as forbidding worship in private homes and sponsoring all church activities and keeping people under strict dictates. They were forced to go to the state established church and do things that were contrary to their conscience. No other churches were allowed, and mandatory attendance of the established church was compelled under the Conventicle Act of 1665. Failure to comply would result in imprisonment and torture. The people did not want freedom from religion, but freedom of religion. **The only real reason to separate the church from the state would be to instill a new morality and establish a new system of beliefs.** Our founding fathers were God-fearing men who understood that for a country to stand it must have a solid foundation; the Bible was the source of this foundation. They believed that God's ways were much higher than Man's ways and held firmly that the Bible was the absolute standard of truth and used the Bible as a source to form our government. . . . Since the Supreme Court has said that Secular Humanism is a religion, why is it being allowed to be taught in schools? The removal of public prayer of those who wish to participate is, in effect, establishing the religion of Humanism over Christianity. This is exactly what our founding fathers tried to stop from happening with the first amendment.[2] [Boldface emphasis added.]

There is much truth in the above article! However, his central theme—that the First Amendment does not mean separation of church and state—is untrue and self-defeating. Note the sentence in boldface which reads, "The only real reason to separate the church from the state would be to instill a new morality and establish a new system of beliefs." **That sentence shows that its author does not want his version of Christianity separated from the state; instead he wants it to be the state.**

Also, the statement that "The 'wall' was understood as one-directional; its purpose was to protect the church from the state. The world was not to corrupt the church, yet the church was free to teach the people Biblical values" is simply not true. The wall was also to keep the church from becoming the state and imposing its religious views upon others against their will. Of course the Christian churches (and non-Christian religions also) are to be free to teach people their values, but only with their consent. People are not to be forced to learn, as is the case when religious ideas are taught in public schools.

Most writers who are against separation of church and state are hoping to make their own church the state church. In some cases they will boldly state that they are working toward America becoming a "theocratic state." It is not actually God they want to rule, however, but the leaders of their denomination.[3] What they actually want is to deny free speech to everyone but themselves, and that is exactly what the First Amendment was designed to prevent. Also, as will be shown later in this chapter, Jesus did not teach that his church should become the government, but rather that his church should be separate from civil governments.

Another important fact that needs to be pointed out is that not all churches claiming to be Christian are truly Christian. Some Christian churches believe that God is a Trinity; others deny this. Some believe that Jesus is both God and the Son of God; others deny this. Some believe that Heaven and Hell are literal places; others deny this. Some believe that Jesus is the sinless, virgin-born Savior; others deny this. Some believe that Jesus died on the cross for our sins; others deny this. Some believe Jesus literally

---

2 "The Myth of Separation of Church and State," Http://www.noapathy.org/tracts/mythofseparation.html.

3 Some of these writers will deny this, insisting that they are for a non-denominational Christian religion to be the state church. But a "non-denominational" church is just a new denomination with a deceptive name.

arose bodily from the grave after three days and three nights; others deny this. Some believe that salvation is by grace through faith, not of works; others believe that it is by works. Some believe that baptism is only for believers, and must be by immersion; others believe that baptism is also for babies, and that sprinkling is sufficient. Some believe that the main day of worship is Sunday; others say it should be Saturday. If two beliefs contradict each other they cannot both be true; someone is not interpreting the Bible correctly. So, clearly, what Christian values and beliefs are to be taught to the world is a subject of great disagreement. The lies of false Christianity are just as wrong and destructive as the lies of Humanism.

This is another reason that freedom of speech is so important: somewhere among all the different teachings, the truth is found. Most people of all these contradictory religions sincerely believe that their beliefs are correct. So, it is obviously possible to be sincerely wrong. But the truth is light that exposes error. Therefore, no religion should be allowed to prevent people of other religions from exercising free speech. Let the issues be freely debated by all the religions with no fear of violence or punishment by government, and along with falsehoods the truth will be presented to everyone. Of course, some will still reject the truth, but the truth will still be presented to the public so that people at least have opportunity to receive it.

To teach that separation of church and state is a myth is a HUGE mistake for another reason also—it unnecessarily confuses and divides Christians on the issue, thereby enabling humanists to remain in control of our children's education. The fact is, Baptists were using the phrase "separation of church and state" to mean "freedom **of** religion" (not "separation **from** religion") long before the First Amendment. For proof simply reread the above article! As its author admits, when Thomas Jefferson spoke of building "a wall of separation between Church and State" he was borrowing words from the Baptists. Separation of church and state has been a Baptist distinctive down through history. In the words of a well-known Baptist historian:

> I venture to give one more distinguishing mark [of a true Baptist church]. We will call it—Complete separation of Church and State. No combination, no mixture of this spiritual religion with a temporal power. "Religious Liberty," for everybody.[4]

Furthermore, that is the meaning many (if not most) Baptists and many others still give the phrase today. Whether anyone likes it or not, this is not likely to change any time soon. Just because the humanists are abusing the phrase doesn't mean that the phrase itself is wrong or a myth. **Why argue over the origin or meaning of this phrase when the real issue is that the humanist religion has unConstitutionally become the established state church of America?**

THE FACT THAT MUST BE FOCUSED ON IS THAT THE HUMANIST CHURCH IS <u>NOT</u> SEPARATE FROM THE STATE, BUT HAS INSTEAD BEEN COMBINED WITH THE STATE AND ESTABLISHED AS THE STATE CHURCH. That illegal union must be relentlessly exposed publicly with great zeal until the Humanist church is totally disestablished. This is the key to getting Humanists out of power. It will not be accomplished without a great fight. But it can and must be done. And there is no other way.

Are Prayer and Bible Reading Main Issues?

Bible reading and prayer should be in every school in which we theists enroll our children. But working to return Bible reading and prayer to pubic schools is a huge mistake, and is based on a terrible misunderstanding of the true nature of public schools. Until theists (especially Christians) wake up to the true nature of public schools, these issues will continue to divide us, and without unity we are going to remain defeated. Bible reading and prayer are the bait Humanists are using to keep us securely in their trap.

Here is how these two issues divide. First of all, as long as these two issues are our battle cry the Jews, Muslims, Hindus, Buddhists, those of other non-Christian religions, and many Christians are going to join with the Humanists to defeat us. Why? Because none of the non-Christian religions pray like Christians do. Muslims exalt the form of praying over the words, and pray toward Mecca to Allah, not to the Jehovah of Christianity. Jews do not pray in Jesus' name. Hindus pray to many gods. And both Hindus and Buddhists

---

4 J.M. Carroll, *The Trail of Blood* (Lexington, Kentucky: Ashland Avenue Baptist Church, 1931), 15, Http://www.biblepreaching.com/trailofblood.html.

pray to idols using incense. Furthermore, many Christians disagree with the wording of other Christians' prayers.

The Bible reading issue also divides and weakens us. Muslims use the Quran, not the Bible, and believe the Christian Bible to be a counterfeit. Hindus and Buddhists also reject the Bible. So again, all of these people are going to vote with the Humanists if this is made an issue. Furthermore, Christians are also deeply divided over the Bible. For instance, what translation of the Bible will be read? The King James Version of 1611? The Catholic Bible? The New International Version? Good News For Modern Man? The New World translation of the Jehovah Witnesses? What translation to use is a major issue that has deeply divided Christianity. Many Christians will absolutely not compromise on this issue even an inch.

Since these two issues keep Christians, Muslims, Hindus, Buddhists, and other theistic religions from uniting against atheism, it is easy to see why Humanists are flaunting their position on these issues so boldly and publicly. These are two of three baits they are effectively using to keep theists in their trap. Reviewing some history is necessary to be able to recognize the third bait.

History of Separation of church and State

It is important to know and accept the fact that there have always been and always will be people advocating their religion as the state religion. Communism is the state religion of China, Russia, Korea, and Cuba. To make Islam the state religion of the world is the goal of Islamic jihad. To become the state religion is also the goal of many church groups that claim to be Christian. While it is true that most of America's forefathers belonged to some form of Christian church, it is not true that all of the founders of this country were wise and spiritual men who wanted freedom of religion. In their days, there was a clash of cultures and beliefs between the different church groups and also between the church groups and atheists and deists, just as there is now.

Much has been written lately about how the humanists are rewriting (changing) history books. Humanists *are*, in fact, rewriting history in an effort to cover up truths that are very detrimental to their movement. However, it is also true that some of the "Christian" groups are covering up embarrassing facts of history, and in so doing they are also strengthening the Humanists' position. Truth does not need to be—and cannot be—defended by lies or by covering up unpleasant facts. Truth just needs to be proclaimed. Mistakes need to be admitted and repented of. In John 8:32, Jesus said: "If ye continue in my word, then are ye my disciples indeed; and ye shall know the truth, and the truth shall make you free." Notice that people must *know* the truth before the truth can make them free. If we would be free from the tyranny of the Humanist religion, we must spread the truth about separation of church and state to every family in America until the USA has regained her freedom. To do this, we ourselves must know the truth.

From Columbus to the First Amendment

While it is true that many[5] of the settlers of the thirteen colonies came to America seeking freedom of religion, in most cases it was only freedom for their *own* church that they sought. They granted no freedom to members of other churches. Most of the colonies established state churches supported by taxation at their very beginnings. In Massachusetts the state church was the Congregational church of the Puritans. In Virginia the state church was the Church of England. In New York it was the Dutch Reformed Church. These state churches all oppressed those of other religious beliefs. People were forced by taxation to support the church-state schools of whatever colony they lived in. People not of the state religion were often fined, beaten, jailed, or banished.

An example: Roger Williams was banished from the Massachusetts Bay Colony because of his Baptist religious beliefs.

---

[5] Certain not all of the settlers were seeking freedom of religion. Some were extremely wicked men—slave traders in some cases—whose only purpose in coming to America was money. They were motivated by pure greed and nothing else.

Banishment in America in those days was something desperately serious. it meant to go and live among the Indians. In this case Williams was received kindly and for quite a while lived among the Indians, and after days proved a great blessing to the colony which had banished him. He saved the colony from destruction by this same tribe of Indians, by his earnest entreaties in their behalf. In this way he returned good for evil.[6]

Another example, also in Massachusetts:

On one occasion one of John Clarke's members was sick. The family lived just across the Massachusetts Bay Colony line and just inside that colony. John Clarke, himself, and a visiting preacher by the name of Crandall and a layman by the name of Obediah Holmes—all three went to visit that sick family. While they were holding some kind of a prayer service with that sick family, some officer or officers of the colony came upon them and arrested them and later carried them before the court for trial. It is also stated, that in order to get a more definite charge against them, they were carried into a religious meeting of their church (Congregationalist), their hands being tied (so the record states). The charge against them was "for not taking off their hats in a religious service." They were all tried and convicted. Gov. Endicott was present. In a rage he said to Clarke, while the trial was going on, "You have denied infants baptism" (this was not the charge against them). "You deserve death. I will not have such trash brought into my jurisdiction." The penalty for all was a fine, or be well-whipped. Crandall's fine (a visitor) was five pounds ($25.00), Clarke's fine (the pastor) was twenty pounds ($100.00). Holmes' fine (the records say he had been a Congregationalist and had joined the Baptists) so his fine was thirty pounds ($.00). Clark's and Crandall's fines were paid by friends. Holmes refused to allow his fine paid, saying he had done no wrong, so was well whipped. The record states that he was "stripped to the waist" and then whipped (with some kind of a special whip) until the blood ran down his body and then his legs until his shoes overflowed. The record goes on to state that his body was so badly gashed and cut that for two weeks he could not lie down, so his body could touch the bed. His sleeping had to be done on his hands or elbows and knees. Of this whipping and other things connected with it I read all records, even Holmes' statement. A thing could hardly have been more brutal. And here in America![7]

So, how did the First Amendment come to be written? Was it because of no reason at all that the various founders of our country decided that America should become the first nation in history to guarantee absolute freedom of religion for everyone? Thinking people realize that that could not possibly have been the case. There were reasons—at least two major reasons—that they ratified this monumental amendment. First of all,

None of the Established Churches Formed a Majority

In their respective colonies where they were established the members of the state churches were the majority of the population. However, in the new nation at large none of theses churches were a majority. This did not mean that these established state churches of the colonies did not want to become the established church for the new nation. That is exactly what they badly wanted, and tried unsuccessfully to obtain.

Congress declared the first amendment to the Constitution to be in force December 15, 1791, which granted religious liberty to all citizens, Baptists are credited with being the leaders in bringing this blessing to the nation. . . . We venture to give one early Congressional incident. The question of whether the United States should have an established church or several established churches, or religious liberty, was being discussed. Several different bills had been offered, one recommending the Church of England as the established church; and another the Congregationalist Church, and yet another the Presbyterian. The Baptists, many of them, though probably none of them members of Congress, were earnestly contending for absolute religious liberty. James Madison (afterwards President) seemingly was their main supporter. Patrick Henry arose and offered a substitute bill for them all, "That four churches (or denominations) instead of one be established"—the Church of England, or Episcopal, Congregationalist, Presbyterian, and the Baptist. Finally when each of the others saw that IT could not be made the sole established church, they each

---

6 Carroll, *Trail of Blood*, 58–59.

7 Ibid., 60–61.

> agreed to accept Henry's compromise. (This compromise bill stated that each person taxed would have the right to say to which denomination of these four his money should go.) The Baptists continued to fight against it all; that any combination of Church and State was against their fundamental principles, that they could not accept it even if voted. Henry pleaded with them, said he was trying to help them, that they could not live without it, but they still protested. The vote was taken—it carried nearly unanimously. But the measure had to be voted on three times. The Baptists, led by Madison and possibly others continued to fight. The second vote came. It also carried almost unanimously, swept by Henry's masterful eloquence. But the third vote had yet to be taken. Now God seemingly intervened. Henry was made Governor of Virginia and left Congress. When the third vote came, deprived of Henry's irresistible eloquence, the vote was lost.
>
> Thus the Baptists came near being an established denomination over their own most solemn protest. This is not the only opportunity the Baptists ever had of becoming established by law, but is probably the nearest they ever came to it.[8]

Patrick Henry no doubt meant well, but his plan would never have succeeded. When a state religion is allowed, one religion will always push the others out, and will rule. That, by the way, is the case today—the Humanist religion rules.

The second reason the First Amendment was ratified is because

Separation of Church and State Had a Champion

Baptists relentlessly pushed for absolute freedom of religion for everyone. Down through the centuries from the days of John the Baptist, Baptists have taught that no one can be converted to Christ against his will, that belief in Christ cannot be forced, that a man converted against his will is of the same opinion still.

Actually, the First Amendment was the second time in history that religious liberty was tried. The first time was in Rhode Island.

> Roger Williams, later, together with others, some of whom, at least, had also been banished from that and other of the colonies among whom was John Clarke, a Baptist preacher, decided to organize a colony of their own. As yet they had no legal authority from England to do such a thing, but they thought this step wiser under existing conditions than to attempt to live in existing colonies with the awful religious restrictions then upon them. So finding a small section of land as yet unclaimed by any existing colony they proceeded to establish themselves on that section of land now known as Rhode Island. That was in the year 1638, ten years later than the Massachusetts Bay Colony, but it was about 25 years later (1663) before they were able to secure a legal charter.
>
> In the year 1651 (?) Roger Williams and John Clarke were sent by the colony to England to secure, if possible legal permission to establish their colony. When they reached England, Oliver Cromwell was in charge of the government, but for some reason he failed to grant their request. Roger Williams returned home to America. John Clarke remained in England to continue to press his plea. Year after year went by. Clarke continued to remain. Finally Cromwell lost his position and Charles II sat upon the throne of England. While Charles is regarded in history as one of the bitterest of persecutors of Christians, he finally, in 1663, granted that charter. So Clarke, after 12 long years of waiting returned home with that charter. So in 1663, the Rhode Island colony became a real legal institution, and the Baptists could write their own constitution.
>
> That Constitution was written. It attracted the attention of the whole wide world. In that Constitution was the world's first declaration of "Religious Liberty."
>
> The battle for absolute religious liberty even in America alone is a great history within itself. For a long time the Baptists seem to have fought that battle entirely alone, but they did not fight it for themselves alone, but for all peoples of every religious faith. Rhode Island, the first Baptist colony, established by a small group of Baptists after 12 years of earnest pleading for permission was the first spot on earth where religious liberty was made the law of the land. The settlement was made in 1638; the colony legally established in 1663.[9]

---

8 Ibid., 64–65.

9 Ibid., 59–60.

America owes a great debt to Baptists for taking the lead in opposing the formation of a tax-supported federal state church during the time leading up to the First Amendment.

> The colonists, whom generations of schoolchildren have learned came for religious freedom, came for a very narrow kind of freedom. With rare exceptions, such as the Baptist followers of Roger Williams in Rhode Island, the colonists came seeking religious freedom for themselves and the right to persecute—or at least banish—anyone who did not share the colony's faith.[10]
>
> Roger William and the Baptists who founded Rhode Island actually spoke as if they believed in religious freedom for all, although for this they were widely distrusted by most of the other colonists who shared what fast became British North America with them.[11]

Aggressive Baptist leadership resulted in the First Amendment to the Constitution. But this achieved religious liberty ***only at the federal level***.

From the First Amendment To the First Public School

Most people do not realize that the First Amendment originally only applied to the federal level of government.

Established Churches Still Existed on the State Level

On the state level the established Protestant churches were still funded by taxes and abused those of other religions, including those of other Protestant denominations. Their schools were also supported by tax money, and they controlled the content of education. There was still no separation of church and state on the state level except in Rhode Island.

> The most sustained post-revolutionary fight over the separation of church and state took place in Connecticut early in the nineteenth century. An alliance of Baptists, Methodists, Anglicans, Jeffersonian Democrats, and others began to challenge that states Congregational establishment. Although Connecticut had long since stopped any form of legal discrimination against other religious groups, the Congregational clergy and lay leaders fought back, seeking to maintain their state financial subsidies and their recognized rank as the "official" religion of the state. Finally, in 1818, they lost and the Congregational Church in Connecticut was officially disestablished, joining the other denominations as an equal partner, dependent as the others were on the voluntary contributions of its own members rather than state tax revenue. It took more than a decade for the two remaining holdouts, Massachusetts and New Hampshire, to follow the Connecticut model, but once Connecticut had fallen, the fight went out of the Congregational leadership and it was only a matter of time before they all gave in.[12]

The significance of this continuing church establishment after the First Amendment is that the established churches really never accepted their disestablishment on either the federal or state levels, and that fact continues to this day. They fought disestablishment on the state level until the bitter end. It took relentless pressure on the state legislatures from the minority churches to accomplish their disestablishment. To this day those disestablished Protestant churches are fighting to regain their position as the official state church. The so-called "Faith-based Inititive" is evidence of this fight.

In fact, as will be seen in the next section of this chapter, they did soon regain establishment for a long period of time in many of the states, only to eventually lose it to the humanists. It was all a matter of power and money. Proud, arrogant men want power over what is taught to other people's children as well as to their own, and they want their indoctrination efforts to be paid for with tax money instead of with their own donations. This desire some Protestant sects have to once again become the state church is the reason they try so hard to convince other Christians that the concept of separation of church and state is a myth. This is a

---

10 James W. Fraser, *Between Church and State: Religion & Public Education in a Multicultural America* (New York: St. Martin Press, 1999), 14.

11 Ibid., 15–16.

12 Ibid., 24.

major mistake on their part, as this is what is keeping humanists in control of public education. ***If all Protestant groups, Catholics, and all other thestic groups would simply admit that it is wrong to have an established church, and would work to honor and enforce the First Amendment, humanism could be disestablished in short order. But if, instead, each group tries to make itself the established church, then humanism is going to continue on in power over us.***

The First Amendment Was Immediately Compromised Even At the Federal Level.

In trying to prove that the separation of church and state is a myth, some writers ask questions and make statements such as these:

> If the basic purpose of the Establishment Clause was "to create a complete and permanent separation of the spheres of religious activity and civil authority by comprehensively forbidding every form of public aid or support for religion," as Justice Rutledge wrote in his dissenting opinion in Everson, then why did the first House of Representatives, after voting up the amendment, ask President Washington to issue a proclamation recommending to the people of the United States "a day of public thanksgiving and prayer, to be observed by acknowledging, with grateful hearts, the many signal favors of Almighty God"?
>
> It was certainly not a commitment to absolute separation of church and state which led President Washington to issue the new nation's first Thanksgiving Day Proclamation. And it was not adherence to an absolute Establishment Clause when Presidents John Adams and James Madison also issued Thanksgiving Day Proclamations. (Jefferson did think they violated the Establishment Clause and federalism. Unlike his two immediate predecessors and Madison, his successor, he refused to issue them.) No commitment to absolute separation of church and state is evident in the First Congress when it set up a congressional chaplain system and voted a $500 annual salary for the Senate and House chaplains. Their principal duties were to offer audible public prayers in Congress. Did the authors of the religion amendment not know what it meant, or if they did, did they immediately proceed to violate it?
>
> Further, no absolute interpretation of the principle of separation of church and state led President Thomas Jefferson to sign a tax-exemption bill for the churches in Alexandria County in 1802. And it was not an absolutist action when in 1803 Jefferson—one year after he wrote his famous "wall of separation" letter to the Danbury, Connecticut, Baptists--concluded a treaty with the Kaskaskia Indians which, in part, called for the United States to build them a Roman Catholic Church and pay their priest.[13]

The above quotation deserves some commentary. Congress did not violate the First Amendment when it asked "President Washington to issue a proclamation recommending to the people of the United States 'a day of public thanksgiving and prayer, to be observed by acknowledging, with grateful hearts, the many signal favors of Almighty God,'" provided it made no law in doing so. If a law was made, then it did violate the First Amendment. The First Amendment protects a president's right to free speech as much as anyone's. A president can exercise that freedom of speech in issuing such a proclamation, even without being asked. Of course, such a proclamation would not be official, but just his personal proclamation. It would have only as much influence as he has as an individual. President Jefferson exercised his freedom of religion by not issuing such a proclamation. Concerning President Jefferson signing "a tax-exemption bill for the churches in Alexandria County in 1802," I haven't been able to obtain the details, but whether a president does or doesn't obey the First Amendment doesn't change what it says or means. When "the First Congress...set up a congressional chaplain system and voted a $500 annual salary for the Senate and House chaplains" it clearly did violate the First Amendment. Also, when President Jefferson "concluded a treaty with the Kaskaskia Indians which, in part, called for the United States to build them a Roman Catholic Church and pay their priest," that was without any shadow of doubt a violation of the First Amendment.

---

13 Robert L. Cord, "Church, State, and the Rihnquist Court: The Court is Doing What the Framers Never Did; Build an Impregnable Wall Between Church and State. (Justice William Rehnquist; United States Supreme Court)," National Review, 1917 August 1992, Http://www.highbeam.com/library/docfree.asp?DOCID=1G1:12666321&ctrlInfo=Round18%3AMode18c%3ADocG%3AResult&ao=.

"Only with the Fourteenth Amendment in 1868 were the protections of the Bill of Rights applied to the states, and not until Everson v. Board of Education in 1947 did the U.S. Supreme Court specifically apply the establishment clause to state legislatures."[14] And Congress did not recognize First Amendment rights as applying to Indians until 1978![15]

So, obviously, **the First Amendment was not the first choice of most of our forefathers. They agreed to it only to keep some other sect beside their own from becoming the state church.** ***The First Amendment was not a conviction with them, and so was easily compromised when they felt it to their advantage to do so.*** Absolute freedom of religion for everyone was the first choice only of the Baptists, who for centuries had been persecuted by state churches.

Half-heartedness Concerning the First Amendment Continues Today

The fact is, we are today in the same situation as our forefathers. ***None*** of the religions in the USA form a majority. Christians, Muslims, Hindus, and Buddhists all disagree on major issues. Christians disagree among themselves on many major issues. Therefore, we theists are ***always*** going to be divided on many major issues. On many major issues theists are ***never*** going to agree with each other. Therefore, ***none*** of the theistic religions—including yours if you are a theist—has any hope whatsoever of ever becoming the established religion of the USA. For the sake of the future of our country, that vain (and sinful) hope must be discarded.

> Most of those who embraced religious disestablishment at the time of the First Amendment had similar ambivalence. We would prefer an establishment of our particular beliefs, many seemed to say, but if we cannot have that, at least give us tolerance and do not establish someone else's beliefs. How little has changed in 220 years![16]

As in the days of our forefathers, ***there is only one thing that can unite theists in this country so that we can cast off our Humanist oppressors, and that is to cast off the desire to become the established religion, and to return to the spirit of the First Amendment—absolute freedom of religion for EVERYONE.*** That is an attainable unity. That is the ONLY unity we can reasonably hope for. Our only choices are these two: (1) we can unite around the First Amendment, and demand that the Humanist religion be disestablished as are all other religions; or (2) we can remain divided by working to make our own sect the state religion in violation of the First Amendment, in which case we may as well resign ourselves to Humanists continuing to brainwash our children with their vile religious and political views until they have made them our enemies.

Justifying Robbery To Educate Our Children

Now we must discuss something that will be very unpleasant for many Christians. ***There is a third bait that Humanists use to keep theists in their trap, and it is a bait so effective that Humanists are arrogant and cocky in total confidence that theists will never have the moral character to be able to break free.*** Humanists feel certain that theists will never return to the spirit of the First Amendment because most theists are hooked on the bait of socialist welfare education. Most theists today want their children's education to be free—paid for with tax money collected by government force from other people. Consider that this is exactly what the members of the old established churches wanted back before the First Amendment. They thought their churches could not survive without tax support. But guess what? They survived just fine being supported by their own donations! They even have plenty of money left over to give to charitable causes.

---

[14] Fraser, *Between Church and State*, 13.

[15] Ibid., 100.

[16] Ibid., 238.

The bitter price of welfare education is the loss of freedom. It is impossible to have a socialist educational system without also having a state established religion. The only way to stop Humanists from brainwashing our children to believe the lies of their pagan, infidel religion is to abolish socialist (deceptively called "public") education. Socialism is illegally legalized robbery. It is evil and wicked to force people by threat of armed government police officers to pay taxes for the teaching of religious ideas which they loathe. Since all education is religious education, let every religion educate its own children at its own expense. The education business is none of the government's business.

> ... it is argued that education of the young is a public good and that it must be paid for by all so that there will be no free riders. These are absolutely fallacious arguments. It can more easily be argued that a poor education in a government monopoly is a public "bad" because it sacrifices the opportunities lost to young people. Should all of life be controlled on the basis of a perceived gain or loss to society? If so, then you have a society of slaves.
>
> And what about free riders? The imposition of taxes does not eliminate the free riders — it merely changes who the free riders will be. And those who usually win in the political arena are the powerful, not the powerless. And what of the ethics of forcing people to pay for things against their will? I cannot force someone else to give me money. That is theft. If I have no right to steal, then I have no right to ask a politician to do this theft on my behalf. When the politician acts for me, it is still theft and the politics involved does not cleanse the action. Large numbers of people who wish to steal from others, are still thieves if they must resort to violence to achieve their ends.
>
> What is the lesson that we teach our children when we do such things? Do we teach them that it is wrong to steal? Or do we teach them that it is OK to steal if they ask a friend to do it for them? Or do we say that it is OK to steal from others if we can outnumber them? No. We must teach our young to find voluntary means to achieve their own goals.[17]

Not only will the privatizing of education end the establishment of the Humanist religion as the state church of America, but private education is much cheaper and better than public (socialist) education. Dr. John T. Wenders (Ph.D., Northwestern University), professor of economics emeritus at the University of Idaho and a senior fellow at the Commonwealth Foundation, summarizes the cost issue as follows:

> All things considered, these various cost comparisons between private and public schools...have a remarkable consistency – the most relevant ones show private school costs to be roughly between 55 and 60 percent of the costs of public schools. Special education considerations raise these only another 6 to 10 percent, to roughly 62 percent. Using the latter figure, this means that roughly 38 percent of public school expenditures are dissipated or wasted. Let us put this waste in perspective.
>
> For 2000-01, NCES estimated total annual current expenditures for public schools to be about $333.8 billion. [13] Assuming an additional 17 percent for capital outlays and interest, this brings total annual estimated U.S. public school expenditures to about $391.7 billion. Applying the waste estimate of 38 percent, this shows that U.S. public education wastes about $148.9 billion annually. That is about 1.57 percent of U.S. gross domestic product, or about $529 per capita in the year 2000. [14]
>
> The waste does not end there. Due to the failure of the public schools, both businesses and institutions of higher education now must spend considerable monies repairing this failure. A rise in the price of one product, or a decline in that product's quality, causes buyers to turn to substitutes. The rise in the demand for remedial education in both community colleges and elsewhere in higher education is one such substitute and reflects a reaction to the decline in the performance of the public schools. Further, it is not a mere coincidence that both the greatest growth in the establishment of community colleges, where remedial education is concentrated, and the surge in the formation of private elementary and secondary schools, came during the 1960-1980 time period when the decline in public school performance was the greatest. This means that the economic cost of public education is not limited to the obvious waste there. Jay Greene found that the waste due to increased spending on remedial education alone conservatively amounted to $16.6 billion annually for the U.S. [15] This further adds to the direct waste due to public

---

[17] Ken Schoolland, "The Free Market and Education," *The Future of Freedom Foundation*, January 1996, Http://www.fff.org/aboutUs/press/schooland.asp.

education and brings the total to at least $166 billion annually, about 1.66 percent of U.S. gross domestic product, or $588 per capita for the year 2000.

The conclusion is inescapable: U.S. public education is much more expensive than private education and, aside from producing an inferior education, the waste there is a very significant drain on the U.S. economy.

In the large, socialism has clearly failed. But in the small, where it has a host from which to draw sustenance, it prospers. Marx predicted that socialism would replace capitalism. It is ironic that socialist institutions survive only as parasites in capitalist systems.[18]

People who believe that education in public schools is ***free*** are like the dog that went hunting with his incompetent master. The master had failed to bring food or a compass, and they got lost in the woods. After several days of hunger, the hunter cut off the dog's tail and boiled it in a pot. The hunter ate the meat and gave the bones to the dog, which wagged the stub of his tail in joy as he ate them, then licked his master's hand in gratitude.

Government schools pretend to be free when they are not. Every penny of expenditure has to first be taken from the people through direct and indirect taxes. Asking the government to provide a service is like taking blood from one arm to put it back into the other arm, and throwing half of the blood on the ground in the process. The costs of government schools far exceed the costs of private schools, especially when taking into account hidden costs, i.e. "free" property upon which they are built, separate pension funds that are often paid from other sources, and taxation that only hits private competitors.

In the private school, by contrast, all these costs must be incorporated in their price. Waste and inefficiency are immediately reflected in higher prices or lower profits—and thus opportunities arise for their competitors. This is not so with government schools. My surveys usually reveal that most people think that more than half of government spending is wasted. Waste in the government sector is usually rewarded with bigger budgets and staff.[19]

Though most people do not realize it, the exceedingly wasteful public school system has drastically lowered the standard of living in this country. **YOU** would be a lot wealthier if all schools were private. And your children would be much better educated. Because of the socialist idea upon which the public school system exists, we are eating our own tail bones instead of eating the fruits of our labor, and little by little we are becoming financially weaker through loss of our own blood.

And, we are—literally—paying for the destruction of our own children. In our greediness to force others to pay for the education of our children, we have been incredibly stupid. We have surrendered control of our children's education to radical atheists and sodomites.

Let us continue with our history lesson to see how this unbelievable error was made.

From the First Public School Until Darwin

Immediately after also being disestablished on the state as well as federal levels, the former state churches began looking for a way around disestablishment. Even some of the religions that had never been established sought a way to become the state-supported, established church. The humanist Unitarian church especially saw opportunity. Unscrupulous religious leaders were determined to somehow gain or regain control over the religious education of other people's children so as to determine the beliefs and culture of the new nation, and they sought to either gain or regain tax funding for their religious educating efforts so that they did not have to pay for them with their own donations. It did not take long for them to find the solution they were looking for in the idea of a government-run, tax-supported, public school system. ***And it was a brilliant solution because it played on the depraved nature of man: specifically,***

---

[18] John T. Wenders, "What a Drag: Inefficient Schools Burden Economy," *Oklahoma Council of Public Affairs* 10, no. 3 (March 2003), Http://www.ocpathink.org/ViewPerspectiveEdition.asp?ID=23.

[19] Schoolland, "The Free Market and Education."

the tendency—the weakness—to be selfish and greedy, to desire to get something without working for it, to steal legally, to get a free education for one's children by forcing other people and other peoples' businesses to pay for it through forced taxation.

Of course, the idea that one can steal without penalty is an illusion, it doesn't actually work out that way. There is always a terrible price to pay for stealing, even if that stealing is made legal by legislation. ***One of the most painful costs of stealing is a loss of liberty***, as will be seen.

Horace Mann

Freedom of religion did not last long in Massachusetts. It was only three or four years after the Congregational Church was disestablished as the state church of Massachusetts that the Unitarian Church was established in its place. This was accomplished under the guise of creating a tax-funded school system to provide a "free" education to all of the children in the state of Massachusetts. Horace Mann, an ardent Unitarian senator, was appointed to the newly formed post of secretary of the Board of Education of Massachusetts in 1836. Historian Jonathan Messerli described Mann's plan as follows:

HORRACE MANN was a radical Unitarian. He conceived the idea of a public school system as a way to teach his humanist religious ideas to the children of other religions at their own expense—to craftily establish the Unitarian Church.

> Parents, citizens, taxpayers, all must be converted to a new religion, which taught that the older informal modes of learning were no longer adequate and that there must be far greater reliance on formal systematic schooling. *Just four years before, the voters of Massachusetts had officially disestablished the old Congregational Church. Now Mann was about to preach a new religion and convince his constituency of the need for a new establishment, a nondenominational institution, the public school, with schoolmasters as a new priestly class,* patriotic exercises as quasi-religious rituals, and a nonsectarian doctrine stressing morality, literacy, and citizenship as a republican creed for all to confess.[20]

This quote is extremely important. ***The public school system of America is an establishment of the atheistic humanist religion as the state religion.*** It has been from the very beginning. The sooner the American people realize this the sooner they will be able to understand why American education is taking the morality and souls of our children to Hell.

Mann held his new position until 1848—twelve years.[21] During this time Mann traveled to Prussia, and came back determined to pattern the Massachusetts public school system after the socialist educational system of Prussia.

Everyone should have realized what Mann was trying to do. He clearly stated from the very beginning that he intended to use the public schools (he called them Common Schools) to teach a new civic religion to tie the nation together. He said that this new religion would use the Bible and teach only the elements of Christianity that everyone agreed on, and who could oppose that? In his last report to the Massachusetts Board of Education, Mann made clear that his public school system was religious. He said:

> It is a matter of notoriety, that the views of the Board of Education,—and my own, perhaps still more than those of the Board,—on the subject of religious instruction in our Public Schools, have been subjected to animadversion. Grave charges have been made

---

20 Messerli, *Horace Mann: A Biography*, 253.

21 Fraser, *Between Church and State*, 25.

against us, that our purpose was to exclude religion; and to exclude that, too, which is the common exponent of religion,—the Bible,—from the Common Schools of the state; or, at least, to derogate from its authority, and destroy its influence in them.[22]

It is still easier to prove that the Massachusetts school system is not anti-Christian nor un-Christian. The Bible is the acknowledged expositor of Christianity. In strictness, Christianity has no other authoritative expounder. This Bible is in our Common Schools, by common consent. Twelve years ago, it was not in all the schools. Contrary to the genius of our government, if not contrary to the express letter of the law, it had been used for sectarian purposes, —to prove one sect to be right, and others to be wrong. Hence, it had been excluded from the schools of some towns, by an express vote. But since the law and the reasons on which it is founded, have been more fully understood; and since sectarian instruction has, to a great extent, ceased to be given, the Bible has been restored.... If the Bible, then, is the exponent of Christianity; if the Bible contains the communications, precepts, and doctrines, which make up the religious system, called and known as Christianity; if the Bible makes known those truths, which according to the faith of Christian, are able to make men wise unto salvation; and if this Bible is in the schools, by what tergiversation in language, or paralogism in logic, can Christianity be said to be shut out from the schools?[23]

I have felt bound to show, that, so far from its being an irreligious, an anti-Christian, or an un-Christian system, it is a system which recognizes religious obligations in their fullest extent; that it is a system which invokes a religious spirit, and can never be fitly administered without such a spirit; that it inculcates the great commands, upon which hang all the law and the prophets; that it welcomes the Bible, and therefore welcomes all the doctrines which the Bible really contains, and that it listens to these doctrines so reverently, that, for the time being, it will not suffer any rash mortal to thrust in his interpolations of their meaning, or overlay the text with any of the "man inventions" which the heart of man has sought out.[24]

This all sounded so good at the time! But with Bible reading and prayer now officially banned from public schools, the bitter truth is undeniable. Mann's schools were religious alright, but the religion was not Christianity but humanist Unitarianism. Mann's God was not the God of the Bible, nor was his Christianity the Christianity of the Bible.[25] The Unitarian humanism taught in the first public school was religion, and the Unitarian humanism being taught in public schools today is still just religion.

Everyone should have realized immediately that ***there is not a single verse in the Bible that everyone agrees on.*** Mann's whole idea of teaching only that on which everyone agreed was pure deception, for it meant that none of the Bible would be taught. But most people were so fixed on the prospect of a "free" education for their children that they never realized the threat Mann's idea posed to their newly gained religious freedom. Nevertheless, a few people did see the threat.

To his critics, Mann's easy solution to the vexing problem of what religion, if any, to teach in the schools was really proposing to make the public schools of Massachusetts a kind of Unitarian parochial school system that would mirror his own deeply held Unitarian beliefs.[26]

Mann's opponents...warned: "The right to mold the political, moral, and religious, opinions of children, is a right exclusively and jealously reserved by our laws to every parent; and for the government to attempt, directly or indirectly, as to these matters, to

---

22 Horace Mann, *The Republic and the School: Horace Mann on the Education of Free Men* (New York: Bureau of Publications, Teachers College, Columbia University, 1957), 101.

23 Ibid., 105–06.

24 Ibid., 110–11.

25 Not only would this new school system teach religion, but it would also teach politics. Said Mann: "[T]hose articles in the creed of republicanism, which are accepted by all, believed in by all, and which form the common basis of our political faith, shall be taught to all. But when the teacher, in the course of his lessons or lectures on the fundamental law, arrives at a controverted text, he is either to read it without comment or remark; or, at most, he is only to say that the passage is the subject of disputation, and that the schoolroom is neither the tribunal to adjudicate, nor the forum to discuss it" Mann, *The Republic and the School*, 97. The reality, of course, is that politics is also religious, and there is not one single political issue that is "accepted by all" and "believed in by all." Some religion's political point of view is going to be taught. That is why the public schools of America are now producing more and more liberal Democrat voters.

26 Fraser, *Between Church and State*, 27.

stand in the parent's place, is an undertaking of very questionable policy" [Report of the Committee on Education, Massachusetts House of Representatives, March 7, 1840, The Common School Journal, 2:15 (August 1, 1840): 227)].[27]

Mann's critics...understood...that a board dominated by Unitarians could not avoid using the book selection process to impose their creed on others.[28]

Living at a time when political and technological revolutions seemed to be ushering in the new dawn of an age of unprecedented human welfare, Mann hoped to accelerate "the agenda of the Almighty," as he referred to his endeavor. to accomplish this, he believed the nation needed new enabling institutions, especially public schools. Phrasing his words in the characteristically hyperbolic rhetoric of his day, he described them as "the greatest invention ever made by man." *What the church had been for medieval man, the public school must now become for democratic and rational man. God would be replaced by the concept of the Public Good, sin and quilt by the more positive virtues of Victorian morality and civic conformity*, and mankind would emancipate itself once and for all, not only from the relentless gnawings of a Puritan conscience but, through its own self-attained enlightenment, from the endemic evils of poverty, ignorance, violence, disease, and war.

All of this was now possible if only reasonable men and women would join together to create a well-managed *system of schooling*, where educators could manipulate and control learning as effectively as the confident new breed of engineers managed the industrial processes at work in their burgeoning textile factories and iron and steel mills. For the first time in the history of western man, *it seemed possible for an intellectual and moral elite to effect mass behavioral changes and bring about a new golden age of enlightened ethics, humanism, and affluence.* Indeed, so dazzling was the prospect, that Mann and his countless co-workers could not conceive of the possibility that those who would follow in their footsteps might actually build a suffocating and sometimes mind-numbing establishmentarian bureaucracy. Nor could they envision that in the hands of lesser individuals, their cherished institution, instead of functioning as a fundamental part of the social solution they sought, could become an integral part of the problem.[29]

In the very same speech Mann would claim that his public schools were Christian but not religious establishments. On the one hand, he claimed his schools were Christian to cover up the fact that by cutting the heart out of Christianity they were allowing only the Unitarian religion to be taught. On the other hand, he claimed his public schools were *not* religious to cover up the fact that they were a violation of the First Amendment. To convince people he was not doing what he obviously was doing he would give strong speeches against what he was doing. Then his friends would stress that he could not possibly be doing what he was doing, since he so strongly opposed it! Consider, for example, Mann's hypocritical tirade against established religion:

The elements of a political education are not bestowed upon any school child, for the purpose of making him vote with this or that political party, when he becomes of age; but for the purpose of enabling him to choose for himself, with which party he will vote. So the religious education which a child receives at school, is not imparted to him, for the purpose of making him join this or that denomination, when he arrives at years of discretion, but for the purpose of enabling him to judge for himself, according to the dictates of his own reason and conscience, what his religious obligations are, and whither they lead. But if a man is taxed to support a school, where religious doctrines are inculcated which he believes to be false, and which he believes that God condemns; then he is excluded from the school by the Divine law, at the same time that he is compelled to support it by the human law. This is a double wrong. It is politically wrong, because, if such a man educates his children at all, he must educate them elsewhere, and thus pay two taxes, while some of this neighbors pay less then their due proportion of one; and it is religiously wrong, because he is constrained, by human power, to promote what he believes the Divine Power forbids. The principle involved in such a course is pregnant with all tyrannical consequences.[30]

The above words prove that Mann was a hypocrite and liar who knew that his public schools were an

[27] Ibid., 29–30.

[28] Ibid., 30.

[29] Messerli, *Horace Mann: A Biography*, xii-xiii.

[30] Mann, *The Republic and the School*, 104.

establishment of his humanist Unitarian religion and that this was a "double wrong." He knew that most people in America considered Unitarianism an un-Christian religion which they believed the "Divine Power forbids." He knew that many people were being forced to support his public schools against their wills, and were therefore double taxed if they insisted on sending their children to a private school. Argued Mann,

> Every man, not on the pauper list, is taxed for their support. But he is not taxed to support them as special religious institutions; if he were, it would satisfy, at once, the largest definition of a Religious Establishment.[31]

Clearly, Mann knew the truth—that his public schools were a Religious Establishment—, but he knew also that he had to hide it, deny it, lie about it if his Unitarian religion was to remain established. Thus his speeches claiming that his schools were religious yet not religious. This tactic is still being used by humanists today! Humanist judges rule that Humanist churches are religious enough to receive non-profit tax status, but not religious enough to be an establishment of religion when their doctrines alone are allowed to be taught in public schools.

But Horace Mann was not the only person to use the public school idea to promote his own religion at the expense of everyone else's religion.

Lyman Beecher

Although Horace Mann is more well known because he was the first secretary of a state board of education, Lyman Beecher is an equally important figure in the history of public education because he and his family and friends were extremely successful in using the public school movement to establish his concept of a new Protestant civic religion as the state church across most of the US west of the Mississippi River. James W. Fraser summarizes this period of history well:

LYMAN BEECHER established his brand of Protestantism in the pubic (socialist) schools out West. This compromise of Christianity with socialism sowed the seeds for the atheists' religion, humanism, to take complete control.

> In 1832, four years before the creation of the Massachusetts Board of Education and Mann's election as its first secretary, another Massachusetts resident, fifty-seven-year-old Lyman Beecher, resigned as pastor of Boston's Hanover Street Congregational Church, left behind his long struggle with New England Unitarians, and moved to a position as president of the newly created Lane Theological Seminary in Cincinnati, Ohio. Beecher took with him his daughters Catharine and the more famous Harriet and his son-in-law Calvin Stowe (Harriet's husband). These leaders provided much of the nucleus of the campaign to build public schools in Ohio...For Lyman Beecher the public schools as they developed in the American midwest were an essential element in his larger campaign to Christianize the nation in the tenets of his ecumenical and evangelical Protestantism.[32]
>
> Many people besides the Beecher clan were involved in building Ohio's common schools. One was Samuel Lewis, a Methodist minister and school reformer. Through the efforts of many like him, the Ohio legislature was convinced to create the office of state Superintendent of Common Schools in 1837, only a year after Mann's secretaryship was created in Massachusetts. As Mann had been the obvious choice for Massachusetts, once the office was created in Ohio, the next logical step was to appoint Lewis to the post....Like Mann or Beecher or Stowe, Lewis never seemed to realize the degree to which the school was being used to re-create a Protestant religious establishment.[33]

---

[31] Ibid., 103.

[32] Fraser, *Between Church and State*, 32.

[33] Ibid., 38.

I disagree with Frazer. I believe that they did realize that they were creating an establishment of religion. Other Protestant ministers, in Indiana Caleb Millis, and in Michigan John Pierce, were also working to establish Protestant public school systems.[34]

Unfortunately for America, the Baptists, who had so strongly led the battle to disestablish the state churches prior to the First Amendment, now, by and large, failed to see what was happening. Or if they did, they now failed to stand by their convictions to expose this dangerous assault against freedom of religion. Or, if they did, there seems to be little mention of it in history.

Catholics, however, did realize what was happening and refused to send their children to public schools to be turned into Protestants. Catholic leaders chose instead to create a system of parochial schools for the education of their youth. The dominant Protestant leaders in charge of state government refused funding to these parochial schools, and the Catholics, rather than submit to the indoctrination of their children in Protestantism, funded their schools with their own donations. The Catholics were therefore paying twice for the education of their children—once by taxation for education they detested and refused to use, and once for funding their own schools. Old School Presbyterians also saw what was happening, and so started their own parochial schools, also paying twice for the education of their children.[35] It was a very unjust situation to say the least, and was a very heavy financial burden on the members of religions that could not with a clear conscience send their children to a school system designed to undermine what their churches taught.

Historian James W. Fraser quotes Calvin Stowe as saying, "Notwithstanding the diversity of sects, there is common ground, on which the sincerely pious of all sects substantially agree" in implementing this new civic religion. Fraser goes on to point out that,

> Of course, the "sincerely pious" did not include Catholics, more creedal Protestants such as Lutherans, many of the Baptists and Methodists, or the considerable numbers of free thinkers and atheists. For Stowe and most of his allies, including in many ways Horace Mann, all of these people were beyond the national consensus and more in need of conversion than serious consideration.[36]

What these "seriously pious" Protestant leaders did not realize was that by watering down their religious teachings to only what "everyone" could agree on, they were preparing the way for their own disempowerment. They would not get away with violating the spirit and substance of the First Amendment forever. Eventually their abuse of other religions would be pointed out in courts of law, and they would lose their power to atheists of the humanist Unitarian religion, now more generally known as Religious Humanism or Secular Humanism. By embracing a system based on the atheistic idea of socialism, they were sowing the seeds that allowed atheists to gain control of education in America.

By advocating a lowest-common-denominator civic religion in order to unite enough of the various Protestant churches to keep themselves in power and to Protestantize the culture of America, these "evangelicals were also secularizing their own faith."[37]

An example of how this "secularizing" (removing God from) happened is seen in the incidents leading up to the passing of a bill in April of 1842 by the New York state legislature "that placed the schools under the control of public officials and a city Board of Education with an explicit prohibition on any sectarian teaching in the schools." This was a result of the private Protestant-led Public School Society, which controlled distribution of government funds to New York schools, having refused funding for Catholic parochial schools. The Catholics pointed out the unfairness of this decision, and demanded their fair share of government funding.

---

[34] Ibid., 39.

[35] Ibid., 44.

[36] Ibid., 33–34.

[37] Ibid., 46.

> The Public School Society fought back, initially seeking some compromise with the Catholics, including an offer to remove any textbook especially offensive to Catholic views. However, in April 1840 the trustees issued a hard line document accusing their opponents of "Religious zeal, degenerating into fanaticism and bigotry." They appealed to the constitutional provisions that "there should be no establishment of religion by law; that the affairs of the State should be kept entirely distinct from, and unconnected with, those of the Church." And most of all, they rejected the notion that Catholics had a right to a share of the school funds since they were taxed for support of the schools. "[I]t should be born in mind that they are taxed not as members of the Roman Catholic Church, but as citizens of the State of New York; and not for the purposes of religion, but for the support of civil government." And the civil government, in the form of an appropriation for the Public School Society, was thus the only appropriate means of spending school funds, its advocates argued.[38]

These arguments, were obviously pure hypocrisy—the Protestants who comprised the Public School Society were actually *doing* what they accused the Catholics of only *attempting*—, and so the Public School Society was justly removed from power by the legislature. Even though the public Board of Education that replaced it was also Protestant controlled, and even though the Catholics were still denied state funding, and even though Protestantism continued to be taught in the public schools of New York, by *hypocritically* appealing to the First Amendment the Protestant leaders of the Public School Society had started a dangerous trend.

> The final compromise became all too common for the future. While the schools of the new Board of Education were more secular than those of the Public School Society by only the barest of margins, the direction was set.... a move toward secularization was begun that never ended.[39]

Remember that secular does not mean non-religious. It merely means that God is excluded. Even though they were doing it in an effort to "Christianize America," by diluting what they taught they were gradually taking the power of God out of it, and planting seeds of defeat. ***Consider that the very arguments the Public School Society used against the Catholics are now being used by the Humanists against the Protestants.*** When the Protestant leaders of the Public School Society correctly pointed out that the First Amendment meant that "there should be no establishment of religion by law; that the affairs of the State should be kept entirely distinct from, and unconnected with, those of the Church," they were advocating separation of church and state, while they themselves were a state church! They were using the First Amendment to protect themselves, but denying that protection to the Catholics. This bit of hypocrisy eventually resulted in their second disestablishment.

It is urgent at this time in history for Protestants to admit that it is wrong to be a state church, that it is wrong to deny freedom to other religions, and that the principle of separation of church and state is a true and right principle taught by Jesus Christ himself. Until Protestants quit trying to regain state church status, they will be unable to use the Humanists' violation of church and state against them to disestablish them.

Is it really freedom of religion that we want, or do we actually want control over the children of people of other religions? Do we really advocate absolute freedom for all to pray according to the dictates of their own consciences, or do we actually want to control the wording and manner of the prayers to which the children of people of other religions will be required to listen? Is it freedom or power that we want?

Even as far back as 1966 the Islamic religion was one of the fastest growing religions on earth when Supreme Court Justice William O. Douglas warned Christians:

> In time Moslems will control some of the school boards. In time devout Moslems may want their prayer in our schools; and if Protestant sects can get their prayers past the barriers of the First Amendment, the same passage would be guaranteed for Moslems."[40]

[38] Ibid., 54.

[39] Ibid., 57.

[40] Ibid., 234.

Do we want our children to hear Muslim prayers broadcast over the school's loudspeakers? Do we want our children to receive instruction in Islam? Is our concern really that our own children receive instruction in the Bible? or is it power to force the children of other religions to study the curriculum we choose that we actually want?

If absolute freedom of religion is what we want then there is only one way to have it: abolish public education. Public schools are a shameful violation of the First Amendment. ***Only in private schools, funded by our own donations, and taught by teachers of our own faith, can our children freely pray and learn the Bible without any compromise or watering down of the truth.*** Evolution can be exposed as the lie it actually is. Discipline can be administered according to the principles laid down in God's Word. Abortion can be shown to be murder, and sodomy shown to be abomination. In private schools funded by private donations we are free to teach what our conscience dictates.

But if power to force the doctrines of a particular Christian sect upon others is actually what we want, then we are doomed forever to slavery. Because of the diversity in this country, we will never be able to obtain the two thirds majority needed to amend the Constitution again to establish any particular theistic sect as the state religion. Furthermore, if establishment is not wrong for Protestants, than it is not wrong for Humanists either. As long as Protestants want to violate the First Amendment themselves, they will be ineffective in pointing out the Humanists' violation of it.

However, ***just as those First Amendment arguments backfired on the hypocritical Public School Society, so they will backfire on the Humanists if only the Humanist Church's own hypocritical use of the First Amendment is relentlessly pointed out publicly.***

Obey the First Amendment. Disestablish all churches, including the Humanist Church. Let the Humanists have the same absolute freedom we give ourselves. Let them teach their vile atheism to their own children if that is their desire. But let them pay for doing so with their own donations, not with tax money. And don't let them force their wicked and deceptive religious dogmas on our children at our expense for even one more day.

From Darwin To the Great Society

Darwin's *Origin of Species*, published in 1859, was a great day in history for humanism. The ideas Darwin espoused were merely pagan religious philosophy, and had all been disproven. But Darwin was able to cloak them in a new veneer of scientific sounding language that made them much more deceptive. The most important thing Darwin did was make it look like the universe and all the creatures on earth could have come into existence without God. If Darwin's Theory of Evolution is right, then the first chapter of the Bible is wrong. And if the first chapter in the Bible is wrong, then how can the remaining chapters be trusted? Suddenly atheism looked much more respectable, and atheists world wide went on the offensive, preaching humanism with an evangelical zeal.

The following is a timeline of humanist organizational activities and accomplishments:

1900 The journal *School Review* recommends that high school biology and zoology courses be consolidated into a unified biology curriculum teaching evolution.[41]

1912 *Elemental Biology* by James E. Peabody and Arthur E. Hunt teaches the evolution theory of Darwin.

1914 Oran L. Raber, a teacher, writes an article for high school mathematics and science teachers telling them it is their duty to their students "to correct for them some of the ideas which previous training in the Sunday school or home had led them." This article was distributed nationally.[42]

1920 The American Civil Liberties Union is founded on January the 19th by a group of over 60 left-wing, socialist radicals led by Unitarian ministers.

---

[41] Ibid., 120–21.

[42] Ibid., 121.

1922 John Dewey's article "Education as a Religion" is published in the August edition of *The New Republic*, p. 64f. Note that Humanists know that education is religion; it cannot be otherwise.

1922 Prompted by the Kentucky Baptist State Board of Missions, the Kentucky legislature passed a law banning the teaching of evolution in public schools.[43] This was a big mistake that set them up for defeat. They banned free speech. Instead, they should have abolished the public schools as being establishments of religion. Baptists should note what compromising on separation of church and state has cost them.

1925 The ACLU placed an ad in the May issue of the Chattanooga Times, stating, "We are looking for a Tennessee teacher who is willing to accept our services in testing this law in the courts." They were, of course, referring to the law banning teaching evolution in the Kentucky public school system. John T. Scopes, a 24 year old science teacher, volunteered to break the law to test it. William Jennings Bryan, a three time presidential candidate, appeared as an expert witness for the prosecution. ACLU lawyer Clarence Darrow represented Scopes. Bryan did a very poor job, and Darrow was able to make him and Christianity also look unscientific, ignorant, and foolish. Scopes was found guilty, but Christianity was made to look anti-science and wrong in the eyes of the public. Charles Francis Potter, a former Baptist evangelist who converted to Unitarianism, "acted as the librarian and Bible expert for Clarence Darrow and the defense during the Scopes evolution trial."[44]

1927 The Humanist Fellowship is organized at the University of Chicago, which in 1935 became the Humanist Press Association, which in 1941 became the American Humanist Association (AHA). The American Humanist Association then became a founding member of the International Humanist and Ethical Union in 1952.

1928 First issue of Potter The *New Humanist* magazine is published. In 1938 *The New Humanist* became *The Humanist Bulletin*, which in 1941 became *The Humanist*.[45]

1930 Charles Francis Potter publishes *Humanism: A New Religion* in which he tells the truth about the public school system. He wrote: **"Education is the most powerful ally of Humanism, and every American public school is a school of Humanism."** Then he asks the question every Christian parent should answer: **"What can the theistic Sunday Schools, meeting for an hour once a week, and teaching only a fraction of the children, do to stem the tide of a five-day program of humanistic teaching?"**[46] Do we really want to learn the answer to that question the hard way? Don't our children mean more to us than that? Actually, we ***are*** learning the answer the hard way; but most people are in denial.

1931 "Dr. Potter's book is offered in combination with a subscription to *The New Humanist* (along with other books, including Robert J. Hutcheon's *Humanism in Religion Examined*)."[47]

1933 The May-June issue of *The New Humanist* published *A Humanist Manifesto* (later know as *Humanist Manifesto I*), which was the bold public statement of faith of this "new" religion. Actually, it was just the old atheist, materialistic religion underlying Communism dressed up in new clothes.

1934 Radical humanist John Dewey publishes *A Common Faith* in which he calls for humanism to be the religion of public schools and of the United States.

1933-45 Franklin Delano Roosevelt becomes president for four terms. "It was an administration that had deeper links to Dewey's notion of faith than to any of the historic religious communities."[48]

---

[43] Richard Stringer-Hye, "Charles Francis Potter" (Boston, MA: Unitarian Universalist Historical Society), 123, Http://www.uua.org/uuhs/duub/articles/charlesfrancispotter.html.

[44] Ibid.

[45] http://www.thehumanist.org/editors.html

[46] Charles Francis Potter, *Humanism: A New Religion* (New York: Simon and Schuster, 1930), 128.

[47] http://www.infidels.org/library/modern/edwin_wilson/manifesto/ch2.html

[48] Fraser, *Between Church and State*, 133.

> In his first diplomatic act of office, President Franklin Deleno Roosevelt...officially recognized the Soviet Union. he chummed around with Joseph Stalin, one of history's greatest mass murderers, calling him "Uncle Joe." With Stalin's agent Alger Hiss at his side, Roosevelt sold out Eastern Europe at Yalta and promised Stalin three votes in the U.N. General Assembly, plus the right to name the No. 2 U.N. official. On Roosevelt's watch, the Soviets took eastern Poland, Moldavia, Lithuania, Latvia, Estonia, and Albania. "Uncle Joe" murdered an estimated twelve to twenty million people, and forced at least 10 million into slave labor.[49]

1945 Vashti McCollum, who later became president of the American Humanist Association (from 1962 to 1965?), won a law suit before the U.S. Supreme Court to prevent Jewish, Protestant, and Roman Catholic teachers from giving religious instruction to those who chose it in the public schools. Wrote Justice Hugo Black in the majority opinion:

> ...the First Amendment has erected a wall between Church and state which must be kept high and impregnable. Here not only are the State 's tax-supported public school buildings used for the dissemination of religious doctrines. The State also affords sectarian groups an invaluable aid in that it helps to provide pupils for their religious classes through use of the State's compulsory public school machinery. This is not separation of Church and State.

He was right. This is another classic example of how, by insisting on violating the First Amendment, theists have set themselves up for defeat at the hands of humanists.

1957 In the case of *Washington Ethical Society v. District of Columbia* (101 U.S. App. D.C. 371), the Washington Ethical Society, a humanist church, which had been denied tax exempt status by the Tax Court, is defined by the U.S. Court of Appeals as a religious organization, and granted its tax exemption. The Court Stated,

> The sole issue raised is whether petitioner falls within the definition of a "church" or a "religious society" .... The taxing authority urges denial of the tax exemption asserting petitioner is not a religious society or church and that it does not use its buildings for religious worship since "religious" and "worship" require a belief in and teaching of a Supreme Being who controls the universe. The position of the tax Court, in denying tax exemption, was that belief in and teaching of the existence of a Divinity is essential to qualify under the statute.... To construe exemptions so strictly that unorthodox or minority forms of worship would be denied the exemption benefits granted to those conforming to the majority beliefs might well raise constitutional issues .... We hold on this record and under the controlling statutory language petitioner qualifies as "a religious corporation or society" ....

1961 Referring to the case of *Washington Ethical Society v. District of Columbia* above, the U.S. Supreme Court declares Secular Humanism to be a religion in the case of *Torcaso v. Watkins* (367 U.S. 488). Roy Torcaso, the appellant, a practicing Humanist in Maryland, refused to declare his belief in Almighty God, as then required by State law in order for him to be commissioned as a notary public. The Court held that the requirement for such an oath "invades appellant's freedom of belief and religion." The Court declared in Torcaso that the "no establishment" clause of the First Amendment reached far more than churches of theistic faiths, that it is not the business of government or its agents to probe beliefs, and that therefore its inquiry is concluded by the fact of the profession of belief. The Court stated:

> We repeat and again reaffirm that neither a State nor the Federal Government can constitutionally force a person to "profess a belief or disbelief in any religion." Neither can constitutionally pass laws or impose requirements which aid all religions as against non-believers, and neither can aid those religions based on a belief in the existence of God as against those religions founded on different beliefs.

In a footnote concerning "religions founded on different beliefs" the Court states"

---

49 Coulter, *Treason*, 155.

Among religions in this country which do not teach what would generally be considered a belief in the existence of God are Buddhism, Taoism, Ethical Culture, Secular Humanism, and others. See Washington Ethical Society v. District of Columbia, 101 U.S. App. D.C. 371, 249 F.2d 127; Fellowship of Humanity v. County of Alameda, 153 Cal. App. 2d 673, 315 P.2d 394; II Encyclopedia of the Social Sciences 293; 4 Encyclopedia Britannica (1957 ed.) 325-327; 21 id., at 797; Archer, Faiths Men Live By (2d ed. revised by Purinton), 120-138, 254-313; 1961 World Almanac 695, 712; Year Book of American Churches for 1961, at 29, 47.

Other court cases confirm that Humanism is a religion:

In *Torcaso v. Watkins*, 367 U.S. 488, 495, n. 11 (1961), we did indeed refer to "SECULAR HUMANISM" as a "religio[n]." [Justice Scalia in *Edwards v. Aguillard*, 482 U.S. 578 (1987) note 6]

This Court has taken notice of the fact that recognized "religions" exist that "do not teach what would generally be considered a belief in the existence of God," *Torcaso v. Watkins*, 367 U.S. 488, 495 n. 11, e. g., "Buddhism, Taoism, Ethical Culture, SECULAR HUMANISM and others." Ibid. See also Washington Ethical Society v. District of Columbia, 101 U.S. App. D.C. 371, 249 F.2d 127 (1957); 2 Encyclopaedia of the Social Sciences 293; J. Archer, Faiths Men Live By 120-138, 254-313 (2d ed. revised by Purinton 1958); Stokes & Pfeffer, supra, n. 3, at 560. [Justice Harlan in *Welsh v. United States* 398 U.S. 333 (1970) note 8]

1962 Realizing that in the *Torcaso v. Watkins* case it had unintentionally set the Humanist Church up for disestablishment, the radical, left-leaning, activist Court corrected its error by declaring that actually, in Torcaso, it rested its decision on "free exercise" grounds, **not** the "Establishment Clause" *(Abington v. Schempp*, 374 U.S. 203, 264-65 (1962) J. Brennan, concurring). ***IT IS ABSOLUTELY AMAZING THAT THEISTS HAVE LET THE COURT GET AWAY WITH THIS BLATANT INJUSTICE!***

1962 The American Civil Liberties Union initiated and won the *Engel v. Vitale* case in behalf of the children of Lawrence Roth, a non-practicing Jew, David Lichtenstein, Monroe Lerner, Lenore Lyons, and Steven Engel. These people objected to their children having to listen to a Christian prayer each day at public school. Justice Black wrote the majority opinion for the U.S. Supreme Court:

...the constitutional prohibition against laws respecting an establishment of religion must at least mean that in this country it is no part of the business of government to compose official prayers.[50]

True, but banning free speech and prohibiting the free exercise of religion is also prohibited by the First Amendment! Still, if a Muslim prayers were being prayed to Allah, would you want your children forced to participate each morning? No matter how the Court ruled, its decision would criminalize some religion or religions, unless it ruled that the existence of public schools, themselves, are the root violation of the First Amendment. The Court's unjust decision was inevitable with the existence of public schools.

1963 Fred Weisgal, an American Civil Liberties Union lawyer, represented Unitarians Edward and Sidney Schempp on behalf of their two public high school students and Madalyn Murray on behalf of her son William in a combined suit before the U.S. Supreme Court to ban all prayer and Bible reading from public schools. Justice Tom Clark wrote the majority opinion:

In both cases the laws require religious exercises and such exercises are being conducted in direct violation of the rights of the appellees and petitioners. Nor are these required exercises mitigated by the fact that the individual students may absent themselves upon parental request, for that fact furnishes no defense to a claim of unconstitutionality under the Establishment Clause.[51]

It is simply not possible to have freedom of religion in a public school. Some religion is going to rule, and in this case the Humanist religion rules.

1965 On January the 12th, liberal Democrat President Lyndon Johnson was able to achieve passage of a bill providing federal aid to education for the first time in American History. Federal aid meant federal

---

50 Fraser, *Between Church and State*, 148.

51 Ibid., 151.

control. Any meaningful parental control of public education was now for all practical purposes totally impossible.

1968 The American Civil Liberties Union initiated and won the *Epperson v. Arkansas* case in which the U.S. Supreme Court ruled that an Arkansas law prohibiting the teaching of evolution in the public schools of Arkansas was unconstitutional.[52]

1981 In *Segraves v. State of California* the Court found that the California State Board of Education's Science Framework, as written and as qualified by its anti-dogmatism policy, gave sufficient accommodation to the views of Segraves, contrary to his contention that class discussion of evolution prohibited his and his children's free exercise of religion. The anti-dogmatism policy provided that class discussions of origins should emphasize that scientific explanations focus on "how", not "ultimate cause," and that any speculative statements concerning origins, both in texts and in classes, should be presented conditionally, not dogmatically. The court's ruling also directed the Board of education to widely disseminate the policy, which in 1989 was expanded to cover all areas of science, not just those concerning issues of origins. (Segraves v. California (1981) Sacramento Superior Court #278978).

1982 In *McLean v. Arkansas Board of Education*, a federal court held that a "balanced treatment" statute violated the Establishment Clause of the U.S. Constitution. The Arkansas statute required public schools to give balanced treatment to "creation-science" and "evolution-science". In a decision that gave a detailed definition of the term "science," the court declared that "creation science" is not in fact a science. The court also found that the statute did not have a secular purpose, noting that the statute used language peculiar to creationist literature in emphasizing origins of life as an aspect of the theory of evolution. While the subject of life's origins is within the province of biology, the scientific community does not consider the subject as part of evolutionary theory, which assumes the existence of life and is directed to an explanation of how life evolved after it originated. The theory of evolution does not presuppose either the absence or the presence of a creator. (McLean v. Arkansas Board of Education (1982) 529 F. Supp. 1255, 50 U.S. Law Week 2412). These opinions of the court , of course, are simply not true.

1987 In *Edwards v. Aguillard*, the U.S. Supreme Court held unconstitutional Louisiana's "Creationism Act." This statute prohibited the teaching of evolution in public schools, except when it was accompanied by instruction in "creation science." The Court found that, by advancing the religious belief that a supernatural being created humankind, which is embraced by the term creation science, the act impermissibly endorses religion. In addition, the Court found that the provision of a comprehensive science education is undermined when it is forbidden to teach evolution except when creation science is also taught. (Segraves v. State of California (1981) Sacramento Superior Court #278978). Again the America Civil Liberties Union was on the side of evolution and against God.[53]

1990 In *Webster v. New Lenox School District*, the Seventh Circuit Court of Appeals found that a school district may prohibit a teacher from teaching creation science, in fulfilling its responsibility to ensure that the First Amendment's establishment clause is not violated, and religious beliefs are not injected into the public school curriculum. The court upheld a district court finding that the school district had not violated Webster's free speech rights when it prohibited him from teaching "creation science," since it is a form of religious advocacy. (Webster v. New Lenox School District #122, 917 F. 2d 1004).[54]

1994 In *Peloza v. Capistrano Unified School Dist.*, 37 F.3d 517 (9th Cir. 1994), Peloza, a high school biology teacher tries to balance the teaching of evolutionism with creationism based on the claim that Secular Humanism (and its core belief, evolutionism) is a religion. **The court emphatically rejected this claim with the most dishonest, deceitful, wicked, and unjust decision ever made in the U.S. Supreme Court, stating:**

---

[52] Ibid., 158 and 226.

[53] Ibid., 162.

[54] "BACKGROUND: Six Significant Court Decisions Regarding Evolution/creation Issues," Http://www.don-lindsay-archive.org/creation/voices/legal/bkgrd.htm.

We reject this claim because neither the Supreme Court, nor this circuit, has ever held that evolutionism or secular humanism are "religions" for Establishment Clause purposes. Indeed, both the dictionary definition of religion and the clear weight of the caselaw are to the contrary. The Supreme Court has held unequivocally that while the belief in a divine creator of the universe is a religious belief, the scientific theory that higher forms of life evolved from lower forms is not. Edwards v. Aguillard, 482 U.S. 578, 107 S.Ct. 2573, 96 L.Ed.2d 510 (1987) (holding unconstitutional, under Establishment Clause, Louisiana's "Balanced Treatment for Creation-Science and Evolution-Science in Public School Instruction Act").

Note 5: See Smith v. Board of School Com'rs of Mobile County, 827 F.2d 684, 690-95 (11th Cir. 1987) (refusing to adopt district court's holding that "secular humanism" is a religion for Establishment Clause purposes; deciding case on other grounds); United States v. Allen, 760 F.2d 447, 450-51 (2d Cir. 1985) (quoting Tribe, American Constitutional Law 827-28 (1978), for the proposition that, while "religion" should be broadly interpreted for Free Exercise Clause purposes, "anything `arguably non-religious' should not be considered religious in applying the establishment clause").

Peloza alleges the school district ordered him to refrain from discussing his religious beliefs with students during "instructional time," and to tell any students who attempted to initiate such conversations with him to consult their parents or clergy. He claims the school district, in the following official reprimand, defined "instructional time" as any time the students are on campus, including lunch break and the time before, between, and after classes:

> You are hereby directed to refrain from any attempt to convert students to Christianity or initiating conversations about your religious beliefs during instructional time, which the District believes includes any time students are required to be on campus as well as the time students immediately arrive for the purposes of attending school for instruction, lunch time, and the time immediately prior to students' departure after the instructional day.

Complaint at 16. Peloza seeks a declaration that this definition of instructional time is too broad, and that he should be allowed to participate in student-initiated discussions of religious matters when he is not actually teaching class.

The school district's interest in avoiding an Establishment Clause violation trumps Peloza's right to free speech.

While at the high school, whether he is in the classroom or outside of it during contract time, Peloza is not just any ordinary citizen. He is a teacher. He is one of those especially respected persons chosen to teach in the high school's classroom. He is clothed with the mantle of one who imparts knowledge and wisdom. His expressions of opinion are all the more believable because he is a teacher. The likelihood of high school students equating his views with those of the school is substantial. To permit him to discuss his religious beliefs with students during school time on school grounds would violate the Establishment Clause of the First Amendment. Such speech would not have a secular purpose, would have the primary effect of advancing religion, and would entangle the school with religion. In sum, it would flunk all three parts of the test articulated in Lemon v. Kurtzman, 403 U.S. 602, 91 S.Ct. 2105, 29 L.Ed.2d 745 (1971). See Roberts v. Madigan, 921 F.2d 1047, 1056-58 (10th Cir. 1990) (teacher could be prohibited from reading Bible during silent reading period, and from stocking two books on Christianity on shelves, because these things could leave students with the impression that Christianity was officially sanctioned), cert. denied, ____ U.S. ____, 112 S.Ct. 3025, 120 L.Ed.2d 896 (1992).

So, according to the Court, teachers and school administrators of the Humanist religion are protected by the "free exercise" clause of the First Amendment as members of tax-exempt religious organizations and as religious conscientious objectors, and are also free to teach their religious views in public schools. But if Christian teachers propagate their views, it is an "establishment clause" violation. Christians are flat out denied freedom of speech. According to the Supreme Court, Humanism IS A RELIGION when it helps Humanism and humanists, but Humanism ISN'T A RELIGION when being one would make Humanism an ESTABLISHED RELIGION as forbidden by the First Amendment Establishment Clause—for Humanism IS established; that no one can honestly deny. A person would have to be a idiot to miss the injustice in this. ***THIS WICKED AND EVIL TRAVESTY OF JUSTICE NEEDS TO BE POINTED OUT TO EVERY CITIZEN OF THE USA. WITH THIS UNJUST RULING THIS COURT SHOWED WITHOUT ANY SHADOW OF DOUBT THAT IT WAS A HUMANIST/ATHEIST ACTIVIST POLITICAL ORGANIZATION AND NOT A TRUE COURT OF JUSTICE. THIS ACTIVIST RULING CAN AND MUST BE OVERTURNED***

NO MATTER WHAT THE COST. PUT ALL OTHER ISSUES ASIDE—THERE IS NO ISSUE MORE IMPORTANT THAN THIS.

1998 An amendment to the Constitution vigorously supported by the Christian Coalition failed to reach the two thirds majority of the House of Representatives needed to proceed to the Senate, even though the vote was 224 to 203 in favor of the amendment. The amendment read:

> To secure the people's right to acknowledge God according to the dictates of conscience: Neither the United States nor any State shall establish any official religion, but the people's right to pray and to recognize their religious beliefs, heritage, or traditions on public property, including schools, shall not be infringed. Neither the United States nor an State shall require any person to join in prayer or other religious activity, prescribe school prayers, discriminate against religion, or deny equal access to a benefit on account of religion.[55]

Notice the last words of that proposed amendment: "or deny equal access to a benefit on account of religion." Again Christians had set themselves up for defeat by desiring federal funds, tax credits, vouchers, for "faith-based" social agencies and church schools. Federal support will always mean federal control. As long as there is a public school system, the official religion of the federal government will be taught. Since the Humanist religion is now the established religion of the United States, the Humanist religion controls education.

It is the wicked desire for tax money for religion education that is keeping Christians in slavery to atheists. Pat Robertson reportedly said on *The 700 Club*, that "The public education movement has also been an anti-Christian movement....We can change education in America if you put Christian principles in and Christian pedagogy in."[56] He was certainly correct in saying that the public education movement has been anti-Christian. But the desire to put Christian principles and Christian pedagogy into public education is not going to succeed. ***Socialism is a Humanist principle, not a Christian principle, so public (socialist) education can never be Christian.***

An amendment with a far better chance of success would be:

> Since all education is by nature religious, government must remain separate from it, otherwise a state church is automatically established in violation of the First Amendment; therefore, no taxes of any kind may be levied for education, and all forms of government support or funding for education are prohibited in the United States of America.

Theists of all theistic religions could vote for such an amendment. And some atheists would probably vote for it also out of fairness. Since the citizens would not be taxed for education, they would have the funds to send their children to the private schools of their choice or to home school them. Due to the fact that government would not have opportunity to waste so much education money, the citizens would also have extra funds to help families that might be going through hard times to educate their children. Only the mistaken belief that public education is "free" might motivate a theist to vote against such an amendment.

Separation of God and State

Does separation of church and state mean that God is excluded from government? Does church have to be combined with the state in order for the state to be run according to godly principles? Can the culture of a country only be Christian if that country has an established Christian church? These are serious questions because: (1) humanists say that separation of church and state does mean that God must be excluded from government; and (2) some Christian groups believe that only by having an established Christian church can a country be run by Christian principles and its culture be Christian. Such Christians are thus anti-separation of church and state. Both of these positions are wrong.

---

[55] Fraser, *Between Church and State*, 183.

[56] Ibid., 187.

The First Amendment Doesn't Separate God From Government

The fact is that every act of humanity is a religious act, showing either faith in the true God or faith in a false, man-made god (such as Evolution). This is true of the acts of individuals, and it is true of the acts of governments. The teachings of some religion are going to prevail on every issue. For example, consider capital punishment. The Bible of Christianity teaches that some crimes are so destructive that they should be capital offenses—in other words, the punishment for committing those crimes should be death. Murder is in this class of crimes. However, the Humanist religion and some of the liberal, humanistic Christian churches say the Bible is wrong on this issue. So, which religion's teaching will be practiced? Shall the murderer be executed or spared to murder again?

The fact is that even a false religion will hold to the truth on some issues. And even the very church which Jesus built, may misunderstand his teachings sometimes and hold to an error. That is why free speech is so important. The First Amendment says that the Humanist Church cannot prevent Christians from expressing their teachings on any subject, including on the subject of capital punishment. Nor may the Christians prevent the Humanists from expressing their teachings. The issue must and may be freely debated by the common people in the streets, and freely debated also in the House of Representatives and in the Senate. If a Christian congressman wants to begin his speech with a prayer, he must be free to do so. If he wants to quote Scripture to prove his points, no one can legally stop him. If the Humanist wants to begin his speech without showing respect to God, no one may force him to do otherwise. If he wants to quote Lenin or Karl Marx to prove his points, no one may stop him. This is called free speech. The truth at least has a chance in a situation like this, for light always drives away darkness, providced it is allowed to shine.

The debate on the issue of capital punishment in Congress would probably go somewhat as follows. The baby-murdering humanists and their friends will say that there is no proof that capital punishment prevents crime. Their atheist friends who have infiltrated the Christian ministry will add that God (the God they really don't even believe exists) is love, and that God would never want the government to kill what He has created. After all, other humanists might add, murderers are born that way; God made them murderers, so we should accept murder as an alternative lifestyle. Anyway, murder is not actually murder if the one being murdered is an unborn baby—a mere fetus. The humanists will then grow passionate together in saying that the only people who should be executed by the government are the Christians who commit the "hate-crime" of pointing out what the Bible says about murder, thus causing murderer bashing.

Bible-believing Christians would respond that, yes, God is love. God loves people so much he does not want them murdered. Therefore God has made murder a capital offense, according to Numbers 35:30-34:

> Whoso killeth any person, the murderer shall be put to death by the mouth of witnesses: but one witness shall not testify against any person to cause him to die. Moreover ye shall take no satisfaction for the life of a murderer, which is guilty of death: but he shall be surely put to death. And ye shall take no satisfaction for him that is fled to the city of his refuge, that he should come again to dwell in the land, until the death of the priest. So ye shall not pollute the land wherein ye are: for blood it defileth the land: and the land cannot be cleansed of the blood that is shed therein, but by the blood of him that shed it. Defile not therefore the land which ye shall inhabit, wherein I dwell: for I the LORD dwell among the children of Israel.

Other Christians would add that humans were not murderers when God created them, but they were created with a free will and therefore able to choose between good and evil. Because of Adam's willful disobedience and subsequent fall into sin men are now born with a depraved nature that is prone to murder and other sins, but that does not mean that God made murderers. To the contrary, "God hath made man upright; but they have sought out many inventions" (Ecc. 7:29). Our depraved hearts may want to murder, but we had better not yield to that wicked desire.

Still other Christians would then point out that the idea that capital punishment does not deter crime is simply closing one's mind to the obvious facts. It does not take a high IQ to realize that if a murderer is executed he will never murder again, nor will he commit any other crime. Capital punishment is the ultimate crime prevention. These Christians could then give hundreds of examples of murderers who were executed and never committed another crime, and hundreds of examples of other murderers who were released by humanist judges, and went out and murdered again and again.

In conclusion, another Christian would point out that the reason humanists want Christians to be executed for using the Bible as a light to expose error is because humanists oppose both free speech and freedom of religion and also oppose freedom in general. Humanists know their lies cannot stand up under open debate. That is why they don't want creationists to be allowed freedom to challenge their evolution lies in public school classrooms. Humanists claim to be pro-choice, but actually they deny the choice of life to innocent babies and to Bible-believing Christians. To humanists, a murderous mom has a right to choose what will happen to the body of their baby—if Mom so chooses she can cut her unborn baby into pieces and flush him down the toilet, and according to humanists that is right and good. Christians, humanists say, should be executed for saying such murder is wrong. In other words, to humanists only criminals have the right to choose.

The humanists may then counter with, "capital punishment is a Christian teaching and therefore forbidden by the First Amendment." A Christian may then respond that just because a teaching is believed by a certain religion does not mean that it is not true. Anyway, to use such humanist logic we could also say that not punishing criminals is a teaching of the humanist religion, and therefore is forbidden by the First Amendment.

Let the above debate take place publicly so that voters can see the participants and hear the arguments, and then let the vote be taken. The truth has a very good chance of prevailing in such circumstances, and our citizens will be safer as a result.

However, let any religion become the government (such as is now the case in public schools), and all meaningful debate will be prohibited by that religion (such as is now the case in public schools). True separation of church and state is essential to freedom. True separation of church and state does not exclude God, nor does it prevent the government from being run according to Christian principles, and is, in fact, the best hope that it will be run according to Christian principles since it gives the truth a chance to prevail.

The First Amendment Doesn't Prevent Christians From Influencing the Culture

A Christian denomination does not have to be established as the state church in order for it to be able to influence the culture of America. Separation of church and state does not prevent your church from being the "salt of the earth." There are *phony* Christian churches, however, that want to be the state church so as to be able to force their corrupt substitute of Christian culture upon the country, using tax money to fund it. This must not be allowed. Let each church fund its own evangelistic efforts. If what your church believes is actually the truth, then you should not resent donating your own time, effort, and funds to spread that truth. The more you give, the more the culture will conform to your liking, provided people are convinced by your arguments. If, however, your arguments are obviously wrong, then perhaps not very many people will accept them. Separation of church and state gives you freedom to try to persuade people to your position, but prevents you from forcing it upon them. Under true separation of church and state, then, the truth has a chance of prevailing in the culture also.

The First Amendment Doesn't Forbid Christians From Engaging In Politics

Another misconception of separation of church and state defines it as separation of the Christian individual from his civil duties. This unscriptural idea teaches that Christians are forbidden by the Bible from involving themselves in even the slightest way in politics. There is not a single verse in the Bible to support that idea. That idea is wrong and has greatly hurt Christianity. Separation of church and state does not at all mean that Christians are not allowed to try to influence political processes and decisions; that is their duty as citizens. If Christians sit idly by and let Humanists win all the elections, appoint justices to the Supreme

Court, hold all government offices, and make all the important decisions, they have no right to complain when their freedoms are lost and they are persecuted and enslaved. Pastors should encourage the capable men in their churches to run for key public positions, to vote according to Biblical principles, etc., so as to influence government to adopt and maintain godly philosophies and laws.

Examples of godly men who were involved in civil government as civil servants include: Joseph, Mordecai, Daniel, Shadrach, Meshach, and Abednigo, and David.

Some people even go so far as to say that it is sin for a Christian to be in the military. However, when Jesus was approached by soldiers who wanted to know what repentance would mean for them, Jesus did not tell them to leave the military. Rather we read:

> And the soldiers likewise demanded of him, saying, And what shall we do? And he said unto them, Do violence to no man, neither accuse any falsely; and be content with your wages. (Luke 3:14)

The fact that Jesus told them to be content with their wages indicates that He did not expect them to cease to be soldiers. Of course, He did expect them to not misuse their power as armed men to harm innocent people; but this is not to be twisted to mean that they may not use the sword against evil doers. Soldiers, policemen, and other government officials are God's ministers to revenge wrongdoing:

> Let every soul be subject unto the higher powers. For there is no power but of God: the powers that be are ordained of God. Whosoever therefore resisteth the power, resisteth the ordinance of God: and they that resist shall receive to themselves damnation. For rulers are not a terror to good works, but to the evil. Wilt thou then not be afraid of the power? do that which is good, and thou shalt have praise of the same: for he is the minister of God to thee for good. But if thou do that which is evil, be afraid; for he beareth not the sword in vain: for he is the minister of God, a revenger to *execute* wrath upon him that doeth evil. Wherefore *ye* must needs be subject, not only for wrath, but also for conscience sake. For for this cause pay ye tribute also: for they are God's ministers, attending continually upon this very thing. Render therefore to all their dues: tribute to whom tribute *is due*; custom to whom custom; fear to whom fear; honour to whom honour. (Rom. 13:1-7)

Civil government is thus clearly ordained of God, and not inherently evil. Each soldier, police officer, and government official is a "minister of God." Thus it is not wrong to be a civil servant. And thus it is not wrong to run for political office. It *is* wrong, however, for a civil servant to forget that he is God's minister, and start thinking and acting like he is God instead. ***A government ruler is not God, nor is government itself God. Government cannot do what only God can do. Government cannot produce wealth. Government cannot produce health. Government cannot educate. Government cannot give people anything without first taking it from them. Government cannot give you or your children a free education.***

While it is Christian duty to vote and influence political processes as much as possible, it is wrong to join with false religions and pagan organizations in attempting to do this. While non-Christian religions may vote with Christians to return to the First Amendment so that all religions can enjoy freedom, it would be a mistake to form ecumenical organizations for this purpose. The strength of the Lord's churches are not in alliances with the world, but in separation from the world and unto the Lord. The Bible is extremely clear about this:

> Be ye not unequally yoked together with unbelievers: for what fellowship hath righteousness with unrighteousness? and what communion hath light with darkness? (2 Cor 6.14)

When Christians yoke up with false religions or pagan organizations in an attempt to accomplish common goals, the end result is that those Christians compromise or remain silent on truths that divide but are vitally important, thus doing more damage than good.

Jesus on Separation of Church and State

The idea of separation of church and state did not originate with humanists, but with the Lord Jesus Christ. For any true Christian, the teachings of Christ are irrevocable and final. Notice how Jesus set forth the principle of separation of church and state in the following verses:

> And when they were come to Capernaum, they that received tribute money came to Peter, and said, Doth not your master pay tribute? He saith, Yes. And when he was come into the house, Jesus prevented him, saying, What thinkest thou, Simon? of whom do the kings of the earth take custom or tribute? of their own children, or of strangers? Peter saith unto him, Of strangers. Jesus saith unto him, Then are the children free. Notwithstanding, lest we should offend them, go thou to the sea, and cast an hook, and take up the fish that first cometh up; and when thou hast opened his mouth, thou shalt find a piece of money: that take, and give them for me and thee (Mat. 17.24-27).

> Then went the Pharisees, and took counsel how they might entangle him in his talk. And they sent out unto him their disciples with the Herodians, saying, Master, we know that thou art true, and teachest the way of God in truth, neither carest thou for any man: for thou regardest not the person of men. Tell us therefore, What thinkest thou? Is it lawful to give tribute unto Caesar, or not? But Jesus perceived their wickedness, and said, Why tempt ye me, ye hypocrites? Shew me the tribute money. And they brought unto him a penny. And he saith unto them, Whose is this image and superscription? They say unto him, Caesar's. Then he saith unto them, Render therefore unto Caesar the things that are Caesar's; and unto God the things that are God's (Mat. 22.15-21).

It is clearly seen in the above verses that Jesus taught separation of church and state. He considered his church to be a sovereign state, but spiritual, not temporal, in nature. His church was not an underground government trying to overthrow the civil government. His church was not to try to become the civil government. Jesus taught that people should pay the taxes they owe the civil government to the civil government; they are obligated to perform their duties as citizens. He taught that people should pay the tithes they owe their church to their church; they are obligated to perform their duties as church members. The government has no authority to collect tithes for the church; nor does the church have authority to collect taxes for the civil government. His church never asked for funding from the civil government. The entire New Testament shows a church that was separate from the state.

Ephesians 5:23 tells us that "Christ is the head of the church." That verse was written after Christ had already assended into Heaven. Christ does not need a vicar. He alone is the head of His church. For a church to enter into union with a civil government thereby making some world ruler other than Jesus its head is to commit spiritual fornication, as is shown in Revelation chapter 17:1-6:

> And there came one of the seven angels which had the seven vials, and talked with me, saying unto me, Come hither; I will shew unto thee the judgment of the great whore that sitteth upon many waters: with whom the kings of the earth have committed fornication, and the inhabitants of the earth have been made drunk with the wine of her fornication. So he carried me away in the spirit into the wilderness: and I saw a woman sit upon a scarlet coloured beast, full of names of blasphemy, having seven heads and ten horns. And the woman was arrayed in purple and scarlet colour, and decked with gold and precious stones and pearls, having a golden cup in her hand full of abominations and filthiness of her fornication: and upon her forehead was a name written, MYSTERY, BABYLON THE GREAT, THE MOTHER OF HARLOTS AND ABOMINATIONS OF THE EARTH. And I saw the woman drunken with the blood of the saints, and with the blood of the martyrs of Jesus: and when I saw her, I wondered with great admiration.

Note in the above Scripture passage that churches which commit such spiritual fornication are called whores and harlots. Such churches always use the political power they gain from such unholy unions to persecute the true saints of God. They are "drunken with the blood of the saints, and with the blood of the martyrs of Jesus." The river of history runs red with the blood shed by such harlot churches. Again, that is why the First Amendment is so important.

Applying Separation of Church and State

THE MOST IMPORTANT FACT CONCERNING EDUCATION IS THIS: IT IS IMPOSSIBLE TO HAVE A PUBLIC SCHOOL SYSTEM WITHOUT ALSO HAVING A STATE CHURCH. Some religion's philosophy of education must be used in any school to the exclusion of other religions' educational philosophies. As the humanists themselves admit, there is no area of life that is not religious.

Public schools are socialist schools, and socialism is legalized robbery based on atheism. Socialism is a doctrine of the humanist religion. Therefore public (tax-funded) schools are fundamentally wrong at their core, AND THAT CANNOT BE FIXED.

There is only one way to stop the present deterioration of education and violation of church and state in this country, and that is by doing away with public schools altogether. It is wrong for government to fund education at any level, including kindergartens, grade schools, middle schools, high schools, and universities, because government funding automatically creates a state church.

Conclusion

JESUS TAUGHT SEPARATION OF CHURCH AND STATE, AND IT IS THE VIOLATION OF HIS TEACHINGS THAT ARE CAUSING ALL OF OUR EDUCATION PROBLEMS. Because tax funded education is socialism, which is based on atheism, it is fundamentally wrong and anti-God at its core, and should not exist. It is, therefore, wrong—lack of love—for Christians to put their children in public schools. It is wrong—theft—for Christians to vote for tax funding of public schools. It is wrong—aiding and abetting the enemy—for Christians to teach in public schools. ***ABOLISHING PUBLIC EDUCATION ON ALL LEVELS IS THE ONLY WAY FOR US TO REGAIN OUR RELIGIOUS FREEDOM.***

Humanists lie in saying they defend separation of church and state. It is amazing that Christians have been so gullible as to believe this huge lie. Opposing separation of church and state is exactly what Humanists want Christians to do; it is what keeps Humanists in power.

The truth is that the Humanist religion was long ago established as the state church of America. Public schools are the Monday through Friday schools of the Humanist religion. Through taxation we are paying for our own children to be brainwashed in the Humanist religious dogmas of evolution and sodomy, and thus turned against their parents and against God.

Public education is socialist education, and by its very nature is religion combined with state, and that cannot be fixed, but must be repented of.

The only hope Christians have of regaining freedom of speech and freedom of religion is to fight for separation of the Humanist religion and all other religions from state, by totally privatizing education.

Chapter 23

IS YOUR MINISTER A HUMANIST?

Wolves In Sheep's Clothing

Approximately fifty percent of the signers of *Humanist Manifesto I & II* claimed to be Christian ministers! Joseph Fletcher, signer of *Humanist Manifesto II* and author of *Situation Ethics—the New Morality*, is a good example. He is a bishop in the Episcopal Church.

The first chapter of *The Humanist Evangel* (Buffalo, New York: Prometheus Books, 1982) by Humanist writer Lucien Saumur, brags that humanists have infiltrated Christian churches in order to subvert them:

> Humanists could pretend to be Christians and to work within the Christian context. They were not above using Christianity as a disguise or as a camouflage for their endeavors. They argued about religion, defending those aspects of religion which served to promote humanism against those aspects which threatened it. They subverted the graphic arts, where religious themes became mere pretexts and where the wretched bodies of the Middle Ages were replaced by the beautiful bodies of the Renaissance. This denial of the Christian ideal of suffering was not recognized as such by the contemporary Christians. It is only in retrospect that the humanist ploy is evident.[414]

That this infiltration and subversion has indeed happened—and is still happening every day—is obvious to anyone schooled in philosophy. Not only do humanists claim to be Christians, they also claim to be Christian preachers and Bible scholars. This being the case, it is important to know how to spot a humanist wolf in sheep's clothing.

> Beware of false prophets, which come to you in sheep's clothing, but inwardly they are ravening wolves. Ye shall know them by their fruits (Mat. 7:15-16).

One way to determine if a minister is a humanist is to listen carefully to how he defines God.

Corliss Lamont, an atheist, a signer of *Humanist Manifesto II*, and at one time Honorary President of the American Humanist Association, Chairman of the National Emergency Civil Liberties Committee, and a director of the American Civil Liberties Union, wrote the following in "Equivocation on Religious Issues" which was published in his book *A Lifetime of Dissent* (Buffalo, New York: Prometheus Books):

> Most important of all among questions of religious belief I consider those of the existence of God and the existence of immortality. And by God I mean a personal God and by immortality I mean personal immortality, survival of the individual after death....It is possible to make a classification of four different groups. *Firstly*, there are those, still powerful in strength and numbers, who affirm the existence of God and immortality. *Secondly*, there is a lesser group which is sincerely agnostic on these questions. *Thirdly*, we have a steadily increasing class of persons who clearly and openly deny the existence of God and immortality. They frankly acknowledge their atheism, since that term most accurately describes their position. Then, *fourthly*, there is that rather large number who in various ways avoid the issue. The greater proportion of these do not actually believe in God or immortality in any ordinary sense of those terms. Most of them, I feel, belong by rights to the third group and ought to be supporting the group. It is this forth and last class that I wish particularly to analyse. The first three divisions for the most part know what they think and say what they think about God and immortality. But I am tempted to believe that the members of the fourth division are somewhat muddled, and at least there can be no doubt that they muddle others.
>
> *The easiest and most frequent way of equivocating on the issue and qualifying for the fourth group is by indulging in the gentle art of redefinition*[415] *[Italics emphasis added].*

The Bible Definition of God

Mr. Lamont is right! Any definition of God in disagreement with the definition of God given in the Bible is really just disguised atheism. The true God is defined in the Bible as follows:

---

[414] Lucien Saumur, *The Humanist Evangel* (Buffalo, New York: Prometheus Books, 1982), ???

[415] Corliss Lamont, *A Lifetime of Dissent* (Buffalo: Prometheus Books), 9–10.

God Is Our Creator

The God of the Bible created everything in six 24 hour days: "For *in* six days the LORD made heaven and earth, the sea, and all that in them *is*" (Ex. 20:11). The argument that the six days were actually thousands (or billions!) of years in which evolution took place is simply atheistic unbelief, for the Genesis account of creation clearly says "the evening and the morning were the first day" (Gen. 1:5).

God Is Separate From His Creation

The God of the Bible "is before all things, and by him all things consist" (Col. 1:17). So God is separate from the universe, matter is not eternal, the universe is not God, and pantheism—the idea that everything is God—is therefore wrong.

God Is Spirit Not Matter

The God of the Bible is spirit, not matter. "God *is* a Spirit: and they that worship him must worship *him* in spirit and in truth" (Joh. 4:24). That spirit is not matter is made very clear in Luke 24:39: "Behold my hands and my feet, that it is I myself: handle me, and see; for a spirit hath not flesh and bones, as ye see me have."

God Is Prayer Hearing and Answering

The God of the Bible hears and answers prayers asked in accordance with His holy will. "Call unto me, and I will answer thee, and show thee great and mighty things, which thou knowest not" (Jer. 33:3).

God Is Unlimited

The God of the Bible is *omniscient*, "Thou, God seeth me" (Gen. 16:13), *omnipresent*, "Do not I fill heaven and earth" (Jer. 23:24), and *omnipotent*, "With God all things are possible" (Mat. 19:26). God can do anything He wills, including creating humans able to choose between good or evil without His intervention. "He hath done whatsoever he hath pleased" (Ps. 115:3). "Lo, this only have I found, that God hath made man upright; but they have sought out many inventions" (Ecc. 7:29).

God Is Absolute and Immutable

The God of the Bible is absolute and immutable. "God is light, and in him is no darkness at all" (1 Joh. 1:5). "For I *am* the LORD, I change not" (Mal. 3:6). Thus we can depend on him!

God Is Holy and Just

"Exalt ye the LORD our God, and worship at his footstool; for he is holy" (Ps. 99:5). "Great and marvellous *are* thy works, Lord God Almighty; just and true *are* thy ways, thou King of saints" (Rev. 15:3). Because God is holy He hates sin. Because He is just, "the soul that sinneth, it shall die" (Eze. 18:4). "The wicked shall be turned into hell, and all the nations that forget God" (Ps. 9:17).

God Is a Trinity

There is only one God, and He is three distinct persons—Father, Son, and Holy Spirit. "There *is* but one God, the Father, of whom *are* all things, and we in him; and one Lord Jesus Christ, by whom *are* all things, and we by him" (1 Cor. 8:6). "For there are three that bear record in heaven, the Father, the Word, and the Holy Ghost: and these three are one" (1 Joh. 5:7).

God Is Living, Personal, and Loving

The God of the Bible is a personal being who loves and cares for the people He created. Therefore God wants to save you from your sins so you will not have to go to Hell. "God commendeth his love toward us, in that, while we were yet sinners, Christ died for us. Much more then, being now justified by his blood, we shall be saved from wrath through him. For if, when we were enemies, we were reconciled to God by the death of his Son, much more, being reconciled, we shall be saved by his life. And not only *so*, but we also joy in God through our Lord Jesus Christ, by whom we have now received the atonement" (Rom 5.8-11). The word atonement implies "at-one-ment." It is the covering and washing away of sin by the blood of Christ so that whosoever believes in Him shall be reconciled with God, and also receive forgiveness, peace, and everlasting life.

God Is Knowable

The God of the Bible can be known by humans. I know him, and so can you. "And this is life eternal, that they might know thee the only true God, and Jesus Christ, whom thou hast sent" (Joh 17.3).

The God of the Bible is the only true God. Any god less then the God of the Bible is not really God at all, but mere delusion. A person believing in a non-God god is for all practical purposes just an atheist even if he does not realize it.

Redefining God Away

Being an atheist himself, Corliss Lamont easily recognizes and lists the following definitions of God as disguised atheism:

Kirsopp Lake's Definition

"God is the sum of all ideal values."

Julian Huxley's Definition

"I wish you here to agree to my giving the name of God to the sum of the forces acting in the cosmos as perceived and grasped by the human mind. We can therefore now say that God is one, but that though one, has several aspects."

Jesse H. Holmes's Definition

"[God is] that unifying element within which moves men to unity in a brotherly world."

Henery Nelson Wieman's Definition

"God is that interaction between individuals, groups, and ages which generates and promotes the greatest possible mutuality of good."

John H. Randall, Jr.'s Definition

"There is no room for God save in the aspirations and imagination of men....We take the word 'God' as the symbol of man's supreme allegiance....faith in God may mean faith in the possibility of sharing ever more fully this vision of the highest perfection."

John Dewey's Definition

"We are in the presence neither of ideals that we completely embodied in existence nor yet of ideals that are mere rootless ideals, fantasies, utopias. There are forces in nature that generate and support ideals.

They are further unified by the action that gives them coherence and solidarity. It is this *active* relation between ideal and actual to which I would give the name *God*. And would not insist that the name *must* be given."

To Corliss Lamont's list of atheists' definitions of God, I will add the following:

John Shelby Spong's Definition

"We have come to the dawning realization that God might not be separate from us but rather deep within us. The sense of God as the sum of all that is, plus something more, grows in acceptability. When theologians are pressed, however, to define that something more, the inadequacy of language becomes gallingly apparent."

Why Atheists Say They Believe In God

Why do some atheists say they believe in God when in fact they do not? The answer to that question is very significant indeed, as Corliss Lamont points out in the following commentary:

> I suppose that the first and fairest question to ask our redefiners is, What is the purpose and value of this complex and bewildering game? I imagine that their chief answer is that they do not wish to cut themeselves off from the great and beautiful tradition that goes under the name of Christianity....They wish to work within the tradition or within the church and win people over gradually to a new and more acceptable idea of God; to evolve a religion relevant to modern conditions while retaining the hollowed and well-loved words of old. All this would be impossible if they acknowledged themselves as atheists....The attitude of the redefinitionists perhaps comes most appropriately under the heading of what is sometimes called "strategy."

In other words, some atheists confess to believe in God so that they will be accepted by Christians so that they can gradually convince those Christians that they should be converts to the "religion" of atheism! And Corliss Lamont is correct to use the term "religion" so, for atheism *is* a religion—a religion of falsehood, lies and deceit. Everyone is religious, and everyone worships someone or thing. Atheists worship Evolution and themselves. That is why Humanists call themselves "religious humanists" as well as atheists.

Lamont's contempt for atheists who claim to be theists provokes him to write yet another truism:

> I wonder what God, if there turns out to be one after all, would think about these people who damn Him with faint praise. Would not He, too, be shocked? And I wonder if He would not be justified in punishing these redefiners for breaking the third commandment, that is, for taking His name in vain....The redefiners mutilate a time-hallowed and well-loved vocabulary, yet provide very little in return for this questionable procedure. For their God concepts have precious little religious value. Their gods cannot be worshipped or prayed to; they do not govern the universe or the earth, or watch over mankind; they do not do anything, nor do they possess personality or mind or consciousness. I cannot imagine any large group of men becoming emotionally aroused over such gods. And these gods are so distant in meaning from the traditional God of Christianity that I doubt whether a continuity that resides merely in the use of the same word is worth bothering about.

How right Mr. Lamont is! To define God as being something which He is not is to imply that God Himself is not. A god without the attributes of God is not God. The redefiners of God are atheists of the most dishonest and deceptive sort. They muddle (mix up in a confused manner) the thinking of everyone they influence.

Important Conclusions

There are important facts made clear by Corliss Lamont which we would be wise to remember:

There Are Phony Christian Preachers

There are atheists who have entered the Christian ministry for the sole purpose of deceiving people into accepting a phony definition of God. The Apostle Paul put it like this:

> I fear, lest by any means, as the serpent beguiled Eve through his subtlety, so your minds should be corrupted from the simplicity that is in Christ. For if he that cometh preacheth another Jesus, whom we have not preached, or *if* ye receive another spirit, which ye have not received, or another gospel, which ye have not accepted, ye might well bear with *him*....such *are* false apostles, deceitful workers, transforming themselves into the apostles of Christ. And no marvel; for Satan himself is transformed into an angel of light. Therefore *it is* no great thing if his minis-

ters also be transformed as the ministers of righteousness; whose end shall be according to their works (2 Cor. 11:3-15).

Because there are phony Christian preachers, the wise soul will beware to carefully distinguish between the real and the phony.

Liberal Religion Is Just Disguised Atheism

Many of the old mainline Protestant religions are now led by atheistic humanists. They do not believe the Bible at all, but simply redefine everything in it to mean whatever they want it to mean. Beware of preachers "having a form of godliness, but denying the power thereof" (2 Tim. 3:5). One atheist accurately described liberal religion as follows:

> Now the increasing number of those who are liberal in religion do not take credal statements in a simple factual sense. They agree that stories of the sun standing still or of devils entering into men or animals belong to a stage that we have passed beyond. But the real difficulty goes deeper. It is that the very idea of an originating or intervening supernatural power is ceasing to have the force that it formerly had. The liberal theologian may feel that his religion is as real and as important to him as it ever was but his idea of a supernatural power is undoubtedly distanced: it has become something more like a philosophical ultimate. If as many people as ever believe in a supernatural power it is a fair statement that they believe in it, or him, less immediately and less continuously than they did, and that there is a wider and wider realm of daily experience in whose working the conception is not invoked.[416]

Even *Humanist Manifesto I & II* classifies liberal religion with atheism, saying: "Free thought, atheism, agnosticism, skepticism, deism, rationalism, ethical culture, and liberal religion all claim to be heir to the humanist tradition."[417]

The Doctrine of Salvation By Works Is Atheism

The Bible says that "by grace are ye saved through faith; and that not of yourselves: it is the gift of God: not of works, lest any man should boast" (Eph. 2:9). But the atheistic *Humanist Manifesto II* declares: "No deity will save us; we must save ourselves."[418] The doctrine of salvation by doing good works is a rejection of the true God, and should be recognized as atheism, even if some claim it to be Christian.

If a person does not yet know God it is because he has not come to God on God's terms: "For he that cometh to God must believe that he is, and *that* he is a rewarder of them that diligently seek him" (Heb. 11:6). Faith in the true God is rewarded instantly by knowledge of His reality. Salvation is not "pie in the sky by and by when you die." Salvation is available right now to every believer: "Behold, NOW is the accepted time; behold, NOW is the day of salvation" (2 Cor. 6:2).

Furthermore, you can KNOW you are saved:

> He that hath the Son hath life; and he that hath not the Son of God hath not life. These things have I written unto you that believe on the name of the Son of God; that ye may **know** that ye **have** eternal life, and that ye may believe on the name of the Son of God (1 Joh. 5:12-13).

The Ultimate Deceivers

If God is "the sum of all that is" or "the sum of the forces acting in the cosmos as perceived and grasped by the human mind" (as some humanist theologians say), then everyone is a theist, and there are no atheists. Madalyn Murray O'Hair and a multitude of Humanists very vocally let us know that that isn't true. There are atheists. There are *open* atheists. There are also *closet* atheists who claim to believe in God but actually do not. There are atheists who have become ministers in Christian churches for the sole purpose of subverting the members and converting them into atheists. Beware of preachers preaching a non-God God.

The Bible Warning

The Bible gives a perfect Description of humanists, and warns us to "turn away" from them.

---

[416] Lionel Elvin, "An Education For Humanity," in *The Humanist Frame*, Ed. Julian Huxley (New York: Harper & Brothers, 1961), 279.

[417] Kurtz, *Humanist Manifestos I & II*, 15.

[418] Ibid., 16.

This know also, that in the last days perilous times shall come. For men shall be lovers of their own selves, covetous, boasters, proud, blasphemers, disobedient to parents, unthankful, unholy, without natural affection, trucebreakers, false accusers, incontinent, fierce, despisers of those that are good, traitors, heady, highminded, lovers of pleasures more than lovers of God; having a form of godliness, but denying the power thereof: from such turn away. For of this sort are they which creep into houses, and lead captive silly women laden with sins, led away with divers lusts, ever learning, and never able to come to the knowledge of the truth. Now as Jannes and Jambres withstood Moses, so do these also resist the truth: men of corrupt minds, reprobate concerning the faith. But they shall proceed no further: for their folly shall be manifest unto all *men* as theirs also was (2 Tim. 3:1-9).

Every one of the adjectives in the above verses fits humanists perfectly, but note especially the following:

* **"Lovers of their own selves"**—most of the magazines targeting women today are teaching woman that they have done enough (even too much) for their husband and children, and that it is now time to take care of self and have some fun by having an affair or deserting their family. That is humanism.
* **"Disobedience to parents"**—humanists are against all authority that stems from God. Humanist ministers teach children to disobey parents, wives to disobey husbands, employees to disobey their employers, citizens to disobey the government, and everyone to disobey the true God, whom they portray as a sadistic monster.
* **"Unthankful"**—humanists enjoy all the benefits of living in the USA, but virtually to a man hate the God that granted the USA all this affluence. Nor are they thankful for all that their parents and grandparents did to pave the way for their success. Nor are they thankful for our Bible-based capitalism economic system that allows them to enjoy so much wealth.
* **"Without natural affection"**—It is not natural for a mother to not love her unborn baby and desire to murder it. It is humanist doctrine that causes women to become so selfish and hateful. These same women have no affection for their husbands, but for strange men or for other woman or even for animals they have an unnatural affection. That is humanism.
* **"False accusers"**—humanists will instantly label anyone who opposed their wicked agenda another "McCarthy," and will call him or her a homosexual, or adulterer, or will find some obscure point of law to say that person has broken. Since they are so well organized, this has worked for them repeatedly in the past. It is time for Americans to quit falling for this trick. After all, the humanists say that homosexuality and adultery are ok, so shouldn't we at least recognize that they are hypocrites when they accuse a conservative of those sins? Even if the conservative they are accusing is actually guilty, does that mean that we should give the reins of government to humanist hypocrites who as a matter of principle live even worse?
* **"Despisers of those that are good"**—humanist despise good people because they view good people as obstacles keeping humanists from achieving their goals, and of course they are correct in so thinking.
* **"Highminded"**—Humanists are elitists. They think they alone are intelligent, and that ordinary American citizens are all morons. You can tell who they are because they are always trying to get laws passed to protect you from yourself. In their opinions you are too ignorant and of too low an IQ to make right choices on your own.
* **"Lovers of pleasures"**—the "if it feels good do it" slogan originated from humanism. What the Bible calls lust and sin, humanists call fun and good. Do you want to do something you know the Bible says is wrong? You can always find a humanist minister who will tell you that the sin you want to do is ok. In fact, a humanist minister will help you get so far down the road to ruin so fast that by the time you wake up to the truth your life will be in shambles. A humanist minister will tear down the standards a church once lived by and lead it into sin. He will replace godly music with Rock music. He will replace the preaching of God's Word with entertainment. Instead of preaching that homosexual sex is an abomination (Lev. 20:13), he will make sodomites leaders in the church.
* **"Creep into houses, and lead captive silly women"**—humanists target women. Almost everyone has heard of the National Organization of Women (NOW), which is a front organization of the American Humanist Association. NOW is run by sodomites who hate marriage and hate the

responsibilities of marriage and motherhood. It is especially easy now for humanists to creep into homes via television soap operas and other programs which are designed to stir up resentment and unholy lusts in women, so as to cause them to destroy their own marriages and homes. They are indeed "silly women" that watch soap operas and read novels that stir up "divers lusts."

* **"Ever learning, and never able to come to the knowledge of the truth"**—since Jesus is "the truth" (John 14:6), and since humanists reject Jesus, humanist are never able to come to the knowledge of the truth. They are always trying to *find themselves.*
* **"Reprobate concerning the faith"**—humanists reject all the basics of the Christian faith: the existence of a true and living triune God as defined in the Scriptures, the Divine inspiration and preservation of the Scriptures, the literal six day creation, the virgin birth of Christ, the Deity of Christ, that Christ died on the cross for our sins as our substitutionary atonement, the bodily resurrection of Christ, the second coming of Christ, the reality of a literal Heaven and a literal Hell, and eternal salvation by grace through faith in the Lord Jesus Christ alone. Humanists reject all these vital basic teachings.

The Bible plainly tells us to "turn away" from such people. After reading to this chapter in this book, you should now be able to identify a humanist by his philosophy, even if he denies being one. If your pastor is a humanist, you no doubt already realize it. You have just read the Bible command to "turn away" from such people, so you also know what action you should take in your relationship with him. All that is necessary now is for you to obey God's command. Get away from that evil man or woman. Find yourself a Bible-believing church pastored by a genuine man of God.

HUMANIST MINISTERS disguise themselves as scientists or Christian ministers. But underneath the cover they are just religious quacks. "Beware of false prophets, which come to you in sheep's clothing, but inwardly they are ravening **wolves**. Ye shall know them by their fruits. Do men gather grapes of thorns, or figs of thistles? Even so every good tree bringeth forth good fruit; but a corrupt tree bringeth forth evil fruit. A good tree cannot bring forth evil fruit, neither *can* a corrupt tree bring forth good fruit. Every tree that bringeth not forth good fruit is hewn down, and cast into the fire. Wherefore by their fruits ye shall know them." (Mat. 7:15-20)

Chapter 24

IS THE DEMOCRAT PARTY HUMANIST?

Yes, It Is the Anti-God Party

The Democrat Party is the anti-God, anti-prayer, anti-Bible, anti-Christian, anti-traditional family, anti-USA-flag, anti-free-speech, pro-socialism, pro-enemy, pro-unborn-baby-murder, pro-pornography, pro-sodomy, pro-whatever-will-divide-the-USA party. Those are just the facts easily observed by anyone who reads newspapers. Those positions are all atheist/liberal/humanist positions. As Ann Coulter has correctly pointed out:

> The fundamental difference between liberals and conservatives is: Conservatives believe man was created in God's image; liberals believe they are God. All their other behavioral ties proceed from this one irreducible minimum. Liberals believe they can murder the unborn because they are gods. They try to forcibly create "equality" through affirmative action and wealth redistribution because they are gods. They can lie, with no higher power to constrain them, because they are gods. They adore pornography and the mechanization of sex because man is just an animal, and they are gods. They revere the U.N. and not the U.S. because they aren't Americans—they are gods.[419]

Christians should vote according to Bible principles, and not according to any party line. Presently, the Republican Party is the most conservative. However, even in the Republican Party there are some humanists. So, no Christian should vote a straight party line without careful study of each candidate first. It is anti-God to vote for a humanist, no matter what his party. But as of this writing most conservative candidates are in the Republican Party, and virtually none are in the Democrat Party. The Democrat Party is spiritually and morally bankrupt. It was long ago hijacked by radical religious humanists, and it is exceedingly unlikely to ever recover from its depravity.

The Bill Clinton Administration

In an editorial titled "New Beginnings" on page 2 of the January/February 1993 issue of *The Humanist* magazine, editor Don Page said concerning the then recent election of Bill Clinton as president of the United States: "This issue of *The Humanist* coincides with the beginning of a new era of hope in Washington and throughout the country." In this same issue of *The Humanist*, Barbara Dority wrote a special editorial in which she stated:

> In the November/December 1992 issue of *The Humanist*, I expressed my hope that the American people had finally had enough of simplistic, moralistic, fundamentalist thinking. "I feel the pendulum beginning to shift," I wrote. Nevertheless, I wasn't prepared for the decisiveness of the election results, the nationwide rejection of hard-line conservative candidates, or the unexpected victories of women and minority candidates in numerous state and local races.[420]

Dority fails to mention that Clinton only received 36 percent of the vote—hardly a decisive victory. Had Ross Perot not split the conservative vote, Clinton would have most likely met decisive defeat. It is also significant to note that Ross Perot was rewarded for making this Democrat victory possible. One of the first bills passed by the Democrat dominated congress put an interstate highway through property owned by Ross Perot, increasing its value by millions of dollars. Nevertheless, in the next few paragraphs of her editorial, Dority gives her version of why Bill Clinton won the election. Leaving no doubt about her joy over Clinton's election, Dority says:

> *Among additional reasons for genuine celebration and relief at Clinton's victory is, of course, the future composition of the Supreme Court.* Justices Harry Blackmun and Byron White (ages 83 and 75, respectively) will both almost certainly retire within the next four years. Two more Bush Supreme Court appointments would have been nothing but disastrous, leaving us with the kind of damage that might have proved virtually irreparable.[421]

---

[419] Coulter, *Treason*, 292.

[420] Barbara Dority, "Power to the People," *The Humanist* 53, no. 1 (January/February 1993): 3.

[421] Ibid., 4.

Just the fact that a Humanist leader should be so elated over Clinton's victory is disturbing. But Dority then went on to make a statement that should make every thinking American sit up and take notice. She said that many of Clinton's campaign promises clearly reflect humanist principles. Furthermore she then proceeded to list those campaign promises so her readers would know exactly which promises she was talking about. Here is what she said:

> ***President-elect Clinton has made many campaign promises which clearly reflect humanist principles***; now it's up to us to hold him to them. He has promised to sign a Workplace Fairness Bill prohibiting permanent replacement of strikers. He has pledged to overturn anti-gay policies in the military, to sign the Family and Medical Leave Act, to revive the child-welfare bill vetoed by Bush, and to fully fund Head Start programs. He has committed himself to freedom of reproductive choice and has promised to sign the Freedom of Choice Act, repeal the gag rule, support testing of the French abortion pill RU-486, and lift the ban on the use of fetal tissue for research purposes.
>
> He has promised to appoint an AIDS policy director to assure better funding for AIDS research and care of AIDS patients. With Al Gore, he has promised environmental reforms, including a rewrite of the Clean Air Act regulations, no expansion of offshore drilling, and tougher penalties for pollution violations. He supports school-based clinics and drug education. He says he'll sign the Motor Voter Bill. He promises health-care reform, a pressing and far-reaching problem particularly resistant to government remedies.
>
> In addition, of course, he has promised to reduce the national debt and to boost inner-city development through national economic strategies: incentives and grants to revitalize urban economies and the expansion of education, job training, and child-care services.[422] [Emphasis added.]

Dority goes on to say that there are a few things Clinton promised that oppose humanist principles: he promised to oppose the legalization of "recreational" drugs, and he promised to support the death-penalty. Also, she felt he didn't promise enough support to blacks and those in poverty. She ends her editorial by saying:

> Notwithstanding all these cautions, concerns, and fears, ***we have made a turn in the road—a turn which alters our view of what lies ahead. We have made a profound and decisive ideological change***; we have also made a long-overdue generational change, the most dramatic since Dwight Eisenhower was replaced by John F. Kennedy. In so doing, we have rejoined the world community and entered the twenty-first century.
>
> I am hopeful that these changes will encourage and inspire more of us to bring our humanist heritage to bear on the burning issues of the day. Free-thought activism is an affair of the heart. Let us resume our work with renewed vigor and hope. ***Now at long last, it is our time.***[423] [Emphasis added.]

And, indeed, it *was* the Humanists' time. There has never been a more anti-Christian, humanist president than Bill Clinton. From his constant lying to his sexcapades with Monica Lewinsky, Clinton lived by humanist principles. And he continues to do so. As Clinton's former counselor, Dick Morris, pointed out:

> By traveling to Dubai, just a few hundred miles from the combat zone, to denounce the American involvement in Iraq as a "big mistake," Bill Clinton has made a big mistake of his own.
>
> Normally, a top leader of the Democratic Party and the spouse of a presidential candidate can and should feel free to say anything he chooses. But a former president of the United States should be more careful before he tells hundreds of thousands of young men and women, many of whom served under him, that they are risking their lives for a mistake.
>
> To do it in the Arab world compounds the error. His denunciation of our war effort so close to the spots where our troops are fighting summons memories of Jane Fonda.[424]

Yet consider this well: Bill Clinton was considered a "moderate" in the Democrat Party! If Hillary Clinton runs for president in the upcoming election (as is predicted), she will be one of the more moderate Democrat candidates even though she is probably the most divisive person in the history of US politics! All of the other candidates are so radical that they cannot hide their contempt for real Americans. When they speak you can almost once again see Nikita Khrushchev pounding his shoe on the table as he told Americans that communism would bury them—humanist beliefs are virtually identical to communism. Hillary is actually just as radical as any other Democrat—perhaps more so—, but is much better at lying about it.

Any way you look at it, the Democrat Party is the radical atheist/humanist/anti-God party. Even the Democrat leadership realizes that this has put their party out of favor with mainstream America. But every year the public school system produces more humanist Democrat voters, gradually making humanism more and more mainstream.

---

422 Ibid.

423 Ibid., 32.

424 Dick Morris, "Bubba Steps Over the Line," *Journal News*, 2001 December 2005, A12.

Democrat Immorality

As these words are being written, the Democrat leadership is disturbed even though their unrelenting attacks upon the Bush administration and upon other Republican leaders is paying off.

> A Pew Research Center poll shows Republican leadership in Congress is down to a 32 percent approval rating. The rating for President Bush hovers under 40 percent—unusual for a second term.
>
> But, paradoxically, Republican public opinion losses do not translate as corresponding Democratic gains.[425]

The main reason that the Democrat Party does not connect with mainstream America is that it has rejected God and God-based morality in favor of Evolution and Situational Ethics, in which humans are considered animals, and right and wrong are determined by the individual instead of by God. For example, in spite of what God says, Democrats consider the murder of unborn babies to be a righteous act and a "fundamental human right."

> Political scientists Bill Galston and Elaine Kamarck have written a report titled "The Politics of Polarization." They say that to win, the Democrats will have to revise their doctrine on national security and on social and moral issues. Mr. Galston and Ms. Kamarck command attention among Democrats because they helped to guide policy for the successful Clinton compain in 1996.[426]

What Galston and Kamarck mean is that the Democrats will have to deceive the American people about what they actually believe in order to win in this next election.

An article in the February 2007 issue of U.S. News and World Report proclaims that "The Dems Get Religion." Here is what it says,

> John Kerry struggled to overcome his secular image in 2004, but the current crop of Democratic presidential front-runners is determined not to repeat his mistakes.
>
> One of New York Sen. Hillary Rodham Clinton's first campaign hires was a top evangelical staffer on Capitol Hill. U.S. News has learned that an aide in Illinois Sen. Barack Obama's office tasked with religious outreach is joining his presidential campaign this week. And former North Carolina Sen. John Edwards is framing poverty relief as a moral issue that's helping to drive his campaign. "Two thousand eight could be the first time since Jimmy Carter that the presidential candidate who's really good on faith issues is the Democrat," says Eric Sapp, a Democratic consultant. So the Democratic primaries could see serious competition among candidates for the faith vote.[427]

Of course, the Dems don't have to get religion—they already have it. The problem is that their religion is the same religion that underlies communism. What they have to do is convince the American public that they have a religion that professes faith in God. There is only one way they can do this, and that is to lie. The Democrats' (im)morals are not going to change. If a person really has morals, those morals don't change. If sodomy is a righteous lifestyle alternative as the Democrats have maintained for a long time now, then sodomy will not suddenly become sin just because an election is coming up. If the Democrats fake change on this issue in order to get votes, then the very change itself will be immoral—and they will change back to what they really believe the moment they are elected to office. The Sodomy Party will be in and sodomy party will begin! Well, actually they already have and it has.

Remember Sodom and Gomorrah

Just in case you've never read it, here is the history behind the word "sodomy."

> ...the men of **Sodom** *were* wicked and sinners before the LORD exceedingly. (Gen. 13:13)

> And there came two angels to **Sodom** at even; and Lot sat in the gate of **Sodom**: and Lot seeing *them* rose up to meet them; and he bowed himself with his face toward the ground; And he said, Behold now, my lords, turn in, I pray you, into your servant's house, and tarry all night, and wash your feet, and ye shall rise up early, and go on your ways. And they said, Nay; but we will abide in the street all night. And he pressed upon them greatly; and they turned in unto him, and entered into his house; and he made them a feast, and did bake unleavened bread, and they did eat. But before they lay down, the men of the city, *even* the men of **Sodom**, compassed the house round, both old and young, all the people from every quarter: And they called unto Lot, and said unto him, Where *are* the men which came in to thee this night? bring them out unto us, that we may know them. And Lot went out at the door unto them, and shut the door after him, and said, I pray you, brethren, do not so

---

425 Daniel Schorr, "Democrats Aren't Gaining Public Support Republicans Are Losing," *Jackson Hole Daily* 27, no. 251 (1925 October 2005): 5.

426 Ibid.

427 Dan Gilgoff, "The Dems Get Religion," *U.S. News & World Report*, 1925 February 2007, Http://www.usnews.com/usnews/news/articles/070225/5evangelicals.b.htm.

wickedly. Behold now, I have two daughters which have not known man; let me, I pray you, bring them out unto you, and do ye to them as *is* good in your eyes: only unto these men do nothing; for therefore came they under the shadow of my roof. And they said, Stand back. And they said *again*, This one *fellow* came in to sojourn, and he will needs be a judge: now will we deal worse with thee, than with them. And they pressed sore upon the man, *even* Lot, and came near to break the door. But the men put forth their hand, and pulled Lot into the house to them, and shut to the door. And they smote the men that *were* at the door of the house with blindness, both small and great: so that they wearied themselves to find the door. And the men said unto Lot, Hast thou here any besides? son in law, and thy sons, and thy daughters, and whatsoever thou hast in the city, bring *them* out of this place: for we will destroy this place, because the cry of them is waxen great before the face of the LORD; and the LORD hath sent us to destroy it. And Lot went out, and spake unto his sons in law, which married his daughters, and said, Up, get you out of this place; for the LORD will destroy this city. But he seemed as one that mocked unto his sons in law. And when the morning arose, then the angels hastened Lot, saying, Arise, take thy wife, and thy two daughters, which are here; lest thou be consumed in the iniquity of the city. And while he lingered, the men laid hold upon his hand, and upon the hand of his wife, and upon the hand of his two daughters; the LORD being merciful unto him: and they brought him forth, and set him without the city. And it came to pass, when they had brought them forth abroad, that he said, Escape for thy life; look not behind thee, neither stay thou in all the plain; escape to the mountain, lest thou be consumed. And Lot said unto them, Oh, not so, my Lord: behold now, thy servant hath found grace in thy sight, and thou hast magnified thy mercy, which thou hast shewed unto me in saving my life; and I cannot escape to the mountain, lest some evil take me, and I die: behold now, this city *is* near to flee unto, and it *is* a little one: Oh, let me escape thither, (*is* it not a little one?) and my soul shall live. And he said unto him, See, I have accepted thee concerning this thing also, that I will not overthrow this city, for the which thou hast spoken. Haste thee, escape thither; for I cannot do any thing till thou be come thither. Therefore the name of the city was called Zoar. The sun was risen upon the earth when Lot entered into Zoar. Then the LORD rained upon **Sodom** and upon Gomorrah brimstone and fire from the LORD out of heaven; and he overthrew those cities, and all the plain, and all the inhabitants of the cities, and that which grew upon the ground. But his wife looked back from behind him, and she became a pillar of salt. And Abraham gat up early in the morning to the place where he stood before the LORD: and he looked toward **Sodom** and Gomorrah, and toward all the land of the plain, and beheld, and, lo, the smoke of the country went up as the smoke of a furnace. (Gen. 19:1-28)

Chapter 25

DOES SLANDER MATTER?

Yes, It Assassinates Free Speech

Most Christians are not aware of the extreme dangers they face in the year 2008. Except God grant us a miracle (which would be no problem for God)—and we had better be praying that He does—, a humanist is certain to be our next president. Tom DeLay, majority leader in the House of Representitives from 1995 to 2005, explains why this is so:

> "When Bush came to power, the Clintonistas didn't just skip town looking for work," said Mr DeLay, who remains an influential and popular figure with the party's Right-wing faithful. "They stayed in Washington and formed dozens of political groups to push their liberal agenda and built the most impressive political coalition I've ever witnessed.
>
> "This is the network that beat conservatives in 2006, and that was just the warm-up."
>
> He is scathing about the lack of unity and leadership in the conservative movement and holds out little prospects that the Republicans can hold on to the White House, despite the creation of his new grouping.
>
> "The Republican party is in total disarray, it's demoralised and it's trying to find itself," he said.
>
> "None of the leading Republican candidates have really caught on, and if the Republicans don't get their act together soon, it will be too late. In the polls, the party's frontrunner is Undecided. And at the moment, Undecided gets my endorsement.
>
> "By contrast, the Democrats are the most united of any party I've seen in years. Hillary Clinton is clearly favourite to win this election."[1]

If a humanist is elected president in 2008, every moral person in the USA will be in danger of going to prison for "hate speech" or for breaking some other humanist designed and enacted law specifically designed to shut up people who oppose humanist religious teachings. What humanists mean by "hate speech" is any "speech" which advocates something humanists "hate." Preaching the gospel of Jesus Christ is hate speech to humanists because Christ taught that only those who believe in Him will go to Heaven. In fact, if you use the Bible in your church at all you are guilty of promoting hate crimes as far as humanists are concerned, because the Bible says, "If a man also lie with mankind, as he lieth with a woman, both of them have committed an abomination: they shall surely be put to death; their blood *shall be* upon them" (Lev. 20:13). What does that verse mean? It means that sodomy is a very major crime and should be punished by death. Let no one misunderstand: it is ***not*** the responsibility of individuals or churches to execute homosexuals. But civil governments ***do*** bear this responsibility. This is not what Christians have decided; that is what God decided. In the eyes of humanists this verse makes the Bible a hate book and makes Bible preachers promoters of hate crimes—because, say humanists, quoting that verse encourages people to bash gays. The fact that many gays (sodomites) are actually very violent individuals who themselves bash people is ignored by humanists. Several years ago in Oklahoma City an out of town man accidentally went into a gay bar. When the man refused their sexual advances, two sodomites followed the man back to his hotel and into his hotel room, and beat him so badly that his blood splattered onto the walls and ceiling. A guard at the hotel in frantically phoning 911 to ask for police assistance, called the two sodomites "fags." For this he was publicly rebuked for using "hate speech"! But no rebuke was given to the two sodomites who had almost beaten a man to death. I listened to this live over the radio as it happened.

To the members of the church in Wichta, Kansas which pickets the funerals of fallen soldiers saying their deaths are the judgement of God upon America for allowing homosexuality: most soldiers and their families

---

[1] Philip Sherwell, "Tom DeLay Targets US Liberals in Media War," *Telegraph.co.Uk*, 2004 November 2007, Http://www.telegraph.co.uk/news/main.jhtml?xml=/news/2007/11/04/wdelay104.xml.

are opposed to homosexuality. So, picketing them is stupid. You may as well picket the funerals of members of your own church. Why picket those who agree with you? That is dumb. In fact, it is dumb to picket anybody's funeral; that is disrespectful, and makes Christianity look bad. You are playing right into the hands of the humanists, who are trying to make Christianity appear to be a hate religion. You are accomplishing the exact opposite of what you intend. Hopefully, people will notice that your church is the only one in the whole USA doing this.

Just to set the record straight, Bible-believing Christians do not hate sodomites, but pray that they find salvation in the Lord Jesus Christ. We invite them into the membership of our churches, requiring only that they meet the qualifications universally required of everyone, which are: (1) that they first repent of their sins (including the sin of sodomy), accepting Jesus Christ as their personal Lord and Savior; and (2) that they then submit themeselves to believer's baptism. Some of the members of the church at Corinth had formerly been sodomites, as the Apostle Paul plainly stated in 1 Cor. 6:9-11:

> Know ye not that the unrighteous shall not inherit the kingdom of God? Be not deceived: neither fornicators, nor idolaters, nor adulterers, nor effeminate, **nor abusers of themselves with mankind**[2], nor thieves, nor covetous, nor drunkards, nor revilers, nor extortioners, shall inherit the kingdom of God. **And such <u>were</u> some of you**: but ye are washed, but ye are sanctified, but ye are justified in the name of the Lord Jesus, and by the Spirit of our God.

Sodomy is a sin like all other sins. People are born sodomites only in the same sense that people are born rapists, or murderers or robbers. That is, all men are born with a depraved nature, but must control it. It is not hate to say that rape, murder, robbery or sodomy are self-destructive sins. Many sodomites have been freed from the sin and bondage of sodomy by Christ, and now live straight clean lives. To deliver that good news to people enslaved to sodomy is love speech, not hate speech.

Humanists constantly claim to be defenders of free speech. They usually say this when they are defending someone's "right" to use profane and vulgar words, or to produce pornography, or to be disrespectful to conservative government officials, or to defend traitors' rights to promote communism or fascism. But in actions they consistently deny free speech to all who disagree with them. They work to silence their critics in whatever way is necessary.

The Fairness Doctrine

Since regaining control of the House and the Senate in 2006, the humanist Democrat Party has been openly working to restore the deceptively named "Fairness Doctrine." Fox News reports that

> Ohio Rep. Dennis Kucinich, who is seeking the Democratic nomination for president in 2008, chairs the House Domestic Policy Subcommittee and plans to revisit the Fairness Doctrine. He said in January that the Fairness Doctrine "derived from the public interest, and that is that there should be an uninhibited marketplace of ideas. That's what the First Amendment is all about."
>
> Rep. Maurice D. Hinchey, D-N.Y., plans to reintroduce his Media Ownership Reform Act (MORA). That bill, introduced in the last Congress, called for the restoration of the Fairness Doctrine and called for broadcast news outlets to investigate issues thoroughly and present their findings in an unbiased way.[3]

There is nothing fair about the Fairness Doctrine; it is what kept conservatives from having a public voice for decades while Democrats controlled all three branches of the government before Ronald Reagan was president. Why is the Fairness Doctrine not fair?

---

2 The greek word translated "abusers of themselves with mankind" is "arsenokoitai" which Strong's Exhaustive Concordance of the Bible defines as, "one who lies with male as with female, sodomite, homosexual."

3 Liza Porteus, "Inhofe Says Boxer, Hillary Clinton Discussed Reining in Conservative Talk Radio Three Years Ago," *FoxNews.Com*, 1926 June 2007, Http://www.foxnews.com/story/0,2933,285933,00.html.

The Fairness Doctrine is Not Fair Because Humanists Control Almost Every Newspaper and Television News Channel in the USA

Except for a few exceptions such as the Daily Oklahoman newspaper in Oklahoma City, humanists control every newspaper in the USA. Except for Fox News, humanists control all of the television news networks, and are totally biased in favor of liberalism/humanism. These liberal/humanist news media churn out a daily mega dose of humanist lies and propaganda with no balance whatsoever. The ***only place*** where conservatives dominate is the in the free market places of talk radio and the Internet. The humanists have multiplied thousands of web sites, but almost no one reads them unless they are doing a search—in which case they really get fed a bill of goods. Instead, most people read the Drudge Report (www.drudgereport.com). Why? Because they trust Matt Drudge to deliver unbiased news, and they know that the liberals/humanists deliver mostly lies and propaganda. "In the spring of 2007, of the 257 news/talk stations owned by the top five commercial station owners, 91 percent of the total weekday talk radio programming was conservative, and only 9 percent was progressive."[4] Liberals are ashamed to admit they are liberals, so they call themselves instead "progressives." A skunk by another name smells the same.

Talk radio is already totally fair. There are no laws that say liberals/humanists cannot start talk radio shows. In fact, they start them all the time, but fail. What prevents humanists from succeeding is their hateful, lying message to which few people want to listen. Liberals/humanists have repeatedly started their own talk shows, but in virtually every case they end up going bankrupt for a lack of listeners. Almost nobody wants to listen to the liberal/humanist glum and doom, hate-and-divide-America message.

To start television news channels takes multiplied millions of dollars, and even if the money is available there are numerous government regulations that make it close to impossible. So the present humanist monopoly of TV news is secure. Do the humanist Democrats plan for the Fairness Doctrine to apply to television stations? Of course not. If television news was made fair, humanists/liberals would immediately lose much of their influence.

The Fairness Doctrine Is Not Fair Because It Makes Talk Radio Unprofitable, Thereby Killing It

The lyingly named Fairness Doctrine was designed to destroy the free market as it applies to talk radio.

> The doctrine had two rules that remained in practice until 2000 — the "personal attack" rule and the "political editorial" rule. The "personal attack" stipulated that when a person or small group was subject to a character attack during a broadcast, stations had to notify them within a week, send them transcripts, and give them an opportunity to respond on air. The "political editorial" rule stipulated that when a station broadcast editorials endorsing or opposing candidates for public office, the candidates who were not endorsed must be notified and allowed an opportunity to respond.

These two rules destroy talk radio because they make it unprofitable. Each radio station ends up having to provide free time for response from liberals/humanists to whom virtually no one wants to listen. Therefore, radio stations end up taking a loss. And they are able to withstand only so much loss until they are no longer able to afford talk radio hosts. It is like telling WalMart that they can't sell only products that people want to buy, but must also make available products that almost no one wants. That would destroy WalMart. So, applying the deceptively named Fairness Doctrine to talk radio would destroy talk radio, thus silencing Rush Limbaugh, Sean Hannity, Michel Savage, and all other conservative talk show hosts who are exposing the humanist/liberal lies. Liberals/humanists don't want to restore fairness, they want to completely destroy fairness.

---

[4] Ibid.

Old-Style, Relentless, Vicious, Low-Tech Slander

In a previous chapter we saw how communists and humanists drove Senator Joseph McCarthy into an early grave, using relentless, vicious slander. Since that time, they have constantly refined this method of attack into a science.

The Character Assassination of Robert Bork

Robert Bork, considered by many the most highly qualified judge in the United States at the time, was nominated to the Supreme Court by President Ronald Reagan on July 1, 1987. Less than an hour later, liberal, humanist, pro-baby-murder, Democrat, Senator Ted Kennedy[5] began the slander of Robert Bork in a nationally televised speech from the Senate floor, saying,

> Robert Bork's America is a land in which women would be forced into back-alley abortions, blacks would sit at segregated lunch counters, rogue police could break down citizens' doors in midnight raids, schoolchildren could not be taught about evolution, writers and artists could be censored at the whim of government.[6]

Immediately humansts nationwide began publish articles attacking Bork as an "extremeist"—a man whose ideas were absolutely wicked. TV ads condemned Bork as a dangerous "extremist." Liberal/humanist news anchors (there were no conservative news anchors then) warned of how Bork would destroy freedom in America. So rapid, and well organized, vicious, and relentless was the slander that President Reagan and conservatives everywhere were stunned. Did the liberal, humanist, Democrats give any facts to prove any of these charges? No, the charges were baseless. But by the time conservatives finally recovered from their shock and began to answer the charges it was too late. Their delay made it look like Bork was actually guilty of the charges, and the Senate voted not to confirm him.

This wicked and horrendous attack against Bork's character was led by two of the American Humanist Associations best known fronts: the American Civil Liberties Union (ACLU)[7] and National Organization for Women (NOW).[8] To this day, humanists continue to slander Robert Bork at every opportunity.

The Character Assassination of Clarence Thomas

Clarence Thomas was nominated to the Supreme Court by President George H.W. Bush on July 2, 1991. Because they suspected that Thomas, a black American, was anti-abortion and against affirmative action and generally conservative in his views, the National Association for the Advancement of Colored People (NAACP), NOW, and the ACLU—all Humanist front organizations—immediately put into action a plan to

---

5 This is the same Ted Kennedy who was expelled from Harvard during his sophomore year for cheating on a Spanish test; who, on Friday 18, 1969, while his wife was at home pregnant, attended a wild party composed of 6 married men and 6 single women on Chappaquiddick island, Mass.; who after consuming at least 2 Heineken beers and 6 rum and cokes was driving with an expired driver's license while taking one of those single women somewhere to do something in the dark of that night; who that evening drove his car off a bridge into a channel, then leaving that young woman in the car to drown, fled the scene of the accident, failing to report the accident to the police for 10 hours. "On August 13, based on a tip from a telephone company employee, The Manchester Union Leader reported that Senator Kennedy had charged 17 long distance telephone calls to his credit card during the hours he claimed to be 'in shock' after the accident." "John Farrar, the rescue diver who examined the Chappaquiddick accident scene, was convinced that Mary Jo Kopechne had not only survived the crash, but had also lived for some time by breathing a pocket of trapped air. Farrar did not believe that she had drowned, but instead had died by asphyxiation as the oxygen in the air she was breathing was used up and replaced with carbon dioxide. "She was alive, easily an hour, maybe two," he said. If that be so, she would have lived if only the accident had been reported. Said George Killen, State Police Detective-Lieutenant, "Senator Kennedy killed that girl the same as if he put a gun to her head and pulled the trigger." (http://www.ytedk.com/)

6 "Robert Bork," *Wikipedia*, 1929 October 2007, Http://en.wikipedia.org/wiki/Robert_Bork.

7 Linda Greenhouse, "A.C.L.U., Reversing Policy, Joins the Opposition to Bork," *The New York Times*, 2001 September 1987, Http://query.nytimes.com/gst/fullpage.html?res=9B0DE0DE1E3CF932A3575AC0A961948260.

8 "In Memoriam: Molly Yard—Honoring an Indomitable NOW President and Civil Rights Pioneer," *NOW.Org*, 1921 September 2005, Http://www.now.org/press/09–05/09–21.html.

block his confirmation. Promised Florence Kennedy at a NOW conference in New York City, "We're going to 'bork' him." By this she obviously meant that they were going to slander him to try to prevent his confirmation—and they did. A woman named Anita Hill, a liberal, humanist Democrat who had formerly worked under Thomas' supervision at the U.S. Department of Education and then followed him to the Equal Employment Opportunity Commission, accused him of making sexually provocative statements to her at both places of employment. Without checking to see if the accusations were true, someone on the confirmation committee leaked the the allegations to Nina Totemberg who was legal correspondant for National Public Radio. Was she a Republican? No, of course not. She was a liberal, humanist Democrat. She was at the time married to former Democrat senator from Colorado, liberal, humanist Floyd Kirk Haskell.[9] She immediately—and no doubt gleefully—made the allegations public. Now world-wide attention was drawn to the confirmation hearing as Anita Hill was called to testify. Shamelessly using the most sexually explicit and vulgar language to a world-wide audience she knew included a multitude of children, Hill actually said the words she was merely accusing Thomas of saying—words too vulgar to repeat. And in so doing Hill sexually harressed thousands and thousands of children. And we have absolute proof that she said them, as she said them publicly with full media coverage. But she gave not one shred of proof that Thomas actually said those words of which she was accusing him. Indeed, she admitted she couldn't prove her allegations, saying, "These incidents took place in his office or mine. They were in the form of private conversations which would not have been overheard by anyone else."[10] True! Something that was never said would not have been overheard by anyone else! This was character assassination at its dirtiest, with its only purpose being to prevent a conservative from becoming a Supreme Court justice. Most people saw through Hill, and Thomas was confirmed to sit on the Supreme Court. But great damage had been done to Thomas' reputation. He told the confirmation committee:

> I think that this today is a travesty. I think that it is disgusting. I think that this hearing should never occur in America. This is a case in which this sleaze, this dirt was searched for by staffers of members of this committee, was then leaked to the media, and this committee and this body validated it and displayed it at prime time over our entire nation. How would any member on this committee, any person in this room, or any person in this country would like sleaze said about him or her in this fashion? Or this dirt dredged up and this gossip and these lies displayed in this manner, how would any person like it? The Supreme Court is not worth it. No job is worth it. I am not here for that. I am here for my name, my family, my life, and my integrity. I think something is dreadfully wrong with this country when any person, any person in this free country would be subjected to this. This is not a closed room. There was an FBI investigation. This is not an opportunity to talk about difficult matters privately or in a closed environment. This is a circus. It's a national disgrace. And from my standpoint, as a black American, it is a high-tech lynching for uppity blacks who in any way deign to think for themselves, to do for themselves, to have different ideas, and it is a message that unless you kowtow to an old order, this is what will happen to you. You will be lynched, destroyed, caricatured by a committee of the U.S. Senate rather than hung from a tree.[11]

Many of these very same liberal, Democrat, humanist congressmen and news reporter character assassins would later defend President Bill Clinton when he was caught in adultery with Monica Lewinsky. Clinton was not just *accused* of dirty talk. He was *actually guilty* of adultery. There was a seman stained dress to prove it. He was also guilty of lying about it under oath—perjury. Yet humanists defended him as a righteous man, saying that what a person does in privite is no one else's business. Humanists defend criminals as though they can do no wrong, yet attempt to make even the most righteous good that conservatives do look evil. They are masters of deceit, expert character assassins, professional slanderers. To this very day, humanists continue to slander Clarence Thomas at every opportunity. They do this to try to bully him into helping their pro-baby-murder agenda. And they do this to make other people fear to oppose them.

---

9 Floyde Haskell was a member of Common Cause, an anti-war organization. At least three members of Common Cause were also members of the American Civil Liberties Union: Winston Perry Bullard, Milton Robert Carr, and Unitarian Fortney Doug Ross. (http://politicalgraveyard.com/group/common-cause.html)

10 Anita F. Hill, "Testimony of Anita F. Hill, Professor of Law, University of Oklahoma, Norman, OK," *Gpoaccess.Gov*, 1911 October 1991, Http://www.gpoaccess.gov/congress/senate/judiciary/sh102–1084pt4/36–40.pdf.

11 "Clarence Thomas," *Wikipedia*, 1930 October 2007, Http://en.wikipedia.org/wiki/Clarence_Thomas.

New-Style, Relentless, Vicious, High-Tech Slander

As the public school system converts more and more of our children into humanists, the Humanist movement gets stronger and stronger. And the stronger the Humanist movement gets, the more agressive and vicious they become. We are now in the high technology age, and the Internet has enabled Humanists to become much more highly organized, and to act much faster against their critics. They have put up multiplied thousands of web sites to promote their atheist religion, and to enable them to communicate more easily with each other, and to slander those who expose them. Several of the most effective, and therefore most dangerous, of the new high tech organizations they have started to refute and defeat Christianity are:

Daily Kos and Yearly Kos

Daily Kos (often referred to as DailyKos or DailyKos.com) is a radical humanist web site founded by Markos Moulitsas Zuniga. The British on-line newspaper Telegraph.co.uk lists Zuniga as the 12th most influencial liberal in the U.S.A. They describe him as follows:

> Founder and chief author of the website Daily Kos, which receives 20 million unique visitors per month. A former US Army artilleryman and consultant for Howard Dean, Moulitsas, 36, described his job as "the sweetest gig in the world". It is also one of the most influential in US politics – ***contributors have included Nancy Pelosi, Ted Kennedy, Jimmy Carter, John Kerry, Harry Reid and Cindy Sheehan***.
>
> Co-author with Jerome Armstrong (Number 62) of Crashing the Gate: Netroots, Grassroots, and the Rise of People-Powered Politics, a definitive examination of the internet's role in transforming politics. ***This year's Yearly Kos convention attracted all the main Democratic candidates*** and Hillary Clinton got a rough ride. ***Kos's status as a liberal powerhouse pushing the Democrats towards the Left*** has been underlined by attacks on it from the likes of Fox's Bill O'Reilly. [Emphasis added.]

The bloggers of DailyKos organize a yearly convention (mentioned in the above quote) where humanists plan out or finalize strategy. While speaking to the Yearly Kos convention in Chicago on August 4, 2007, Senator Hillary Clinton bragged,

> We are certainly better prepared and more focused on, you know, taking our arguments, and making them effective, and disseminating them widely, and really putting together a network, uh, in the blogosphere, in a lot of the new progressive infrastructure, ***institutions that I helped to start and support like Media Matters*** and ***Center for American Progress***.[12] [Emphasis added.]

These two instituutions Hillary "helped to start and support" need to be closely examined and remembered.

Media Matters For America

This organization would be more truthfully named Slander Matters for America. Says the Media Matters web site about itself:

> Media Matters for America is a Web-based, not-for-profit, 501(c)(3) progressive research and information center dedicated to comprehensively monitoring, analyzing, and correcting conservative misinformation in the U.S. media.
>
> Launched in May 2004, Media Matters for America put in place, for the first time, the means to systematically monitor a cross section of print, broadcast, cable, radio, and Internet media outlets for conservative misinformation — news or commentary that is not accurate, reliable, or credible and that forwards the conservative agenda — every day, in real time.
>
> Using the website www.mediamatters.org as the principal vehicle for disseminating research and information, Media Matters posts rapid-response items as well as longer research and analytic reports documenting conservative misinformation throughout the media. Additionally, Media Matters works daily to notify activists, journalists, pundits, and the general public about instances of misinformation, providing them with the resources to rebut false claims and to take direct action against offending media institutions.[13]

So, clearly, Media Matters is not a non-partisan organization, but is by its own admission an anti-

---

[12] Neal Sheppard, "Hillary Clinton Told YearlyKos Convention She Helped Start Media Matters," *NewsBusters*, 2001 October 2007, Http://www.newsbusters.org/blogs/noel-sheppard/2007/10/01/hillary-clinton-told-yearlykos-convention-she-helped-start-media-matt.

[13] http://mediamatters.org/about_us/

conservative organization whose purpose is to immediately rebut and discredit anyone who exposes humanists as the liars and traitors that they are, thereby helping Hillary Clinton in her quest to become the next president of the United States. Their purpose is to refute "conservative" information as "misinformation." Obviously, they do not expose "liberal misinformation" as that would require exposing themselves as liars and deceivers.

But the ultimate goal of Media Matters is not just to discredit but to silence opposing viewpoints. In spite of their loud claims to the contrary, humanists hate freedom of speech, and work relentlessley to stomp it out. Here is another quote from the Media Matters web site:

> Contact advertisers. ***If a news outlet has a habit of presenting conservative misinformation, contact companies that financially support or advertise on it and request they withdraw their support.*** Identify the companies whose advertisements appear most often, or visit the news outlet's website to determine who provides financial support.[14]

That is a very clear statement of intent. Whatever conservatives say is automatically considered misinformation whether it is true or not. Media Matters wants to cut off all funding so as to silence the critics of their godless religion.

Center for American Progress

Center for American Progress is the Hillary Clinton administration working zealeously to undermine conservative critics in preparation to take over the white house. Telegraph.co.uk lists John Podesta, president of Center for American Progress, as the 11th most influencial liberal in America. They describe him and Center for American Progress as follows:

> ***Bill Clinton's former chief of staff*** remains a pivotal player in the Democratic party. Head of the Centre for American Progress, funded by George Soros, A fanatical X-Files aficionado, he has not publicly endorsed Hillary Clinton's presidential bid but ***his think tank is packed with former Clinton staffers itching to return to the White House in a Hillary Clinton administration.***
>
> Battle tested in the trenches of the Clinton-Gingrich wars of the 1990s and a vehement defender of Bill Clinton during the Lewinsky scandal, he is likely to play a major role in any Democratic administration. ***Released a report detailing how Right-wingers dominate talk radio and calling for restrictive legislation*** – making him a target of derision from conservatives. If a Democrat wins, his think tank could enjoy the same influence that AEI and Heritage Foundation enjoyed in the Bush years. [Emphasis added.]

Center for American Progress and many other humanist organizations are funded by George Soros. Telegraph.co.uk lists him as the 15th most influncial liberal in the U.S.A., and says,

> Soros, 78, has given millions from his $11 billion fortune to Democratic-supporting organisations, such as MoveOn.org, the Centre for American Progress and America Coming Together, leading the Republican party to claim he has "purchased the Democratic party". Certain to be a source of controversy – and hard cash exceeding the $15.5 million he spent last time – once again in the 2008 campaign.

MoveOn.org

Telegraph.co.uk describes MoveOn.org as a "liberal pressure group" that supports "democratic political candidates with tens of millions of dollars in advertising and thousands of hours of telephone canvassing and knocking on doors." It was founded by millionaire Wes Boyd and his wife Joan Blades. Telegraph.co.uk lists them as the 20th most influencial liberals in the U.S.A.

The December 10, 2004 issue of FrontPageMag.com reported that

> In a December 9th e-mail signed by "Eli Pariser, Justin Ruben, and the whole MoveOn PAC team," the Soros front group stated: "In the last year, grassroots contributors like us gave more than $300 million to the Kerry campaign and the DNC, and proved that the Party doesn't need corporate cash to be competitive. ***Now it's our Party: we bought it, we own it, and we're going to take it back.***"[15] [Emphasis added.]

---

[14] "What You Can Do," *MediaMatters.Org*, 1922 August 2007, Http://mediamatters.org/items/200508220010.

[15] Ben Johnson, "MoveOn: 'We Bought' the Democratic Party," *FrontPageMag.Com*, 1910 December 2004, Http://www.frontpagemag.com/Articles/Read.aspx?GUID={89BC7BB2–298F-4B8D-99DF-A9EA273A0559}.

On September 10, 2007, in an effort to refute what they believed would be a report from General David H. Petraeus, the commander of our troops in Iraq, that the war against terrorism in Iraq was succeeding, MoveOn.org placed a full-page ad in the New York Times calling him "General Betray Us," and accusing him of "cooking the books for the White House." They placed this ad before he delivered his report, thus criticizing his report before they even know what it said. This ad caused a very negative backlash against MoveOn.org from the American public, which the Democrats in congress could not ignore.

On September 20, 2007, Republican Senator John Cornyn III of Texas introduced a resolution to "strongly condemn personal attacks on the honor and integrity of General Petraeus."

> The goal was to put Democrats in a corner, forcing them to risk angering anti-war voters OR face potential political fallout for NOT condemning an attack on a respected military leader.
>
> Democrats countered with a proposed resolution of their own, condemning the MoveOn ad, but also those run in the past by conservative groups attacking the patriotism of Democrats, including 2004 Presidential nominee John Kerry.
>
> "They're all disgraceful ads and we ought to treat them the same way," said Sen. Carl Levin, a Democrat from Michigan. "They impugn the honor, integrity and patriotism of real patriots."
>
> The Democrats' resolution failed. The one proposed by Republicans passed 72-25. ***Of the Democrats running for president, sens. Hillary Clinton of New York and Christopher Dodd of Connecticut voted against the resolution.*** Sens. Barack Obama of Illinois and Joseph Biden of Delaware did not vote.[16]

The resolution passed with all 49 Republican senators and 22 Democrat senators supporting, and a similar bill passed the House by a vote of 341 to 79. Tim Harper of thestar.com said,

> The "General Betray Us" controversy has also peeled back the curtain on MoveOn, which boasts a huge array of firepower for a cyber-organization that has only 17 employees, no central office and is being run by a guy who is still in his 20s.... Today, it is run out of New York by Eli Pariser, a 26-year-old precocious child of 1960s activists who moved from anti-globalization rallies to more pragmatic political fundraising and partisan battle.

This is an example of how humanists portray themselves as being far more numerous than they actually are, and far more credible then they possibly could be. Nevertheless,

> MoveOn.org is continuing to push the theme of betrayal. It expanded its ad campaign with TV spots targeting President Bush specifically, and other Republican leaders, including presidential candidate Rudy Giuliani, the former mayor of New York.[17]
>
> It has one television ad in heavy rotation attacking the Bush "betrayal of trust" with last week's troop reduction announcement and going after Giuliani as "a big fan of George Bush's war" who didn't bother showing up for work as a member of the bipartisan Iraq Study Group created to give Bush a way ahead on the war.[18]

Actually, such attacks on President Bush is nothing new for MoveOn.org.

> During the 2004 campaign, MoveOn...had to withdraw one ad that compared Bush to Hitler.[19]

The backlash to the General Betray Us ad exposed the Democrats as unpatriotic, and dealt them a stinging defeat. For this they wanted revenge badly. Thus, only seven days later, overconfident in their ability to make slander look true, they attempted to get that revenge by destroying Rush Limbaugh.

---

[16] Don Gonyea, "Anger Over 'Betray Us' Ad Simmers on Hill," *National Public Radio*, 1922 September 2007, Http://www.npr.org/templates/story/story.php?storyId=14623512.

[17] Ibid.

[18] Tim Harper, "Putting the Moves on MoveOn.Org," *Thestar.Com*, 1923 September 2007, Http://www.thestar.com/article/259511.

[19] Ibid.

Recent Victims of Humanist Slander

America is in the midst of a civil war, and sadly it is no longer just a war of words and ideas. Humanists want their atheist religion to reign over every aspect of life, and are willing to use force if necessary to make it happen. One by one they are taking us down, like mad wolves take down a buffalo.

The Character Assassination of Rush Limbaugh

Humanists especially hate Rush Limbaugh because he is very talented in exposing their lies and hypocrasy, and because he has a very large audience.

On Thursday September 27, 2007, Hillary Clinton's Media Matters for America falsely claimed on its web site that "during the September 26 broadcast of Rush Limbaugh's nationally syndicated radio show, he called service members who advocate U.S. withdrawal from Iraq "phony soldiers."[20]

Harry "Wave-the-White-Flag" Reid

On Monday October 1, 2007, acting upon the Media Matters report, Senate Majority Leader Harry Reid (D-Nev.) asked all senators to sign an intimidating letter he and other Democrat senators had co-written to Clear Channel Communications CEO Mark Mays demanding that he repudiate Rush Limbaugh for allegedly calling U.S. troops opposed to the war in Iraq "phony soldiers." Said Reid, "I ask my colleagues, Democrat and Republican alike, to join together against this irresponsible, hateful, and unpatriotic attack by calling upon Rush Limbaugh to give our troops the apology they deserve."[21] Reid issued this accusation from the senate, knowing that slander issued from the senate is immune from prosecution. Forty-one Democrat senators signed the letter, and sent it to Mays. But were the accusations true? No, the context of Limbaugh's reveals that they were just lies. The phony soldiers Rush had referred to were actually phony soldiers—men claiming to be soldiers when in truth they weren't, but which humanist news reporters had been dishonestly quoting as being actual soldiers. This context was not hard for Limbaugh to prove. As one lady commented concerning Senator Reid:

> What an idiot - how did Reid get his job? Limbaugh has had the full audio and transcript of all this on his website since last week - available for anyone to see. None of what Reid says is even remotely close to what was said. Reid is either illiterate or a liar.[22]

Limbaugh responded to Senator Reid, "If anybody in this country has been trying to demoralize the troops, it is you, sir, and your members of the Democrat Party. You have waved the white flag of defeat."

When Mays received the letter, he gave it to Limbaugh who promptly put it up for auction on Ebay, promising his 20 million listeners that he would match every dollar of the final bid with a dollar of his own to be given to the Marine Corps-Law Enforcement Foundation to help with its charible work with the

---

20 A.J. Walzer, "Limbaugh: Service Members Who Support U.S. Withdrawal Are 'phony Soldiers'," *MEDIA MATTERS for America*, 1927 September 2007, Http://mediamatters.org/items/200709270010?f=h_top.

21 Mark Silva, "Senate Leader Demands Apology of Rush Limbaugh," *Baltimoresun.Com*, 2001 October 2007, Http://weblogs.baltimoresun.com/news/politics/blog/2007/10/senate_leader_demands_apology.html.

22 Ibid.

children of fallen Marines. Limbaugh also challenged the Democrat senators that signed the letter to match it with a dollar of their own. Amazingly, the top bid for the letter was $2,100,000.00! Matching with his own funds as promised, Limbaugh sent a 4.2 million dollar check to help the children of fallen marines! Even more amazingly, shortly before bidding ceased, Senator Reid attempted to take credit for raising the money! From the senate floor he said,

Harry "I'm-Gonna-Make-Sure-We-Lose" Reid

> More than $2 million, this is going to really help. And that's, again, an understatement. There's only a little bit of time left. -- so I would ask those that are wanting to do more, that they can go to the Harry Reid, search -- actually go on say "Harry Reid letter," this will come up on eBay. I encourage anyone interested in this with the means to do so to consider bidding on this letter and contributing to this worthwhile cause. I strongly believe that when we can put our differences aside, even Harry Reid and Rush Limbaugh, we should do that and try to accomplish good things for the American people.

Limbaugh responded:

> Senator Reid, let me be clear about this one more time -- actually, as many times as it takes. It wasn't your letter that raised this money. It was your abuse of power that is responsible for raising this money. No other letter you have written would be... People wouldn't pay a dime for it, Senator! This one represents an abuse of power: a federal government official, a US senator, getting hold -- after besmirching me and smearing me by name personally from the Senate floor, gets hold -- of the CEO of my syndication partner and asks him to "confer" with me about something Senator Reid thought was said that was improper? Words? First Amendment? Free speech? That, sir, is an abuse of power. That is why your letter is historic, not because you signed it, not because 40 other people signed it, not because you wrote it. It is because of what that letter represents: a full-fledged, undeniable, 100% abuse of power, and that's how this letter will be remembered by historians forever.... The 41 Democrats who signed the letter wanted Mark Mays, CEO of Clear Channel, my syndication partner, to "confer" with me about what I had said. When you run a business that's federally regulated, and the Senate majority leader tells you that he wants you to confer with me, what he means is, "You get him to stop criticizing us! You get him to apologize. You make him." There's an implied "or else," when the Senate majority leader calls a CEO of a broadcast company and says those things. That's the abuse of power. That is the arrogant abuse of power and an attempt to essentially negate what I do, and to render me unable to do it.
>
> Um, put our differences aside? Okay. Where is the apology for calling me "unpatriotic"? Where's the apology for repeating a smear and a bunch of lies from Media Matters for America?[23]

In spite of Reid encouraging people to bid on the letter, appearantly not one of the Democrats that signed the slanderous letter, including Reid, gave even a cent to the Marine Corps-Law Enforcement Foundation. As usual, Reid's talk was just empty humanist hypocrisy.

The Character Assassination of Our Troops

Is anyone still not convinced that liberal, humanist, Democrat leaders are hypocrites? "I Support the Troops" is the title of an article by A. Whitney Brown[24] on the Democrats favorite blog site, the Daily Kos. Here is what the article says:

> ...what I mean when I say I support our troops is that I actually pay for their food, their ammo, their upkeep, transport, everything. I pay for all of it.
>
> And I do that not only because I'm a patriotic American, although I am, but also because they take 35% out of my check every week and if I don't pay it I will end up in jail.

---

23 "Senator Reid: You Win, Rush," *Rushlimbaugh.Com*, 1919 October 2007, Http://www.rushlimbaugh.com/home/daily/site_101907/content/01125109.guest.html.

24 A comment made to this article indicates that AWhitney Brown may be a pen name.

> That is what I mean by 'I support our troops'. I mean I am involuntarily, under threat of prison, forced to pay for their support. . . .
>
> So yes, I resent my support for the killing of Iraqis for which I get not even a memento or trophy. But do I still support the individual men and women who have given so much to serve their country?
>
> No. I think they're a bunch of idiots. I also think they're morally retarded. Because they sign a contract that says they will kill whoever you tell me to kill. And that is morally retarded.
>
> Friends, the most important moral decision a man makes in the course of a day is "Who am I going to kill today?"
>
> That's a decision you should agonize over, dream about, rehearse in your mind for hours, not just leave up to some hare-brained President you didn't even vote for.
>
> A man's killing list is a very personal matter. It should be between him and those persistent voices in his head.
>
> So to sum up, I don't like our troops, I don't like what they're doing, I don't like their fat, whining families, and yet, I support them. Thank God I live in a free country. Thank You.[25]

Just to make sure his position was clear, Brown added in the comment section after his article: "And yes, I'm anti-military." And thank you, Mr. Brown, for explaining to us so clearly what our Democrat senators actually mean when they say they support our troops!

Do liberal, humanist, Democrats believe in free speech or are they working with mad rage to stomp it out? Failing in their attempt to intimidate Mark Mays, Hillary Clinton's Media Matters put up a web page to make it easy for humanists to intimidate the individual radio stations carrying Limbaugh's broadcasts. The web page is titled, "Contact Your Local Rush Limbaugh Radio Station Today," which, after condemning Limbaugh in no uncertain terms, says, "It's time to take action. Use this online directory of Limbaugh's radio affiliates -- contact your local station directly and let them know what you think of his despicable comments."[26] A drop down menu then lists links for all the states, which in a few clicks gives the name, title, e-mail address, phone number, and fax number of each station manager they want to be intimidated. Underneigh this is a paragraph that says, "When contacting the media, please be polite and professional. Express your specific concerns regarding that particular news report or commentary, and be sure to indicate exactly what you would like the media outlet to do differently in the future."[27]

And, of course, what possibly can these radio station managers do differently except not run Limbaugh's broadcasts? Humanists hate free speech because their ideas cannot hold up under the light of the truth.

The Character Assassination of Ann Coulter

Doing a Google search on "Ann Coulter" finds 1,570,000 web pages (as of November 1, 2007)! Most of them are on humanist web sites and condemn her. Of these, most are almost idential in content. Could that be because their owners all answer to the same leader? Could it be that just a few people own those multitude of web sites, and use them for propaganda purposes? Very likely. Many of the web pages are just a list of out-of-context quotes from Coulter in a not so subtle attempt to discredit her. Generally these web pages enable readers to leave comments without identifying themselves, and many of those comments attack Coulter using such hateful, and vile language that it is not fit to reprint. After one such web page, a more sane reader commented:

> Liberals. When they can't argue with the facts, quickly resort to personal attacks.
>
> If Coulter is so "off the wall", why ARE liberals so afraid of her (and Rush and all the rest)? Why can't they just ignore her like conservatives ignore, uh, what's his name, that guy that used to be on Air America? I guess I've forgotten (see liberals, that's how it's done).[28]

---

25 A Whitney Brown, "I Support the Troops," *Daily Kos*, 1923 July 2007, Http://www.dailykos.com/story/2007/7/23/114037/956.

26 "Contact Your Local Rush Limbaugh Radio Station Today," *Media Matter for America Web Site*, November 2007, Http://mediamatters.org/action_center/limbaugh_stations/.

27 http://mediamatters.org/action_center/limbaugh_stations/index?qstate=ok will take you to the Media Matters web page for the Oklahoma radio stations.

28 "Ann Blames Clinton, Carter for 9/11 and Dreams of Denying Women the Vote," *The New York Observer*, 2002 October 2007,

Of course, the fact is that Coulter isn't off the wall. What upsets the liberals/humanists so much is that she is telling the truth about them, and has the guts to call them what they are: TRAITORS. And she has the brains and training to document their treason in very easy to read and entertaining prose. She is a lawyer, and she writes very carefully and precisely, knowing that if she cannot prove what she writes the ACLU will probably have her in court before she receives the first royalty on a book. Her book *TREASON: Liberal Treachery from the Cold War to the War on Terrorism*, quoted in the chapter about the ACLU, should be required reading before a person is allowed to vote. If a person can still vote Democrat after reading and checking out the facts given in *TREASON*, that person is not a true American.

One of Anne's fans pointed out, "The Loony Left has NO sense of humor. Ann loves to get their goat; and it's SOOOO easy."[29] All she has to do is point out the facts in a clear and frank manner that exposes how silly, hypocritical, and wicked their arguments are. The Amazon web page for *Treason*, lists a whooping 2030 customer reviews (as of Oct. 31, 2007)! Individual reviewers usually give her either five stars or only one. Her writing is so good that people either love her or hate her. Many reviewers are humanists, who probably haven't even read her book, but simply want to give her book a low rating to discourage people from reading its exposure of them.

Humansts' attempts to silence Coulter have been so many that a book could be written about them. So far, humanists have succeeded in getting her columns dropped from: USA Today, the Arizona Star, The Gazette of Cedar Rapids, Iowa, the Augusta Chronicle of Augusta, Georgia, Yes! Weekly of Greensboro, North Carolina, The Times of Shreveport, Louisiana, The Oakland Press of Oakland County, Michigan, The Mountian Press of Sevierville, Tennessee, and the New Era of Lancaster, Pennsylvania. Several advertisers have been pressured into pulling their advertisements from her web site: Verizon, Sallie Mae, and Netbank.[30]

Hillary Clinton's Media Matters for America has started a petition to silence Ann Coulter and other conservatives which are exposing them. Here is what it says:

Hate has no place on the airwaves

Recently, the major television networks have given a platform to conservative hate merchants like Ann Coulter, Glenn Beck, and Melanie Morgan.

Coulter's column is distributed by Universal Press Syndicate, one of the country's largest syndicates. Beck was recently hired by CNN Headline News. Morgan broadcasts from a radio station owned by Disney. And all three -- and countless others like them -- are regularly given guest spots on cable-news networks.

The fact that these right-wing pundits -- who have called for the execution of public officials and others -- are given a platform in the major media is unprecedented.

We, the undersigned, urge the media to stop allowing these hate merchants to spread their venom and abuse. America deserves to hear honest, reasoned debate, not rants from professional hatemongers.

Please sign this petition (with complete contact information) to show that the American public does not endorse the hate speech that these pundits are spewing.

Urge your friends to sign the petition here.

33913 people have already added their names.[31]

Manufactured scandal of the week; humanists manufacture a new scandal just about every week. Any "speech" humanists "hate" is "hate speech" to humanists. So, they brand almost every statement Coulter makes as "hate speech." As they do with all the more influencial conservatives, Media Matters for America monitors every word Coulter speaks or writes looking for anything they can take out of context to attempt to discredit her. As of this writing, humanists are accusing Coulter of "hate speech" because, during an

---

Http://www.observer.com/2007/coulter-culture.

29 Ibid.

30 http://en.wikipedia.org/wiki/Ann_Coulter as of 6 November 2007.

31 http://mediamatters.org/hatefree

interview on Donny Deutsch's CNBC show, The Big Idea, on October 8, 2007, she answered "Yes" to this direct question from Deutsch, who is a Jew: "Christian — so we should be Christian? It would be better if we were all Christian?"

Deutsch, was obviously fishing for something he could use against Coulter, and so asked her one loaded question after another. Finally, he asked a question that produced the answer he wanted: "Let's wipe Israel off the earth. I mean, what, no Jews?" Coulter answered, "No, we think — we just want Jews to be perfected, as they say." Deutsch said that he was offended by this comment, and said Coulter's words were "hateful...anti-Semitic." Coulter responded, "No, no, no, no, no. I don't want you being offended by this.... We consider ourselves perfected Christians. For me to say that for you to become a Christian is to become a perfected Christian is not offensive at all."[32]

Within two days Media Matter for America had posted a web page[33] to exploit this into a major issue to divide conservative Jews from Conservative Gentiles. On this web page, to really make Christians look bad, they deceptively quote what a Jewish writer says as though it was said by a Christian. Taking their cue from Media Matters, Humanists world wide branded Coulter as anti-Semitic on their web sites.[34] Many conservative Jews recognized this as the usual divide-in-order-to-defeat humanist tactic, and publicly stated that Coulter's remarks were not anti-Semitic. However, sadly, many other conservative Jews took the bait.

So now on thousands of humanist and Jewish web sites Coulter is being branded "anti-Semitic," "a pig...so hateful it is beyond the study of man," "a neo-fascist," "a heretic preacher of dual covenant theology," "vomit," "a gnarley headed hoe," "a buffoon," "a demagogue," "a bleached-blond skank with no body fat and a prominent Adam's Apple," "an evil pshyco," "a sick individual, beyond crazed," "a vicious troll," "an unclovcen harlot," "a crazy aunt," "a fraud," and a lot of other bad things too vulgar to reprint.[35] One writer said what many others implied, "I hope this woman wakes up one morning and everything she belives [*sic*] is wrong starts to happen to her." And all of that hatred from the very people who are demanding that Coulter be silenced because of "hate speech"!

A few words to conservative Jews. Is it wise to let atheists divide you from Christian friends? You should always be suspicious of the motives of atheists.

Why is it so offensive for Coulter to say that she would like for all Americans to be Christians? People of all religions wish that all people believed exactly like them. That does not necessarily mean that they hate other people. Do you not write articles to convince people to believe like you? Should we Gentiles be offended by that? I mean, do you mean to say we are wrong and need to change our way of thinking? How dare you! You spewer of hate-speech! Those last three sentences are sarcasm, of course. Say whatever you want and it will not offend me, so long as you don't take up a sword to try to force me to believe it, and provided you don't try to keep me from saying what I believe.

Did Coulter pull out a sword and try to decapitate Deutsch? No. Instead she said, "Would you like to come to church with me, Donny?" That does not sound like anti-Semitism to me. Instead that sounds like a genuine accepting of Donny (a Jew) as a person, and a desire to have him become a part of her church. What is wrong with that?

Especially after Coulter explained that ***everyone*** needs to be perfected, not just Jews, why does that upset you? Do you not believe that Muslims need to be perfected? For instance, what about the Muslims who

---

32 "Columnist Ann Coulter Shocks Cable TV Show, Declaring 'Jews Need to Be Perfected by Becoming Christians'," *FoxNews.Com*, 1911 October 2007, Http://www.foxnews.com/story/0,2933,301216,00.html.

33 http://mediamatters.org/items/200710100008

34 Remember that on the Internet you cannot easily know where the webmaster of a web site is located. He may rent space on a server of a web hosting company in the USA, but he, himself, may be in Russian, or North Korea or anywhere in the world; a person knowledgeable in Internet technology can easily put up a new web site in a foreign country in just a few hours. And one person can maintain many different web sites. So, just because there are many different humanist web sites, does not mean that there are actually that many humanists.

35 I'm not going to document these nasty quotes since there are thousands of such quotes on the internet. Do a search. You do not have time to read them all. Warning: some use words and pornographic pictures that are vulgar beyond comprehension.

have declared war on you and want to wipe you off the face of the earth? Are they perfect? Or do you think they need to be perfected? If you answer that they are perfect, then why do you complain when they blow you up? If you answer that they are not perfect, does that make you a hate monger? What about evangelical Christians like Ann Coulter? Are they perfect? Or do you think they need to be perfected?

Do you think Jews are perfect? Do Jews never sin? If Jews are sinners like everyone else then they are not perfect and need to be perfected.

Here is how the Bible says we can be perfected:

> For *it is* not possible that the blood of bulls and of goats should take away sins. Wherefore when he cometh into the world, he saith, Sacrifice and offering thou wouldest not, but a body hast thou prepared me: in burnt offerings and *sacrifices* for sin thou hast had no pleasure. Then said I, Lo, I come (in the volume of the book it is written of me,) to do thy will, O God. Above when he said, Sacrifice and offering and burnt offerings and *offering* for sin thou wouldest not, neither hadst pleasure *therein*; which are offered by the law; then said he, Lo, I come to do thy will, O God. He taketh away the first, that he may establish the second. By the which will we are sanctified through the offering of the body of Jesus Christ once *for all*. And every priest standeth daily ministering and offering oftentimes the same sacrifices, which can never take away sins: but this man, after he had offered one sacrifice for sins for ever, sat down on the right hand of God; from henceforth expecting till his enemies be made his footstool. For by one offering he hath **perfected** for ever them that are sanctified."

So you can see that Christians believe that people of all nationalities need to be perfected, and can be "perfected for ever" through faith in Christ. Keeping the law cannot perfect us simply because we (us Gentiles along with you Jews) do not keep it. Some of us try to keep it, but all of us fail miserably. We are all sinners, including you. We cannot perfect ourselves. The Bible teaches that only in the Messiah can we (whatever our nationality) be considered perfect, and that because He died for our sins, and His perfect righteousness becomes eternally ours the moment we trust Him as Lord and Savior.

Penina Taylor, a young Jewish lady, wrote an article for Arutz Sheva titled "Thank You, Ann Coulter," in which she thanks Ann Coulter for "getting the Jewish community upset about something that it should be upset about...."

In trying to explain why Jews should be upset, Penina gave a good Bible lesson! She said:

> Let me give you a little Bible lesson here. Evangelical Christians who are calling themselves Zionists and who give moral and financial support to Israel do so because they believe with every fiber of their beings that the Christian Bible - what they call the Old and New Testaments - are the word of God. They believe every word of it, literally. That's why they are generally very good, moral people and that is also why they believe, in no uncertain terms, that anyone who does not believe in Jesus will go to Hell. That includes the Jews.[36]

So, that is why Jews should be upset! Not because Christians believe that "anyone" who does not believe in Jesus will go to Hell, but because "that includes the Jews." She then lists the following verses from the New Testament to prove that the Bible actually does teach this: John 3:17-18 and 36; 5:24; 6:40 and 54-56; 17:3; Acts 13:46; 4:12; 6:23; 2 Thessalonians 1:8-10; 1 John 5:11-12. Read them and you will see that she is correct.[37] "Anyone" does indeed mean "anyone."

I am a Christian and unashamedly confess that Miss Taylor has stated exactly what I believe: anyone, including each of my own children and closest friends, who does not place his or her faith in Jesus as the Messiah will go to Hell. ***Now let me ask you a question: since I sincerely believe that, what is love? to just remain silent and let you go to Hell? or to try to persuade you to believe the truth so that you can go to Heaven?*** Please open your eyes and notice that Bible-believing Christians—the only genuine kind—are not trying to decapitate unbelievers, but rather trying to keep them out of Hell by showing them the way to Heaven, by persuasion not force. That is not hate, that is love. If that

---

36 Penina Taylor, "Thank You, Ann Coulter," *Arutz Sheva*, 1914 October 2007, Http://www.israelnationalnews.com/Articles/Article.aspx/7475.

37 One Jewish reader of Miss Taylor's article rebuked her for posting them, as though Jews shouldn't be allowed to see those verses. (YOUR LEADERS FORBID YOU TO READ THOSE VERSES! To them, YOU ARE SO DUMB AND GULLIBLE THAT YOU WILL FOR CERTAIN BE DECEIVED. SO DON'T READ THOSE VERSES! YOU ARE NOT ALLOWED! AND YOU ARE FORBIDDEN TO TALK TO MISSIONARIES TOO. They want to totally control your spiritual life. Not the Torah, but your rabbis' interpretation of it only is what they want you to believe. Also, don't read Isaiah chapter 53 which prophesies that the Messiah would suffer for your sins; you can't understand that passage of Scripture either. You are too dumb. And you don't have the proper education. And Isaiah was probably anti-Semitic too, since he said that Jews actually have sins, implying that Jews also need perfecting.

is offensive to you, then you are immature and need to grow up. Throw off that pride. People who are not your enemies are your friends. A person doesn't have to agree with you on every point to be your friend; all he has to do to be your friend is have genuine good will toward you.

Another serious question (in answering please be honest with your own self): do you love Christians enough to try to persuade them to believe what you think to be the truth? or do you just hope that Christians go to Hell? Who hates whom? If you are really a loving person, then why aren't you a missionary for your own religion? "...thou shalt love thy neighbour as thyself: I *am* the LORD" (Lev. 19:18 in your Scriptures). Some German Christians knew about the slaughter of Jews during the holocaust, and just remained silent as Jews were marched past them to their deaths, and that was wrong. (Yes! I do believe it was wrong.) Do you then think it is ok for Jews to remain silent as other people march past them into Hell, because religion is a "personal thing." According to who is it a personal thing? That is like saying with Cain, "Am I my brother's keeper?" (Genesis 4:9). Let me tell you, ***that*** is the kind of selfish thinking that is offensive. If you truly believe that modern Judahism is the way to Heaven, then show some love and compassion to the lost. It would pay to give serious thought to Luke 10:25-37.

Yet another vital question: is what you believe so lacking in proof that you must forbid free speech in Israel and try to end it in America? The problem seems to be that your religious leaders know that what they teach cannot stand up to being exposed by the light from your own Scriptures. Without freedom of speech you are an enslaved people—chained by darkness. If you knew the truth, it would make you free (John 8:31-59), but when free speech is banned you have no opportunity to know truth. You can't be free without freedom. I love you, and want you to be free. But only you can make the decision to allow the free speech that is necessary for freedom to exist. If you are so insecure in your religious beliefs that you fear they cannot stand up under serious debate, then the reason is probably because down in your heart you sense that your beliefs are wrong. That is the only reason you fear missionaries.

I fully expect that for what I have just written your rabbis will try to persuade you to hate me, just as they have stirred people up to hate Ann Coulter and all evangelical Christians. That is ok. My love and support for Israel is unconditional. I love Israel and the Israeli people because they (you my dear Jewish friends) are my Savior's kinsmen, and because the New Testament which your religious leaders hate teaches me to love the Jews. Isn't that amazing?! Our gospel (good news) is "to the Jew first."

> I am not ashamed of the gospel of Christ: for it is the power of God unto salvation to every one that believeth; to the **Jew first**, and also to the Greek. For therein is the righteousness of God revealed from faith to faith: as it is written, The just shall live by faith. (Romans 1:16)

> For the **love of Christ constraineth us**; because we thus judge, that if one died for all, then were all dead: and *that* he died for all, that they which live should not henceforth live unto themselves, but unto him which died for them, and rose again. Wherefore henceforth know we no man after the flesh: yea, though we have known Christ after the flesh, yet now henceforth know we *him* no more. Therefore if any man *be* in Christ, *he is* a new creature: old things are passed away; behold, all things are become new. And all things *are* of God, who hath reconciled us to himself by Jesus Christ, and hath given to us the ministry of reconciliation; to wit, that God was in Christ, reconciling the world unto himself, not imputing their trespasses unto them; and hath committed unto us the word of reconciliation. **Now then we are ambassadors for Christ, as though God did beseech you by us: we pray you in Christ's stead, be ye reconciled to God. For he hath made him to be sin for us, who knew no sin; that we might be made the righteousness of God in him.** (2 Cor. 5:14-21)

> For the **Jews** require a sign, and the Greeks seek after wisdom: but we preach Christ crucified, unto the **Jews** a stumblingblock, and unto the Greeks foolishness; but unto them which are called, both **Jews** and Greeks, Christ the power of God, and the wisdom of God. (1 Cor. 1:22-24)

Every individual who has so unjustly maligned Ann Coulter owes her an apology.

Hate Crimes

All of the victims of slander discussed so far were to some degree or another harmed by humanist slander. Nevertheless, they remain free to defend their views. Perhaps Robert Bork was hurt the worst, as the slander against him kept him from becoming a Supreme Court justice. Clarence Thomas made it to the Supreme Court, but his character was forever marred in the eyes of those people who believed the slander against him. So far, the communication skills of Rush Limbaugh and Ann Coulter have enabled them to survive all assaults, and to become champions of conservatives who lack a platform from which to voice their opinions.

But at least twice humanists have instigated criminal investigations against Rush Limbaugh. They wanted to put him in prison over minor infraction of the law that they had tried to make look like major felonies. This should alarm us. Humanist congressmen love to pass laws to force the enactment of their agenda. There are now so many laws that no one can possibly know all of them. Without any doubt, each and every American is breaking some law which he or she does not even realize exists—unjust laws that have been passed for the specific purpose of someday imprisoning people who oppose the atheist humanist religion.

One such law deserving special attention is H.R. 1592, also known as the The Matthew Shepard Act or the Local Law Enforcement Hate Crimes Prevention Act. Liberal, humanist legislators have been trying unsuccessfully to get this bill passed for 10 years. But since Democrats have regained control of the House and Senate, this bill has now been passed.

> On September 27, the Senate passed by voice vote a bill that would expand federal hate crimes coverage to include sexual orientation, gender, gender identity, and disability.
>
> The vote came after a successful vote (60-39) to stop debate and add the amendment to the Department of Defense bill. . . .
>
> The amendment, The Matthew Shepard Act (or the Local Law Enforcement Hate Crimes Prevention Act), will expand coverage to include gender, gay, lesbian, bisexual, transgender and individuals with disabilities. It also provide grants to state and local communities to combat violent crimes committed by juveniles, train law enforcement officers, or to assist in state and local investigations and prosecutions of bias motivated crimes.[38]

This bill is the most dangerous threat to religious freedom in America since the establishment of the public school system. Louis Shelton of Traditional Values Coalition correctly summed up the danger:

> In 2003, the Canadian House of Commons passed a bill that added "sexual orientation" to the list of groups protected against so-called "hate speech." Violators can be sentenced to up to five years in prison for uttering words critical of homosexual sodomy.
>
> Homosexual activists are actually monitoring the sermons of Christian pastors to make sure they do not openly criticize homosexuality.
>
> H.R. 1592 is laying the legal framework for this kind of persecution in the U.S. Once homosexuality and cross-dressing become federally-protected minority groups, the full force of the federal law enforcement can be brought down upon anyone who "incites" potential violence against a homosexual. For example, a pastor's sermon from Romans 1 about homosexuality could be considered an incitement to such violence if some deranged churchgoer then goes out and beats up a homosexual.
>
> If signed into law, H.R. 1592 will usher in the death of religious freedom and speech in this nation. Any critical comments about homosexual sodomy will be considered "hate speech" and outside the bounds of First Amendment protections. It has already happened in Canada and it will happen here if H.R. 1592 and other laws like it are not soundly defeated.[39]

And Dr. Shelton is not alone in recognizing the danger of this bill.

> Many Christian leaders fear that the hate crime bill will inhibit pastors from speaking about homosexuality as a biblical sin and be interpreted in a way that bans even peaceful speech against the lifestyle. As example, leaders have pointed to hate-crime laws in England, Sweden and Canada, where Christians have been prosecuted for breaking these laws.
>
> Furthermore, in the United States, 11 Christians in Pennsylvania were prosecuted under the state's hate crimes law shortly after "sexual orientation" was added as a victim category several years ago. According to reports, the ten adults and one teenager were singing hymns and carrying signs peacefully at a homosexual celebration in Philadelphia when they were arrested.
>
> "The Hate Crimes Act will be the first step to criminalize our rights as Christians to believe that some behaviors are sinful," Dr. James C. Dobson, founder and chairman of Focus on the Family, said in a message for a petition to oppose the bill.[40]

---

[38] Tyler Lewis, "Senate Passes Hate Crimes Bill," *Civilrights.Org*, 1927 September 2007, Http://www.civilrights.org/press_room/buzz_clips/civilrightsorg-stories/senate-passes-hate-crimes-bill.html.

[39] Louis P. Sheldon, "TVC Chairman Speaks Out On Dangers Of H.R. 1592 To Free Speech/Religion," *The Traditional Values Coalition*, 1918 April 2007, Http://www.traditionalvalues.org/modules.php?sid=3059.

[40] Michelle Vu, "Bush Prepared to Veto 'Hate Crimes' Bill," *The Christian Post*, 2007, 10 March 2007, Http://www.christianpost.com/article/20071003/29558_Bush_Prepared_to_Veto_'Hate_Crimes'_Bill.htm.

Only one man can prevent this bill from becoming law: President George W. Bush.

> WASHINGTON – President Bush is ready to veto a contentious hate crimes bill that was attached last week to a massive defense spending bill, said the White House on Tuesday.
>
> The Senate had attached the hate crimes legislation to the high-priority defense spending bill – which includes funding for the Iraq War – in a political maneuver to pressure Bush to pass the amendment.
>
> However, the White House said Bush will not sign the hate crimes bill into law.
>
> "The president has said overwhelmingly that these are two separate issues – that they should not be combined; and the president has reiterated his commitment to vetoing the hate crimes provision," said White House spokesman Tim Goeglein on Tuesday, according to OneNewsNow.[41]

But during 2008 President Bush's term in office will expire, and he will step down to be replaced by a new president. If the new president is a humanist, this bill will almost certainly become law. So the danger is very, very real. Now is the time to begin preparing for the next election. Begin warning your family members and friends and neighbors now while you still have the chance.

Readers that believe the danger is being exaggerated had perhaps best buckle their seat belts before reading the next chapter.

---

41 Ibid.

Federal
Hate Bill
Means
Funeral
For Free
Speech

Chapter 26

IS YOUR CHILD GAY?

Be Aware That He or She Is Being Seduced

The U.S.A. is rushing madly toward the edge of a cliff. Waiting for us at the bottom of that cliff is the legalization of sodomy, the banning of free speech to protect sodomites from criticism, and severe religious oppression such as we have never known before. If we elect to plunge over that cliff on election day November 4, 2008, there will most likely be no return. We citizens are literally deciding if we want to remain a free people. Actually, we could be deciding before November 4, 2008 if we choose wrong in the primaries. This year the primaries are exceedingly crucial.

Sodom, California

On January 1, 2008, the religion of atheism—and its doctrine that sodomy is righteousness instead of sin—becomes officially protected from criticism by the government in the public schools of California. The free speech of theists who believe that sodomy is sin has been officially banned. Only the doctrines of the humanist religion may be taught or practiced. Voicing the opposing views of other religions are decreed to be "hate-crimes."

SB 777

This bill passed the Democrat majority California State Assembly September the 11th by a 21-to-15 vote, and was signed into law by Governor Arnold Schwarzenegger on October the12th 2007.

What SB 777 Does

The lead author of this bill was Senator Sheila Kuehl. The bill was sponsored by Equality California, a homosexual organization. A document on Equality California's web site explains what the bill does:

> SB 777 would update and explicitly list all the prohibited categories of discrimination in publicly funded K-12 schools and institutions of higher education. Those categories include:
>
> - Disability
> - Gender
> - Nationality
> - Race or ethnicity
> - Religion
> - Sexual orientation
> - Any other characteristic that is contained in the definition of hate crimes set forth in Section 422.55 of the Penal Code
>
> In addition, SB 777 would reference already codified definitions of these protected bases as follows:
>
> - with the person's assigned sex at birth.
> - "**Nationality**" includes citizenship, country of origin, and national origin.
> - "**Race or ethnicity**" includes ancestry, color, and ethnic background.
> - "**Religion**" includes all aspects of religious belief, observance, and practice, and includes agnosticism and atheism.
> - "**Sexual orientation**" means heterosexuality, homosexuality, or bisexuality.
> - **Disability, gender, nationality, race or ethnicity, religion, sexual orientation, or any other characteristic contained in the definition of hate crimes set forth in Section 422.55 of the Penal Code** includes a perception that the person has any of those characteristics or that the person is associated with a person who has, or is perceived to have, any of those characteristics.
>
> Finally, SB 777 would standardize various nondiscrimination statutes throughout the Education Code by amending those laws with a reference to the characteristics contained in the general prohibition of discrimination in Section 220. This will remedy deficiencies in protection for many students and confusion that exists for implementation and compliance by teachers and school administrators. Another advantage to this approach is

that whenever additional protected categories are added to Section 220, these other educational laws will be updated automatically to include all the recognized civil rights protections that exist in the Education Code.

Specifically, the bill links the following Education Code sections to the characteristics listed in the general prohibition against discrimination in Section 220:

- Section 235. Prohibiting discrimination in the operation of alternative schools and charter schools.
- Section 260. Establishing the responsibility of school district governing boards to ensure that school district programs and activities are free from discrimination.
- Section 50. Prohibiting bias in teacher instruction or school sponsored activities.
- Section 66251. Guaranteeing equal opportunity in postsecondary educational institutions.
- Section 66270. Prohibiting discrimination in the programs and activities of postsecondary institutions.[42]

This document needs to be examined carefully.

SB 777 Declared Atheism and Agnosticism To Be Religions!

This is exactly what this book has been proving over and over again. Humanism and atheism are the same thing—they are an anti-God ***religion***. This is the most important fact in this chapter; understanding this is the key to victory. As a religion the teaching of their doctrines may not legally be funded by government, as that violates the First Amendment. Also, according to the First Amendment, "Congress shall make no law respecting an establishment of religion, or prohibiting the free exercise thereof..." Since public schools receive federal funding, SB 777 is the type of law that the First Amendment forbids. SB 777 even more firmly establishes humanism/atheism as the official state church, and at the same time prohibits the free exercise of other religions. This violation of the First Amendment must not be allowed to be ignored. ***This is the key—THE ONLY KEY—to stopping this vile, wicked, anti-God, humanist religion. Disestablish the humanist church, and it will collapse. Make humanists use their own funds instead of tax fund to pay for the teaching of their vile religion, and it will be reduced to insignificance. [If you haven't yet read chapter 22 of this book, be sure to do so].***

SB 777 Protects Atheism and Agnosticism From Criticism

By specifically naming atheism and agnosticism, SB 777 give them special status above other religions. Therefore, if Christians or other theists say that atheism is wrong and is rebellion against God, they can be charged with committing a hate crime. But atheists can talk against Christianity and other theist religions all they want with impunity. SB 777 therefore bans free speech, except for the established humanist church.

SB 777 Protects the Act of Sodomy

This bill redefines gender. Gender no longer means male and female. Now it "means sex: and includes a person's gender identity and gender-related appearance and behavior" (Emphasis added). So, if a person identifies him or her self as a homosexual, or bi-sexual, and dresses like the opposite sex, and behaves like homosexuals behave, no one is allowed to say that is wrong. And how do homosexuals behave? Well, you already know from going to the web page given in chapter one. But for more in depth information, Paul Cameron of Family Research Institute has written an excellent article titled "Medical Consequences of What Homosexuals Do," which explains what they do and the consquences. Since this is the type behavior that homosexuals are trying to seduce children into, parents need to understand what the consquences are going to be if their children are unable to resist the seduction. You can find the article on the web at this URL:

Http://www.familyresearchinst.org/Default.aspx?tabid=73

---

[42] Senator Sheila Kuehl, "FACT SHEET: STUDENT CIVIL RIGHTS ACT (SB 777)," *Equality California* (2007), Http://www.eqca.org/atf/cf/%7B687DF34F-6480–4BCD-9C2B-1F33FD8E1294%7D/SB%20777%20FACT%20SHEET.PDF.

Please go there now and read the very sobering facts.

Consider that even in *Little Black Book* distributed by homosexuals to encourage such behavior, it says, "As you can see, it can be hard to be sure you sure you are safe from all STDs. If you are having sex, get tested every 3-6 months!" Sure, and if the test shows that you have AIDS, then what?

Just like all other humanist practices, sodomy is insanity. Do a web search for "bug chasers gift givers." Doing such a search, I found an article titled "Bug Chaser & Gift Giver Parties" on the About.com:Gay Life website. A copyright notice at the bottom of the page says that About, Inc. is "a part of The New York Times Company. Fitting! Here is what the article says (I'm combining several paragraphs into one to save space):

> Deliberately Transmitting HIV. What is a "bug chaser?" A bug chaser is a gay man who deliberately attempts to contract HIV by having unprotected sex with a man or group of men who are known to have the virus. What is a "gift giver?" A gift giver is an HIV positive gay man who deliberately transmits the virus, often times to bug chasers, or those willing to contract it. What are bug parties? Bug parties are sex parties often ranging from a few to as much as 30 people. Unsafe sex with every participant at the party is encouraged. . . . Why do people participate in bug parties? Many psychologists theorize that participation in bug parties is actually an anxiety disorder where the non-infected individuals fear getting HIV so greatly that they would rather contract it and free themselves of the anxiety of living in fear. These parties are also seen as a sort of club for those living with HIV. Infecting a HIV negative and willing participant initiates them into their world.[43]

The question is: does anyone have a right to engage in behavior that on-purpose spreads fatal diseases? Is this not murder? Yes, it is. One homosexual even admitted it, saying, "If I know that he's negative and I'm [haveing sex with] him, it sort of gets me off. I'm murdering him in a sense, killing him slowly, and that's sort of, as sick as it sounds, exciting to me."[44]

SB 777 Sanctions Extra-Marital Sex

According to SB 777, "'**Sexual orientation**' means heterosexuality, homosexuality, or bisexuality." Bisexuality means having sex with both men and women. As long as there are laws against polygamy, this cannot be done without having extra-marital sex. This law therefore implies that marriage is not important and is of no value. And of course we know that many homosexuals have literally hundreds of sex partners, and they certainly don't bother to marry each other first.

> A survey conducted by the homosexual magazine Genre found that 24 percent of the respondents said they had had more than a hundred sexual partners in their lifetime. The magazine noted that several respondents suggested including a category of those who had more than a thousand sexual partners.[45]

So, this law sanctions fornication and adultery, and says that no one may say that fornication is wrong.

What if a bi-sexual pressures your child to have sex with him or her? If you child says, No, that is wrong!, then your child can be punished for discriminating against bi-sexuals. What if your son is approached by some homosexual boys in the now bi-gender bathroom, and told to lower his pants so they can "love him." If he refuses stating that sodomy is sinful behavior, he will be punished for discriminating against homosexuals. And no teacher can come to his rescue without risking his or her career. For parents to send a child into such an environment is child abuse, pure and simple.

It needs to be pointed out that discrimination against a person for committing sodomy is much different from discrimination against a person because of his skin color or nationality. It is ***not*** a sin to be a Jew or to have black skin. It ***is*** a sin to commit sodomy. Sodomy is a sin just like murder and rape are sins. It is necessary to discriminate against murder and rape and sodomy, as these are very harmful and destructive actions that destroy civilization if left unpunished and thus encouraged. No one has the right to sodomize.

---

43 Ramone Johnson, "Bug Chaser & Gift Giver Parties," *About.com: Gay Life*, Http://gaylife.about.com/cs/gay101/a/bugparties.htm.

44 Gregory A. Freeman, "Bug Chasers: The Men Who Long to be HIV+," *Rolling Stone*, 1923 January 2003, Http://www.shoutwire.com/viewstory/16216/Bug_Chasers_Men_Who_Want_To_Be_HIV_Positive.

45 Timothy J. Dailey, "The Negative Health Effects of Homosexuality," *Family Research Council*, no. 232, Http://www.frc.org/get.cfm?i=IS01B1.

SB 777 Forces Boys and Girls To Use the Same Bathrooms and Locker Rooms

Humanism is mental and moral insanity. It is absolutely insane to force boys and girls to use the same bathroom. It is inevitable that a boy and a girl will find themselves in such a bathroom alone with each other, having no privacy. Will girls have to use urinals like boys? It would be interesting to know how they can do that. In spite of what humanists teach, there is a very big difference in the way boys and girls are made. Will boys urinate in a urinal in front of girls, or will millions of dollars worth of urinals have to be removed and replaced with millions of dollars worth of toilets with stalls? Who is going to pay for all this? Mark my words, rape will take place in such bathrooms! This is worse than insane! It is evil and wicked to the core—it is the ***ultimate*** of the ultimate child abuse. Humanists claim to be defenders of the right to privacy, but then they pass laws to deny privacy to everyone. Humanism is hypocrisy.

SB 777 Provides For Protecting Other Sins In the Future

Some sodomites have sex with animals and even with dead bodies. Other homosexuals want sex only with young boys. Sodomites argue that they can't help it; they were born that way. Murderers could just as truthfully as homosexuals say the same thing—that they were born to murder, and therefore should not be discriminated against. Rapists could say the same, that they were born to rape, and so should not be discriminated against. Senator Kuehl says that "Another advantage to this [SB 777] approach is that whenever <u>additional protected categories</u> are added to Section 220, these other educational laws will be updated automatically to include all the recognized civil rights protections that exist in the Education Code." So, these people obviously have plans to legalize other sinful behavior in the future. People who ignore this warning should remember it when some sodomite rapes the corpse of a loved one lying in state at a funeral home, or when they find a homosexual in their barn sexually mounting their favorite horse, or when they learn that some sodomites have raped their son. When sodomy is concerned, an ounce of prevention is worth a trillion tons of cure. It is doubtful that the emotional damage homosexual rape causes to a child can ever be completely repaired.

SB 777 Protects Sodomy Even in Alternative and Charter Schools. This bill will protect sodomy in every school in California that receives government funding. This includes "alternative schools and charter schools," and any other school that receives government funding. Remember, government funding always means government control. That is why theists should never seek or accept any government funding for their schools. THIS IS ALSO WHY THE SO-CALLED "FAITH-BASED INITIATIVE" IS A MISTAKE AND WILL NOT HAVE THE DESIRED EFFECT, BUT WILL INSTEAD FURTHER ENSLAVE THEISTS IN THE U.S.A.

Right now these laws will not apply to totally privately funded private schools or to totally privately funded home-schooled children. But eventually they will. If it is wrong to discriminate against sodomy in public schools, then it is also wrong to discriminate against sodomy in private schools and in private homes. Changing this law to make it universal will be the next step.

> The European Human Rights Court just a few weeks ago concluded in a case involving similar objections that parents do not have an "exclusive" right to lead their children's education and any parental "wish" to have their children grow up without adverse influences "could not take priority over compulsory school attendance."
>
> That court said a German family had no right to provide homeschooling for their children.
>
> In the case that originated in Germany, homeschooling parents Fritz and Marianna Konrad argued for that right because they said Germany's compulsory school attendance endangered their children's religious upbringing and promotes teaching inconsistent with the family's Christian faith.
>
> But the court concluded, "The parents' right to education did not go as far as to deprive their children of that experience."
>
> "The (German) Federal Constitutional Court stressed the general interest of society to avoid the emergence of parallel societies based on separate philosophical convictions and the importance of integrating minorities into society," the European ruling said.[46]

THEISTS, BE THEY CHRISTIANS OR NOT, CANNOT ALLOW ANY LAW SUCH AS THIS TO GO INTO EFFECT IN THE U.S.A, WITHOUT ALSO PLACING THEMSELVES AT GREAT RISK OF GOING TO PRISON FOR "HATE

[46] "'Gay' Groups: We Have Rights to Your Children!" *WorldNetDaily*, 2006 October 2006, Http://www.wnd.com/news/article.asp?ARTICLE_ID=52311.

CRIMES." ***Now is not the time to hesitate or to be lazy—IMMEDIATE action is vital for our own well being, to say nothing about the well being of our children!***

You could go to jail. Already on the state level it has get to the federal level.

On January 14, 2005 a "Diversity Book bag" containing a book titled *Who's In a Family* by Robert Skutch was sent home from the kindergarten of Estabrook Elementary School in Lexington, Massachusetts in the hands of the five year old son of David and Tonia Parker. The Parkers were alarmed at the homosexual contents of this bag. They did not want their son exposed to homosexuality, especially at his young age. They wrote to the principle of the school, "The real question is—do parents have the right to exclude/shield their children from these contrary values being pushed upon young children in elementary school....Do you commit to us that [son's name] will not be subjected to homosexual family values at Estabrook?" Numerous e-mails were thereafter exchanged over a period of three months between the Parkers and the school, but the school administrators would not agree to exclude the Parker's son from homosexual discussions.

On April 27, 2005, the Parkers were invited to a face-to-face discussion about the issue at the school. As the meeting seemed at a stalemate, the Principal and Director of Education seemed to change course. Although they had claimed they "did not have the authority" to allow David Parker to be informed when his 6-year-old son was exposed to discussions of homosexuality, they suggested that the Superintendent did have the authority to agree -- at least until the full process of appealing to the School Committee went through.

So they had David hand-write an agreement, which they discussed with Superintendent William Hurley over the telephone, and then faxed to him. David was led to believe that Hurley was going to sign this - but instead he called back saying he rejected it, and they decided to have David arrested for trespassing.[47]

David Parker hand cuffed in court after spending a night in jail for insisting that his five-year-old son not be taught about homosexuality.

The police were called, and David Parker was arrested and taken to jail. He was not allowed to call his lawyer. The next day he stood handcuffed (see photo right) before Judge Robert McKenna in Concord District Court.

When he informed Judge Robert McKenna that he had not been allowed to call his lawyer, the judge scolded him for not being respectful. Parker was released on $1,000 surety bond. He was officially informed that he may not set foot on any school property in Lexington, or he will be arrested again for trespassing. A hearing was set for June 1, followed by court appearances on Aug. 2 and Sept. 19.[48]

Parker wisely refused to plea bargain[49], and refused to plead guilty to false charges—which would have been dishonest. Thus began a series of enormously expensive (over $200,000) legal proceedings. Large numbers of parents gathered in support of the Parkers, and the case drew nationwide media attention. On October 20, 2005 the Middlesex County District Attorney dropped the charges against David Parker. However, the Parkers were informed that their request to opt-out their son from homosexual discussions was denied, and that if they didn't like it they should home school.

---

47 "Lexington, Mass., Father of 6-Year-Old Arrested, Spends Night in Jail," *MassResistance* (2005), Http://www.massresistance.org/docs/parker/main.html.

48 Ibid.

49 Never ever plead guilty to a crime you did not commit. Not only would doing so be dishonest, but also could result in you ending up in prison. Lawyers who want you to lie are wicked people who cannot be trusted.

In April of 2006, the Parkers filed a federal civil rights lawsuit against the Lexington school system to appeal this ruling. In August of 2006 the Lexington school system filed a 57 page motion to dismiss the Parker's lawsuit. In September of 2006 the Parker's lawyers filed a rebuttal to the motion to dismiss the lawsuit. That same month the American Civil Liberties Union and major homosexual groups (Human Rights Campaign, Massachusetts Teachers Association, Gay and Lesbian Advocates and Defenders), plus local gay organizations filed a brief in federal court opposing the Parker's lawsuit. In October of 2006 the Lexington school system filed a rebuttal to the Parker's rebuttal.

On February 7, 2007, the lawsuit began with school and ACLU lawyers arguing that the case should be dismissed.

> "Once I have elected to send my child to public school, my fundamental right does not allow me to direct what my child is exposed to in the public school," the [school's] lawyer said. Once you send your child to a public school, you give up your ability to control what is taught to your child, he asserted.
>
> The ACLU lawyer also spoke, and said that because of the publicity surrounding this lawsuit, "teachers have been chilled - they are afraid to open their mouths on things they have been teaching." ... She added that "it is a tremendous bonus [for children in the schools] to be exposed to ideas different from their parents." She also said that "the exposure of children to ideas that their parents abhor" has nothing to do with a violation of religious freedom.[50]

On February 23, 2007 U.S. District Judge Mark L. Wolf decided in favor of the school and ACLU, and dismissed the lawsuit! WorldNetDaily summed up what happened like this:

> A federal judge in Massachusetts has ordered the "gay" agenda taught to Christians who attend a public school in Massachusetts, finding that they need the teachings to be "engaged and productive citizens."
>
> U.S. District Judge Mark L. Wolf yesterday dismissed a civil rights lawsuit brought by David Parker, ordering that it is reasonable, indeed there is an obligation, for public schools to teach young children to accept and endorse homosexuality.
>
> Wolf essentially adopted the reasoning in a brief submitted by a number of homosexual-advocacy groups, who said "the rights of religious freedom and parental control over the upbringing of children ... would undermine teaching and learning..."[51]

You or your child could be beaten or worse. Sodomites respond viciously when it is pointed out that they tend to be violent people. Not all of them are violent, but many of them are. They use threats and violence to intimidate individuals, businesses, organizations, and politicians in order to force their will on others. Here is an example:

> On May 17, 2006 - the two-year anniversary of same-sex "marriage" in Massachusetts - David Parker's first-grade son, Jacob, was beaten up at the Estabrook Elementary School in Lexington during recess, receiving multiple blows to the chest, stomach, and genital area.
>
> During the recess period, a group of 8-10 kids suddenly surrounded Jacob and grabbed him. He was taken around the corner of the school building out of sight of the patrolling aides, with the taunting and encouragement of other kids. Jacob was then positioned against the wall for what appeared to be a well planned and coordinated assault. Many children stood, watched silently, and did nothing as the beating commenced.
>
> The group of kids surrounded Jacob and he was beaten and punched. Then, as he fell to the ground, another child was heard saying to the group of children, "Now you all can finish him off," and as he was down on his hands and knees, the beating continued on his back. Then, fortunately, one little girl ran to contact the oblivious playground aides to stop it.[52]

The school at first acknowledged the facts about the beating, but later radically changed the story and worked with gay activists to demean the Parkers.

February 2005 (the year before the above incident), an incident in the same school prompted a family to pull their child from the school in the middle of the school year, and move out of the area. Like the Parkers, Mr. and Mrs. Montalvos

> told the school they wanted to opt-out of the diversity book bag, which the schools EXPRESSLY told them they could do. Furthermore, the parents requested that the principal please respect their values and morals and remove their children from any material or discussion, whether oral or written, in the classroom pertaining to such subjects. The book bag was sent home with their kindergarten son anyway, even though the parents made these requests in writing to the Estabrook principal.

---

[50] "Contention Inside and Outside as David Parker's Civil Rights Lawsuit Begins in Federal Court," *MassResistance*, 2007 February 2007, Http://www.massresistance.org/docs/parker_lawsuit/hearing_020707/index.html.

[51] Bob Unruh, "Judge Orders 'gay' Agenda Taught to Christian Children," *WorldNetDaily*, 1924 February 2007, Http://wnd.com/news/article.asp?ARTICLE_ID=54420.

[52] "David Parker's First-Grade Son Surrounded and Beaten up at School," *MassResistance* (2005), Http://www.massresistance.org/docs/parker/parker_son_incident/index.html.

Further discussions with the principal revealed that all children at Estabrook have access to books about lesbian and gay-headed relationships in each and every classroom, and that any teacher or adult can read these books to children any time they wish, with no thought of notifying their parents.

Instead of respecting the Montalvos values and beliefs, the principal seemed to think the problem was the Montalvos, and suggested the parents attend a workshop entitled, "How and why to talk with your children about diversity" which was held at Diamond Middle School on February 8th.... Many of the teachers and parents at this meeting were in favor of teaching acceptance and normalization of homosexuality. When Mr. Montalvos discussed his belief system and his legal rights to shield his own children from these materials and discussions in the public schools, a parent told him to leave and to place his children in a private or religious school. One of the Estabrook staff members had to physically restrain this parent as she was apparently preparing to physically attack.[53]

Therefore, the Montalvos family left Lexington, concluding that this school was not a safe place to have their children.

Here is another example of homosexual violence:

Arlington, VA (Aug. 28, 2007) -- Last week Parents and Friends of Ex-Gays & Gays (PFOX) exhibited at the Arlington County Fair in Arlington, Virginia. PFOX has exhibited at this county fair for the past four years and hands out materials on same-sex attraction and tolerance for the ex-gay community to a hungry public. A local gay group also exhibits there and distributes materials on gay rights.

As happens every year, gay activists disrupted our booth activities. They screamed obscenities, threw our materials from the exhibit table to the ground, insisted we recognize their same-sex "spouses," demanded that PFOX leave, and hit a PFOX volunteer because he is ex-gay.

When we explained that the county's sexual orientation law allows both the gay booth and our ex-gay booth to exhibit, the unhappy gays insisted that sexual orientation laws on hate crimes and discrimination do not apply to ex-gays -- only gays -- and no tolerance should be extended to former homosexuals.

All the gays who stopped by our booth that week insisted that no one could change their sexual orientation from gay to straight, although they knew of people who had changed in mid-life from heterosexual to a gay lifestyle or had changed their gender.

The gays became infuriated when our ex-gay volunteers testified about leaving homosexuality. They adamantly refused to accept the ex-gays' sexual orientation. One gay man went so far as to hit our ex-gay volunteer because he refused to recant his ex-gay testimony. We summoned a police officer, who ejected the gay man off of the fairgrounds. Our ex-gay volunteer decided not to press assault charges against the gay man because he wanted to turn the other check as Jesus had done.[54]

Paul Cameron of Family Research Institute has done extensive study of violence committed by homosexuals. He found that

Although the total number of victims dispatched by a given killer is often in doubt, (e.g., homosexual Henry Lucas claimed that he killed 350), it appears that the modern world record for serial killing is held by a Russian homosexual, Andrei Chikatilo, who was convicted in 1992 of raping, murdering and eating parts of at least 21 boys, 17 women and 14 girls. The pathology of eating one's sexual victims also characterized Milwaukee's Jeffrey Dahmer in 1992. He not only killed 17 young men and boys, but cooked and ate their body parts.

The top six U.S. male serial killers were all gay:

- Donald Harvey claimed 37 victims in Kentucky;
- John Wayne Gacy raped and killed 33 boys in Chicago, burying them under his house and in his yard;
- Patrick Kearney accounted for 32, cutting his victims into small pieces after sex and leaving them in trash bags along the Los Angeles freeways;
- Bruce Davis molested and killed 27 young men and boys in Illinois;
- A gay sex-murder-torture ring (Corll-Henley-Brooks) sent 27 Texas men and boys to their grave; and
- Juan Corona was convicted of murdering 25 migrant workers (he "made love" with their corpses).[55]

Humanist "love" is just selfish lust; it is hatred feigning to be love. And if a person rejects what God says about sex, then it is logical for that person to also reject what God says about human life.

AB 394

Governor Arnold Schwarzenegger also signed a second pro-sodomy bill into law.

The second sexual indoctrination bill that Schwarzenegger signed, AB 394, will promote transsexuality, bisexuality, and homosexuality to students, <u>parents</u>, and teachers through school <u>training programs</u> against 'harassment'" and 'discrimination.'"

Moralists can read between the bold lines on that second bill. It means that those who express the biblical position on homosexuality could face lawsuits.[56] [Underline emphasis added.]

---

[53] Gerry Wambolt, "Family Left Lexington School System Over Homosexuality in David Parker's Elementary School" (2005), MassResistance.

[54] "GAYS ASSAULT EX-GAYS AT COUNTY FAIR," *Venus Magazine*, 1928 August 2007, Http://venusmagazine.org/Gay%20Assault%20PFOX.html.

[55] Paul Cameron, "Violence and Homosexuality," *Family Research Institute* (2006), Http://www.familyresearchinst.org/Default.aspx?tabid=74.

[56] Grant Swank, "CA Schools: Pull Christian Kids Out," *The Conservative Voice*, 2007, 22 October 2007, Http://www.theconservativevoice.com/article/28694.html.

Of course students, parents, and teachers will have to be taught what sodomy is in order to not discriminate against it. Parents should note that if they are going to have to attend school training programs against harassment and discrimination, this is going to force them to waste time in a very unpleasant way. Consider how much more unpleasant it will be for their children to be under the authority of sodomite teachers as they teach them sodomy. The pressure and intimidation on your children and their classmates to do wrong to please the teacher and be like their friends will be immense. Many children won't be unable to resist it.

Christians Reactions To SB 777 and AB 394

There are basically two reactions to the passage of these two pro-sodomy laws from the Christians in California: some are calling for a referendum, and others are urging parents to immediately pull their children from public schools. Both of these actions are absolutely essential. For the reason explained in the section above this one, parents who have their children in private schools or are home schooling them, ***are also put at risk by this law, and must help defeat it.***

The Call For a Referendum

According to the Save Our Kids web site (saveourkids.net), which is a web site of Capitol Resource Family Impact (CRFI), they have "filed a referendum to prevent the implementation of SB 777. CRFI is calling on every concerned citizen to join them in this huge undertaking." They add that,

> The Attorney General has given us clearance to begin collecting signatures. Petitions have been printed and are being distributed throughout the state. If you have already signed up to receive petitions, they should arrive in the mail shortly.[57]

This is a very expensive and labor intensive undertaking. CRFI explains:

> Here is a brief summary of why we cannot post the petitions on our web site:
>
> -- The petitions are 17 x 14 and are 4 fold, like a booklet. Most citizens do not have printers that can print 17 x 14 paper.
>
> -- Because this is a referendum (not an initiative), we must include the entire text of SB 777. The bill is over 30 pages long, thus making the referendum petition very long.
>
> -- Many of the local county election offices, where referendum petitions are turned in, would reject petitions not in the specific print layout. We cannot risk invalidating thousands of vital signatures because the petitions were not printed properly or printed on separate pages and stapled together.
>
> -- We have consulted with both our attorneys and consultants and they are all in agreement that we must not put them online. These are the same very experienced consultants that conducted the Save Our License initiative and were very involved in the Davis recall effort.
>
> -- Because most people cannot print the petitions and we cannot staple them (they must be in a booklet format), we are forced to print the petitions ourselves and then distribute them.[58]

So the referendum process has been made very hard and expensive—obviously to try to discourage it from happening. The will of the people doesn't matter to whoever made such rules. Getting their own way is all that matters.

Also, what about AB 394? Sadly, it appears that there is not enough money and manpower to stop both bills.

UPDATE: according to the sodomite website Advocate.com,

> The Student Civil Rights Act, which went into effect on January 1, prohibits in publicly funded schools and activities discrimination that is based on religion, race, disability, gender, or sexual orientation. Opponents, led by the Alliance Defense Fund and Advocates for Faith and Freedom, were able to garner just 350,000 signatures, far fewer than the necessary 433,000 to qualify for a June referendum.[59]

So Californians have lost their freedom of speech, and Califonia children have been placed in great danger.

---

57 "Help Us Repeal SB 777 to Protect Our Kids," *MassResistence* (2007), Http://www.saveourkids.net/.

58 "Update on Petitions," *MassResistence* (2007), Http://www.saveourkids.net/news.html?news_id=13&start=0&category_id=1&parent_id=1&arcyear=&arcmonth=.

59 "Petition Against Students' Rights Falls Short," *Advocate.Com*, 1915 January 2008, Http://www.advocate.com/news_detail_ektid51608.asp.

The Call For an Exodus

The second reaction to these two pro-sodomy bills being signed into law is a call for Christians to pull their children from public schools to either place them in private schools or home school them. Actually, if Christian parents truly love their children they have no choice but to do this—anything less is child abuse.

> Christians in California are outraged that their ***children in public schools will be indoctrinated pro-homosexuality in all its aspects. Therefore, believers are urged to pull their students immediately out of all public schools for home schooling or private schools****. . . .*
>
> CRI's legislative liaison Meredith Turney said: "SB 777 will result in reverse discrimination against students with religious and traditional family values. These students have lost their voice as the direct result of Gov. Schwarzenegger's unbelievable decision. The terms 'mom and dad' or 'husband and wife' could promote discrimination against homosexuals if a same-sex couple is not also featured."
>
> "Parents want the assurance that when their children go to school they will learn the fundamentals of reading, writing and arithmetic – not social indoctrination regarding alternative sexual lifestyles. Now that SB 777 is law, schools will in fact become indoctrination centers for sexual experimentation," she said per WorldNetDaily.com's Bob Unruh.
>
> WorldNetDaily reports: "Ray Moore, a spokesman for Exodus Mandate, which advocates Christians give up on public schools and either school their children at home or send them to Christian schools, agreed with Thomasson, and went further. ***"This really is a call to conservative and Christian pro-family groups to give up this absurd idea of public school reform,' he told WND. 'It can't be done. The longer they talk about saving public schools, the longer they prolong this agony, when they could be setting up new schools.'"***
>
> Christians must act as a united block—and quickly. There is no time to lose. There is no Christian who can absent himself from the cause.[60] [Emphasis added.]

Moore is totally correct. Many (perhaps most) public school teachers are humanists, and they believe sodomy is a righteous lifestyle. Such teachers are not fit to teach children. Stopping these two bills from taking effect will not change the beliefs of those teachers. A complete change of teachers and administrators is essential.

The Call For Abolishment

The above two reactions are vital, but they are not enough. They are defensive measures only, and will not solve the problem. They buy a little time, but leave parents in financial straits. Parents will be forced to pay for both the teaching of truth to their own children, and the teaching of lies and immorality to other people's children. That is religious oppression. The parasite cancer of humanist socialism will continue to eat the flesh of the United States of America, sapping her vitality and dragging her ever closer to death. ***The best defense now is an all-out offense.***

The public school system is based on socialism, and that cannot be fixed except by abandoning the public school system altogether. Socialism is stealing—sin. Sin cannot be reformed, but must be forsaken. Get away from it, and never return to it. The cancer of socialism can only thrive on a free-enterprise host, and then only until it has killed that host. Only major surgery can save the U.S.A.: THE PUBLIC SCHOOL SYSTEM MUST BE ABOLISHED. ***Mark this well, most people will be very hard pressed to send their children to private schools while at the same time being heavily taxed to support public schools. Go all the way to deliver them from such tyranny by abolishing the public school system or else all other efforts will be in vain.***

One major obstacle must be recognized and overcome. Most parents know the Public Schools are a horrible mess, but they have been taught to have faith in government instead of in God. They cannot imagine private education being financially possible for them. Churches across America must teach these people to have faith in God, instead of in Uncle Sam. Evangelism is essential; every person in the United States must be reached with the gospel!

---

[60] Swank, "CA Schools: Pull Christian Kids Out."

Gomorrah, U.S.A.

So far in this chapter we have discussed only the state of California. But in 2006 the Sodomy Party won, and now the sodomy party has begun at the federal level of government. Every person in the U.S.A. is directly effected.

On September 27, 2007, Rep. Barney Frank, one of two openly homosexual members of Congress, introduced H.R. 3685, also called the Employment Non-Discrimination Act of 2007.[61] By November 8, 2007 this bill had been through all the required steps, and was passed by a vote of 235-184 in the House of Representatives, and was sent to the Senate, where Massachusetts Democrat Edward Kennedy plans to introduce a similar bill.[62] H.R. 3685 is "the first federal ban on job discrimination against gays, lesbians and bisexuals."[63] The Library of Congress Thomas summary of the bill begins as follows:

> Employment Non-Discrimination Act of 2007 - (Sec. 4) Makes it an unlawful employment practice for covered entities (employers, employment agencies, labor organizations, or joint labor-management committees) to discriminate against an individual on the basis of actual or perceived sexual orientation, including actions based on the actual or perceived sexual orientation of a person with whom the individual associates or has associated. Prohibits preferential treatment or quotas. Allows only disparate treatment claims.
>
> (Sec. 5) Makes it an unlawful employment practice to discriminate against an individual because the individual opposed any practice made an unlawful employment practice by this Act or made a charge, testified, assisted, or participated in any manner in an investigation, proceeding, or hearing under this Act.
>
> (Sec. 6) Makes this Act inapplicable to a corporation, association, educational institution, or society that is exempt from religious discrimination provisions under the Civil Rights Act of 1964.
>
> (Sec. 7) Makes this Act inapplicable to the relationship between the United States and members of the Armed Forces, including the Coast Guard. Declares that this Act does not repeal or modify any federal, state, territorial, or local law creating a special right or preference concerning employment for a veteran.[64]

At first glance this bill doesn't seem so bad. It doesn't apply to religious institutions or the military. Of course, because those are the two groups most likely to oppose the bill; humanists are willing to get what they want one step at a time. For now, H.R. 3685 only applies to "employers, employment agencies, labor organizations, or joint labor-management committees." For most people, since it doesn't apply to them personally they will not worry about it. But there is a problem with that kind of thinking.

Who Is an Employer?

Suppose you need someone to babysit your three year old son. Guess what? If you hire a baby sitter, that makes you an employer! So, let's say, two strange sodomite men dismount their Harley in front of your house in answer to your ad. One is wearing an earring, a tongue stud, multiple bead necklaces, a see-through lace blouse unbuttoned half way down his hairy chest, and skin tight pants which reveal a high state of arousal. The other is wearing long, permed, bleached blond hair, make up, painted fingernails, a low-cut blouse, a mini-skirt, and high heel shoes. They hug, paw, and lip kiss during the interview. Watching two men lip kiss is sickening. They ogle your son, and stress how much they "love" little boys. When you tell them you were expecting for a girl to apply for the job, they frown angrily, and inform you of their rights under the Employment Non-Discrimination Act.

You are now in a serious dilemma. You have a gut feeling that you would be a stupid fool to risk your three year old son with these people. But if you refuse to hire one of them based upon "actual or perceived sexual orientation," you face being charged with a federal crime, having to pay a huge fine, doing time in a federal prison, and having a criminal record for the rest of your life. **Who do you sacrifice on the alter of political correctness to the insane humanist religion? You or your son?**

---

[61] http://thomas.loc.gov/cgi-bin/bdquery/z?d110:h.r.03685:

[62] Andrew Miga, "House Passes Job Bias Ban Against Gays," *MyWay*, 2007 November 2007, Http://apnews.myway.com/article/20071107/D8SP50200.html.

[63] Ibid.

[64] "Employment Non-Discrimination Act of 2007," *Library of Congress Thomas*, 2007 November 2007, Http://thomas.loc.gov/cgi-bin/bdquery/z?d110:HR03685:@@@D&summ2=m&.

UPDATE

At least one commentator has reported that H.R. 3685 has been defeated. That is incorrect. As of Jan. 24, 2008, the bill is still very much alive. According to the Library of Congress Thomas website, the latest action on the bill occurred "11/13/2007: Read the second time. Placed on Senate Legislative Calendar under General Orders. Calendar No. 479." However, even if the bill were defeated, it would not change the danger posed by a humanist being elected as president, because this bill has already been introduced 14 times. Humanists are simply never going to take "no you may not sodomize" for an answer. They intend to keep introducing this bill until it becomes law.

A pro-sodomy bill similar to the ones recently passed in California was introduced in the U.S. House of Representatives by Linda T. Sanchez of California July 23, 2007. It is bill number H.R. 3132, and has been given the title Safe Schools Improvement Act of 2007. And there are many others. Go to http://thomas.loc.gov/cgi-bin/thomas and type in "gender" or "sexual orientation" and see how many bills come up. You will—are at least should be—greatly alarmed.

Conclusions

Several important lessons need to be learned from this chapter.

Compromise With Wickedness Brings Defeat

Sodomites are driven by insatiable wanton lust. Concessions from godly people never satisfy them, but rather provoke them to demand more. They don't want equality—***THEY WANT SUPERIORITY AND OUR CHILDREN***. The only way they can multiply is by seducing the children of heterosexuals. And the fact that their movement is growing by leaps and bounds proves that they are excellent seducers. They view each compromise we make as another step toward producing more sex objects.

> Protections for transgender workers were in the original [Employment Non-Discrimination Act of 2007] bill. But Democratic leaders found they would lose support from moderate and conservative Democrats by including transgender employees in the final bill.
>
> "That's a bridge too far," said Rep. Rick Boucher, D-Va. "It's better to take it one step at a time."[65]

So, don't be deluded into thinking that this is the last step of their demands; it is just the beginning. Their goal is to totally silence us as they seduce or coerce as many of our children as possible into being their sex partners.

Fake Tolerance Is Intolerance

Humanists love the word "tolerance," that is, when it applies to others being tolerant of their wicked acts. They, however, are totally intolerant of any opinions contrary to their own. They are especially intolerant of God's opinion as voiced in the Bible. As in just about every realm of life, humanists are hypocrites in their use of "tolerance." Another example of an intolerant group demanding tolerance, but giving no tolerance in return was pointed out by Michael Bresciani in an article for The Conservative Voice:

> Tolerance is a word that is sailing around at the speed of stupidity. The confusion it creates is apparent when Islamic groups like CAIR go about pointing out every perceived insult to Islam in America even as America and the rest of the world are not afforded a speck of tolerance in return, in fact the doctrine and ideology of Islam forbids it. A cartoon, a negative statement about Muhammad or refusal to convert to Islam can result in death. Yet there are Americans who also watch for any and all possible intolerant language as it pertains to Islam. Double standards notwithstanding; this is the stupidity connected to the word "tolerance" that betrays its obvious lack of wisdom and social importance.[66]

And who are those "Americans" who watch for any and all possible intolerant language as it pertains to Islam? The humanists, of course. Liberal, humanist, Democrats always take the side of America's enemies.

---

[65] Miga, "House Passes Job Bias Ban Against Gays."

[66] Michael Bresciani, "California Passes SB 777 - Here Come the Language Police," *The Conservative Voice*, 1918 October 2007, Http://www.theconservativevoice.com/article/28720.html.

But you will be looking a long time trying to find any tolerance from them for Bible-believing Christians. Humanists are bigots with great hatred of Christianity.

Fiscal Republicans Are Democrats

Liberal Republicans generally claim to be fiscal conservatives, meaning that they are not conservatives on the more important social issues like abortion and homosexuality.

Arnold Schwarzenegger

Arnold Schwarzenegger is an example of this type Republican. Telegraph.co.uk recently named him the 8th most influential "liberal" in the U.S.A., right after Michael Moore! The Republicans of California chose him to represent them because they thought that since he was running on the Republican ticket he must be a conservative. Or perhaps they supported him because they felt he had the best chance of winning—which is not wise. Why not pick a true conservative and help him win; rather than a liberal who will oppose you once he wins. They ignored his marriage to Maria Shriver of the radically liberal Kennedy clan. They also ignored the Drudge Report headline article on Tuesday September 23, 2003, exposing the fact that Schwarzenegger posed in the nude for Robert Mapplethorpe, a man notorious for photographing "men engaging in homosexual acts."[67] Now they feel betrayed.

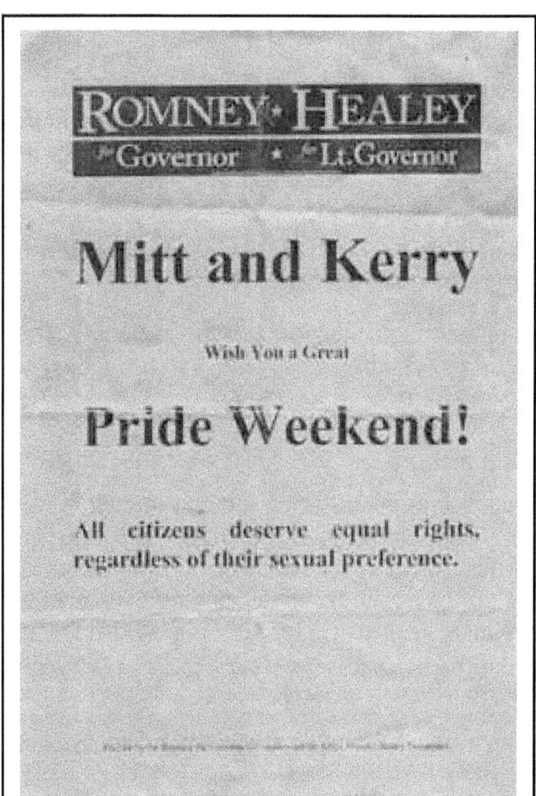

Mitt Romney

Mitt Romney, former governor of Massachusetts, has been portraying himself as a Reagan conservative, but his record reveals a very liberal/humanist position instead.

Mitt Romney's Record in Massachusetts

MassResistance, also of Massachusetts, has a long extensively documented article about Romney on their web site. The article is written by Brian Camenker, and is titled "The Mitt Romney Deception" and details his long history of supporting the radical liberal, humanist, sodomite agenda. Says Camenker:

> Romney was probably the most pro-abortion and pro-gay rights Republican official in the nation for the last decade. The idea that he has suddenly become a conservative after a decade of liberal actions and statements would be merely amusing were it not for the fact that he's running for the presidency and that many conservatives are falling for this act....Romney has supported abortion since before the 1972 Roe v. Wade ruling![68]

Camenker lists the following facts about Romney. (1)Romney campaigned for Governor of Massachusetts as a pro-choice candidate, and was endorsed by the New York-based Republican Pro-Choice Coalition; (2) Romney supported some embryonic stem cell research; (3) Romney approved of the abortion pill and

---

[67] Matt Drudge, "CAMPAIGN CHASES EROTIC MAPPLETHORPE NUDE PHOTOS OF SCHWARZENEGGER," *Drudge Report*, 1923 September 2003, Http://www.drudgereportarchives.com/data/2003/09/24/20030924_204603_arnold.htm.

[68] Brian Camenker, "The Mitt Romney Deception," *MassResistance*, 1920 November 2006, Http://www.massresistance.org/docs/marriage/romney/record/index.html.

supported legalization of RU-486; (4) Romney signed a proclamation to celebrate the anniversary of Baird v. Eisenstadt, a 1972 court ruling legalizing birth control for ***unmarried*** people; (5) Romney twice sought and received the endorsement of the homosexual Log Cabin Republican Club; (6) Romney's campaign distributed bright pink flyers during Boston's Gay Pride that declared 'Mitt and Kerry [running mate Kerry Healey] wish you a great Pride weekend! All citizens deserve equal rights, regardless of their sexual preference.' (7) Romney supported the Federal Employment Non-Discrimination Act (ENDA), a pro-gay bill; (8) Romney advocated homosexual couples' right to bear or adopt children; (9) Romney promised to "support and endorse efforts to provide domestic partnership benefits to gay and lesbian couples"; (10) Romney supported and promoted legalizing homosexual civil unions; (11) Romney opposed the Boy Scouts' Ban on Homosexual Scoutmasters; (12) Romney barred Boy Scouts from public participation in the 2002 Olympics; (13) Romney appointed prominent homosexual activists to key positions in his administration; (14) Romney appointed prominent homosexual activists and Democrats as judges—he passed over GOP lawyers for three-quarters of the 36 judicial vacancies he filled, instead choosing registered Democrats or independents -- including two gay lawyers who have supported expanded same-sex rights; (15) Romney "nominated Stephen Abany to a District Court. Abany has been a key player in the Massachusetts Lesbian and Gay Bar Association which, in its own words, is 'dedicated to ensuring that the Massachusetts Supreme Judicial Court decision on marriage equality is upheld, and that any anti-gay amendment or legislation is defeated'"; (16) during his final days as governor, Romney bucked tradition by not appointing any new judges, but instead left it to his liberal Democrat replacement to appoint them; (17) Romney's Commission on Gay and Lesbian Youth used huge taxpayer funding to promote homosexuality in the public schools; (18) Romney issued a proclamation celebrating gay "Youth Pride Day"; (19) under Romney's leadership, the Massachusetts Department of Education continued to be rabidly pro-homosexual. The Department's web site is full of "How To" information for homosexual activists within the public schools.; (20) Romney's Department of Public Health contributed to the *The Little Black Book: Queer in the 21st Century*.... Distributed to middle-school and high-school students at a GLSEN [Gay, Lesbian and Straight Education Network] conference at Brookline High School, it discussed highly dangerous homosexual practices such as fisting and what homosexuals call "water sports." ... here's one quote: "There is little risk of STD infection and no risk of HIV infection from playing with pee"; *(21)* Romney opposed federal legislation that would stop public schools from promoting homosexuality; *(22)* The Massachusetts Department of Social Services, run by the Romney administration, honored a homosexual "married" couple (two men) as their adoptive "Parents of the Year" for 2006; *(23)* Romney refused to endorse the original 2002 Mass. constitutional amendment absolutely defining marriage as one man and one women; (24) After the Massachusetts Supreme Court ruling that same-sex "marriages" were protected by the Massachusetts Constitution, Romney issued altered marriage licenses and ordered town clerks to issue the licenses and Justices of the Peace to perform same-sex marriages when requested, or be fired; (25) Romney favored "Assault" Weapons Ban; (26) Romney supported minimum wage laws; (27) Romney imposed "socialized" health care on Massachusetts.

> "David Parker's dilemma ... threatens the parental rights and religious freedom of every Massachusetts parent, and indirectly every parent in America," said John Haskins of the Parents' Rights Coalition.
>
> "As the Lexington schools themselves are arguing, the state's right to force pro-homosexuality indoctrination on other people's children arises directly from former Gov. Mitt Romney's nakedly false and unconstitutional declaration that homosexual marriage is now legal."
>
> Haskins said when the Massachusetts state Supreme Court demanded homosexual marriages in the state, it didn't have the constitutional or legal authority to order the governor to act or to order the Legislature to make any changes, and the creation of same-sex marriages in Massachusetts actually was accomplished by executive order from Romney.[69]

After all this radical humanist activity, Romney is now trying to convince American conservatives that he is a social conservative.[70] That is downright dishonest. Spend a few hours browsing the www.massresistance.org website. You will be stunned.

---

[69] Unruh, "Judge Orders 'gay' Agenda Taught to Christian Children."

[70] Camenker, "The Mitt Romney Deception."

Mitt Romney's "Faith In America" Speech

On December the 6th 2007, Romney gave a speech to try to convince the American people to overlook his Mormon religion and elect him as president. He correctly addressed a topic "fundamental to America's greatness: our religious liberty." Later Romney almost identifies America's greatest violation of religious freedom. He said,

> We separate church and state affairs in this country, and for good reason. No religion should dictate to the state nor should the state interfere with the free practice of religion. But in recent years, the notion of the separation of church and state has been taken by some well beyond its original meaning. They seek to remove from the public domain any acknowledgment of God. Religion is seen as merely a private affair with no place in public life. It is as if they are intent on establishing a new religion in America — the religion of secularism. They are wrong.

But actually Romney, himself, is wrong. It is not "as if" atheistic Humanists are "intent on establishing a new religion in America"; they have already done so, as I am sure Romney very well knows. The secular (meaning "leaving God out") religion of Humanism is America's established state church, and with its "hate crimes" bills threatens to deny freedom of speech to all who disagree with them. Other religious teachings are banned. Romney backed those "hate crimes" bills while he was governor.

While most churches have their Sunday Schools, the Humanist church has its Monday through Friday public schools, brainwashing our children in their sodomite, atheist religion five days a week, and Romney has fully supported this. Romney has shown himself to be of that "new" humanist religion in practice if not profession. What he has done in the very recent past speaks so loud that what he says now has no credit. It is impossible not to believe that his sudden professed change from a radically liberal humanist to a social conservative is for political gain only—to get the vote of the religion right—, and is therefore not genuine. He speaks of "the breakdown of the family," as though he thinks we have totally forgotten that it was his executive order started same-sex marriage in Massachusetts. No Republican has done more to hurt the traditional family than Romney.

IMPORTANT UPDATE: On Dec. 17, 2007, on NBC's Meet the Press, Mitt Romney reaffirmed his support for the pro-sodomy Employment Non-Discrimination Act (ENDA). Romney used these same non-discrimination laws as the basis for legalizing gay marriage in Massachusetts. In trying to get the Christian vote he claimed to have changed his position to opposing ENDA, BUT NOW HE REVEALS THAT HE OPPOSES IT ONLY ON THE FEDERAL LEVEL; ON THE STATE LEVEL HE STILL SUPPORTS IT![71]

Rudy Giuliani

Rudy Giuliani is another liberal, humanist Democrat running as a Republican. He advocated "passage of the Clinton semi-auto ban and supported passage of federal gun-owner licensing. As gun owners know, he also championed lawsuits to hold legal firearms manufacturers responsible for criminals who use firearms to commit violent crime."[72] Giuliani is also openly pro-abortion. Concerning homosexual issues, Giuliani has been photographed in drag. Do a web search on "Rudy Giuiani dressed in drag," and watch the videos. Can you imagine how embarrassing and disgusting it would be to have your president giving speeches dressed as a woman?! What more does one need to know about him? It would be better to not vote at all than to vote for such a man. He is, however, at least honest about his pro abortion and pro sodomy stand, while Romney lies about it.

John McCain

The OnTheIssues website lists John McCain as a "Populist-Leaning Conservative." But he is conservative only on fiscal issues. On social issues he is liberal humanist. In fact, he flip flops so much on so many issues, that it is hard to know if he actually has a stand other than whatever stand will get votes at the moment.

---

[71] ttp://race42008.com/2007/12/31/mitt-romney-flip-flop-or-slip-on-enda/#comment-217049

[72] Frank Miniter, "Presidential Candidates Ask for NRA Support," *National Rifle Association Website* (2007), Http://www.nrapublications.org/celebration/default.asp.

McCain has long been the favorite Republican of the liberal press because he often takes very liberal positions, thus helping the Democrats pass bills. The ultra-liberal New York Times newspaper recently endorce McCain, so that shows what camp he is actually in..

McCain on Freedom of Speech

McCain is very weak on defence of First Ammendment rights.

> Arizona Senator John McCain has been widely criticized for fighting for and passing the McCain-Feingold Campaign Reform Act of 2002, a law that prohibits organizations, such as the NRA, from running issue ads that name a federal candidate within 30 days of a primary or caucus or 60 days of a general election. The NRA was in the forefront in its opposition to the law's free-speech ban.[73]

How can banning people from exposing the truth about dishonest, corrupt candidates be considered "campaign finance reform"? This reveals a disregard for the First Amendment. Disregard for the First Amendment is the number one problem we face in the USA.

McCain on Abortion

Judging from statements on McCain website, I was convinced that he took a strong pro-life stand. But further research shows that that is not the case. He supports federal funding of emryonic stem cell research. He says that he has "come to the conclusion that the exceptions for rape, incest, and the life of the mother are legitimate exceptions" to an outright ban on abortions."[74] McCain said in 1999, "I'd love to see a point where Roe vs. Wade is irrelevant, and could be repealed because abortion is no longer necessary. But certainly in the short term, or even the long term, I would not support repeal of Roe vs. Wade, which would then force women in America to [undergo] illegal and dangerous operations."[75]

> KEYES [to McCain]: What you would say if your daughter was ever in a position where she might need an abortion? You answered [earlier today] that the choice would be up to her and then that you'd have a family conference. That displayed a profound lack of understanding of the basic issue of principle involved in abortion. After all, if your daughter said she was contemplating killing her grandmother for the inheritance, you wouldn't say, "Let's have a family conference." You'd look at her and say "Just Say No," because that is morally wrong. It is God's choice that that child is in the womb. And for us to usurp that choice in contradiction of our declaration of principles is just as wrong.
>
> McCAIN: I am proud of my pro-life record in public life, and I will continue to maintain it. I will not draw my children into this discussion. As a leader of a pro-life party with a pro-life position, I will persuade young Americans [to] understand the importance of the preservation of the rights of the unborn.

Note that McCain did not agree with Keyes, but instead gave a non-answer answer. He has no real conviction against abortion.

So, as president, McCain would not do anything to stop abortion, but instead would say that it was not his responsibility as he passed the issue off to the states.

McCain on Gay Marriage

July 13, 2004, saying that a ban on same-sex marriage would be "unRepublican," McCain voted against the very badly needed Federal Marriage Amendment which would have banned gay-marriage by defining marriage in the United States as a union of one man and one woman.[76] In explaining why he voted against it he said, "It would prevent States, many of which are grappling with the definition of marriage, from deciding that gays and lesbians should be allowed to marry."[77] To which I answer, Of course! That is exactly what needs to be done. In August of 2005 he supported the Arizona initiative to ban gay marriage,[78] which he

---

[73] Ibid.

[74] http://www.ontheissues.org/2008/John_McCain_Abortion.htm

[75] Ibid.

[76] John McCain, "MCCAIN STATEMENT ON THE FEDERAL MARRIAGE AMENDMENT," *Senate Website*, 1913 July 2004, Http://mccain.senate.gov/press_office/view_article.cfm?ID=246.

[77] http://www.ontheissues.org/2008/John_McCain_Civil_Rights.htm

[78] Elvia Diaz, "Gay-Marriage Ban Initiative Wins Support from McCain," *The Arizona Republic*, 1926 August 2005, Http://www.azcentral.com/arizonarepublic/news/articles/0826initiatives26.html.

probably knew was going to fail anyway, but gave him a bragging point when addressing conservatives. He can be both for and against same-sex marriage, depending on the audience. McCain said in an interview with Reuters that he would be "comfortable with a homosexual as president of the United States."[79] On this issue—one of the most important issues facing the next president— McCain is liberal humanist.

McCain on Illegal Immigration

McCain has also taken a very dangerous position on immigration. He fought very hard for passage of Comprehensive Immigration Reform Act of 2007 (S. 1348), which would have given legal status and a path to citizenship for approximately 12 million people presently living in the United States illegally. He said, "In the short term, [a hard line on immigration] probably galvanizes our base. In the long term, if you alienate the Hispanics, you'll pay a heavy price."[80] Perhaps, but you still have to do what is right. Our soldiers may pay a heavy price for defending our liberties. But they are willing to take that risk because their love for our country overrides their love of self.

One of McCain's former aides is reported to have said, "Yes, he's a social conservative, but his heart isn't in this stuff, but he has to pretend [that it is], and he's not a good enough actor to pull it off. He just can't fake it well enough."[81] That is the most dangerous kind of "conservative," because you never know when he will betray what is right in exchange for votes.

McCain on Evolution

Q: Do you believe in evolution?

McCAIN: Yes.[82]

Ron Paul

The OnTheIssues website lists Ron Paul as a "Moderate Libertarian." Ron Paul seems to take a social conservative stand on many issues. Upon a first reading, what he says sounds great, but much of what he says breaks down under critical examination, and he is seen voting like a Democrat. He has what I call a live and let sin philosophy.

Ron Paul On Abortion

Ron Paul says he is against abortion, but examine carefully the context of what he says:

> In Congress, I have authored legislation that seeks to define life as beginning at conception, HR 1094.
>
> I am also the prime sponsor of HR 300, which would negate the effect of Roe v Wade by removing the ability of federal courts to interfere with state legislation to protect life. This is a practical, direct approach to ending federal court tyranny which threatens our constitutional republic and has caused the deaths of 45 million of the unborn.[83]

So, while on the one hand he says he is against abortion, on the other hand, he wants to let each individual state decide to allow it or ban it. So, as president, he would not work to solve this problem, but would simply push it off on the governors. Now, I am very strong on states rights myself, but ***abortion is NOT a state issue. "Life" has been declared to be a federal issue by section 1 of the 14th Amendment of the Constitution*** which was passed by Congress June 13, 1866, and was ratified July 9, 1868. Here is what it says:

---

79 http://www.ontheissues.org/2008/John_McCain_Civil_Rights.htm

80 Steve Benen, "McCain 'Trying to Square the Circle'," *The Carpetbagger Report*, 2003 January 2007, Http://www.thecarpetbaggerreport.com/archives/9509.html.

81 Ibid.

82 http://www.ontheissues.org/2008/John_McCain_Education.htm

83 Ron Paul, "Life and Liberty," *Ron Paul 2008* (2007), Http://www.ronpaul2008.com/issues/life-and-liberty/.

All persons born or naturalized in the United States, and subject to the jurisdiction thereof, are citizens of the United States and of the State wherein they reside. No State shall make or enforce any law which shall abridge the privileges or immunities of citizens of the United States; nor shall any State deprive any person of life, liberty, or property, without due process of law; nor deny to any person within its jurisdiction the equal protection of the laws.[84]

So, obviously, no state has authority to pass a law that deprives a person of life. Abortion deprives persons of life! In no way did humanist judges have the authority to supersede the Constitution with *Roe v. Wade*.

Do you see the word "privacy" in those Constitution words? No. There is nothing there about a "right to privacy." What is protected is LIFE. The "right to privacy" idea did not come from the Constitution, but from the depraved humanist "ethics" of a few unjust judges, who called evil good.

Roe v. Wade is an illegal ruling. And we need a president with enough guts to honor and enforce the Constitution by prosecuting the abortionists who are violating the laws contained in the Constitution itself. Abortion is a federal felony. What if a state decided to legalize euthanasia of elderly parents? Let's say that Idaho made it legal in Idaho for anyone to murder anyone over the age of sixty, but the other states voted for murder to be illegal in their states. A person in Oklahoma could then take his mother to Idaho on her sixtieth birthday, and legally murder her without receiving any punishment. A person from Idaho visiting his mother in Oklahoma, however, would be in grave trouble if he murdered his mother there.

Now, back to babies. If just one state allows the murder of unborn babies, then the women from all the other states could go there to legally murder their babies. How would Paul's HR 300 and states rights stand help stop the murders? Ron Paul's claim that he "never votes for legislation unless the proposed measure is expressly authorized by the Constitution" doesn't seem to mean that he honors the Constitution when abortion is concerned.

Ron Paul On Sodomite Rights

The American View interviewed Ron Paul and asked him,

Is homosexuality a sin? Paul says he's "not as judgmental about that probably because of my medical background. I don't see it in [such] simplistic terms. I think it's a complex issue to think it's a sin or other problems with the way people are born. It's too complex to give an answer as simple as that [that homosexuality is a sin.]"

Does he believe God says homosexuality is a sin? "Well, I believe a lot of people understand it that way but I think everybody is God's child, too, so, you know, I have trouble with that."[85]

So, Ron Paul has trouble accepting what the Bible says about sodomy being a sin. He doesn't think homosexuality is sin. He thinks that people are "born" that way. Wow! Just examining his web site one would expect the opposite.

A web search found this conversation on the web site of a homosexual named Brian:

Dear Ron Paul,

As a gay man, I would really like to see you take a strong stance on gay rights as you have done with the war and immigration. I read that you are a libertarian and when I googled that term this is what I found:

Libertarianism is a political philosophy maintaining that all persons are the absolute owners of their own lives, and should be free to do whatever they wish with their persons or property, provided they allow others the same liberty and avoid abusing their liberty.

How can you NOT support gay rights and equality if you truly believe the above statement?

Sincerely,
Brian

Response from campaign:

Dr. Paul voted against the Federal Marriage Amendment, one of only a few Republicans to do so.

---

84 "The Constitution: Amendments 11–27," *Archives.Gov*, Http://www.archives.gov/national-archives-experience/charters/constitution_amendments_11–27.html.

85 John Lofton, "Excerpts From Our Exclusive Ron Paul Interview," *The American View* (2007), Http://theamericanview.com/index.php?id=916&PHPSESSID=4d627613baced8c2c91c6ff2b6bc2f25.

> Thanks for contacting us,
> [name removed]
> Ron Paul 2008[86]

This seems to be implying that Ron Paul is for gay rights. I sent an e-mail to the Ron Paul campaign asking for clarification on this issue. They answered:

> In a recent interview, Dr. Paul had this to say on the issue of gay rights: "I don't see rights as gay rights, women's rights, minority rights. I see only one kind of rights: the individual's. The individual has a right to their life and their liberty, and everyone should be treated equally."

This is just riding the fence, trying to get voters from both sides. The issue is not whether gays have the same rights as other individuals, but rather do any individuals have the right to commit sodomy, and do individuals committing sodomy have a right no other sinners have, that is, the right to be protected by the government from criticism of their wicked behavior. Rapists are individuals also; do they have such a right? No. Robbers are individuals also. Do they have such a right? No. Murderers are individuals also, do they have such a right? No.

Sodomy is a major issue facing the next president. Ron Paul either hasn't thought this issue out well (in which case he should not be president), or else he is on the sodomite's side (in which case he should not be president).

Ron Paul On Same-Sex Marriage

On this issue Paul again takes a stand that amounts to no stand. He says,

> Mr. Speaker, while I oppose federal efforts to redefine marriage as something other than a union between one man and one woman, I do not believe a constitutional amendment is either a necessary or proper way to defend marriage....
>
> If I were in Congress in 1996, I would have voted for the Defense of Marriage Act, which used Congress's constitutional authority to define what official state documents other states have to recognize under the Full Faith and Credit Clause, to ensure that no state would be forced to recognize a "same sex" marriage license issued in another state. This Congress, I was an original cosponsor of the Marriage Protection Act, HR 3313, that removes challenges to the Defense of Marriage Act from federal courts' jurisdiction. If I were a member of the Texas legislature, I would do all I could to oppose any attempt by rogue judges to impose a new definition of marriage on the people of my state.[87]

In other words, he believes that this is an issue that should be decided by the States. As president, he would do nothing about this problem, except pass it off to the governors. That is wrong! Non-moral issues are decided by the states, but moral issues must be decided at the federal level. Sodomy is a very basic moral problem like murder or rape or slavery. States cannot be allowed to say that rape, or murder, or slavery, or sodomy is legal.

Ron Paul On Prostitution

A brothel owner near Carson City, Nevada has endorsed Ron Paul! OK, so what does the Ron Paul campaign people say about that?

> A spokesman for Paul says the politician with a libertarian streak doesn't condone prostitution on a personal level. But, he says, "it's not the role of federal government and it's not in the constitution for federal government to regulate these things."[88]

Is that all you are going to say, Ron Paul? What kind of leadership are you showing here? Immorality is this country's biggest problem right now. It is destroying America. Don't you think you should at least issue a strong condemnation? Who can conscientiously vote for a person endored by a brothel owner?

Ron Paul On Israel

Ron Paul says that his foreign policy would be good for Israel. But Muslims and other Jew-hating groups think otherwise. Here is what one Muslim web site (MuslimsVoteRonPaul.com) has to say:

---

86 Brian, "My Correspondence With Ron Paul About Gay Rights," *In Repair*, 1931 May 2007, Http://inrepair.net/2007/05/31/my-correspondence-with-ron-paul-about-gay-rights/.

87 Ron Paul, "The Federal Marriage Amendment Is a Very Bad Idea," *LewisRockwell.Com*, 2001 October 2004, Http://www.lewrockwell.com/paul/paul207.html.

88 "Nevada Brothel Owner Endorses Ron Paul," *NBC11.Com*, 1926 November 2007, Http://www.nbc11.com/politics/14693483/detail.html#.

In the spin room after the Republican debate on Tuesday evening in Dearborn, Mich., a reporter from the Arab-American News asked Ron Paul what he thought of the term "Islamic fascism."

"It's a false term to make people think we're fighting Hitler," Paul responded. "It's war propaganda designed to generate fear so that the war has to be spread."

Why should YOU vote for Ron Paul?

Assalaamu Alaikum Brothers and Sisters,

You can help by sharing and sending this note to all the Muslims you know as well as by registering as a Republican and voting for Ron Paul in the Republican primaries in your state. Here's why: Muslims and Americans have an unique window of opportunity for the 2008 election. There is a candidate running as a Republican that would work to completely cut off the funding to Israel, remove ALL US troops from Arab lands, and repeal the Patriot Act. He's a Republican with Libertarian views named Ron Paul. Ron Paul's policies ranging from monetary to foreign are top notch.[89]

All this makes one wonder just who the people are that are helping Ron Paul raise cash so fast.

Mel Gibson's Jew-hating, Holocaust denying dad has endorsed Paul.

Hutton Gibson, father of actor Mel Gibson, has endorsed Rep. Ron Paul (R., Texas) for president. "I intend to tell my 10 children and my 48 grandchildren that the only way to save the country is to vote for Ron Paul in 2008," says Gibson, who appears in the video endorsement sitting on a sofa wearing a "Legalize Freedom" t-shirt.[90]

And what about the anti-Semitic Klu Klux Klan people? They also support Ron Paul.

A LoneStarTimes.com investigation has conclusively established that a leading figure in the American neo-Nazi/White-Supremacist movement has provided financial support to Ron Paul's 2008 Presidential campaign.

The individual in question is Don Black, the founder, owner and operator of Stormfront, a "white power" web site that both professional journalists and watch-dog groups have identified as the premier English-language racist/hate-site on the Internet....

The evidence is as follows:

* Black proudly and openly identifies himself as Stormfront's guiding hand, and publishes a contact address on the Internet– PO Box 6637, West Palm Beach, FL, 33405

* A search by LST of public databases indicates that there is only one "Don Black" residing in West Palm Beach, Florida, zip code 33405

* A 7/16/01 USA Today article identifies Black's wife as being named "Chloe"

* That same article identifies Chloe as being the ex-wife of close Black associate and former "Grand Wizard" of the Ku Klux Klan, David Duke

* Minutes of a 9/7/07 City of West Palm Beach code-compliance hearing identify "Chloe H. Duke" as owning a residential property located at 203 Lakeland Drive

* According to Federal Election Commission records, on 9/30/07 the Ron Paul presidential campaign received a $500 contribution from a Mr. Don Black, who lists his address as 203 Lakeland Drive and identifies his occupation as "self-employed/web site manager."[91]

A quick check reveals that as of November 18, 2007, numerous articles supporting Ron Paul for president appear on both Stormfront.com and DavidDuke.com.

Ron Paul says, "Too often we give foreign aid and intervene on behalf of governments that are despised. Then, we become despised." It is impossible to believe that Paul is not including Israel in that statement.

I sent this e-mail to Paul's campaign headquarters: "There are numerous posts on the web claiming that Dr. Paul hates Jews and will offer neither aid nor support to the state of Israel. Is this true?" They answered:

He does not hate Jews, see his issue statement denouncing racism:

http://www.ronpaul2008.com/issues/racism/

He plans on ending military aid and funding to all nations in the Middle East, including Israel's enemies. We should not be involved in directing Israel's foreign policy.

It is good to hear him say that he does not hate the Jews, but he doesn't seem to love them much either. He is right that we should not be directing Israel's foreign policy. And he is also right in stating that by giving military aid to both Israel and Israel's enemies, we have made the situation worse, not better. What we should do is give Israel massive military aid with no strings attached, and give Israel's enemies nothing except the promise that we will come to Israel's aid if Israel is attacked. A quick look at a globe and demographic statistics show that

---

89 "Why Should YOU Vote for Ron Paul," *MuslimsVoteRonPaul.Com* (2007), Http://muslimsvoteronpaul.com/.

90 Susan Davis, "Paul Picks Up Backing From Mel Gibson's Dad," *Washington Wire*, 1914 November 2007, Http://blogs.wsj.com/washwire/2007/11/14/paul-picks-up-backing-from-mel-gibsons-dad/.

91 Matt Bramanti, Editor, "LST: Neo-Nazi Leader Gives Ron Paul $500," *LoneStarTimes.Com*, 1925 October 2007, Http://lonestartimes.com/2007/10/25/rpb1/.

> 22 Arab and/or Muslim [Iran is not considered Arab] nations completely engulf Israel.... The Arab countries occupy 640 times the land mass as does Israel and outnumber the Jews of Israel by nearly fifty to one.[92]

And those 22 nations all want to drive Israel into the sea. According to Numbers 24:9, God promises to bless those who bless Israel, and to curse those who curse Israel. The U.S. has been mightily blessed when she has taken Israel's side, and has suffered greatly when taking stands that harmed Israel.[93] It is vital to our interest that our next president be sincerely for Israel.

Ron Paul On Evolution

I sent the following question in an e-mail to Paul's campaign headquarters:

> Does Dr. Paul believe in evolution? This is my second e-mail asking this question. I'm assuming that the answer is yes, since he didn't raise his hand in the debate when it was asked who does not believe in evolution.

Their answer:

> Congressman Paul believes in evolution.

So, we have it straight from his headquarters—Ron Paul ***does*** believe in evolution. This means he does not believe the very first chapter of the Bible, and therefore probably doubts the truthfulness of the rest of the Bible also. That is why he refuses to accept what Bible verses such as Lev. 18:22; 20:13; and Romans 1:26-27) say about sodomy; he just doesn't really believe the Bible is true. Believing evolution makes him a practical humanist, and that means that he will make many decisions based on that very wrong world-view.

"Who Does Not Believe In Evolution?"

At the GOP presidential debate on Thursday May 3, 2007, Chris Matthews asked the candidates to raise their hands if they do not believe in evolution. Only three raised their hands: Mike Huckabee, Sam Brownback, and Tom Tancredo. All the rest, therefore, do believe in evolution, and that makes them humanists in practice if not in profession, and no Christian should consider voting for them.

Sam Brownback has dropped out of the race, and so has Tom Tancredo. Alan Keyes has since announced that he is also a candidate, so I sent him an e-mail asking this question: "Do you believe in a literal six-day creation by the living, personal, Triune God?" Dr. Keyes' director of correspondance, DeeAnn Stone, replied with this answer: "Yes, he does."

So, for Bible-believing Christians, the field has been narrowed down to two men: Mike Huckabee, and Alan Keyes. These are the only two men we can be sure actually believe in God. I could vote for either of these two men. I could not vote for Romney or Giuliani or McCain under any conditions—even if it meant not voting at all. The OnTheIssues website lists Alan Keyes as a "Libertarian-Leaning Conservative,"[94] and lists Mike Huckabee as a "Hard Core Conservative."[95] Of all the candidates for president, Mike Huckabee is the most conservative, and is the person I believe is the most qualified to be president.

Rush Limbaugh Hating Mike Huckabee

It is very sad that Rush Limbaugh, Ann Coulter, Sean Hannity, and some of the other conservative leaders have decided that fiscal conservatism is more important than social conservatism, and have therefore given their support to social liberals. Actually, I have examined Huckabee's record, and I am not convinced that Huckabee is that weak on the fiscal side of conservatism. Huckabee is against the greed shown by many leading Republican during the past 20 years are so. That does not make him weak on the fiscal side of conservatism. It appears to me that the real reason that Rush, Ann, and Shawn don't like Huckabee is because he is a "Bible believer." Rush has shown his contempt of Bible believers before. Rush tells off color

---

[92] "HISTORY of Israel & 'Palestine'," *Masada2000.Org*, Http://www.masada2000.org/historical.html.

[93] For an excellent discussion of what our relation to Israel should be, read *Don't Mess with Israel* by Jame L. Milton. This 43 page booklet is available free on-line at: http://www.biblebaptistpublications.org/israeljews.html

[94] http://www.ontheissues.org/Alan_Keyes.htm

[95] http://www.ontheissues.org/Mike_Huckabee.htm

jokes, cusses, smokes. Such things are not conservatism, Rush; they are humanism. When is comes to social issues, Rush is really more of a libertarian than he is a conservative. That, I believe, is the main reason why he doesn't like Huckabee. Rush claims that Huckabee is attempting to redefine conservatism, but Rush is the one who is trying to redefine conservatism. Huckabee is much more a Reagan conservative than Rush.

Rush has no children. So, the sodomy in public schools doesn't affect him personally. He is more concerned about his own pocketbook. Here is how he defines conservatism:

> Conservatism is a set of principles and ideals, kind of like the Constitution. They don't float, they don't bend, they don't shape. You don't rewrite them to fit the social mores or depravity of the day or what have you. Conservatism is what it is. Conservatism seeks to balance the budget, not by raising taxes, but by cutting government and reducing the size of government.

There is not one word about social issues in Rush's defination. Rush says he is pro-life. He talks like he is against same-sex marriage. But, when it comes time to vote, fiscal issues are more important to him; and he is willing to support a pro-sodomite candidate. His value system is out of balance. In my book a poor virgin is better than a rich harlot. Having lots of money doen't make you right, and certainly doesn't make you good. Rush is openly against McCain and Huckabee, saying that if either of them become the Republican candidate for president it will spit the Republican party. Rush says, "I don't think Congressman Paul has a snowball's chance." So, that leaves only Rudy Giuliani—a man who dresses in drag—, and Mitt Romney—the man who brought gay marriage to Massachusetts. Rush is the one about to split the Republican party.

> Rush and crew should listen up: the Evangelical/Republican marriage could very well be on the rocks. This large and important block of voters who put George W. Bush in the White House twice could well be close to saying bye-bye to the party of Lincoln and Reagan, and conservative talk radio could be the reason why. And don't let us kid ourselves, without W's overwhelming support from Evangelicals, Al Gore would be President and the term "Lock Box" wouldn't be a punch line.
>
> Why in the world would Evangelicals bolt? The answer is simple—Rush and crew have demonstrated the values Evangelicals hold dear don't matter nearly as much as economic and foreign policy positions. No one in the Republican field is more committed to the causes that matter most to the Evangelical community than Huckabee—the former Baptist minister who is pro-life (and always has been), pro-traditional family and even open to amending the Constitution to define marriage as solely between one man and one woman. Huckabee believes in abstinence education and is very pro-states rights. These positions connect with Evangelicals and frankly are more important to many in these communities than tax breaks for billionaires, border fences or amnesty accusations.
>
> The three tenants of the Reagan revolution seem to be dissolving into just two pillars in the hearts and minds of Limbaugh, Hannity and the like. While trickle down economics and strong foreign policy are very important to the posse, strong social conservatism seems to be optional. Many in the world of conservative talk radio seem to care much more about economic and foreign policy issues, and much less about the issues that matter most to the Evangelical community.[96]

Those of us with children, are very concerned about the sodomy being promoted in public schools—we don't want our children or grandchildren molested or seduced into becoming homosexuals. Rush says that abortion and same-sex marriage aren't the only issues to be concerned about. True, but they are the main issues. America is turning into Sodom and Gomorrah. It would be better to be a poor but righteous nation than to be a rich Sodom and Gomorrah. Now that Fred Thompson has dropped out of the race, Huckabee and Keyes are the only social conservatives left. Keyes is not getting anywhere. So that leaves only Huckabee. If Rush can't support Huckabee now, than Rush is just not truly a social conservative, and we should no longer lend him our support. If he is just talking conservative between elections so as to gain our confidence to be able to steer us into supporting liberal, humanist, pro sodomites during elections, then that is treason to the conservative cause, and we must tell him bye. I for one will never vote for a candidate who is pro-abortion or pro-sodomy. Never! That is liberal, not conservative, no matter what Rush says.

Mick Huckabee On the Issues

Huckabee is undeniably the strongest social conservative among the leading Republican candidates. As previously stated, Giuliani, Romney, and McCain cannot honestly be called social conservatives. On social issues, they are radical liberals. And, frankly, I don't see that they are that strong on fiscal conservatism

---

96 Greg Taylor, "Huckabee Hatin' Could Backfire on GOP," *Yahoo! News*, 1924 January 2008, Http://news.yahoo.com/s/realclearpolitics/20080124/cm_rcp/huckabee_hatin_could_backfire_1.

either, at least not the kind of fiscal conservatism that benefits the common man instead of just multi-millionaires. Huckabee has taken the strongest stand of all the candidates against illegal immigration.

Fred Thompson (who has recently dropped out of the race) makes the same mistake as Ron Paul on abortion. On November the 18th 2007, "Thompson said Roe v. Wade, the landmark Supreme Court decision allowing legal abortion, should be overturned, with states allowed to decide whether to permit abortions."[97] Huckabee immediately responded, rejecting that idea:

> "It's the logic of the Civil War," Huckabee said Sunday, comparing abortion rights to slavery. "If morality is the point here, and if it's right or wrong, not just a political question, then you can't have 50 different versions of what's right and what's wrong.... For those of us for whom this is a moral question, you can't simply have 50 different versions of what's right," he said in an interview on Fox News Sunday.

Huckabee is right. And the issues—murder and sodomy—are even more serious than slavery.

Huckabee has taken the strongest stand of all the candidates against sodomy. If you had to pick, would you rather your child be enslaved, murdered, or sodomized? At least with slavery you might be able to free your child later. With abortion your child is dead. And I would rather be murdered myself than have my child sodomized. These are issues on which there can be no compromise. I've had enough experience with sodomite activists to know that they are not going to accept "No, you may not sodomize" for an answer. They threatened to murder Beverly Hodges, our city council representative in Oklahoma City if she wouldn't stop voting against them. They threatened me also. The truth of what we are up against needs to be faced. The only way to stop these people is to make sodomy a capital offense, as the Bible says it should be: "If a man also lie with mankind, as he lieth with a woman, both of them have committed an abomination: they shall surely be put to death; their blood *shall be* upon them" (Lev. 20:13). It is really sad that it has come to this, but it has. The sodomites are not going to give us any peace until we submit to the idea of them being able to legally sodomize our children without rebuke. A country cannot ignore abominable wickedness like America has for the last 20 years without criminals eventually ruling over her. I read once of a couple that bought a baby python for a pet. They still had it many years later, it having grown so slowly that they didn't realize the danger it now posed. Until, one day they found it in their new born baby's crib, the baby crushed, dead, and being swallowed. I wonder if they had mercy on the poor snake; after all **he** *really was* born that way. What about the children being seduced by these sex perverts? Is there no mercy for them? Does it matter to you if your child is sodomized and perhaps given AIDS?

> Some activists contend that 'real homosexuals' are not the ones molesting pupils, but a different kind of person -- 'pedophiles.' Considerable evidence against such a dichotomy exists. Consider the 1996 homosexual scandal in Australia. When accused "To a man, each ...so far has claimed to be a homosexual with an interest in young men but not a pedophile, despite evidence that each has had sex with boys barely into their teenage years and younger." The news report noted that this was the same claim made by "lesbian school teacher Lee Dunbar who was recently jailed for having committed indecent acts upon one of her pupils when the girl was less than 14 years old." Dunbar had first engaged in a sexual affair with the mother of the victim, and only then turned to the daughter. In England, a male teacher who molested a girl pupil, was married, a father of two, worked as a male prostitute, and had also kissed and propositioned at least one male pupil demonstrating sexual flexibility in age and kind of sexual object choice. Or consider the 5 cases of HIV+ male teachers who molested boys – from New Zealand: Leef (45) who molested 5 boys between 13 and 15; a name-suppressed man who molested 6 boys aged 12 to 16; from Denmark: a name-suppressed man who molested 7 pre-teen boys, at least one of which he apparently infected; and from the U.S., McFarlane who molested 6 boys aged 7 to 9 yr., and Lepley who molested a 16 year-old boy. Obviously, these perpetrators got HIV from sex with other men, not from their victims (nor was Mutie, the HIV+ Kenyan school teacher who declared he "would not die alone", a 'pedophile' because he raped 5 elementary girls. Further, the testimony (for whatever its worth) of the perpetrators indicates the perpetrators are self declared 'homosexuals:' Thus Stratton, convicted of abusing boys 11 and 12 yr., was married and declared himself "bisexual" "with a predominance towards homosexuality") and Curran, convicted of molesting 9 boys aged 8 to 12 yr., said he was a "gay person" with a "sexual preference for people over age 65". Of course, excuses abounded. Misenti, who had his penis excised and dressed like a woman, declared he was a "she" and only molested 6 boy pupils because he "desperately wanted affirmation of his womanhood".[98]

And there is no end to stories like this.[99] Here is a recent one you'll probably remember:

---

97 "Huckabee: Abortion not States' Call," *USA Today*, 1918 November 2007, Http://www.usatoday.com/news/politics/election2008/2007–11–18-huckabee_N.htm?csp=34.

98 Paul Cameron, "Teacher-Pupil Sex Across the World: How Much Is Homosexual?" *The Empirical Journal of Same-Sex Sexual Behavior* (2007), Http://www.ejssb.org./resources/ejssb_CameronP_WorldwideTeacherPupilSexualInteractions$5B1$5D.pdf.

99 Get on the web and check out this link: http://www.familyresearchinst.org/Default.aspx?tabid=71

> The Missouri pizzaman in whose apartment two kidnapped boys were found by police last month has now been charged with 69 counts of forcible sodomy and two counts of kidnapping. All charges are felonies each carrying a possible life in prison sentence.
>
> Prosecutor Robert McCullough said 18 of the counts against Michael J. Devlin relate to 13-year-old Ben Ownby, who disappeared Jan. 8 and was found Jan. 12. The other 51 charges are related to Shawn Hornbeck, now 15, who was abducted when he was 11 years old.[100]

What sodomites do to themselves is depressingly sad, but what they do to children is unbearably sad. They should be called "sads" not "gays." Is it being intolerant to tell a rapist to repent and stop his unacceptable behavior or else you will have to separate your family from him, and perhaps call the police? Is one a bigot to tell a robber to stop robbing or else he cannot be right with God? We are all sinners. God saves repentant sodomites just as He saves repentant liars or adulterers or drug dealers. Is God a hater and bigot for giving the Bible that condemns self-destructive behavior in no uncertain terms? What is so awful about the modern gay movement is that it encourages rebellion instead of repentence. It discourages instead of giving hope. It blames instead of taking responsibility. It insures defeat by sin instead of supporting people to victory over sin. It pulls down instead of lifting up. It denies the truth instead of admitting it. "He that covereth his sins shall not prosper: but whoso **confesseth** and **forsaketh** *them* shall have **mercy**" (Prov. 28:13).

One of the Gay, Lesbian, Straight Education Network's (GLSEN) Jump-Start Guides for starting and running a Gay Straight Alliance club in a public school. The battlefields are public school classrooms, just as Humanists boast, and our children will be the spoils of war.

After the Election

Having said all the above, I don't think Huckabee has faced the fact that the humanist religion is established as the state church in public schools. Neither does he seem to see that as a grave violation of the First Amendment, which is destroying America. Perhaps he knows it in his heart, but hasn't yet decided what to do about it. Whatever the case may be, humanism must be disestablished as state church, or else the advance of the humanist religion will continue until we are destroyed. So, we must not let up pressure once a president has been elected. Our trust must be in God, not in a mortal man.

If we succeed in getting a true conservative elected to the presidency, we will have won a very important battle. But that will not be the end of the war—not by a long shot. The war will just have begun. They humanists will try to destroy him by slander or by violence. They will try to Bork him or McCarthy him.

Also, just because a presidential candidate is personally against abortion and same-sex marriage does not mean that he will be able to stop those problems just by being elected president. To hope that is to be naive. For instance, how will he gather the necessary two-thirds support in both houses of Congress to amend the Constitution to outlaw abortion and same-sex marriage when Democrats are the majority in both houses? And after that, three-quarters of the state legislatures will have to approve it before it will become law. We Christians have been too apathetic and too naive for too long, and have allowed things to get too far out of hand. This is going to be a long war which we cannot win without the faith in God needed to take the seemingly impossible necessary steps, and to fight relentlessly until TOTAL victory is won. Only God can give us such great victory. And God wants to give us such victory, but it is up to us—no faith no victory. "And this is the victory that overcometh the world, *even* our faith" (1 John 5:4). We must trust in

---

[100] Charles Montaldo, "Devlin Faces 69 Counts of Sodomy," *Charles Montaldo's Crime / Punishment Blog*, 2006 November 2007, Http://crime.about.com/b/2007/02/06/devlin-faces-69-counts-of-sodomy.htm.

God, not in men, not in government, not in a president. We must never say that the needed changes cannot be made. Be not faithless, but believing.

Also, it is essential that Christians realize that it is not the duty of government to make the culture Christian, nor could government do so. That is the duty of Christians. Jesus said, "Ye are the salt of the earth: but if the salt have lost his savour, wherewith shall it be salted? it is thenceforth good for nothing, but to be cast out, and to be trodden under foot of men" (Mat. 5:4). Salt is a preservative, but if it has lost its saltiness it is worthless. A Christian who has lost his Christlikeness is also worthless—he or she will either have no influence or bad influence. Were Jesus in the USA today, He would not be sitting on a couch watching immoral TV shows while the world goes to Hell. He would read His Bible and pray every day. He would set aside lots of time every week to evangelize. He would make time to minister to individual people. Nothing—absolutely nothing—will take the place of visiting people in their homes, making friends with them, living a holy life before them, telling them what a difference Christ has made in your life and can make also in their lives, and presenting the Gospel to them. Light drives away darkness. Present the light of the Gospel to the world, and the humanists will run like cockroaches back into their holes.

Rudy Giuliani dressed in drag.

Chapter 27

WHAT MUST WE DO?

A Plan of Action

What must we do to prevent the sodomite Humanist religion from destroying our children, grandchildren, and country?

What Churches Must Do

Churches must **immediately** acknowledge the danger and take proper action or else they will suffer great loss. Some states have just a few days to prevent pro-sodomy "hate-crimes" bills from going into effect. In California two "hate-crimes" bills have already passed and have been signed by the governor. They must be overturned before Janurary 1, 2008. [UPDATE: it is too late for Californians; they acted to late. Let's not the rest of us make the same mistake.] Here are the most important actions that are needed.

Really, Actually Have Faith In God

There is hope provided we act ***now***! "**I can do <u>all</u> things** through **Christ** which strengtheneth me" (Phil. 4:13). Do not say that what ***must*** be done ***cannot*** be done. That is a certain road to defeat, which in this case will mean religious oppression, and for some of us may literally mean imprisonment. Say rather, "with men this is impossible; but **with God <u>all</u> things are possible**" (Mat. 19:26). Let us be as Caleb, not as the men who were defeated without a fight by their own unbelief.

> And Caleb stilled the people before Moses, and said, **Let us go up <u>at once</u>**, and possess it; for **we are <u>well able</u> to overcome it**. But the men that went up with him said, We be not able to go up against the people; for they *are* stronger than we. And they brought up an evil report of the land which they had searched unto the children of Israel, saying, The land, through which we have gone to search it, *is* a land that eateth up the inhabitants thereof; and all the people that we saw in it *are* men of a great stature. And there we saw the giants, the sons of Anak, *which come* of the giants: and we were in our own sight as grasshoppers, and so we were in their sight. (Numbers 13:30-33)

Because they are well organized, there seems to be many more humanists than there actually are. Because they constantly honor each other with various awards (such as the Nobel Peace Prize) they seem to be creditable when in fact they are phonies. Let us not be impressed. Let us not be intimidated. Let us not be "in our own sight as grasshoppers."

Declare War On Humanism

Humanists have declared war on Christians, but Christians have not declared war in return. This is first and foremost a spiritual war, but it is also a political war. By declaring war we face reality.

Declaring war implies a willingness to sacrifice to achieve victory. War takes money, time, and great effort. We must not be reluctant, but put our ***whole*** heart into this war. "Come with me, and see my **zeal** for the **LORD**" (2 Kings 10:16).

Declare war realizing that defeat is not an option. In our present case, defeat will mean total loss of religious liberty, and for many of us it may mean imprisonment or execution. For our children and grandchildren defeat will mean being turned into sodomite sex objects.

In war nothing takes the place of TOTAL victory. The humanist threat to stop us from preaching the word of God must be TOTALLY removed. Their movement to turn our children into sodomites must be TOTALLY stopped. Our preachers must be TOTALLY freed from being silenced by illegal laws (e.g. tax-exemption laws). The establishment of the humanist religion as state church must be TOTALLY ended. We must DEMAND that the First Amendment be TOTALLY honored in all aspects.

Righteous people suffer their worse setbacks when they have mercy on poisonous snakes, who then come back to bite them. When you get a snake cornered you must keep chopping at his head until it actually comes off. And then you grind the head to pulp, so it can't still bite you out of reflex. I once read about a man who was bitten by the head he had chopped off of a snake. In this case the snake is the movement declaring God to be wrong in saying that sodomy is sin—there is no such thing as a "right" to sin. Not all sodomites are atheists, but sodomy springs from atheism. For the sake of the children, we must exhibit great unrelenting zeal in stopping this movement. Among the children we save will be our own.

> Now Elisha was fallen sick of his sickness whereof he died. And Joash the king of Israel came down unto him, and wept over his face, and said, O my father, my father, the chariot of Israel, and the horsemen thereof. And Elisha said unto him, Take bow and arrows. And he took unto him bow and arrows. And he said to the king of Israel, Put thine hand upon the bow. And he put his hand *upon it*: and Elisha put his hands upon the king's hands. And he said, Open the window eastward. And he opened *it*. Then Elisha said, Shoot. And he shot. And he said, The arrow of the LORD'S deliverance, and the arrow of deliverance from Syria: for thou shalt smite the Syrians in Aphek, till thou have consumed *them*. And he said, Take the arrows. And he took *them*. And he said unto the king of Israel, Smite upon the ground. And he smote thrice, and stayed. And the man of God was wroth with him, and said, Thou shouldest have smitten five or six times; then hadst thou smitten Syria till thou hadst consumed *it*: whereas now thou shalt smite Syria *but* thrice. (2 Kings 13:14-19)

The half heartedness of King Joash hundreds of years ago is why Syria is still around plotting war against Israel right now! Half heartedness in operation Desert Storm is why we are in Iraq right now. That half heartedness has cost us billions of dollars and thousands of lives. Be half hearted in defeating humanism and it will be right back to bite you so soon it will make dizzy.

Something You Can Do Right Now!

Actually, this is something for individuals to do, not for churches. But I insert it here because it is so urgent. Please do this right now. Do this and watch things turn around fast:

- Send all your friends the link to the www.MassResistance.com web site, and ask them to forward it to all their friends.
- Do a web search for "Rudy Giuliani dressed in drag." Send links to the photos you find to your friends and family members. Print out a few of the pictures you find, and show them to your neighbors. Warn them also about Mitt Romney and Ron Paul's pro-gay rights stands also. See chaper 26 of this book.
- Send the link to the free on-line version of chapter 26 of this book to all your friends and family members. Ask them to first read chapter 26, and then the whole book beginning with chapter one. The link is on the last page of this chapter.
- Go to www.dayspringpublisher.com and sign up for the free True Liberty Newsletter, to be kept informed about important legislation and events concerning freedom or religion, freedom of speech, church and state, education, the First Amendment, etc.

Break Out of the Tax-Exemption Muzzle

Non-profit, tax-exempt status is automatic for all churches as long as the First Amendment is honored by the government; a civil government has no authority to tax churches. However, our government is not honoring the First Amendment. Illegal IRS rules declare that tax exemption is government support, and that therefore the government has the power to say how the money donated to churches is spent. That is an outrageous ruling based on a lie. Tax exemption is not government support; it is the government not oppressing religion. To tax churches a law has to be passed concerning an establishment of religion. That is forbidden by the First Amendment. The IRS has decided that God's money does not actually belong to God but is the property of the government. That is an illegal decision. Christians have already paid taxes on the money they make. The money left is therefore their own to do with as they please. When they give a portion of that money to their church (which is the house of God), that money becomes the property of God. It is not the property of the civil government, and the government has no authority over that money whatsoever.

For the government to try to claim ownership is robbery. The government does not own that money, and has no authority to say how it is spent.

So, what should churches do now that the I.R.S. denies them freedom of speech by saying that they will lose their tax-exempt status if they try to influence an election? Here are the choices: (1) remain tax exempt by keeping silent and not trying to influence any elections; (2) claim tax exempt status, but speak out in defiance of the I.R.S. and risk going to prison; (3) don't claim tax exempt status (pay the tax) so that the church can remain free to speak out boldly on all public issues.

The results of a church choosing to remain silent will be that wicked people will eventually gain control of government, and will then use government power to oppress Christians.

The results of a church choosing to claim tax exempt status, but speak out in defiance of the I.R.S. will very likely be that that church will be closed, its building sold to pay the taxes the I.R.S. claims it owes, and the leaders of that church may go to prison.

The results of a church choosing to not claim tax exempt status—to pay the tax demanded by the I.R.S.—will be that that church may have less funds to work with, but will remain free to use those funds to enlighten voters so that they know how to vote in such a way as to preserve freedom in this nation.

For many years now most churches have chosen to remain silent so as to retain tax-exempt status, and the results have been disastrous. This choice has muzzled our pastors. They have become like the "dumb dogs" that "cannot bark" mentioned in Isaiah 56:10. The I.R.S. appears to be carefully selective to enforce their ruling only on theist churches, and not on atheist, humanist churches. The atheist, humanist churches have, therefore, been extremely vocal to influence politics. Because Christian preachers have remained silent while the atheist, humanist preachers have radically spoken out to influence every election, atheist humanists have taken over much of our government, and now threaten to destroy Christianity in America. Do a search on political topics and thousands of atheist, humanist religion web sites will come up, but virtually no web sites of theistic churches. Yet there are many thousands of church web sites in the U.S.A. This cowardize to speak out on vital issues of the day is a shame and disgrace. It is like we don't really believe what the Bible says, and so are not willing to stand up for it at all. We should be willing to die for it, but we obviously haven't been willing to pay any price whatsoever—especial if the price is actual money.

A handful of churches have claimed tax-exempt status, but continue to speak out on political issues. Several of these churches have already been closed by the I.R.S. and their buildings sold, and their leaders discredited in the eyes of the public. This has not proven to be a wise course of action.

It is time to try the third option of simply paying the tax—temporarily— so that our preachers are not muzzled. Jesus has given us the answer to this problem, but we have not listened. Mat. 17:24-27 indicts that Jesus would have churches pay the tax in situations such as churches face in the U.S.A. today, so that they can be free to influence the moral direction of the nation. The most prudent course of action seems to be: (1) pay the tax for now, trusting God to provide a "fish" with money in its mouth to enable the church to do so; (2) use the freedom this buys your church to vigorously influence the political process to overturn this outrageous ruling; (3) visit your senators and representatives and tell them that your church has elected to pay tax in order to be free to get this illegal law rescinded. Tell them that you consider it an illegal law that violates the First Amendment. Ask them to promise to do everything in their power to have this extremely unjust I.R.S. ruling rescinded; (4) monitor them closely and ralley the community to vote them out of office if they will not so promise, or if they do not fulfill their promise; (5) get busy evangelizing your community so as to find that fish with money in its mouth! In other words, get busy winning people to Christ, and the extra money needed to pay that tax will be provided. This is a very simple and easy solution, but the results will be immediate and dramatic. Such Christian activism will easily determine the outcome of most elections. All it takes is a little faith in God.

Of course, this will only work if we act soon enough. If we wait until for-profit organizations also are banned from influencing an election, it will be too late.

Wage Spiritual Warfare In the Streets

Preach the gospel of Jesus Christ to every person in the USA before November 4, 2008! This war cannot be won inside the walls of our churches. This is a war for the hearts minds and souls of men. We must go into the streets and homes of America to persuade people of the truth one person at a time. With much love and compassion, we must start obeying the Great Commission of Mat. 28:18-20:

> And Jesus came and spake unto them, saying, All power is given unto me in heaven and in earth. Go ye therefore, and teach all nations, baptizing them in the name of the Father, and of the Son, and of the Holy Ghost: teaching them to observe all things whatsoever I have commanded you: and, lo, I am with you alway, *even* unto the end of the world. Amen.

To be sure, humanists will try to stop us from doing this, for it will mean their eventual defeat, but we have orders from the King of kings, and we must "obey God rather than men" (Acts 5:29). Everyone must have the gospel presented to them before November 4, 2008; let not even one home be left unevangelized.

Open the Church Door Wide To Repentant Sinners

The church of the Lord Jesus Christ is composed of sinners. The apostle Paul said, "This *is* a faithful saying, and worthy of all acceptation, that **Christ** Jesus came into the world to **save sinners**; of whom I am chief" (1 Tim. 1:15). Jesus said, "I say unto you, that likewise joy shall be in heaven over one **sinner** that repenteth, more than over ninety and nine just persons, which need no repentance. Likewise, I say unto you, there is joy in the presence of the angels of God over one **sinner** that repenteth" (Luke 15:9. Jesus also said,

> And, behold, a woman in the city, which was a **sinner**, when she knew that *Jesus* sat at meat in the Pharisee's house, brought an alabaster box of ointment, and stood at his feet behind *him* weeping, and began to wash his feet with tears, and did wipe *them* with the hairs of her head, and kissed his feet, and anointed *them* with the ointment. Now when the Pharisee which had bidden him saw *it*, he spake within himself, saying, This man, if he were a prophet, would have known who and what manner of woman *this is* that toucheth him: for she is a **sinner**. And Jesus answering said unto him, Simon, I have somewhat to say unto thee. And he saith, Master, say on. There was a certain creditor which had two debtors: the one owed five hundred pence, and the other fifty. And when they had nothing to pay, he frankly forgave them both. Tell me therefore, which of them will love him most? Simon answered and said, I suppose that *he*, to whom he forgave most. And he said unto him, Thou hast rightly judged. And he turned to the woman, and said unto Simon, Seest thou this woman? I entered into thine house, thou gavest me no water for my feet: but she hath washed my feet with tears, and wiped *them* with the hairs of her head. Thou gavest me no kiss: but this woman since the time I came in hath not ceased to kiss my feet. My head with oil thou didst not anoint: but this woman hath anointed my feet with ointment. Wherefore I say unto thee, **Her sins, which are many, are forgiven; for she loved much: but to whom little is forgiven, *the same* loveth little.** And he said unto her, Thy sins are forgiven. And they that sat at meat with him began to say within themselves, Who is this that forgiveth sins also? And he said to the woman, **Thy faith hath saved thee; go in peace**. (Luke 7: 37-50)

What kind of sinner was she? A fornicator? or Adulteress? Possibly. A lesbian? A drug addict? A thief? A prostitute? Jesus said, "her sins, which are many." Perhaps she was guilty of all those sins. "…the **blood** of Jesus Christ his Son cleanseth us from **all** sin" (1 John 1:7) at the very moment we place our faith in Him. A born-again sodomite is no longer a sodomite! And he or she will love Christ deeply. The people that love Christ the most are those who realize the immensity of their sins and the depth of love that motivated Christ to die for them that they might have forgiveness. Truly repentent and born-again ex-sodomites make great church members because they will love Jesus for saving them from the bondage of that sinful, life-destroying lifestyle.

Help Your Members Rescue Their Children

Make it immediately possible for your members to pull their children out of the anti-God, anti-Christian, sodomite influence they are under in public schools. Don't wait until their children are seduced into sodomy and turned against God and against His church. Then it will be too late. Either start a school in your church, or start a church-sponsored, home-school support group. Open the church door wide to repentant sinners. The next sinner to walk through that door might be your daughter or your son.

Work To Disestablish the Humanist Religon As State Church

Work relentlessly to get the humanist church disestablished so as to relieve Americans of having to pay the billions of dollars of tax money presently being used by humanists to make atheist, humanst Democrat voters out of our children, so that that money can be used by parents as they see fit to provide a real education for their children.

The disbanding of public education is what Humanists fear the most. The wise among them are warning the others to be nice to the religious Right and not push them too far too fast lest Christians and other theists realize that the abolition of public education is the only way to prevent Humanists from completely destroying the worship of God in this country. Here is an example of what these humanists are saying:

> I may find much to disagree with in many of the claims of the religious Right; I may find creationism to be bad science and wrong-headed; I may find Robertson and Reed and many of their allies mean-spirited and dangerous in their political agenda; but I will fight with all my strength to be sure that their children, and more likely the children of their followers, are treated with as much respect as my own children or any other child in the public schools of this nation**. . . .Anything less invites a retreat into private schools and ultimately undermines public education**. . . . Michael Apple has brilliantly stated the case for a more tolerant, open, and welcoming school. . . .: "When school bureaucracies do not listen respectfully to criticism, when our definition of 'professionalism' are used to exclude power-sharing arrangement, when a curriculum seems imposed, when community members feel their voices are ignored—**all of this makes rightist arguments seem sensible, even among those people who are not usually sympathetic to such ideological positions" This statement applies with considerable force to the issue of religion in the schools**. . . . Apple continues: "Making schools more open and responsive is not 'just' important because it may raise achievement scores or it may get more parents involved in supporting what 'we' want. **It is also absolutely crucial for interrupting the growth of rightest social movements.**"[101] [Emphasis added.]

Interpretation: they think we are dumb to believe in the Creator God, but they know that if we wake up soon enough to how they are using public schools to rule over us and destroy us, it will result in a major defeat to their religion. They realize that keeping our children in public schools is "absolutely crucial for interrupting the growth of rightest social movements," because public schools are set up to make Democrat voters out of our children. So, to keep us from getting angry and disestablishing their anti-God religion, they will be nice to our children while they brainwash them! Note the fear these two humanists have that the God-fearing Right might wake up and realize that getting government out of the education business by privatizing education is the only way to rescue our children and nation from atheistic Humanism. They know that there is ***no other way*** to disestablish their pagan Humanist religion.

Remember their boast:

> . . . every American public school is a school of Humanism. What can the theistic Sunday Schools, meeting for an hour once a week, and teaching only a fraction of the children, do to stem the tide of a five-day program of humanistic teaching?[102]

Helping your church members transfer their children out of public schools into private or home schools will rescue their children, but this alone is not enough to stop our loss of freedoms. Public schools are very effectively destroying children's faith in God and making them into voters who hate Christianity. They receive billions of dollars of tax money to fund their war against us. Public school has got to go. Now is our opportunity if ever there is going to be one—with their sodomy they have pushed many people too far. But many others do not yet realize what sodomites actually do and are seducing our children into doing. Educating our neighbors and friends and family members to the truth will be most effective.

---

[101] Fraser, *Between Church and State*, 238–39.

[102] Potter, *A New Religion*, 128.

Encourage Married Couples To Have Children

It does not take a high I.Q. to realize that it takes voters to win elections. The more voters voting on your side the more success you will have winning elections. Yet many pastors actually teach the married couples in their church to disobey the very first commandment God gave to humans. Here it is again:

> So God created man in his *own* image, in the image of God created he him; male and female created he them. And God blessed them, and God said unto them, Be fruitful, and multiply, and replenish the earth, and subdue it: and have dominion over the fish of the sea, and over the fowl of the air, and over every living thing that moveth upon the earth. (Gen. 1:27-28)

Disobeying this command will eventually cost us in the voting booths. Larry Eastland of the LEA Management Group LLC, a public research organization, has pointed out that

> In the 2008 election, 24,408,960 in the Voting Age Population will be missing because of abortions between 1973-90. . . .
>
> • There are 19,748,000 Democrats who are not with us today. (49.37 percent of 40 million).
>
> • There are 13,900,000 Republican who are not with us today. (34.75 percent of 40 million).
>
> • By comparison, then, the Democrats have lost 5,848,000 more voters than the Republicans have.
>
> ***
>
> These numbers will not change. They are based on individual choices made--aggregated nationally--as long as 30 years ago. Look inside these numbers at where the political impact is felt most. Do Democrats realize that millions of Missing Voters--due to the abortion policies they advocate--gave George W. Bush the margin of victory in 2000?
>
> The number of abortions accumulate in size and political impact as the years roll along. Like an avalanche that picks up speed, mass, and power as it thunders down a mountain, the number of Missing Voters from abortion changes the landscape of politics. . . .
>
> Here's what we know from several generations of social science research about children:
>
> • They tend to absorb the values of their parents.
>
> • They tend to have the same political views as their family (parents, siblings, immediate relatives) and share common views on political causes.
>
> • They tend to develop the same lifestyle as their family.
>
> ***
>
> • Six out of 10 Americans call themselves conservatives. Only a quarter of them are having abortions.
>
> • A little more than one-third of Americans call themselves liberals. More than four in 10 are having abortions.
>
> • This means that liberals are having one third more abortions than conservatives.

Eastland goes on to give data to show that

> in the actual popular vote for president in the 2000 general election in Florida, George W. Bush was declared the winner by 537 votes. But if the 260,962 Missing Voters of Florida had been present to vote, Al Gore would have won by 45,366 votes. Missing Voters--through decisions made in the 1970s and early 1980s, encouraged and emboldened by the feminist movement at the height of its power--altered the outcome of the U.S. presidency a generation later, in a way proponents of legal abortion could not have imagined.
>
> Examining these results through a partisan political lens, the Democrats have given the Republicans a decided advantage in electoral politics, one that grows with each election. Moreover, it is an advantage that they can never regain. Even if abortion were declared illegal today, and every single person complied with the decision, the advantage would continue to grow until the 2020 election, and would stay at that level throughout the voting lifetime of most Americans living today.[103]

The fact that Republicans had ***fewer*** abortions than Democrats is the only reason Republicans have any chance at all of retaking control of the government. But the fact is many Republicans did have abortions and

---

[103] Larry L. Eastland, "The Empty Cradle Will Rock: How Abortion is Costing the Democrats Voters--Literally," *OpinionJournal.Com*, 1928 June 2007, Http://www.opinionjournal.com/extra/?id=110005277.

also practiced many other forms of birth-control, and this has hurt us badly. Had Republicans not had any abortions, and had they not practiced birth control of any kind, they would now so outnumber Democrats that the Democrats would not even rate being discussed. One of the main reasons Christians are in their present predicament is because in the bedroom they have often practiced humanism instead of Christianity. They have had no faith in God. They need to be taught better than this in church.

What Individuals Must Do

In the end, it is what individuals do that makes the difference. If you move a grain of sand you have changed the world. Your every decision and every thing you do makes a difference. "But thanks *be* to God, which giveth us the victory through our Lord Jesus Christ. Therefore, my beloved brethren, be ye stedfast, unmoveable, always abounding in the work of the Lord, forasmuch as ye know that your labour is not in vain in the Lord" (1 Cor. 15:58). "And let us not be weary in well doing: for in due season we shall reap, if we faint not" (Gal. 6:9).

Love and Worship God

The most effective way to defeat the Humanist religion is to love and worship God, sing praises to His name, pray and meditate in His word daily; then, as you go about your daily life with a smile on your face and melody in your heart, testify to those you meet concerning God's marvelous grace and power to save. God will fight this powerful enemy for us if we will just trust in His omnipotent power. Consider God's words through the prophet Jahaziel to the children of Israel when they were hopelessly outnumbered by strong enemies (the Moabites, Edomites, and Amorites):

> Thus saith the LORD unto you, Be not afraid nor dismayed by reason of this great multitude; for **the battle is not yours, but God's**.... Ye shall not need to fight in this battle: set yourselves, stand ye still, and see the salvation of the LORD with you, O Judah and Jerusalem: fear not, nor be dismayed; to morrow go out against them: for the LORD will be with you.... Believe in the LORD your God, so shall ye be established; believe his prophets, so shall ye prosper. ... And when he had consulted with the people, he appointed singers unto the LORD, and that should praise the beauty of holiness, as they went out before the army, and to say, Praise the LORD; for his mercy endureth for ever. And when they began to sing and to praise, the LORD set ambushments against the children of Ammon, Moab, and mount Seir, which were come against Judah; and they were smitten. For the children of Ammon and Moab stood up against the inhabitants of mount Seir, utterly to slay and destroy them: and when they had made an end of the inhabitants of Seir, every one helped to destroy another. And when Judah came toward the watch tower in the wilderness, they looked unto the multitude, and, behold, they were dead bodies fallen to the earth, and none escaped. (2 Chronicles 20:15-24)

Do you see what God did?! He told the Israelites to get together on the battle field to sing songs of praise, and then, while they were singing, God caused the enemies of Israel to get in a fight with themselves, so that they killed each other to the last man! Israel went out against the enemy, but it was God that fought and won the battle. Note that "Ye shall not need to fight in this battle." True, we are to "go out against them," but only to *stand still and see the salvation of the Lord.*

As David told Goliath,

> Thou comest to me with a sword, and with a spear, and with a shield: but I come to thee in the name of the LORD of hosts, the God of the armies of Israel, whom thou hast defied. This day will the LORD deliver thee into mine hand; and I will smite thee, and take thine head from thee; and I will give the carcases of the host of the Philistines this day unto the fowls of the air, and to the wild beasts of the earth; that all the earth may know that there is a God in Israel. And all this assembly shall know that the LORD saveth not with sword and spear: for **the battle is the LORD's**, and he **will** give you into our hands. (1 Samuel 17:45-47)

And remember the words of Jonathan to his armor bearer: "... there is **no restraint** to the LORD to save by many **or by few**" (I Samuel 14:6). After saying those words, they two alone were used of God to bring a great victory to hopelessly outnumbered Israel. Don't neglect your political duties, but don't put your confidence in politics. Our strength is not in numbers, but in God.

Be Sure You Know the True God

The most important thing you can do for your children, grandchildren, and country is to become personally acquainted with God.

> These words spake Jesus, and lifted up his eyes to heaven, and said, Father, the hour is come; glorify thy Son, that thy Son also may glorify thee: as thou hast given him power over all flesh, that he should give **eternal life** to as many as thou hast given him. And this is life eternal, that they might know thee the only true God, and Jesus Christ, whom thou hast sent. (John 17:1-3)

After you know God as your Heavenly Father and personal Lord and Savior, you can introduce your family and friends to Him so that they also might have eternal life.

Is it actually possible to **KNOW** right **NOW** that you **HAVE** ***eternal*** life? **Yes, it is!**

> And this is the record, that God hath given to us **eternal** life, and this life is in his Son. He that hath the Son hath life; and he that hath not the Son of God hath not life. These things have I written unto you that believe on the name of the Son of God; that ye may **know** that ye have **eternal** life, and that ye may believe on the name of the Son of God. (1 John 5:11-13)

The reason we can "have" eternal life and "know it," is because salvation is by grace through faith in Christ—not of works.

> For by **grace** are ye saved through **faith**; and that not of yourselves: it is the gift of God: **not of works**, lest any man should boast. (Ephesians 2:8-9)

Thank God, you do not have to save yourself (for that is not in your power). God provided salvation by sending His only begotten Son to die on the cross for our sins (1 Cor. 10:1-4). All you must do is "Believe on the Lord Jesus Christ, and thou shalt be saved" (Acts 16:31). God, who cannot lie, promised

> **That if thou shalt confess with thy mouth the Lord Jesus, and shalt believe in thine heart that God hath raised him from the dead, thou shalt be saved.** For with the heart man believeth unto righteousness; and with the mouth confession is made unto salvation. For the scripture saith, Whosoever believeth on him shall not be ashamed. For there is no difference between the Jew and the Greek: for the same Lord over all is rich unto all that call upon him. For **whosoever** shall call upon the name of the Lord shall be saved. (Romans 10:9-13)

So call upon the Lord Jesus Christ to save you now! And He will.

Read Your Bible and Pray Daily

Once you have been born into the family of God, it is important that you allow Him to guide your thinking. In these days of war for the hearts, minds and souls of men, it is essential that we have the peace, tranquility, guidance, and inner strength that comes only from having a quiet, unrushed personal time of prayer and meditation in God's Word daily.

> **Blessed** is the man that walketh not in the counsel of the ungodly, nor standeth in the way of sinners, nor sitteth in the seat of the scornful. But his delight is in the law of the LORD; and in his law doth he meditate day and night. And he shall be like a tree planted by the rivers of water, that bringeth forth his fruit in his season; **his leaf also shall not wither; and whatsoever he doeth shall prosper**. The ungodly are not so: but are like the chaff which the wind driveth away. Therefore the ungodly shall not stand in the judgment, nor sinners in the congregation of the righteous. (Ps. 1:1-5)

> This book of the law shall not depart out of thy mouth; but thou shalt meditate therein day and night, that thou mayest observe to do according to all that is written therein: for then thou shalt make thy way **prosperous**, and then thou shalt have **good success**. (Joshua 1:8)

Actually, it is the faith or lack of faith of God's people—not what the humanists do—that will determine the fate of this nation. God will fight our battles and win the victories for us, provided we show genuine faith in Him.

> If my people, which are called by my name, shall humble themselves, and pray, and seek my face, and turn from their wicked ways; then will I hear from heaven, and will forgive their sin, and will heal their land. (2 Chronicles 7:14)

Learn More About the Issues

This book only begins to expose the humanist lies that are being taught to our children in public schools.

None Dare Call It Education

For additional exposure of how humanism has destroyed real education in public schools read John A. Stormer's excellent book *None Dare Call It Education.* In his book, Stormer documents in detail how humanists educators have rewritten text books to completely change history so as to deceive our children into accepting their dream of a one-world socialist government. He gives example after example of how these lies in text books are being used to undermine America's foundations so as to rob our great nation of her sovereignty.

Institute In Creation Research

Many excellent books by Dr. Henry Morris and many other scientists are available from the Institute In Creation Research web site at: http://www.icr.org. Also, many excellent articles, books, and videos can be downloaded for free from this same web site at http://www.icr.org/index.php?module=articles&action=all&ID=2

With the wealth of scientific evidence against evolution, there is really no excuse for anyone to believe the evolution myth.

Join and Attend a Bible-believing Church

The church of the living God is the "pillar and ground of the truth" (1 Tim. 3:15). In the fight against errors and lies, the most effective organizations on earth are the Lord's churches. It is true that there are many humanist churches falsely claiming to be Christian. Not every "church" is a genuine church. But that does not excuse you from finding and joining and supporting a sound Bible-believing church. The benefit to you, your spouse, and your children will be immense.

Conduct a Family Devotion Daily

Do everything in your power to teach your children Bible principles.

> Hear, O Israel: The LORD our God is one LORD: and thou shalt love the LORD thy God with all thine heart, and with all thy soul, and with all thy might. And these words, which I command thee this day, shall be in thine heart: **and thou shalt teach them diligently unto thy children**, and shalt talk of them when thou sittest in thine house, and when thou walkest by the way, and when thou liest down, and when thou risest up. And thou shalt bind them for a sign upon thine hand, and they shall be as frontlets between thine eyes. And thou shalt write them upon the posts of thy house, and on thy gates. (Deut. 6:4-9)

If you want your children to know and live by the truths of God's Word, you must teach them those truths in your home, showing them that they are indeed true.

Withdraw Your Child From Public School

It is abuse to send your children to a school you know will teach them atheistic beliefs and immoral practices. In public school your children will be taught that sodomy and other sexual perversions are normal and right. They will be taught that evolution is true and the Bible is a lie. They will be taught that only uneducated fools believe in God. You should love your children too much to allow them to be so confused and misled. The chance that they will be able to stand up under the pressure that will be put upon them and still retain their faith in God is virtually zero. They are children, not adults. They will be asked many hard questions they will not know how to answer. Until they are intimately acquainted with the true and genuine they will not be able to recognize the counterfeit and phony. Doubts will be sown in their minds. Children pretty much believe what their teachers tell them without question. Their minds are still being molded. They are not yet able to distinguish the wheat from the tares—to know truth from error. You must protect them from the wolves, not throw them to the wolves. Either place your children in a carefully selected private Christian school, or else home school them yourself.

Be Fruitful and Multiply

If you are married, one of the most important things you can do is to stop practicing humanism in your bedroom. Throw out your birth control pills and contraceptives, and start having babies to raise for the glory of God. Have faith in God. He will provide. Let the humanists practice birth control—there are too many of them already. But there will never be too many Christians. By simply obeying God in this one area of life, we can be more and mightier then they in just a few short generations.

> So God created man in his own image, in the image of God created he him; male and female created he them. And God blessed them, and God said unto them, **Be fruitful, and multiply**, and replenish the earth, and subdue it: and have dominion over the fish of the sea, and over the fowl of the air, and over every living thing that moveth upon the earth. (Gen. 1:27-28)

> **And the children of Israel were fruitful, and increased abundantly, and multiplied, and waxed exceeding mighty; and the land was filled with them.** Now there arose up a new king over Egypt, which knew not Joseph. And he said unto his people, Behold, the people of the children of Israel are more and mightier than we: come on, let us deal wisely with them; lest they multiply, and it come to pass, that, when there falleth out any war, they join also unto our enemies, and fight against us, and so get them up out of the land. (Ex. 1:7-10)

Like Pharaoh, king of Egypt, the humanists are doing everything in their power to keep us from reproducing, because they know that the more of us there are the more votes and political power we wield. Let us not fall for their tricks in selfishness and unbelief, thereby losing our freedoms. Children are blessings, not curses!

Vote According To Bible Principles

If you have not yet registered to vote, register today! A Christian should vote in every election, and should vote according to Bible principles, and not by strict party line. Often just one or two votes make the difference between having a godly man in office or having a devil rule over us.

The Democrat Party has been taking a rapidly intensifying, militant anti-God, humanist stand for many decades. No Bible-believing Christian can vote Democrat. The whole Democrat platform is anti-Christian.

The position of the Republican Party is at present the closest to what the Bible teaches. However, humanist Republicans are just as wicked as humanist Democrats. In some cases it may be best to vote for an independent candidate. But in other cases independent candidates are also humanists. So, there is no way around taking the time to examine the beliefs and voting record of each candidate. You simply ***must*** take the time to prepare to vote godly.

It is wrong to vote according to how much money some politician promises to put in your pocket. Government is not God, and can't put money into your pocket. Vote for what is right according to God's Word—vote by the principles found in the Bible!

Vote Humanists Out of Office

Ask each of your congressmen point blank if they believe in evolution. If they answer, "Yes," vote them out of office. Ask them point blank if they believe in the literal six day creation as recorded in the book of Genesis. Evolution is the root doctrine of the humanist religion. Belief in evolution makes a person a humanist. Evolution is a "world view" (basic concept of life) in direct opposition to the Bible. Every decision made based on that erroneous world view will also be wrong. Make sure you vote only for people who believe in God and who believe the Bible is true.

Consider Running For Public Office Yourself

Civil servants are ministers of God. Is God calling you to run for public office? If yes, then surrender to God's call. It will not be an easy road ahead for you. You will be a target of humanists. They will hate you and try to destroy you. Even though they are hypocrites themselves, humanists will try to find and expose every trace of hypocrisy in you. So you must confess and forsake all sin before entering the public arena. But if God is calling you, it is your duty and privilege and honor to surrender to God's call. As Mordecai told Esther,

> For if thou altogether holdest thy peace at this time, then shall there enlargement and deliverance arise to the Jews from another place; but thou and thy father's house shall be destroyed: and **who knoweth whether thou art come to the kingdom for such a time as this**? (Esther 4:14)

Perhaps you have come to your particular place in life to be used of God to bring deliverance to this country. Please do whatever you can, for unlike the Jews there is no deliverance promised the USA from "another place." If **you** don't do what God wants **you** to do, this country may be destroyed. If not you, who? If not now, when?

Contact Your Congressmen About Key Issues

Phone your congressman about key issues. Ask to talk to him personally. Urge him to vote according to Bible principles. Better yet, make a personal visit to his office, give him a copy of this book, and ask him to commit to reading it.

Influence the Judiciary

The judiciary has proven to be the weakest branch of our government. The Supreme Court has been especially easy for humanists to use to subvert justice. One humanist president may be able to appoint many Supreme Court justices, who then sit in the Court for life, thwarting the intent of the original framers of the Constitution and of the American people. Almost all of our loss of liberty over the last 100 years has been caused by unjust, activist judges, who are legislating instead of judging. There are several things we should fight to achieve.

Term Limits For Judges

There needs to be term limits for all federal judges, especially for Supreme Court justices. This will require an amendment to the Constitution to achieve, but should be a diligently worked for goal. A presidental appointment to the Supreme Court should be for no more than four years, and a Supreme Court justice should be able to be appointed no more than twice. This way a really corrupt, one-term president can only do four years of damage to the judiciary.

Constitution Honoring Judges Only

This is extremely important! Even if you never contact your congressmen on any other issue, make sure you do contact them when a judge is being selected to serve on the Supreme Court. Let your congressmen know in a respectful but firm way that you will work to remove them from office if they vote to confirm any judge who does not swear to honor and make all judgements in accordance to the original meaning of the Constitution, and to not make any judgements in accordance to United Nations' or other foreign governments laws. Your phone calls and letters to your congressmen do count. And so do your votes, as your congressmen very well know.

Impeach Ruth Ginsburg

This woman is the most unAmerican person to ever sit on the Supreme Court. She "served as the ACLU's General Counsel from 1973–1980, and on the National Board of Directors from 1974–1980."[104] She is an internationalist, and her loyalty is to the International Humanist and Ethical Union headquarters of her Humanist religion, and not the United States of America. She speaks of the Constitution as a "living" document, meaning that a judge should be able to change its original meaning to suit the present circumstances. That just simply means that if she doesn't like the original meaning, she says it means something else. That is being unjust and wicked. She must go. We must work to have her and any other "living document" justice like her impeached immediately.

Investigate the American Humanist Association

The American Humanist Association is the heart and soul of America's problems. It is the planner of much of the subversion and treason taking place in this country—the head of the humanist snake. This dangerous organization and all its fronts—especially the American Civil Liberties Union—needs to be investigated by the FBI and other law enforcement agencies for their subversive, treasonist, anti-America activities, and its leaders brought to justice. Be wise! These highly organized Humanists hate us and are out to destroy us. If they ever gain enough power to kill us they will do so with no more compassion than they show a baby when it is stabbed it in the back of the head and its brains sucked out in partial-birth abortion. The subversive actives of these wicked people must be stopped. They are working to have all outspoken Christians put in prison for "hate crimes." It is literally going to be either them or us. Ask you Congressmen to have them investigated; and keep asking each week until action is taken.

Work To Disestablish the Humanist Religion

Personally ask your Congressmen to submit a bill to force the courts to regard humanism a "religion" as that word is used in the establishment clause of the First Amendment. It is exceedingly unjust and wicked for the humanist religion to be declared a "religion" for tax exemption purposes, but "not a religion" when it puts humanism in the same position as theistic religions in regards to the establishment clause. If the establisment clause doesn't apply to humanism, neither should tax exemption. Humanism is a religion. Humanism is presently illegally established as the state church in direct violation of the First Amendment, and that must end immediately.

Distribute This Book

The time is very short. Please help us distribute this book to every family in the USA before November 4, 2008. The entire contents of this book may be read for free on our publisher's web site:

http://www.dayspringpublisher.com/psh.html

If you have a web site, please post this entire book (not just a link to it) on your web site. If you just absolutely can't do that, then post on your website the above link to the book on dayspringpublisher.com.[105]

Now e-mail the link to your friends, and encourage them to post it on their web sites also.

Next, e-mail the link to all your city, state, and national government officials, to your local newspaper editors, radio stations, tv stations, and to everyone you know who is running for public offices. Perhaps if they get enough e-mails containing links to this book, they will read it.

---

[104] "The Justices of the Supreme Court," *SupremeCourtUS.Gov*, Http://www.supremecourtus.gov/about/biographiescurrent.pdf.

[105] Please read the copyright notice. You may (and are encouraged) to post this book on your web site, but the contents may not be changed without written notice. The entire book must be posted "as is."

However, please do not send this link in spam!

This book is also available in inexpensive e-book format as well as printed form online from www.Amazon.com.

Generous volume discounts are available to those who would like to distribute this book on a grassroots level during election campaigns, or to all the families in their church, or to the members of their local PTA, etc. For discounted pricing send email to: manager@dayspringpublisher.com

Amazon.com will drop ship printed copies of this book to all your relatives, friends, co-workers, children and grandchildren who do not have computers.

And take courage in this important fact:

> ...the most High ruleth in the kingdom of men, and giveth it to whomsoever he will....whose dominion is an everlasting dominion, and his kingdom is from generation to generation: and all the inhabitants of the earth are reputed as nothing: and he doeth according to his will in the army of heaven, and among the inhabitants of the earth: and none can stay his hand, or say unto him, What doest thou? ...whose works are truth, and his ways judgment: and those that walk in pride he is able to abase. (Dan. 4:32-37)

Caution: the following link connects to a terribly nasty, pornographic, homosexual book that was distributed to public school children. Of course, we do NOT condone the pornography; WE CONDEMN IT TOTALLY. We provide this link only so that parents can see the depth of depravity being taught to children by GLSEN and other Humanist groups. We are NOT trying to pervert you by providing this link, but are trying to alert you to what Humanists are showing to GRADE SCHOOL CHILDREN to pervert them. GLSEN is the sodomite group working together with the ACLU to start GSA clubs in every public school in the United States. If they are not in your public school yet they most likely will be soon.

The link to The Little Black Book—Queer in the 21st Century:

http://www.massresistance.org/docs/issues/black_book/black_book_inside.html

The link to chapter 26 of this book:

http://www.dayspringpublisher.com/psh-26.pdf

If Margaret Sanger is the most wicked woman ever to live, then who is the most wicked person, male or female? I believe it has to be Charles Darwin. It was Darwin that put the evil ideas into the heads of Hitler, Lenin, Mao, Sanger, and all the baby-slaughtering Humanists of today. By cleverly cloking his atheist religion's dogma in scientific-sounding language, he has deceived more people into going to Hell than any person in history. This man's ideas inspired all of the modern mass-murdering movements except Islam, including Nazism and its holocaust of six million Jews plus perhaps five million of other nationalities, Communism and its slaughter of tens of millions who opposed it, and the abortion slaughter of over 40 million innocent babies. So, clearly, Darwin reigns as the most evil person of all time. And blood continues to drip from his hands.

CHARLES DARWIN

(before the beard)

WORKS CITED

"30 Years of Abortion and Its Impact on Women---National Symposia." *Americans United for Life Website* (2003). Http://unitedforlife.org/30_year_symposia/symposia.htm.

"ACLU Letter to the Senate Urging Opposition to Cloture Motion on Nomination of Judge Samuel Alito." *ACLU Web Site*, 1927 January 2006. Http://www.aclu.org/scotus/2005/23964leg20060127.html.

"Ann Blames Clinton, Carter for 9/11 and Dreams of Denying Women the Vote." *The New York Observer*, 2002 October 2007. Http://www.observer.com/2007/coulter-culture.

"Anthony D. Romero, Executive Director." *ACLU.Org*. Http://www.aclu.org/about/staff/13279res20030205.html.

"Anthony Romeo." *Pbs.Org*. Http://www.pbs.org/now/politics/romero.html.

Associated Press. "ACLU to Defend Pedophile Group." *Wired News*, 1931 August 2000. Http://www.wired.com/news/politics/0,1283,38540,00.html.

"BACKGROUND: Six Significant Court Decisions Regarding Evolution/creation Issues." Http://www.don-lindsay-archive.org/creation/voices/legal/bkgrd.htm.

Beaman, Roderick T. "THE AMERICAN CIVIL LIBERTIES UNION: Uncomfortable Truths About the Origins." *Ether Zone*, 1916 September 2004. Http://www.etherzone.com/2004/beam091604.shtml.

Benen, Steve. "McCain 'Trying to Square the Circle'." *The Carpetbagger Report*, 2003 January 2007. Http://www.thecarpetbaggerreport.com/archives/9509.html.

Bramanti, Matt, Editor. "LST: Neo-Nazi Leader Gives Ron Paul $500." *LoneStarTimes.Com*, 1925 October 2007. Http://lonestartimes.com/2007/10/25/rpb1/.

Bresciani, Michael. "California Passes SB 777 - Here Come the Language Police." *The Conservative Voice*, 1918 October 2007. Http://www.theconservativevoice.com/article/28720.html.

Brian. "My Correspondence With Ron Paul About Gay Rights." *In Repair*, 1931 May 2007. Http://inrepair.net/2007/05/31/my-correspondence-with-ron-paul-about-gay-rights/.

Brown, A Whitney. "I Support the Troops." *Daily Kos*, 1923 July 2007. Http://www.dailykos.com/story/2007/7/23/114037/956.

Camenker, Brian. "The Mitt Romney Deception." *MassResistance*, 1920 November 2006. Http://www.massresistance.org/docs/marriage/romney/record/index.html.

Cameron, Paul. "Teacher-Pupil Sex Across the World: How Much Is Homosexual?" *The Empirical Journal of Same-Sex Sexual Behavior* (2007). Http://www.ejssb.org./resources/ejssb_CameronP_WorldwideTeacherPupilSexualInteractions$5B1$5D.pdf.

__________. "Violence and Homosexuality." *Family Research Institute* (2006). Http://www.familyresearchinst.org/Default.aspx?tabid=74.

Carroll, J.M. *The Trail of Blood*. Lexington, Kentucky: Ashland Avenue Baptist Church, 1931. Http://www.biblepreaching.com/trailofblood.html.

Cattrill, Robert C. "Roger Baldwin: Founder, American Civil Liberties Union." *Harvard Square Library*. Http://www.harvardsquarelibrary.org/unitarians/baldwin.html.

"Celebrate 50 Years of Defending Freedom at the ICLU." *Indiana Civil Liberties Union* (2003, 17 October). Http://www.iclu.org/news/news_article.asp?ID=71.

Cheating and Succeeding: Record Number of Top High School Students Take Ethical Shortcuts. Lake Forest, IL: Who's Who Among American High School Students, 2000. Http://www.eci-whoswho.com/highschool/frame.html.

Chesler, Ellen. *Woman of Valor: Margaret Sanger and the Birth Control Movement in America*. New York: Simon & Schuster, 1992. 639 pp.

"Clarence Thomas." *Wikipedia*, 1930 October 2007. Http://en.wikipedia.org/wiki/Clarence_Thomas.

Cloud, John. "The Battle Over Gay Teens." *Time*, 2002 October 2005. Http://www.time.com/time/magazine/article/0,9171,1112856,00.html.

Coates, Ta-Nehisi Paul. "Anthony Romero." *Time*, 1913 August 2005. Http://www.time.com/time/nation/article/0,8599,1093634,00.html.

"Columnist Ann Coulter Shocks Cable TV Show, Declaring 'Jews Need to Be Perfected by Becoming Christians'." *FoxNews.Com*, 1911 October 2007. Http://www.foxnews.com/story/0,2933,301216,00.html.

Coms, Stephanie. "Recent Survey Says Most College Students Cheat." *Arizona Daily Wildcat*, 1921 September 1998. Http://wildcat.arizona.edu/papers/92/20/01_2_m.html.

"The Constitution: Amendments 11–27." *Archives.Gov*. Http://www.archives.gov/national-archives-experience/charters/constitution_amendments_11–27.html.

"Contact Your Local Rush Limbaugh Radio Station Today." *Media Matter for America Web Site*, November 2007. Http://mediamatters.org/action_center/limbaugh_stations/.

"Contention Inside and Outside as David Parker's Civil Rights Lawsuit Begins in Federal Court." *MassResistance*, 2007 February 2007. Http://www.massresistance.org/docs/parker_lawsuit/hearing_020707/index.html.

Cooney, Timothy J. *Telling Right From Wrong: What Is Moral, What is Immoral, and What Is Neither One Nor the Other*. Buffalo, New York: Prometheus Books, 1985.

Cord, Robert L. "Church, State, and the Rihnquist Court: The Court is Doing What the Framers Never Did; Build an Impregnable Wall Between Church and State. (Justice William Rehnquist; United States Supreme Court)." National Review, 1917 August 1992. Http://www.highbeam.com/library/docfree.asp?DOCID=1G1:12666321&ctrlInfo=Round18%3AMode18c%3ADocG%3AResult&ao=.

Coulter, Ann. *TREASON: Liberal Treachery from the Cold War to the War on Terrorism*. New York, New York: Three Rivers Press, 2003.

Dailey, Timothy J. "The Negative Health Effects of Homosexuality." *Family Research Council*, no. 232. Http://www.frc.org/get.cfm?i=IS01B1.

"David Parker's First-Grade Son Surrounded and Beaten up at School." *MassResistance* (2005). Http://www.massresistance.org/docs/parker/parker_son_incident/index.html.

Davidson, Robert F. *Philosophies Men Live By*. New York: Dryden Press, 1953.

Davis, Susan. "Paul Picks Up Backing From Mel Gibson's Dad." *Washington Wire*, 1914 November 2007. Http://blogs.wsj.com/washwire/2007/11/14/paul-picks-up-backing-from-mel-gibsons-dad/.

Dewey, John. "My Pedigodic Creed." In *John Dewey on Education*, editor Reginald D. Archamoault. New York: Random House, 1964.

Diaz, Elvia. "Gay-Marriage Ban Initiative Wins Support from McCain." *The Arizona Republic*, 1926 August 2005. Http://www.azcentral.com/arizonarepublic/news/articles/0826initiatives26.html.

Dority, Barbara. "Power to the People." *The Humanist* 53, no. 1 (January/February 1993).

Drudge, Matt. "CAMPAIGN CHASES EROTIC MAPPLETHORPE NUDE PHOTOS OF SCHWARZENEGGER." *Drudge Report*, 1923 September 2003. Http://www.drudgereportarchives.com/data/2003/09/24/20030924_204603_arnold.htm.

Eastland, Larry L. "The Empty Cradle Will Rock: How Abortion is Costing the Democrats Voters--Literally." *OpinionJournal.Com*, 1928 June 2007. Http://www.opinionjournal.com/extra/?id=110005277.

Elvin, Lionel. "An Education For Humanity." In *The Humanist Frame*, Ed. Julian Huxley. New York: Harper & Brothers, 1961.

"Employment Non-Discrimination Act of 2007." *Library of Congress Thomas*, 2007 November 2007. Http://thomas.loc.gov/cgi-bin/bdquery/z?d110:HR03685:@@@D&summ2=m&.

Ericson, Edward L. *The Humanist Way: An Introduction to Ethical Humanist Religion*. With a foreword by Isaac Asimov. New York: The Continuum Publishing Company, 1988. 205 pp.

Everett, Carol. "Interview With the Scarlet Lady." *Rutherford* 2, no. 4 (April 1993): 8.

Fletcher, Joseph. "Humanist Ethics: The Groundwork." In *Humanist Ethics*, 258–9. Buffalo, New York: Prometheus Books, c1980. 303.

__________. *Religioethical Issues*. Edited by Marvin Kohl, 17. Buffalo, New York: Prometheus Books, 1978.

Flynn, Elizabeth Gurley. "Do You Believe in Patriotism?" *The Masses*, March 1916. Http://www.marxists.org/subject/women/authors/flynn/1916/patriotism.htm.

Fraser, James W. *Between Church and State: Religion & Public Education in a Multicultural America*, 278. New York: St. Martin Press, 1999.

Freeman, Gregory A. "Bug Chasers: The Men Who Long to be HIV+." *Rolling Stone*, 1923 January 2003. Http://www.shoutwire.com/viewstory/16216/Bug_Chasers_Men_Who_Want_To_Be_HIV_Positive.

Freundlich, Naomi. "When the Cure May Make You Sicker." *BusinessWeek Online*, 1916 March 1998. Http://www.businessweek.com/archives/1998/b3569025.arc.htm?campaign_id=search.

Gallegos, Gilbert. "Pressure Can Provide Incentive to Cheat." *The Albuquerque Tribune*, 1920 December 2002. Http://www.abqtrib.com/extras/education/121899_playing.shtml.

"'Gay' Groups: We Have Rights to Your Children!" *WorldNetDaily*, 2006 October 2006. Http://www.wnd.com/news/article.asp?ARTICLE_ID=52311.

"GAYS ASSAULT EX-GAYS AT COUNTY FAIR." *Venus Magazine*, 1928 August 2007. Http://venusmagazine.org/Gay%20Assault%20PFOX.html.

Gilgoff, Dan. "The Dems Get Religion." *U.S. News & World Report*, 1925 February 2007. Http://www.usnews.com/usnews/news/articles/070225/5evangelicals.b.htm.

"The GLSEN Jump-Start Guide for Gay-Straight Alliances." *GLSEN*. Http://www.glsen.org/cgi-bin/iowa/all/news/record/2226.html.

Gonyea, Don. "Anger Over 'Betray Us' Ad Simmers on Hill." *National Public Radio*, 1922 September 2007. Http://www.npr.org/templates/story/story.php?storyId=14623512.

Greenhouse, Linda. "A.C.L.U., Reversing Policy, Joins the Opposition to Bork." *The New York Times*, 2001 September 1987. Http://query.nytimes.com/gst/fullpage.html?res=9B0DE0DE1E3CF932A3575AC0A961948260.

Harper, Tim. "Putting the Moves on MoveOn.Org." *Thestar.Com*, 1923 September 2007. Http://www.thestar.com/article/259511.

"Help Us Repeal SB 777 to Protect Our Kids." *MassResistence* (2007). Http://www.saveourkids.net/.

Hill, Anita F. "Testimony of Anita F. Hill, Professor of Law, University of Oklahoma, Norman, OK." *Gpoaccess.Gov*, 1911 October 1991. Http://www.gpoaccess.gov/congress/senate/judiciary/sh102–1084pt4/36–40.pdf.

"HISTORY of Israel & 'Palestine'." *Masada2000.Org*. Http://www.masada2000.org/historical.html.

"Huckabee: Abortion not States' Call." *USA Today*, 1918 November 2007. Http://www.usatoday.com/news/politics/election2008/2007–11–18-huckabee_N.htm?csp=34.

The Humanist, November/December 1991.

"In Memoriam: Molly Yard—Honoring an Indomitable NOW President and Civil Rights Pioneer." *NOW.Org*, 1921 September 2005. Http://www.now.org/press/09–05/09–21.html.

Johnson, Ben. "MoveOn: 'We Bought' the Democratic Party." *FrontPageMag.Com*, 1910 December 2004. Http://www.frontpagemag.com/Articles/Read.aspx?GUID={89BC7BB2–298F-4B8D-99DF-A9EA273A0559}.

Johnson, Ramone. "Bug Chaser & Gift Giver Parties." *About.com: Gay Life*. Http://gaylife.about.com/cs/gay101/a/bugparties.htm.

"The Justices of the Supreme Court." *SupremeCourtUS.Gov*. Http://www.supremecourtus.gov/about/biographiescurrent.pdf.

Key, Ellen. *The Woman Rebel*, May 1914.

Kuehl, Senator Sheila. "FACT SHEET: STUDENT CIVIL RIGHTS ACT (SB 777)." *Equality California* (2007). Http://www.eqca.org/atf/cf/%7B687DF34F-6480–4BCD-9C2B-1F33FD8E1294%7D/SB%20777%20FACT%20SHEET.PDF.

Kurtz, Paul, ed. *Humanist Manifestos I & II*. Buffalo, New York: Prometheus Books, 1981. 31 pp. Http://www.humanism.net/documents/manifesto1.html and http://www.humanism.net/documents/manifesto2.http.

LaHaye, Tim. "Sex Education Belongs in the Home." In *Teenage Sexuality: Opposing Viewpoints*, edited by David Bender, Bruno Leone, Neal Bernards, and Lynn Hall. Opposing Viewpoints. St. Paul, Minnesota: Greenhaven Press, 1988.

Lamont, Corliss. *The Illusion of Immortality*. John Dewey. 1935. Half-Moon Foundation, Inc. New York: The Continuum Publishing Company, 1990. 303 pp.

__________. *A Lifetime of Dissent*. Buffalo: Prometheus Books.

Lamson, Peggy. *Roger Baldwin: Founder of the American Civil Liberties Union*. Boston: Houghton Mifflin Company, 1976. 304 pp.

Leo, John. "A Judge with no Agenda." *U.S. News and World Report* 139, no. 2 (18 July 2005).

"Lesbian Gay Bisexual Transgender Project—Schools & Youth." *ACLU*. Http://www.aclu.org/lgbt/youth/index.html.

Lewis, Tyler. "Senate Passes Hate Crimes Bill." *Civilrights.Org*, 1927 September 2007. Http://www.civilrights.org/press_room/buzz_clips/civilrightsorg-stories/senate-passes-hate-crimes-bill.html.

"Lexington, Mass., Father of 6-Year-Old Arrested, Spends Night in Jail." *MassResistance* (2005). Http://www.massresistance.org/docs/parker/main.html.

Lofton, John. "Excerpts From Our Exclusive Ron Paul Interview." *The American View* (2007). Http://theamericanview.com/index.php?id=916&PHPSESSID=4d627613baced8c2c91c6ff2b6bc2f25.

Mann, Horace. *The Republic and the School: Horace Mann on the Education of Free Men*. New York: Bureau of Publications, Teachers College, Columbia University, 1957.

Margaret Sanger, the Woman Rebel and the Rise of the Birth Control Movement in the United States. Edited by Alex Baskin. New York: Stony Brook, Archives of Social History, State University of New York, 1976.

McCain, John. "MCCAIN STATEMENT ON THE FEDERAL MARRIAGE AMENDMENT." *Senate Website*, 1913 July 2004. Http://mccain.senate.gov/press_office/view_article.cfm?ID=246.

McCallister, Patrick. "Answering the Biblical Right with Biblical Socialism." *Socialist*, no. July/August (1995).

Messerli, Jonathan. *Horace Mann: A Biography*. New York: Alfred A. Knopf, 1972.

Miga, Andrew. "House Passes Job Bias Ban Against Gays." *MyWay*, 2007 November 2007. Http://apnews.myway.com/article/20071107/D8SP50200.html.

Miller, G. Tyler, Jr. *Living in the Environment: Problems, Connections and Solutions*, 757. Stamford, Connecticut: Wadsworth Publishing Co., 1994.

Miniter, Frank. "Presidential Candidates Ask for NRA Support." *National Rifle Association Website* (2007). Http://www.nrapublications.org/celebration/default.asp.

Montaldo, Charles. "Devlin Faces 69 Counts of Sodomy." *Charles Montaldo's Crime / Punishment Blog*, 2006 November 2007. Http://crime.about.com/b/2007/02/06/devlin-faces-69-counts-of-sodomy.htm.

Morris, Arval A. "Infanticide and the Value of Life." In *Religioethical Issues*, edited by Marvin Kohl, 17. Buffalo, New York: Prometheus Books, 1978.

Morris, Dick. "Bubba Steps Over the Line." *Journal News*, 2001 December 2005.

"The Myth of Separation of Church and State." Http://www.noapathy.org/tracts/mythofseparation.html.

"National Education Association." *Wikipedia*. Http://en.wikipedia.org/wiki/National_Education_Association.

"NEA Endorses Kerry for President." *USA Today*, 2005 July 2004. Http://www.usatoday.com/news/politicselections/nation/president/2004–07–05-nea-kerry_x.htm.

"Nevada Brothel Owner Endorses Ron Paul." *NBC11.Com*, 1926 November 2007. Http://www.nbc11.com/politics/14693483/detail.html#.

Paul, Ron. "The Federal Marriage Amendment Is a Very Bad Idea." *LewisRockwell.Com*, 2001 October 2004. Http://www.lewrockwell.com/paul/paul207.html.

__________. "Life and Liberty." *Ron Paul 2008* (2007). Http://www.ronpaul2008.com/issues/life-and-liberty/.

"Petition Against Students' Rights Falls Short." *Advocate.Com*, 1915 January 2008. Http://www.advocate.com/news_detail_ektid51608.asp.

Porteus, Liza. "Inhofe Says Boxer, Hillary Clinton Discussed Reining in Conservative Talk Radio Three Years Ago." *FoxNews.Com*, 1926 June 2007. Http://www.foxnews.com/story/0,2933,285933,00.html.

Potter, Charles Francis. *Humanism: A New Religion*. New York: Simon and Schuster, 1930.

"Robert Bork." *Wikipedia*, 1929 October 2007. Http://en.wikipedia.org/wiki/Robert_Bork.

Rogers, Carl. "Personal Thoughts on Teaching and Learning." In *The Carl Rogers Reader*. Boston: Houghton Mifflin Company, 1989.

"Safety Information." *Prozac Web Site; Eli Lilly and Company* (2006). Www.prozac.com/common_pages/safety_information.jsp?reqNavId=undefined.

Saumur, Lucien. *The Humanist Evangel*. Buffalo, New York: Prometheus Books, 1982.

Savage, Michel. *The Enemy Within: Saving America from the Liberal Assault on Our Schools, Faith, and Military*. Nashville, Tennessee: Nelson Current, 2003.

Schoolland, Ken. "The Free Market and Education." *The Future of Freedom Foundation*, January 1996. Http://www.fff.org/aboutUs/press/schooland.asp.

Schorr, Daniel. "Democrats Aren't Gaining Public Support Republicans Are Losing." *Jackson Hole Daily* 27, no. 251 (1925 October 2005).

"Senator Reid: You Win, Rush." *Rushlimbaugh.Com*, 1919 October 2007. Http://www.rushlimbaugh.com/home/daily/site_101907/content/01125109.guest.html.

Sheldon, Louis P. "TVC Chairman Speaks Out On Dangers Of H.R. 1592 To Free Speech/Religion." *The Traditional Values Coalition*, 1918 April 2007. Http://www.traditionalvalues.org/modules.php?sid=3059.

Sherwell, Philip. "Tom DeLay Targets US Liberals in Media War." *Telegraph.co.Uk*, 2004 November 2007. Http://www.telegraph.co.uk/news/main.jhtml?xml=/news/2007/11/04/wdelay104.xml.

Silva, Mark. "Senate Leader Demands Apology of Rush Limbaugh." *Baltimoresun.Com*, 2001 October 2007. Http://weblogs.baltimoresun.com/news/politics/blog/2007/10/senate_leader_demands_apology.html.

Smith, Lawrence. "Our 14-Year-Old Son Died from Ritalin Use." *National Alliance Against Mandated Mental Health Screening & Psychiatric Drugging of Children*. Http://www.ritalindeath.com/index.htm.

Spengler. "Spain's Elections Show Why Radical Islam Can Win." *Asia Times Online*, 1916 March 2004. Http://www.atimes.com/atimes/Front_Page/FC16Aa01.html.

__________. "Why Radical Islam Might Defeat the West." *Asian Times Online*, 1909 July 2003. Http://www.atimes.com/atimes/Middle_East/EG08Ak02.html.

Stringer-Hye, Richard. "Charles Francis Potter." Boston, MA: Unitarian Universalist Historical Society. Http://www.uua.org/uuhs/duub/articles/charlesfrancispotter.html.

Swank, Grant. "CA Schools: Pull Christian Kids Out." *The Conservative Voice*, 2007, 22 October 2007. Http://www.theconservativevoice.com/article/28694.html.

Taft, Senator Robert A. "Congress Should not Enact a National Compulsory Medical Insurance Law." *Congressional Digest* xxvii (March 1949): 79, 81. As Reprinted in Materials on American National Government. New York: Oxford University Press, *1952, pp. 522.*

Taylor, Greg. "Huckabee Hatin' Could Backfire on GOP." Yahoo! News, 1924 January 2008. Http://news.yahoo.com/s/realclearpolitics/20080124/cm_rcp/huckabee_hatin_could_backfire_1.

Taylor, Penina. "Thank You, Ann Coulter." *Arutz Sheva*, 1914 October 2007. Http://www.israelnationalnews.com/Articles/Article.aspx/7475.

"'Teachers' Pets: The NEA Gave $65 Million in Its Members' Dues to Left-Liberal Groups Last Year." *OpinionJournal*, 2006, 1 March 2006. Http://www.opinionjournal.com/editorial/feature.html?id=110007761.

Unruh, Bob. "Judge Orders 'gay' Agenda Taught to Christian Children." *WorldNetDaily*, 1924 February 2007. Http://wnd.com/news/article.asp?ARTICLE_ID=54420.

"Update on Petitions." *MassResistence* (2007). Http://www.saveourkids.net/news.html?news_id=13&start=0&category_id=1&parent_id=1&arcyear=&arcmonth=.

Vu, Michelle. "Bush Prepared to Veto 'Hate Crimes' Bill." *The Christian Post*, 2007, 10 March 2007. Http://www.christianpost.com/article/20071003/29558_Bush_Prepared_to_Veto_'Hate_Crimes'_Bill.htm.

Walzer, A.J. "Limbaugh: Service Members Who Support U.S. Withdrawal Are 'phony Soldiers'." *MEDIA MATTERS for America*, 1927 September 2007. Http://mediamatters.org/items/200709270010?f=h_top.

Wambolt, Gerry. "Family Left Lexington School System Over Homosexuality in David Parker's Elementary School," 2005. MassResistance.

Wattenberg, Ben J. *The Birth Dearth*. New York: Pharos Books, 1987. 214 pp.

Wells, H.G. *The Pivot of Civilization*. New York: Brentano, 1922.

Wenders, John T. "What a Drag: Inefficient Schools Burden Economy." *Oklahoma Council of Public Affairs* 10, no. 3 (March 2003). Http://www.ocpathink.org/ViewPerspectiveEdition.asp?ID=23.

"What You Can Do." *MediaMatters.Org*, 1922 August 2007. Http://mediamatters.org/items/200508220010.

"What's Your Problem?" *ACLU*, 2007, 3 January 2007. Http://www.aclu.org/lgbt/youth/28754res20070301.html#4.

"Why Should YOU Vote for Ron Paul." *MuslimsVoteRonPaul.Com* (2007). Http://muslimsvoteronpaul.com/.

Wm. Robert Johnston. "Summary of Registered Abortions Worldwide, Through 2000." *Johnston's Archive* (2001). Http://www.johnstonsarchive.net/policy/abortion/wrjp333sd.html.

INDEX

A FREE GIFT FOR YOUR FRIENDS!

Help prevent a child from being seduced into sodomy and atheism. Please help us warn people of the danger of the Humanist religion. Cut out the cards below and give them to your friends and family members. More copies of this page are available on our publisher's web site: **www.dayspringpublisher.com**

FREE e-book!
Please tell your friends!

PUBLIC SCHOOL HELL
the Humanist religion established as state church

exposing the promotion of sodomy in public schools

www.dayspringpublisher.com

FREE e-book!
Please tell your friends!

PUBLIC SCHOOL HELL
the Humanist religion established as state church

exposing the promotion of sodomy in public schools

www.dayspringpublisher.com

FREE e-book!
Please tell your friends!

PUBLIC SCHOOL HELL
the Humanist religion established as state church

exposing the promotion of sodomy in public schools

www.dayspringpublisher.com

FREE e-book!
Please tell your friends!

PUBLIC SCHOOL HELL
the Humanist religion established as state church

exposing the promotion of sodomy in public schools

www.dayspringpublisher.com

FREE e-book!
Please tell your friends!

PUBLIC SCHOOL HELL
the Humanist religion established as state church

exposing the promotion of sodomy in public schools

www.dayspringpublisher.com

FREE e-book!
Please tell your friends!

PUBLIC SCHOOL HELL
the Humanist religion established as state church

exposing the promotion of sodomy in public schools

www.dayspringpublisher.com

FREE e-book!
Please tell your friends!

PUBLIC SCHOOL HELL
the Humanist religion established as state church

exposing the promotion of sodomy in public schools

www.dayspringpublisher.com

FREE e-book!
Please tell your friends!

PUBLIC SCHOOL HELL
the Humanist religion established as state church

exposing the promotion of sodomy in public schools

www.dayspringpublisher.com

A FREE GIFT FOR YOUR FRIENDS!

Help prevent a child from being seduced into sodomy and atheism. Please help us warn people of the danger of the Humanist religion. Cut out the cards below and give them to your friends and family members. More copies of this page are available on our publisher's web site: **www.dayspringpublisher.com**

FREE e-book!
Please tell your friends!

PUBLIC SCHOOL HELL
the Humanist religion established as state church

exposing the promotion of sodomy in public schools

www.dayspringpublisher.com

FREE e-book!
Please tell your friends!

PUBLIC SCHOOL HELL
the Humanist religion established as state church

exposing the promotion of sodomy in public schools

www.dayspringpublisher.com

FREE e-book!
Please tell your friends!

PUBLIC SCHOOL HELL
the Humanist religion established as state church

exposing the promotion of sodomy in public schools

www.dayspringpublisher.com

FREE e-book!
Please tell your friends!

PUBLIC SCHOOL HELL
the Humanist religion established as state church

exposing the promotion of sodomy in public schools

www.dayspringpublisher.com

FREE e-book!
Please tell your friends!

PUBLIC SCHOOL HELL
the Humanist religion established as state church

exposing the promotion of sodomy in public schools

www.dayspringpublisher.com

FREE e-book!
Please tell your friends!

PUBLIC SCHOOL HELL
the Humanist religion established as state church

exposing the promotion of sodomy in public schools

www.dayspringpublisher.com

FREE e-book!
Please tell your friends!

PUBLIC SCHOOL HELL
the Humanist religion established as state church

exposing the promotion of sodomy in public schools

www.dayspringpublisher.com

FREE e-book!
Please tell your friends!

PUBLIC SCHOOL HELL
the Humanist religion established as state church

exposing the promotion of sodomy in public schools

www.dayspringpublisher.com

www.ingramcontent.com/pod-product-compliance
Ingram Content Group UK Ltd.
Pitfield, Milton Keynes, MK11 3LW, UK
UKHW051127260726
13967UKWH00010B/2915

9 780977 999682